W9-BYZ-306

poetrySPEAKS
EXPANDED

poetrySPEAKS

EXPANDED

HEAR

POETS FROM TENNYSON TO PLATH READ THEIR OWN WORK

• Elise Paschen & Rebekah Presson Mosby *Editors* • Dominique Raccah *Series Editor*

• Robert Pinsky, Rita Dove & Dana Gioia *Advisory Editors* • Charles Osgood *Narrator*

© 2007 by Sourcebooks, Inc.
Cover design © 2007 by Sourcebooks, Inc.
Cover photo © Corbis

Sourcebooks and the colophon are registered trademarks of
Sourcebooks, Inc.
If the CDs included with this book are missing, broken, or defec-
tive, please email customer.service@sourcebooks.com for a
replacement. Please include your name and address, and the
ISBN number located on the back cover of this book.

Published by Sourcebooks MediaFusion, an imprint of Sourcebooks, Inc.
P.O. Box 4410, Naperville, Illinois   60567-4410
(630) 961-3900
FAX: (630) 961-2168
www.sourcebooks.com

Library of Congress Cataloging-in-Publication Data is on file with
the publisher.

Printed and bound in Canada
TC   10 9 8 7 6 5 4 3 2 1

To all poets and teachers of poetry

Contents

Track List

Disc 1

1. **Introduction by Charles Osgood**
2. **Alfred, Lord Tennyson**
3. *from* "The Bugle Song"
4. *from* The Charge of the Light Brigade
5. **Robert Browning**
6. How They Brought the Good News from Ghent to Aix
7. **Walt Whitman**
8. *from* America
9. **William Butler Yeats**
10. Yeats On "The Lake Isle Of Innisfree"
11. The Lake Isle of Innisfree
12. Coole Park and Ballylee, 1931
13. **Gertrude Stein**
14. Christian Berard
15. She Bowed to Her Brother
16. **Robert Frost**
17. The Oven Bird
18. The Road Not Taken
19. Stopping by Woods on a Snowy Evening
20. Nothing Gold Can Stay
21. The Silken Tent
22. **Carl Sandburg**
23. Grass
24. Cool Tombs
25. 107 *from* The People, Yes
26. **Wallace Stevens**
27. So-And-So Reclining on Her Couch
28. Not Ideas About the Thing But the Thing Itself
29. **James Joyce**
30. *from* Anna Livia Plurabelle *from* Finnegans Wake
31. **William Carlos Williams**
32. Queen-Anne's-Lace
33. To Elsie
34. The Red Wheelbarrow
35. **Ezra Pound**
36. Cantico Del Sole
37. Hugh Selwyn Mauberley
38. XLV *from* The Cantos
39. **H.D.**
40. *from* Helen in Egypt
41. **Robinson Jeffers**
42. The Day Is a Poem (September 19, 1939)
43. Oh, Lovely Rock
44. **John Crowe Ransom**
45. Captain Carpenter
46. Bells for John Whiteside's Daughter
47. **T.S. Eliot**
48. The Love Song of J. Alfred Prufrock
49. La Figlia Che Piange

Disc 2

1. **Edna St. Vincent Millay**
2. Recuerdo
3. I Shall Forget You Presently, My Dear
4. Childhood Is the Kingdom Where Nobody Dies
5. **Dorothy Parker**
6. One Perfect Rose
7. Résumé
8. Afternoon
9. **E. E. Cummings**
10. *from* anyone lived in a pretty how town
11. as freedom is a breakfastfood
12. **Robert Graves**
13. The Castle
14. To Juan at the Winter Solstice
15. The Blue-Fly
16. **Louise Bogan**
17. The Dream
18. Song for the Last Act
19. **Melvin B. Tolson**
20. An Ex-Judge at the Bar
21. Dark Symphony
22. **Laura (Riding) Jackson**
23. Death as Death
24. Nothing So Far
25. **Langston Hughes**
26. The Negro Speaks of Rivers
27. Mother to Son
28. The Weary Blues
29. Harlem [2]
30. **Ogden Nash**
31. I Do, I Will, I Have
32. I Must Tell You About My Novel
33. **W. H. Auden**
34. In Memory of W. B. Yeats
35. Musée des Beaux Arts
36. If I Could Tell You
37. **Louis MacNeice**
38. Conversation
39. Meeting Point
40. **Theodore Roethke**
41. My Papa's Waltz
42. The Waking
43. I Knew a Woman
44. **Elizabeth Bishop**
45. The Fish
46. *from* Crusoe in England
47. **May Swenson**
48. Question
49. The Watch
50. **Robert Hayden**
51. Those Winter Sundays
52. El-Hajj Malik El-Shabazz (Malcolm X)
53. **Muriel Rukeyser**
54. Night Feeding
55. The Poem as Mask
56. Waiting for Icarus

Disc 3

1. **William Stafford**
2. The Star in the Hills
3. Traveling Through the Dark
4. **Randall Jarrell**
5. The Death of the Ball Turret Gunner
6. Seele im Raum
7. **John Berryman**
8. The Ball Poem
9. 4 *from* The Dream Songs
10. 22 *from* The Dream Songs
11. **Dylan Thomas**
12. Fern Hill
13. Among Those Killed in the Dawn Raid Was a Man Aged a Hundred
14. **Robert Lowell**
15. Skunk Hour
16. Home After Three Months Away
17. **Gwendolyn Brooks**
18. A Song in the Front Yard
19. kitchenette building
20. We Real Cool
21. **Robert Duncan**
22. Poetry, A Natural Thing
23. Often I Am Permitted to Return to a Meadow
24. **Jack Kerouac**
25. MacDougal Street Blues: Canto Uno
26. *from* Book of Haikus
27. **Philip Larkin**
28. Places, Loved Ones
29. The Old Fools
30. **Denise Levertov**
31. The Secret
32. Her Sadness
33. **Allen Ginsberg**
34. *from* Howl
35. A Supermarket in California
36. **Frank O'Hara**
37. Ave Maria
38. Poem (Lana Turner Has Collapsed!)
39. **Anne Sexton**
40. The Truth the Dead Know
41. *from* The Operation
42. **Ted Hughes**
43. The Thought-Fox
44. February 17
45. **Etheridge Knight**
46. The Idea of Ancestry
47. Belly Song
48. **Sylvia Plath**
49. Daddy
50. Lady Lazarus

Tracks in bold contain narration by Charles Osgood

Note from the Publisher

Poetry speaks to each of us at another level, below our consciousness. Like music, it reaches inside to touch us. While most of us first experience poetry read aloud as children, we almost never hear a poem once we've grown up. Yet spoken poetry can be a visceral and immediate experience. *Poetry Speaks Expanded* is an attempt to create (or perhaps recreate) that experience. It is our hope that this book will be the beginning of a journey for you. In *Poetry Speaks Expanded*, you can hear Alfred, Lord Tennyson and T.S. Eliot, Gertrude Stein and Gwendolyn Brooks, and forty-three other poets reading their own poetry. You can hear recordings of the great voices of twentieth-century (and some of nineteenth-century) English and American poetry, some of them rare.

Poetry Speaks Expanded is also a book about and by poets. In it you will find many different schools of poetry and many different types of poets. You will read and hear Victorians and Imagists, Modernists and poets from the Harlem Renaissance, Black Mountain poets and Beat poets, Confessional poets and poets from the Black Arts Movement. In the forty-seven poets represented here, no two are alike. Their voices are different, their styles unique, their language as individual as a fingerprint. The range and quality of poetry included in this book, the culmination of four years' work, is due largely to the team that put it together. We first enlisted Elise Paschen, then the executive director of the Poetry Society of America, and Rebekah Presson Mosby, host of NPR's *New Letters on the Air* for twelve years, to edit *Poetry Speaks Expanded*. Robert Pinsky and Rita Dove, two former U.S. Poet Laureates, and Dana Gioia, a poet and critic who would later become Chairman of the National Endowment for the Arts, then joined the project as advisors, providing their considerable talents and expertise in selecting the poets who would be featured.

The poets represented in *Poetry Speaks Expanded* are all deceased. This allowed the editors to review the entire body of work of any poet considered for inclusion. Paschen and Mosby, together with advisors Pinsky, Dove, and Gioia, and Sourcebooks' editors, first compiled a list of more than sixty poets. We then asked each editor to narrow that list to forty. There was, perhaps surprisingly, a great deal of consistency in the selections. Because *Poetry Speaks Expanded* is an attempt to collect some of the best poetry ever written, as read by the poets themselves, we omitted any poets for whom no audio was available (much to our chagrin, that removed such notable poets as Hart Crane and Emily Dickinson). To finalize the list, we reviewed all of the selections again and erred on the side of range. That is, we thought it important to represent as many different styles of poetry as possible. In this way, we arrived at the forty-seven historic poets you see included here, from Tennyson to Plath, all of whom you can hear reading their own poetry on the three accompanying audio CDs.

The book you are holding is the second edition of *Poetry Speaks*. Since we published the original in 2001, we've heard from thousands of readers expressing their appreciation for the chance to discover the voices of poets, and asking for more. *Poetry Speaks Expanded* adds more poets and their works, in print and audio. It includes rare recordings of Jack Kerouac reading his Haiku poetry, May Swenson rehearsing her poem "The Watch," and James Joyce reading the "Anna Livia Plurabelle" episode from *Finnegans*

Wake, published here for the first time with the matching passages from the book.

Each chapter is about a specific poet. The chapters are arranged in chronological order by birth date. We begin with a short biography—meant to be an introduction to the poet's life. Next you will find an essay about the poet written by a prominent living poet. These essays can help you gain a very different insight into each of the poets. They are also meant to introduce you, albeit via prose, to some of the great poets writing today, from W.S. Merwin, Seamus Heaney, Robert Bly, and Jorie Graham to Billy Collins, Sonia Sanchez, and Al Young. Our essayists were also instrumental in selecting the poems to be included for each poet. At the back of *Poetry Speaks Expanded*, you will find brief biographies of each of these essayists, so that you may further explore their work. Many of the chapters also include rare handwritten manuscripts, letters, or photographs that will enhance your understanding of the poets.

Finally, you will find for each poet a set of his or her poems arranged in chronological order (by when they are thought to have first been published). A selection of these poems is also on the audio, and thus have audio track numbers listed next to the poem's title. For these, you will hear how the poet thought the poem should be read at a specific time and place. The additional poems are there for you to enjoy and perhaps read for yourself once you have experienced the poet's own voice. Our hope is that you will want to go further in exploring these poets once you are introduced.

There are many different ways to use and enjoy *Poetry Speaks Expanded*. You may want to read a chapter from beginning to end before listening to the poet read his or her poems. Or you may decide to pick out an individual poem—one that has special meaning for you or whose meaning eludes you—and listen to the poet read the poem aloud while going back to the text to reread it with a new perspective. You may start with all the poets you know or you may start with those who are new to you. Here's the important part: the book and the audio should be used together.

As you will undoubtedly note, some readings are very different from the published versions, especially those recorded near or before publication, such as Anne Sexton's "The Operation" and Elizabeth Bishop's "Crusoe in England." In fact, differences in printed and recorded versions are the norm, not the exception. Thus, readings very often do not precisely match the published poem. Poets are constant revisers and they sometimes change a poem even in the middle of a reading. This is yet another level of understanding that can't be achieved by simply reading or listening to a poem. It is also a good argument for listening to the poet read the poem him or herself. You will also find that the voice of the poet may change across different readings since readings may take place at a different time of life or in different venues. So you will hear Bishop early in life and then an older, more assured poet.

For some readings, the poets have provided a brief introduction, which we have included. You can hear Langston Hughes explain how he wrote "The Negro Speaks of Rivers" or W.B. Yeats provide the background for "The Lake Isle of Innisfree."

Finally, some of these poets and recordings are very old. Three of the recordings, of Tennyson, Robert Browning, and Walt Whitman, date back to the nineteenth century. Tennyson was around eighty years old when Thomas Edison recorded him on wax cylinders. These recordings can be hard to hear and understand. They are a bit easier to understand if you follow along with the poet in your book.

I welcome you now to *Poetry Speaks Expanded*.

Dominique Raccah
Publisher

Introduction

A poem can change your life. In poems, we discover the words and images to understand and interpret the world. Whether writing birth songs or elegies, love vows or political anthems, lyric outbursts or vast narratives, great poets throughout the ages transform ordinary experience, thought, and emotion into something memorable.

A poet regards the page differently than the prose writer. As the French poet Paul Valéry wrote, "Poetry is to prose as dancing is to walking." The poet, when writing, considers the borders of a right and left margin and chooses where to begin and end the line. "Verse" derives from the Latin *versus*, or "turn," as in turn of the plough, furrow, or line of writing. Unlike the prose writer, who will continue writing the sentence until the typewriter or computer pulls the line over to the left margin, the poet "carves" the line onto the page.

Just as poetry differs from prose on the page, poems have a unique power when read aloud. Poets are attuned to sound as they "make" their poems or, in Robert Frost's words, create "the sound of sense." Hearing poetry read aloud, the listener may glimpse the poet's psyche. Recited well, poetry can even mesmerize.

Recall the first time you heard a poem read out loud: perhaps your mother or father recited "Stopping by Woods on a Snowy Evening" when you were young. Or maybe, when older, a high school teacher read to the class T.S. Eliot's "The Love Song of J. Alfred Prufrock" or Gwendolyn Brooks' "We Real Cool." What if we could hear Eliot or Brooks, Frost or W.B. Yeats recite poems in their own voices? Yeats wrote, "I wanted all my poetry to be spoken on a stage or sung....I have spent my life in clearing out of poetry every phrase written for the eye, and bringing all back to syntax that is for the ear alone." The force of a poem is empowered by the voice behind the poem.

I remember the first time I heard Yeats reciting his poetry. I had researched a script for a Bloomsday Joyce/Yeats tribute in New York City. The program concluded with a recording of Yeats reading "The Lake Isle of Innisfree." Although I had studied and written about the poem, it was not until after hearing Yeats's sonorous tone, his inflections and rhythm, that the work gained new dimension. When I later visited the Lake Isle of Innisfree in Ireland, the memory of Yeats's voice reverberated through the landscape. The sound of the author's voice resurrects the poet vividly in the imagination.

Poetry spoken aloud recalls the oral origins of poetry. In every culture, poetry emerges before writing. In traditional Native American societies, poetry was expressed in prayers and ceremonies, as in the Navajo Blessingway Chants. In Babylon, in the early twenty-first century B.C., court entertainers sang for King Shulgi early versions of the *Epic of Gilgamesh*. During the fifth century B.C. in Greece, Homeric bards recited *The Iliad* from memory. These early spoken performances have been revived in our own day as we witness the popularity of Slam, Hip Hop, Rap, and Cowboy poetry, as well as more traditional poetry readings.

The force of modern poetry resides in this union of the written and the spoken word. With this insight in mind, we have compiled in *Poetry Speaks* a collection that features memorable poems of the last century and a half—works that, remarkably, have also been recorded in the poets' own voices. Here is a rare mix of poems for the eye and the ear, where the lover of poetry may act as both reader and listener. We hope that you will discover, in these pages and on these discs, poems that change your life.

Elise Paschen

poetrySPEAKS
EXPANDED

Alfred, Lord Tennyson

(1809–1892) b. Somersby, England

Disc 1

Tracks 2–4

Alfred, Lord Tennyson, probably the most popular English poet of his day, was born the fourth of twelve children on August 6, 1809. The financial comfort of the Tennyson household was precarious. Tennyson's father, rector of a local church, practically disowned by his wealthy family, appears to have taken recourse to alcohol and drugs. As an escape from this dark atmosphere, Tennyson turned to writing poetry at the age of eight.

In 1827, Tennyson published *Poems by Two Brothers*, a compilation of poems written by Tennyson and his older brother, Charles, and a few written by his brother Frederick. That same year, Tennyson enrolled at Trinity College, Cambridge, where he continued to write poetry, winning the 1828 Chancellor's Gold Medal for his poem "Timbuctoo." While at Cambridge, he joined the Apostles, an exclusive intellectual society, and became acquainted with Arthur Hallam, another brilliant Victorian man of letters who was to become Tennyson's dearest friend and perhaps his greatest inspiration. In 1830, Tennyson published the volume, *Poems, Chiefly Lyrical,* to universal acclaim, but soon after began a decline. In 1831, his father died and left his family to cope with numerous debts, forcing Tennyson to withdraw from Trinity College and return home. He published another volume, *Poems,* in 1832, but it received mostly unfavorable reviews. Then, in 1833, Hallam died unexpectedly while traveling with his father. Tennyson's grief, poverty, and family problems (his brother Edward was committed to a mental asylum the same year Hallam died) conspired to distract Tennyson from the literary world, and though he continued to write, he published nothing for the rest of the decade. During this time, Tennyson attempted to court Emily Sellwood, the daughter of a family friend of the Hallams. Tennyson and Sellwood were engaged briefly in 1838, nine years after Arthur Hallam introduced the two, but they were officially separated in 1840 for financial reasons. Caught in a web of misfortunes, Tennyson had reached his life's low point.

Prospects improved in 1842, when Tennyson's friends convinced him to publish the two-volume *Poems.* The book was a success and helped stabilize Tennyson's finances as well as his spirits. However, he chose to invest nearly all of his money in a business venture that failed and he lost essentially everything. In 1845, he received a government pension based on his literary accomplishments and financial need. In 1847, he published the book-length poem, *The Princess,* to great acclaim, and three years later, his finances were finally stable enough for him to marry Emily Sellwood. In 1850, he published *In Memoriam,* a brilliant lyric sequence memorializing Hallam, and the poem established Tennyson as the greatest poet of the day. Few were surprised when he was appointed Poet Laureate after William Wordsworth's death.

While Poet Laureate, Tennyson lived happily with his wife and published such works as *Maud, and Other Poems,* "Charge of the Light Brigade," and *Idylls of the King,* all of which maintained or enhanced his reputation while helping shape Victorian tastes. In 1883, he was granted a barony and a seat in the House of Lords by the crown, the first person ever to receive such a position based merely on literary prowess. Tennyson died peacefully at his home on October 6, 1892, and was buried in the Poet's Corner of Westminster Abbey.

Anthony Hecht on Alfred, Lord Tennyson

> *And still she slept an azure-lidded sleep,*
> *In blanchéd linen, smooth, and lavendered...*
> > —*Keats*
>
> *Her limbs are delicate as an eyelid,*
> *Love has blinded him with tears...*
> > —*Yeats*
>
> *Music that gentlier on the spirit lies*
> *Than tired eyelids upon tired eyes...*
> > —*Tennyson*

Here are three eyelid poets (of the three, Tennyson was the most enamoured of the word), all aiming at the same sense of delicacy, beautiful softness, and vulnerability. Yeats might well have had Keats and Tennyson lurking somewhere in the storages of his mind. The three have more than eyelids in common: they were all, at least at some points in their careers, lullingly musical in their commerce with the English language.

In his biography of Auden, Humphrey Carpenter reports that the poet, "began editing a selection of Tennyson's poetry for a New York publisher; in his introduction to the volume, he wrote of Tennyson: 'He had the finest ear, perhaps, of any English poet; he was also undoubtedly the stupidest.' This earned the comment from T.S. Eliot that if Auden had been a better scholar he would have known many stupider."

One must puzzle about Auden's accusation. Tennyson's biographer, Robert Bernard Martin, reports in connection with the poet's student years at Cambridge that, "Though he was no true intellectual he early cast his lot with those who were," meaning The Apostles, among others. But Martin also declares, "His instincts were deeply conservative, but otherwise tended to confuse political thought with xeno-phobic patriotism," which Auden would have deplored; but it is worth adding that

Auden had little sympathy with the moods of nostalgia and regret that characterize so much of Tennyson's most beautiful lyrics.

When Thomas Hardy wished to strike the note of forlorn abandonment, he summons Tennyson by name, and slyly echoes him:

> *The bower we shrined to Tennyson,*
> *Gentlemen,*
> *Is roof-wrecked; damps there drip upon*
> *Sagged seats, the creeper-nails are rust,*
> *The spider is sole denizen;*
> *Even she who voiced those rhymes is dust,*
> *Gentlemen!*

Surely those rusty nails recall the opening of "Mariana":

> *With blackest moss the flower-pots*
> *Were thickly crusted, one and all;*
> *The rusted nails fell from the knots*
> *That held the pear to the gable-wall.*

But Tennyson could convey many moods, from the heroic ("Ulysses") to the lethargic ("The Lotus-Eaters") to the neurotic ("Maud" and "Saint Simeon Stylites"). I want here to reflect upon one of his most beautiful, erotic, and languorous songs from *The Princess,* "Now Sleeps the Crimson Petal":

> *Now sleeps the crimson petal, now the white;*
> *Nor waves the cypress in the palace walk;*
> *Nor winks the gold fin in the porphyry font.*
> *The fire-fly wakens; waken thou with me.*
>
> *Now droops the milk-white peacock like a ghost,*
> *And like a ghost she glimmers on to me.*

Now lies the Earth all Danaë to the stars,
And all thy heart lies open unto me.

Now slides the silent meteor on, and leaves
A shining furrow, as thy thoughts in me.

Now folds the lily all her sweetness up,
And slips into the bosom of the lake.
So fold thyself, my dearest, thou, and slip
Into my bosom and be lost in me.

Our finest Tennyson critic, Christopher Ricks, observes of this poem, "Tennyson succeeds in the hardest task of all: distinguishing love from lust in erotic poetry." He also informed me that the poem is a species of Ghazal, and some of its leading images and details—crimson and white petals, cypress and palace, peacock, stars, and lilies—are commonly to be found in Persian love poetry; and while Tennyson assured a questioner that he knew no Persian, one of his close friends was Edward FitzGerald, translator of *The Rubaiyat.*

Tennyson was rarely careless (he was one of the most scrupulous of revisers) so that we must puzzle about the pronoun "she" in the sixth line, which can refer only to the peacock, which is male. I will attempt to account for this anomaly by suggesting that there is something equivocal about gender throughout the song. In context, it is read *sotto voce* by the princess as she sits beside her half-conscious prince, with whom, against her firm resolve, she is falling in love. I want to propose that in the course of this brief poem there is a deliberate and conscious shift from the masculine to the feminine posture of the mind, that the first eight lines present an invitation to love, protected by the privacy conferred by dusk, and encouraged by the veiled and ghostly obscurity surrounding the peacock, and the yielding posture of Danaë (who thwarts the imprisonment of a puritanical father, the agent of prudery and repression) and at one with the waking fireflies. But beginning with the ninth line, the mode of expression—with the furrowing and planting of thought, its earthen fertility, and the invitation to enter the bosom of the speaker—appears to shift to the feminine. And I would suggest that this shift is indicative of the change in the princess herself who initially founded a female university from which men were sternly excluded; an institution invaded by the prince and two of his friends, all disguised as women; they are exposed, and the prince sues for the love of the princess, only to be coldly informed that she has foresworn marriage; the prince and his fellows are wounded in a tourney, whereupon the princess, aroused by sympathy for his plight, begins to yield to the softnesses of affection. The story is in fact that of Shakespeare's *Love's Labour's Lost,* with the genders reversed. As Martin says, "The story begins lightheartedly…with a direct inversion of all the accepted roles for men, now taken by women," but in which at the end the old familiar erotic impulses win their way through to a happy ending.

Handwritten manuscript by Tennyson of "The Rose"

Ulysses

It little profits that an idle king,
By this still hearth, among these barren crags,
Match'd with an aged wife, I mete and dole
Unequal laws unto a savage race,
That hoard, and sleep, and feed, and know not me.
I cannot rest from travel; I will drink
Life to the lees. All times I have enjoy'd
Greatly, have suffer'd greatly, both with those
That loved me, and alone; on shore, and when
Thro' scudding drifts the rainy Hyades
Vext the dim sea. I am become a name;
For always roaming with a hungry heart
Much have I seen and known,—cities of men
And manners, climates, councils, governments,
Myself not least, but honor'd of them all,—
And drunk delight of battle with my peers,
Far on the ringing plains of windy Troy.
I am a part of all that I have met;
Yet all experience is an arch wherethro'
Gleams that untravell'd world whose margin fades
For ever and for ever when I move.
How dull it is to pause, to make an end,
To rust unburnish'd, not to shine in use!
As tho' to breathe were life. Life piled on life
Were all too little, and of one to me
Little remains; but every hour is saved
From that eternal silence, something more,
A bringer of new things; and vile it were
For some three suns to store and hoard myself,
And this grey spirit yearning in desire
To follow knowledge like a sinking star,
Beyond the utmost bound of human thought.

This is my son, mine own Telemachus,
To whom I leave the sceptre and the isle,—
Well-loved of me, discerning to fulfil
This labor, by slow prudence to make mild
A rugged people, and thro' soft degrees
Subdue them to the useful and the good.
Most blameless is he, centred in the sphere
Of common duties, decent not to fail
In offices of tenderness, and pay
Meet adoration to my household gods,
When I am gone. He works his work, I mine.
    There lies the port; the vessel puffs her sail;
There gloom the dark, broad seas. My mariners,
Souls that have toil'd, and wrought, and thought with me,—
That ever with a frolic welcome took
The thunder and the sunshine, and opposed
Free hearts, free foreheads,—you and I are old;
Old age hath yet his honor and his toil.
Death closes all; but something ere the end,
Some work of noble note, may yet be done,
Not unbecoming men that strove with Gods.
The lights begin to twinkle from the rocks;
The long day wanes; the slow moon climbs; the deep
Moans round with many voices. Come, my friends.
'T is not too late to seek a newer world.
Push off, and sitting well in order smite
The sounding furrows; for my purpose holds
To sail beyond the sunset, and the baths
Of all the western stars, until I die.
It may be that the gulfs will wash us down;
It may be we shall touch the Happy Isles,
And see the great Achilles, whom we knew.
Tho' much is taken, much abides; and tho'
We are not now that strength which in old days
Moved earth and heaven, that which we are, we are,—
One equal temper of heroic hearts,
Made weak by time and fate, but strong in will
To strive, to seek, to find, and not to yield.

[1842]

"The Bugle Song"

from The Princess

DISC 1, TRACK 3

The splendor falls on castle walls
    And snowy summits old in story;
The long light shakes across the lakes,
    And the wild cataract leaps in glory.
Blow, bugle, blow, set the wild echoes flying,
Blow, bugle; answer, echoes, dying, dying, dying.

    O, hark, O, hear! how thin and clear,
        And thinner, clearer, farther going!
    O, sweet and far from cliff and scar
        The horns of Elfland faintly blowing!
Blow, let us hear the purple glens replying,
Blow, bugle; answer, echoes, dying, dying, dying.

    O love, they die in yon rich sky,
        They faint on hill or field or river;
    Our echoes roll from soul to soul,
        And grow for ever and for ever.
Blow, bugle, blow, set the wild echoes flying,
And answer, echoes, answer, dying, dying, dying.

[1850]

The Charge of the Light Brigade

DISC 1, TRACK 4

1

Half a league, half a league,
Half a league onward,
All in the valley of Death
    Rode the six hundred.
"Forward, the Light Brigade!
Charge for the guns!" he said.
Into the valley of Death
    Rode the six hundred.

2

"Forward, the Light Brigade!"
Was there a man dismay'd?
Not tho' the soldier knew
    Some one had blunder'd.
    Theirs not to make reply,
    Theirs not to reason why,
    Theirs but to do and die.
    Into the valley of Death
        Rode the six hundred.

3

Cannon to right of them,
Cannon to left of them,
Cannon in front of them
    Volley'd and thunder'd;
Storm'd at with shot and shell,
Boldly they rode and well,
Into the jaws of Death,
Into the mouth of hell
    Rode the six hundred.

4

Flash'd all their sabres bare,
Flash'd as they turn'd in air
Sabring the gunners there,
Charging an army, while
　　All the world wonder'd.
Plunged in the battery-smoke
Right thro' the line they broke;
Cossack and Russian
Reel'd from the sabre-stroke
　　Shatter'd and sunder'd.
Then they rode back, but not,
　　Not the six hundred.

5

Cannon to right of them,
Cannon to left of them,
Cannon behind them
　　Volley'd and thunder'd;
Storm'd at with shot and shell,
While horse and hero fell,
They that had fought so well
Came thro' the jaws of Death,
Back from the mouth of hell,
All that was left of them,
　　Left of six hundred.

6

When can their glory fade?
O the wild charge they made!
　　All the world wonder'd.
Honour the charge they made!
Honour the Light Brigade,
　　Noble six hundred!

[1854]

Tithonus

The woods decay, the woods decay and fall,
The vapors weep their burthen to the ground,
Man comes and tills the field and lies beneath,
And after many a summer dies the swan.
Me only cruel immortality
Consumes; I wither slowly in thine arms,
Here at the quiet limit of the world,
A white-hair'd shadow roaming like a dream
The ever-silent spaces of the East,
Far-folded mists, and gleaming halls of morn.
　　Alas! for this gray shadow, once a man—
So glorious in his beauty and thy choice,
Who madest him thy chosen, that he seem'd
To his great heart none other than a God!
I ask'd thee, "Give me immortality."
Then didst thou grant mine asking with a smile,
Like wealthy men who care not how they give.
But thy strong Hours indignant work'd their wills,
And beat me down and marr'd and wasted me,
And tho' they could not end me, left me maim'd
To dwell in presence of immortal youth,
Immortal age beside immortal youth,
And all I was in ashes. Can thy love,
Thy beauty, make amends, tho' even now,
Close over us, the silver star, thy guide,
Shines in those tremulous eyes that fill with tears
To hear me? Let me go; take back thy gift.
Why should a man desire in any way
To vary from the kindly race of men,
Or pass beyond the goal of ordinance
Where all should pause, as is most meet for all?
　　A soft air fans the cloud apart; there comes
A glimpse of that dark world where I was born.
Once more the old mysterious glimmer steals
From thy pure brows, and from thy shoulders pure,
And bosom beating with a heart renew'd.

Thy cheek begins to redden thro' the gloom,
Thy sweet eyes brighten slowly close to mine.
Ere yet they blind the stars, and the wild team
Which love thee, yearning for thy yoke, arise,
And shake the darkness from their loosen'd manes,
And beat the twilight into flakes of fire.

Lo! ever thus thou growest beautiful
In silence, then before thine answer given
Departest, and thy tears are on my cheek.

Why wilt thou ever scare me with thy tears,
And make me tremble lest a saying learnt,
In days far-off, on that dark earth, be true?
"The Gods themselves cannot recall their gifts."

Ay me! ay me! with what another heart
In days far-off, and with what other eyes
I used to watch—if I be he that watch'd—
The lucid outline forming round thee; saw
The dim curls kindle into sunny rings;
Changed with thy mystic change, and felt my blood
Glow with the glow that slowly crimson'd all
Thy presence and thy portals, while I lay,
Mouth, forehead, eyelids, growing dewy-warm
With kisses balmier than half-opening buds
Of April, and could hear the lips that kiss'd
Whispering I knew not what of wild and sweet,
Like that strange song I heard Apollo sing,
While Ilion like a mist rose into towers.

Yet hold me not for ever in thine East;
How can my nature longer mix with thine?
Coldly thy rosy shadows bathe me, cold
Are all thy lights, and cold my wrinkled feet
Upon thy glimmering thresholds, when the steam
Floats up from those dim fields about the homes
Of happy men that have the power to die,
And grassy barrows of the happier dead.
Release me, and restore me to the ground.
Thou seest all things, thou wilt see my grave;
Thou wilt renew thy beauty morn by morn,
I earth in earth forget these empty courts,
And thee returning on thy silver wheels.

[1860]

Crossing the Bar

Sunset and evening star,
    And one clear call for me!
And may there be no moaning of the bar,
    When I put out to sea,

But such a tide as moving seems asleep,
    Too full for sound and foam,
When that which drew from out the boundless deep
    Turns again home.

Twilight and evening bell,
    And after that the dark!
And may there be no sadness of farewell,
    When I embark;

For tho' from out our bourne of Time and Place
    The flood may bear me far,
I hope to see my Pilot face to face
    When I have crost the bar.

[1889]

Robert Browning

(1812–1889) b. Camberwell, England

Disc 1

Tracks 5–6

Robert Browning was born in Camberwell, a suburb of London, on May 7, 1812. His father, also named Robert, was a bank clerk who possessed an extensive library, while his mother, Sara, was a religious woman with an artistic sensibility. As a child, Browning attended a nearby boarding school and then, at the age of sixteen, enrolled in the recently founded University of London. Browning remained at the University for less than a year; he preferred to receive his instruction—in foreign languages, music, even boxing—from private tutors at home. He read omnivorously, and some critics say that the breadth and peculiarities of Browning's education may help explain what some of Browning's contemporaries would refer to as his work's "obscurity." Poetry appealed to Browning from the start, and by the time he was twenty, his ambition was to become a great poet. His family supported him in this pursuit.

Browning's first published work, *Pauline,* a long poem in blank verse modeled after the passionate work of Percy Bysshe Shelley, failed to receive much positive notice when it appeared anonymously in 1833. Perhaps the most telling response to the confessional, flamboyant *Pauline* came from the famous Victorian essayist and philosopher John Stuart Mill, who declared the poem's author self-indulgent. This dismissal supposedly humiliated Browning so much that he swore never again to write in the confessional vein. His next book, *Paracelsus,* a long blank-verse dramatic monologue, appeared in 1835 to warm reviews. In 1840, he published the notoriously obscure, difficult, and publicly derided *Sordello, A Poem in Six Books.* Thought by many to be incomprehensible, it would take Browning almost twenty years to remove the tarnish that this poem (long since reassessed as one of the century's finest long poems) brought to his reputation. Between 1841 and 1846, Browning published four books—collections of his shorter poems for the most part, many of which would go on to become his most widely known works. In January 1845, Browning began his correspondence with Elizabeth Barrett after reading her *Poems* (1844). They met in May and married in September of 1846, relocating to Florence where they lived in near seclusion in the Mediterranean air that proved helpful to Elizabeth's ill health. She gave birth to a son on March 9, 1849.

Browning wrote less while in Italy with his wife, but what he did write, the collection of short poems entitled *Men and Women,* almost fully revived his reputation when it appeared in 1855. Elizabeth died in June of 1861, and Browning returned to London thereafter. His next collection, 1864's *Dramatis Personae,* reflected his profound grief. Many of the poems in the book take the form of dramatic monologues, a form that Browning had been partial to and with which he will always be associated. From 1868 to 1869, Browning published the centerpiece of his poetical accomplishments, the twelve-book novel in verse, *The Ring and the Book.* He continued to publish new work throughout the remainder of his life; in fact, his last book, *Asolando,* a collection of lyrics, narratives, and dramatic monologues, was published the day of his death, December 12, 1889. Browning was buried in Westminster Abbey, as the cemetery in which his wife had been buried had since been closed to new burials.

Edward Hirsch on Robert Browning

Edward Hirsch on Robert Browning

Robert Browning contained multitudes. A voracious reader, a zealous and prolific writer—he is the Victorian poet who lived most by forgetting himself, by deploying his imagination across the centuries. He took the radical liberty in his work of fashioning other selves, of dramatizing voices from the bloody precincts of history, from "the dangerous edge of things." "Often lyric in expression, always Dramatic in principle," he said decidedly about his own poetry, "and so many utterances of so many imaginary persons, not mine."

Browning's poetry is a superb gallery—a veritable pageant—of colorful figures. His poems are specific occasions in which an imaginary or historical character speaks to an imaginary listener or audience, as in the key dramatic lyrics of "My Last Duchess," "Andrea del Sarto," and "The Bishop Orders His Tomb at St. Praxed's Church." There are so many distinctive voices calling out in his work, so many angles and perspectives, that it comes as a bit of a shock to hear his own tentative voice reciting—misreading—"How They Brought the Good News from Ghent to Aix," which he recorded on a wax cylinder in the summer of 1889, when he was already an old man. It was as if he was entering the modern era, conversing with posterity, reminding us that there was a historical Robert Browning who animated so many other living presences. But he was always happiest concealing, projecting, and dispersing himself like a secret into the voices of others.

Browning understood the great ductility of the human imagination, and his supreme source is Shakespeare. He was the leading post-Romantic exponent of the dramatic monologue, a medium which he employed to probe the deep mysteries of identity. He was especially compelled by the permeable borders of consciousness, by those who crossed the boundaries of ordinary morality, such as lunatics and criminals. One might say that he was healthily obsessed by obsession, by aberrant and cruel behavior, by moral cynicism bordering on madness. He characterized insanity as an incapacity to recognize one's own derangement, as in *Pippa Passes* (1841):

I think my mind is touched—suspect
All is not sound: but is not knowing that,
What constitutes one sane or otherwise?

One thing that makes Browning's work seem so modern is how unusually alert it is to nuances of voice, to its own intonations, its characteristic verbal strategies. His self-conscious use of a dramatic persona, and his literary development of the monologue, had considerable influence on poets to come. He stands behind W.B. Yeats's use of "masks," and T.S. Eliot's explorations in persona, and Ezra Pound's pathbreaking *Personae* (1909). These poets learned something crucial from him about how to create a phantasmagoria through words, how to dramatize perspectives on the truth.

Browning thought that all poetry consists of "putting the infinite within the finite." His work suggests that—to adapt one of Yeats's favorite sayings—we can embody truth but we cannot know it. He gives us characters perceived, feelings explored, moments expanding toward the infinite. Jorge Luis Borges, who was a great admirer of Browning's work, understood the way that the English poet explored so many other identities in order to discover and become himself, to stitch and unstitch a solitary fate, which was his own character. Thus, the conclusion to Borges's poem "Browning Resolves to Be a Poet":

Stanzas IX and X of "How They Brought the Good News from Ghent to Aix" handwritten by Browning

I will be the face I half-see and forget,
I will be Judas who accepts the blessed destiny of being a traitor,
I will be Caliban in the swamp,
I will be a mercenary dying without fear or faith,
I will be Polycrates, horrified to see the ring returned by destiny,
I will be the friend who hates me.
Persia will grant me the nightingale, Rome the sword.
Agonies, masks, and resurrections will weave and unweave my fate
*   and at some point I will be Robert Browning.*
(tr. Alastair Reid)

A caricature of Browning as the Pied Piper, circa 1865

My Last Duchess
Ferrara

That's my last Duchess painted on the wall,
Looking as if she were alive; I call
That piece a wonder, now: Frà Pandolf's hands
Worked busily a day, and there she stands.
Will't please you sit and look at her? I said
"Frà Pandolf" by design, for never read
Strangers like you that pictured countenance,
The depth and passion of its earnest glance,
But to myself they turned (since none puts by
The curtain I have drawn for you, but I)
And seemed as they would ask me, if they durst,
How such a glance came there; so, not the first
Are you to turn and ask thus. Sir, 'twas not
Her husband's presence only, called that spot
Of joy into the Duchess' cheek: perhaps
Frà Pandolf chanced to say "Her mantle laps
Over my Lady's wrist too much," or "Paint
Must never hope to reproduce the faint
Half-flush that dies along her throat;" such stuff
Was courtesy, she thought, and cause enough
For calling up that spot of joy. She had
A heart…how shall I say?…too soon made glad,
Too easily impressed; she liked whate'er
She looked on, and her looks went everywhere.
Sir, 'twas all one! My favor at her breast,
The dropping of the daylight in the West,
The bough of cherries some officious fool
Broke in the orchard for her, the white mule
She rode with round the terrace—all and each
Would draw from her alike the approving speech,
Or blush, at least. She thanked men,—good; but thanked
Somehow…I know not how…as if she ranked
My gift of a nine-hundred-years-old name
With anybody's gift. Who'd stoop to blame

This sort of trifling? Even had you skill
In speech—(which I have not)—to make your will
Quite clear to such an one, and say "Just this
Or that in you disgusts me; here you miss,
Or there exceed the mark"—and if she let
Herself be lessoned so, nor plainly set
Her wits to yours, forsooth, and made excuse,
—E'en then would be some stooping, and I choose
Never to stoop. Oh, Sir, she smiled, no doubt,
Whene'er I passed her; but who passed without
Much the same smile? This grew; I gave commands;
Then all smiles stopped together. There she stands
As if alive. Will't please you rise? We'll meet
The company below, then. I repeat,
The Count your Master's known munificence
Is ample warrant that no just pretence
Of mine for dowry will be disallowed;
Though his fair daughter's self, as I avowed
At starting, is my object. Nay, we'll go
Together down, Sir! Notice Neptune, though,
Taming a sea-horse, thought a rarity,
Which Claus of Innsbruck cast in bronze for me.

[1842]

Soliloquy of the Spanish Cloister

I

Gr-r-r—there go, my heart's abhorrence!
    Water your damned flower-pots, do!
If hate killed men, Brother Lawrence,
    God's blood, would not mine kill you!
What? your myrtle-bush wants trimming?
    Oh, that rose has prior claims—
Needs its leaden vase filled brimming?
    Hell dry you up with its flames!

II

At the meal we sit together:
    Salve tibi! I must hear
Wise talk of the kind of weather,
    Sort of season, time of year:
Not a plenteous cork-crop: scarcely
    Dare we hope oak-galls, I doubt;
What's the Latin name for "parsley"?
    What's the Greek name for Swine's Snout?

III

Whew! We'll have our platter burnished,
    Laid with care on our own shelf!
With a fire-new spoon we're furnished,
    And a goblet for ourself,
Rinsed like something sacrificial
    Ere 'tis fit to touch our chaps—
Marked with L. for our initial!
    (He-he! There his lily snaps!)

IV

Saint, forsooth! While brown Dolores
    Squats outside the Convent bank,
With Sanchicha, telling stories,
    Steeping tresses in the tank,
Blue-black, lustrous, thick like horse-hairs,
    —Can't I see his dead eye glow,
Bright as 'twere a Barbary corsair's?
    (That is, if he'd let it show!)

V

When he finishes refection,
    Knife and fork he never lays
Cross-wise, to my recollection,
    As do I, in Jesu's praise.
I, the Trinity illustrate,
    Drinking watered orange-pulp—
In three sips the Arian frustrate;
    While he drains his at one gulp!

VI

Oh, those melons! If he's able
    We're to have a feast; so nice!
One goes to the Abbot's table,
    All of us get each a slice.
How go on your flowers? None double?
    Not one fruit-sort can you spy?
Strange!—And I, too, at such trouble,
    Keep them close-nipped on the sly!

VII

There's a great text in Galatians,
    Once you trip on it, entails
Twenty-nine distinct damnations,
    One sure, if another fails:
If I trip him just a-dying,
    Sure of Heaven as sure can be,
Spin him round and send him flying
    Off to Hell, a Manichee?

VIII

Or, my scrofulous French novel
    On grey paper with blunt type!
Simply glance at it, you grovel
    Hand and foot in Belial's gripe:
If I double down its pages
    At the woeful sixteenth print,
When he gathers his greengages,
    Ope a sieve and slip it in't?

IX

Or, there's Satan!—one might venture
    Pledge one's soul to him, yet leave
Such a flaw in the indenture
    As he'd miss till, past retrieve,
Blasted lay that rose-acacia
    We're so proud of! *Hy, Zy, Hine...*
'St, there's Vespers! *Plena gratiâ*
    Ave, Virgo! Gr-r-r—you swine!

[1842]

Meeting at Night

The grey sea and the long black land;
And the yellow half-moon large and low;
And the startled little waves that leap
In fiery ringlets from their sleep,
As I gain the cove with pushing prow,
And quench its speed i' the slushy sand.

Then a mile of warm sea-scented beach;
Three fields to cross till a farm appears;
A tap at the pane, the quick sharp scratch
And blue spurt of a lighted match,
And a voice less loud, through its joys and fears,
Than the two hearts beating each to each!

[1845]

"How They Brought the Good News from Ghent to Aix"
[16—]

I

I sprang to the stirrup, and Joris, and he;
I galloped, Dirck galloped, we galloped all three;
"Good speed!" cried the watch, as the gate-bolts undrew;
"Speed!" echoed the wall to us galloping through;
Behind shut the postern, the lights sank to rest,
And into the midnight we galloped abreast.

II

Not a word to each other; we kept the great pace
Neck by neck, stride by stride, never changing our place;
I turned in my saddle and made its girths tight,
Then shortened each stirrup, and set the pique right,
Rebuckled the cheek-strap, chained slacker the bit,
Nor galloped less steadily Roland a whit.

III

'Twas moonset at starting; but while we drew near
Lokeren, the cocks crew and twilight dawned clear;
At Boom, a great yellow star came out to see;
At Düffeld, 'twas morning as plain as could be;
And from Mecheln church-steeple we heard the half-chime,
So Joris broke silence with, "Yet there is time!"

IV

At Aerschot, up leaped of a sudden the sun,
And against him the cattle stood black every one,
To stare thro' the mist at us galloping past,
And I saw my stout galloper Roland at last,
With resolute shoulders, each butting away
The haze, as some bluff river headland its spray.

V

And his low head and crest, just one sharp ear bent back
For my voice, and the other pricked out on his track;
And one eye's black intelligence, —ever that glance
O'er its white edge at me, his own master, askance!
And the thick heavy spume-flakes which aye and anon
His fierce lips shook upwards in galloping on.

VI

By Hasselt, Dirck groaned; and cried Joris, "Stay spur!
Your Roos galloped bravely, the fault's not in her,
We'll remember at Aix"—for one heard the quick wheeze
Of her chest, saw the stretched neck and staggering knees,
And sunk tail, and horrible heave of the flank,
As down on her haunches she shuddered and sank.

VII

So we were left galloping, Joris and I,
Past Looz and past Tongres, no cloud in the sky;
The broad sun above laughed a pitiless laugh,
'Neath our feet broke the brittle bright stubble like chaff;
Till over by Dalhem a dome-spire sprang white,
And "Gallop," gasped Joris, "for Aix is in sight!"

VIII

"How they'll greet us!"—and all in a moment his roan
Rolled neck and croup over, lay dead as a stone;
And there was my Roland to bear the whole weight
Of the news which alone could save Aix from her fate,
With his nostrils like pits full of blood to the brim,
And with circles of red for his eye-sockets' rim.

IX

Then I cast loose my buffcoat, each holster let fall,
Shook off both my jack-boots, let go belt and all,
Stood up in the stirrup, leaned, patted his ear,
Called my Roland his pet-name, my horse without peer;
Clapped my hands, laughed and sang, any noise, bad or good,
Till at length into Aix Roland galloped and stood.

X

And all I remember is, friends flocking round
As I sat with his head 'twixt my knees on the ground;
And no voice but was praising this Roland of mine,
As I poured down his throat our last measure of wine,
Which (the burgesses voted by common consent)
Was no more than his due who brought good news from Ghent.

[1845]

Walt Whitman

(1819–1892) b. West Hills, New York, United States

Disc 1
Tracks 7–8

Walt Whitman, perhaps the first uniquely "American" poet, was born in West Hills, New York (Long Island), on May 31, 1819. He was the second of nine children born to Walter and Louisa Whitman. The family moved to Brooklyn, where Whitman briefly attended public school, but he soon left it behind in order to enter the printer's trade. He returned to Long Island in 1836 and worked as a teacher, but made journalism his full-time career in 1841, relocating once again to Brooklyn. It was during this period that Whitman first began publishing short stories and poems.

In 1846, Whitman left Brooklyn to become the editor of a newly launched New Orleans paper, the *Crescent*. His brief sojourn in New Orleans exposed him to the reality of slavery and the auction block. His poem, "I Sing the Body Electric," incorporated his experience of witnessing one such slave auction. Whitman's stay in New Orleans lasted only three months, as his employers were dubious of his unorthodox views on slavery and "free soil" (that slavery should not be allowed into any new territories). Returning to Brooklyn by way of St. Louis and Chicago, he founded his own free-soil paper, but it proved to be a short-lived venture.

Throughout this period, Whitman had been refining and creating his own poetic style. In 1855, the first edition of *Leaves of Grass* appeared, containing "Song of Myself." The book was a response to Ralph Waldo Emerson's challenge: "I look in vain for the poet whom I describe...we have yet had no genius in America...[who] knew the value of our incomparable materials." When Whitman sent Emerson his book, Emerson responded with great praise: "I greet you at the beginning of a great career." A second edition of *Leaves of Grass*, with more than twenty new poems, appeared in 1856 with Emerson's blurb slapped on the spine (unbeknownst to Emerson). Whitman would continue to revise and add to *Leaves of Grass* throughout the rest of his life, releasing numerous editions.

During the Civil War, Whitman nursed wounded soldiers in New York City and Washington, D.C., where he would care for thousands of soldiers in makeshift hospitals. In 1862, he headed to Virginia to seek out his brother George, whom he feared was dead. Relief upon finding George alive turned to horror as Whitman came upon "a heap of amputated feet, legs, arms, hands, etc., a full load for a one-horse cart." His firsthand experience of the horrifying aftereffects of battle and the journal he kept during this time, led to Whitman's collection of powerful Civil War poems, *Drum-Taps*.

Whitman stayed in Washington after the war, taking a job in the Department of the Interior—a position he lost when the new Secretary of the Interior, James Harlan, read *Leaves of Grass* and declared it "indecent." William Douglas O'Connor, Whitman's friend and a journalist, was incensed and wrote a fifty-page pamphlet attacking Harlan and sanctifying Whitman. O'Connor's paper changed public perception of the poet, and the title, "The Good Gray Poet," became Whitman's sobriquet. In 1873, after a stroke, he moved to a working-class section of Camden, New Jersey, where he lived with his brother George and his wife. He regularly received visitors and admirers, including, most notably, Oscar Wilde. His 1882 version of *Leaves of Grass* enabled him to purchase a small house in Camden. A final volume, entitled *Good-bye, My Fancy*, appeared in 1891. He died on March 26, 1892, at his Camden home. Though often condemned and dismissed in his day, there can be little doubt that Whitman revolutionized the face of poetry forever by inventing a uniquely American voice.

Galway Kinnell on Walt Whitman

I heard the music of Whitman's poetry for the first time when I was living alone in a little village in France in 1956, far away from the sounds of my mother tongue. Up to then, Whitman's poetry had sounded to me like declamatory prose, but in these new circumstances, I was astonished by the clarity and beauty of certain poems, and suddenly I felt very much connected to Whitman. I read him for an hour or so nearly every day, and when I wasn't reading, a turn of phrase of his was often rolling around in my mouth.

The music of his poetry put me in mind of a mother and her baby talking to each other and understanding each other perfectly, but using no words, simply crooning the sounds words would have when their time came. Meanings are deeply embedded in Whitman's words. It is as if each word had been pressed while still wet upon a part of reality, and then taken into the poem bearing its contours. Individual words seem to fuse together, the line a long continuous cadenced flow. There in the village of St. Martin de la Cluze, I began to feel that if I were to hear a poem of Whitman's recited through closed doors, with the intelligibility of the words muffled, I would still understand him. Osip Mandelstam said the Russian language is "speaking flesh"; Whitman's English felt to me something like that.

> *Not words, not music or rhyme I want,*
> *not custom or lecture, not even the best,*
> *Only the lull I like, the hum of your valvéd voice.*

The songs mothers sing to their babies often have verses that echo each other in sound and tune, and Whitman depended on similar repetitions. The form he most often wrote has the imposing name, *parallelismus membrorum,* meaning the use of repetitions of thought, patterns, syntax, word order, rhythmic structure, words, phrases, clauses, or whatever in consecutive lines. It is a form that sprang up independently all over the world, especially for religious uses. In it, the mind thinks in "grooves" and may fall into a rhythmic "zone." Just as the "zone" allows athletes to perform beyond their normal capacities, so language's powerful cadenced music, flowing through Whitman's precise and astounding vocabulary, touches upon knowledge beyond the grasp of hard thinking or systematic logic. Lines composed in parallel structure are like the acts of friction of stick rubbed against stick in the production of "forced fire": finally wisps of smoke, then a scatter of sparks, then flame.

> I too lived, Brooklyn of ample hills was mine,
> I too walked the streets of Manhattan island, and bathed in the waters around it,
> I too felt the curious abrupt questionings stir within me,
> In the day, among crowds of people, sometimes they came upon me,
> In my walks home late at night, or as I lay in my bed, they came upon me,
> I too had been struck from the float forever held in solution,
> I too had received identity by my body,
> That I was, I knew was of my body—and what I should be, I knew I should be of my body.

Though akin musically to babies' croonings, Whitman's "language experiment," as he called *Leaves of Grass*, is fully adult in that it can evoke complex states of feeling with exactness and subtlety. The riddling repetitions in the final three lines of the passage quoted above from "Crossing Brooklyn Ferry" contribute to a remarkable virtuoso performance that keeps what he is saying just opaque enough for it to elude those readers who prefer not to see it and yet clear enough to be understood by more enlightened readers in his time or in time to come.

Ten years ago, a wax cylinder turned up with a thirty-four–second recording on it of Whitman's poem "America." Many think it is a recording of Whitman's own voice. The recording, which is included on Disc One, was first played publicly in 1992, at the Whitman centenary celebration at the Cathedral of St. John the Divine. The poem began:

> Centre of equal daughters, equal sons,
> All, all alike endear'd, grown, ungrown, young or old...

As we listened, my first thought was that this could not be how Whitman sounded. Two vowels seem to have a slight nasal tone (Whitman had asserted that a nasal tone in a voice is offensive); the principal words of the poem are solid blocks of sound, not fluid elements in that continuous flow that I had imagined; and the voice that I had hoped for sounds a little like the voice of a generic old-timer. Later, I thought, this would not be the first case of a disparity between the inspired voice on the page and the poet's actual voice; and furthermore, Whitman's age and illness, combined with Edison's then still primitive technology, could have produced the not-unpleasant geezering of a voice that may once have been glorious.

So, is the voice in the recording Whitman's? Each of you will have your own impression. For myself, I yield to mammals with keener hearing than ours. As soon as the recording began, several bats flew down out of the gloom of the cathedral's vaulted ceiling, and while the poem was being read they flitted about, seemingly both musing and attentive, and when the poem ended, they returned to their shadows.

Handwritten note from Whitman to Henry Wadsworth Longfellow requesting his autograph, dated February 20, 1881

from Song of Myself

1

I celebrate myself,
And what I assume you shall assume,
For every atom belonging to me, as good belongs to you.

I loafe and invite my soul,
I lean and loafe at my ease, observing a spear of summer
    grass.

2

Houses and rooms are full of perfumes—the shelves are
    crowded with perfumes,
I breathe the fragrance myself, and know it and like it,
The distillation would intoxicate me also, but I shall not
    let it.

The atmosphere is not a perfume—it has not taste of the
    distillation, it is odorless,
It is for my mouth forever—I am in love with it,
I will go to the bank by the wood, and become
    undisguised and naked,
I am mad for it to be in contact with me.

The smoke of my own breath,
Echoes, ripples, and buzzed whispers, love-root,
    silk-thread, crotch and vine,
My respiration and inspiration, the beating of my heart,
    the passing of blood and air through my lungs,
The sniff of green leaves and dry leaves, and of the shore
    and dark-colored sea-rocks, and of hay in the barn,
The sound of the belched words of my voice, words
    loosed to the eddies of the wind,
A few light kisses, a few embraces, a reaching around
    of arms,
The play of shine and shade on the trees as the supple
    boughs wag,
The delight alone or in a rush of the streets, or along
    the fields and hillsides,

The feeling of health, the full-noon trill, the song of
    me rising from bed and meeting the sun.

Have you reckoned a thousand acres much? Have you
    reckoned the earth much?
Have you practiced so long to learn to read?
Have you felt so proud to get at the meaning of
    poems?

Stop this day and night with me and you shall possess
    the origin of all poems,
You shall possess the good of the earth and sun—there
    are millions of suns left,
You shall no longer take things at second or third
    hand, nor look through the eyes of the dead, nor
    feed on the spectres in books,
You shall not look through my eyes either, nor take
    things from me,
You shall listen to all sides and filter them from
    yourself.
…

5

I believe in you my soul—the other I am must not
    abase itself to you,
And you must not be abased to the other.

Loafe with me on the grass—loose the stop from your
    throat,
Not words, not music or rhyme I want—not custom or
    lecture, not even the best,
Only the lull I like, the hum of your valved voice.

I mind how once we lay such a transparent summer
    morning,
How you settled your head athwart my hips and gently
    turned over upon me,
And parted the shirt from my bosom-bone, and
    plunged your tongue to my bare-stript heart,
And reached till you felt my beard, and reached till you
    held my feet.

Swiftly arose and spread around me the peace and
    knowledge that pass all the argument of the earth,
And I know that the hand of God is the elderhand of
    my own,

And I know that the spirit of God is the brother of my
   own,
And that all the men ever born are also my brothers,
   and the women my sisters and lovers,
And that a kelson of the creation is love,
And limitless are leaves stiff or drooping in the fields,
And brown ants in the little wells beneath them,
And mossy scabs of the worm fence, and heaped stones,
   elder, and mullen and poke-weed.

6
A child said, What is the grass? fetching it to me with
   full hands,
How could I answer the child? I do not know what it is
   any more than he.

I guess it must be the flag of my disposition, out of
   hopeful green stuff woven.

Or I guess it is the handkerchief of the Lord,
A scented gift and remembrancer designedly dropped,
Bearing the owner's name someway in the corners, that
   we may see and remark, and say Whose?

Or I guess the grass is itself a child, the produced babe
   of the vegetation.

Or I guess it is a uniform hieroglyphic,
And it means, Sprouting alike in broad zones and
   narrow zones,
Growing among black folks as among white,
Kanuck, Tuckahoe, Congressman, Cuff, I give them the
   same, I receive them the same.

And now it seems to me the beautiful uncut hair of
   graves.

Tenderly will I use you curling grass,
It may be you transpire from the breasts of young men,
It may be if I had known them I would have loved
   them,
It may be you are from old people and from women,
   and from offspring taken soon out of their mothers'
   laps,
And here you are the mothers' laps.

This grass is very dark to be from the white heads of old
   mothers,
Darker than the colorless beards of old men,
Dark to come from under the faint red roofs of mouths.

O I perceive after all so many uttering tongues!
And I perceive they do not come from the roofs of
   mouths for nothing.

I wish I could translate the hints about the dead young
   men and women
And the hints about old men and mothers, and the
   offspring taken soon out of their laps.

What do you think has become of the young and old
   men?
And what do you think has become of the women and
   children?

They are alive and well somewhere,
The smallest sprout shows there is really no death,
And if ever there was it led forward life, and does not
   wait at the end to arrest it,
And ceased the moment life appeared.

All goes onward and outward—and nothing collapses,
And to die is different from what any one supposed, and
   luckier.
…

20
Who goes there! hankering, gross, mystical, nude?
How is it I extract strength from the beef I eat?

What is a man anyhow? what am I? and what are you?
All I mark as my own you shall offset it with your own,
Else it were time lost listening to me.

I do not snivel that snivel the world over,
That months are vacuums and the ground but wallow
   and filth,
That life is a suck and a sell, and nothing remains at the
   end but threadbare crape and tears.

Whimpering and truckling fold with powders for
    invalids—conformity goes to the fourth-removed,
I cock my hat as I please indoors or out.

Shall I pray? shall I venerate and be ceremonious?
I have pried through the strata and analyzed to a hair,
And counselled with doctors and calculated close and
    found no sweeter fat than sticks to my own bones.

In all people I see myself, none more and not one a
    barley-corn less,
And the good or bad I say of myself I say of them.

And I know I am solid and sound,
To me the converging objects of the universe
    perpetually flow,
All are written to me, and I must get what the writing
    means.

And I know I am deathless,
I know this orbit of mine cannot be swept by a
    carpenter's compass,
I know I shall not pass like a child's carlacue cut with
    a burnt stick at night.

I know I am august,
I do not trouble my spirit to vindicate itself or be
    understood,
I see that the elementary laws never apologize,
I reckon I behave no prouder than the level I plant
    my house by after all.

I exist as I am, that is enough,
If no other in the world be aware I sit content,
And if each and all be aware I sit content.

One world is aware, and by far the largest to me, and
    that is myself,
And whether I come to my own today or in ten
    thousand or ten million years,
I can cheerfully take it now, or with equal
    cheerfulness I can wait.

My foothold is tenoned and mortised in granite,
I laugh at what you call dissolution,
And I know the amplitude of time.
…

24

Walt Whitman, an American, one of the roughs, a
    kosmos,
Disorderly fleshy and sensual, eating drinking and
    breeding,
No sentimentalist—no stander above men and women
    or apart from them—no more modest than
    immodest.

Unscrew the locks from the doors!
Unscrew the doors themselves from their jambs!

Whoever degrades another degrades me, and whatever
    is done or said returns at last to me,
And whatever I do or say I also return.

Through me the afflatus surging and surging—through
    me the current and index.

I speak the pass-word primeval—I give the sign of
    democracy,
By God! I will accept nothing which all cannot have
    their counterpart of on the same terms.

Through me many long dumb voices,
Voices of the interminable generations of slaves,
Voices of prostitutes and of deformed persons,
Voices of the diseased and despairing, and of thieves
    and dwarfs,
Voices of cycles of preparation and accretion,
And of the threads that connect the stars—and of
    wombs, and of the father-stuff,
And of the rights of them the others are down upon,
Of the trivial and flat and foolish and despised,
Of fog in the air and beetles rolling balls of dung.

Through me forbidden voices,
Voices of sexes and lusts—voices veiled, and I remove
    the veil,
Voices indecent by me clarified and transfigured.

I do not press my finger across my mouth,
I keep as delicate around the bowels as around the
    head and heart,
Copulation is no more rank to me than death is.

I believe in the flesh and the appetites,
Seeing hearing and feeling are miracles, and each
    part and tag of me is a miracle.

Divine am I inside and out, and I make holy whatever
    I touch or am touched from,
The scent of these arm-pits is aroma finer than
    prayer,
This head is more than churches or bibles or creeds.

If I worship one thing more than another it shall be
    the spread of my own body, or any part of it.
Translucent mould of me it shall be you,
Shaded ledges and rests, firm masculine coulter, it
    shall be you,
Whatever goes to the tilth of me it shall be you,
You my rich blood, your milky stream pale strippings
    of my life,
Breast that presses against other breasts it shall be
    you,
My brain it shall be your occult convolutions,
Root of washed sweet-flag, timorous pond-snipe, nest
    of guarded duplicate eggs, it shall be you,
Mixed tussled hay of head and beard and brawn it
    shall be you,
Trickling sap of maple, fibre of manly wheat, it shall
    be you,
Sun so generous it shall be you,
Vapors lighting and shading my face it shall be you,
You sweaty brooks and dews it shall be you,
Winds whose soft-tickling genitals rub against me it
    shall be you,
Broad muscular fields, branches of live oak, loving
    lounger in my winding paths, it shall be you,
Hands I have taken, face I have kissed, mortal I have
    ever touched, it shall be you.

I dote on myself—there is that lot of me, and all so
    luscious,
Each moment and whatever happens thrills me with
    joy.

I cannot tell how my ankles bend, nor whence the
    cause of my faintest wish,
Nor the cause of the friendship I emit, nor the cause
    of the friendship I take again.

To walk up my stoop is unaccountable, I pause to
    consider if it really be,
That I eat and drink is spectacle enough for the great
    authors and schools,
A morning-glory at my window satisfies me more
    than the metaphysics of books.

To behold the daybreak!
The little light fades the immense and diaphanous
    shadows,
The air tastes good to my palate.
Hefts of the moving world at innocent gambols,
    silently rising, freshly exuding,
Scooting obliquely high and low.

Something I cannot see puts upward libidinous
    prongs,
Seas of bright juice suffuse heaven.

The earth by the sky staid with—the daily close of
    their junction,
The heaved challenge from the east that moment
    over my head,
The mocking taunt, See then whether you shall be
    master!
…

51
The past and present wilt—I have filled them and
    emptied them,
And proceed to fill my next fold of the future.

Listener up there! what have you to confide to me?
Look in my face while I snuff the sidle of evening,
Talk honestly, for no one else hears you, and I stay
    only a minute longer.

Do I contradict myself?
Very well then, I contradict myself,
I am large—I contain multitudes.

I concentrate toward them that are nigh—I wait on
the door-slab.

Who has done his day's work and will soonest be
through with his supper?
Who wishes to walk with me?

Will you speak before I am gone? Will you prove
already too late?

52

The spotted hawk swoops by and accuses me—he
complains of my gab and my loitering.
I too am not a bit tamed—I too am untranslatable,
I sound my barbaric yawp over the roofs of the world.

The last scud of day holds back for me,
It flings my likeness after the rest and true as any on
the shadowed wilds,
It coaxes me to the vapor and the dusk.

I depart as air—I shake my white locks at the
runaway sun,
I effuse my flesh in eddies and drift it in lacy jags.

I bequeath myself to the dirt to grow from the grass I
love,
If you want me again look for me under your
boot-soles.

You will hardly know who I am or what I mean,
But I shall be good health to you nevertheless,
And filter and fibre your blood.

Failing to fetch me at first keep encouraged,
Missing me one place search another,
I stop some where waiting for you.

[1855]

Crossing Brooklyn Ferry

1

Flood-tide below me! I see you, face to face!
Clouds of the west! sun there half an hour high! I see
you also face to face.

Crowds of men and women attired in the usual
costumes! how curious you are to me!
On the ferry-boats, the hundreds and hundreds that
cross, returning home, are more curious to me than
you suppose,
And you that shall cross from shore to shore years hence,
are more to me, and more in my meditations, than
you might suppose.

2

The impalpable sustenance of me from all things, at all
hours of the day,
The simple, compact, well-joined scheme—myself
disintegrated, every one disintegrated, yet part of the
scheme,
The similitudes of the past, and those of the future,
The glories strung like beads on my smallest sights and
hearings—on the walk in the street, and the passage
over the river,
The current rushing so swiftly, and swimming with me
far away,
The others that are to follow me, the ties between me
and them,
The certainty of others—the life, love, sight, hearing of
others.

Others will enter the gates of the ferry, and cross from
shore to shore,
Others will watch the run of the flood-tide,
Others will see the shipping of Manhattan north and
west, and the heights of Brooklyn to the south and
east,

Others will see the islands large and small,
Fifty years hence, others will see them as they cross,
   the sun half an hour high,
A hundred years hence, or ever so many hundred years
   hence, others will see them,
Will enjoy the sunset, the pouring-in of the flood-tide,
   the falling-back to the sea of the ebb-tide.

3
It avails not, neither time or place—distance avails not,
I am with you, you men and women of a generation, or
   ever so many generations hence,
Just as you feel when you look on the river and sky, so I
   felt,
Just as any of you is one of a living crowd, I was one of
   a crowd,
Just as you are refreshed by the gladness of the river,
   and the bright flow, I was refreshed,
Just as you stand and lean on the rail, yet hurry with
   the swift current, I stood, yet was hurried,
Just as you look on the numberless masts of ships, and
   the thick-stemmed pipes of steamboats, I looked.

I too many and many a time crossed the river, of old,
Watched the December sea-gulls—saw them high in the
   air, floating with motionless wings, oscillating their
   bodies,
Saw how the glistening yellow lit up parts of their
   bodies, and left the rest in strong shadow,
Saw the slow-wheeling circles, and the gradual edging
   toward the south,
Saw the reflection of the summer sky in the water,
Had my eyes dazzled by the shimmering track of beams,
Looked at the fine centrifugal spokes of light round the
   shape of my head in the sunlit water,
Looked on the haze on the hills southward and south-
   westward,
Looked on the vapor as it flew in fleeces tinged with
   violet,

Looked toward the lower bay to notice the arriving
   ships,
Saw their approach, saw aboard those that were near
   me,
Saw the white sails of schooners and sloops, saw the
   ships at anchor,
The sailors at work in the rigging, or out astride the
   spars,
The round masts, the swinging motion of the hulls, the
   slender serpentine pennants,
The large and small steamers in motion, the pilots in
   their pilot-houses,
The white wake left by the passage, the quick tremulous
   whirl of the wheels,
The flags of all nations, the falling of them at sunset,
The scallop-edged waves in the twilight, the ladled cups,
   the frolicsome crests and glistening,
The stretch afar growing dimmer and dimmer, the gray
   walls of the granite storehouses by the docks,
On the river the shadowy group, the big steam-tug
   closely flanked on each side by the barges—the
   hay-boat, the belated lighter,
On the neighboring shore, the fires from the foundry
   chimneys burning high and glaringly into the night,
Casting their flicker of black, contrasted with wild red
   and yellow light, over the tops of houses, and down
   into the clefts of streets.

4
These, and all else, were to me the same as they are to
   you,
I loved well those cities,
I loved well the stately and rapid river,
The men and women I saw were all near to me,
Others the same—others who look back on me, because
   I looked forward to them,
(The time will come, though I stop here to-day and
   to-night.)

5

What is it, then, between us?
What is the count of the scores or hundreds of years
    between us?

Whatever it is, it avails not—distance avails not, and
    place avails not,
I too lived, Brooklyn of ample hills was mine,
I too walked the streets of Manhattan island, and
    bathed in the waters around it,
I too felt the curious abrupt questionings stir within me,
In the day, among crowds of people, sometimes they
    came upon me,
In my walks home late at night, or as I lay in my bed,
    they came upon me,
I too had been struck from the float forever held in
    solution,
I too had received identity by my body,
That I was, I knew was of my body—and what I should
    be, I knew I should be of my body.

6

It is not upon you alone the dark patches fall,
The dark threw patches down upon me also,
The best I had done seemed to me blank and
    suspicious,
My great thoughts, as I supposed them, were they not
    in reality meagre?
Nor is it you alone who know what it is to be evil,
I am he who knew what it was to be evil,
I too knitted the old knot of contrariety,
Blabbed, blushed, resented, lied, stole, grudged,
Had guile, anger, lust, hot wishes I dared not speak,
Was wayward, vain, greedy, shallow, sly, a solitary
    committer, a coward, a malignant person,
The wolf, the snake, the hog, not wanting in me,
The cheating look, the frivolous word, the adulterous
    wish, not wanting,
Refusals, hates, postponements, meanness, laziness,
    none of these wanting,

Was one with the rest, the days and haps of the rest,
Was called by my nighest name by clear loud voices of
    young men as they saw me approaching or passing,
Felt their arms on my neck as I stood, or the negligent
    leaning of their flesh against me as I sat,
Saw many I loved in the street, or ferry-boat, or public
    assembly, yet never told them a word,
Lived the same life with the rest, the same old laughing,
    gnawing, sleeping,
Played the part that still looks back on the actor or
    actress,
The same old role, the role that is what we make it, as
    great as we like,
Or as small as we like, or both great and small.

7

Closer yet I approach you,
What thought you have of me, I had as much of you—
    I laid in my stores in advance,
I considered long and seriously of you before you were
    born.

Who was to know what should come home to me?
Who knows but I am enjoying this?
Who knows, for all the distance, but I am as good as
    looking at you now, for all you cannot see me?

8

Ah, what can ever be more stately and admirable to me
    than my mast-hemm'd Manhattan,
My river and sunset, and my scallop-edged waves of
    flood-tide,
The sea-gulls oscillating their bodies, the hay-boat in the
    twilight, and the belated lighter;
What gods can exceed these that clasp me by the hand,
    and with voices I love call me promptly and loudly by
    my nighest name as I approach?
What is more subtle than this which ties me to the
    woman or man that looks in my face,

Which fuses me into you now, and pours my meaning
into you?

We understand, then, do we not?
What I promised without mentioning it, have you not
accepted?
What the study could not teach—what the preaching
could not accomplish is accomplished, is it not?

9
Flow on, river! flow with the flood-tide, and ebb with
the ebb-tide!
Frolic on, crested and scallop-edged waves!
Gorgeous clouds of the sunset! drench with your
splendor me, or the men and women generations
after me!
Cross from shore to shore, countless crowds of
passengers!
Stand up, talls masts of Mannahatta!—stand up,
beautiful hills of Brooklyn!
Throb, baffled and curious brain! throw out questions
and answers!
Suspend here and everywhere, eternal float of solution!
Blab, blush, lie, steal, you or I or any one after us!
Gaze, loving and thirsting eyes, in the house, or street,
or public assembly!
Sound out, voices of young men! loudly and musically
call me by my nighest name!
Live, old life! play the part that looks back on the actor
or actress!
Play the old role, the role that is great or small,
according as one makes it!
Consider, you who peruse me, whether I may not in
unknown ways be looking upon you!
Be firm, rail over the river, to support those who lean
idly, yet haste with the hasting current!
Fly on, sea-birds! fly sideways, or wheel in large circles
high in the air!

Receive the summer-sky, you water! and faithfully
hold it, till all downcast eyes have time to take it
from you!
Diverge, fine spokes of light, from the shape of my
head, or any one's head, in the sun-lit water!
Come on, ships from the lower bay! pass up or down,
white-sailed schooners, sloops, lighters!
Flaunt away, flags of all nations! be duly lowered at
sunset!
Burn high your fires, foundry chimneys! cast black
shadows at nightfall! cast red and yellow light over
the tops of the houses!
Appearances, now or henceforth, indicate what you are,
You necessary film, continue to envelop the soul,
About my body for me, and your body for you, be hung
our divinest aromas,
Thrive, cities! bring your freight, bring your shows,
ample and sufficient rivers,
Expand, being than which none else is perhaps more
spiritual,
Keep your places, objects than which none else is more
lasting.

You have waited, you always wait, you dumb, beautiful
ministers,
We receive you with free sense at last, and are insatiate
henceforward,
Not you any more shall be able to foil us, or withhold
yourselves from us,
We use you, and do not cast you aside—we plant you
permanently within us,
We fathom you not—we love you—there is perfection in
you also,
You furnish your parts toward eternity,
Great or small, you furnish your parts toward the soul.

[1856]

Bivouac on a Mountain Side

I see before me now, a traveling army halting,
Below, a fertile valley spread, with barns, and the orchards of summer,
Behind, the terraced sides of a mountain, abrupt in places, rising high,
Broken, with rocks, with clinging cedars, with tall shapes, dingily seen,
The numerous camp-fires scatter'd near and far, some away up on the mountain,
The shadowy forms of men and horses, looming, large-sized, flickering,
And over all, the sky—the sky! far, far out of reach, studded with the eternal stars.

[1865]

The Last Invocation

At the last, tenderly,
From the walls of the powerful fortress'd house,
From the clasp of the knitted locks, from the keep of the well-closed doors,
Let me be wafted.

Let me glide noiselessly forth;
With the key of softness under the locks—with a whisper,
Set ope the doors O soul.

Tenderly—be not impatient,
(Strong is your hold O mortal flesh,
Strong is your hold O love.)

[1871]

America

DISC 1, TRACK 8

Centre of equal daughters, equal sons,
All, all alike endear'd, grown, ungrown, young or old,
Strong, ample, fair, enduring, capable, rich,
Perennial with the Earth, with Freedom, Law and Love,
A grand, sane, towering, seated Mother,
Chair'd in the adamant of Time.

[1888]

William Butler Yeats

(1865–1939) b. Dublin, Ireland

Disc 1
Tracks 9–12

William Butler Yeats, born in Dublin on June 13, 1865, is considered by many the greatest poet of the twentieth century. Born into the Irish Protestant middle class, Yeats was the son of John Butler Yeats, a Dublin lawyer turned artist, and Susan Mary Pollexfen, the eldest daughter of a Sligo family in the shipping and milling business. Yeats received no formal education until he was eleven, when he attended the Godolphin Grammar School in Hammersmith, just outside of London. He then attended Erasmus High School in Dublin, where he studied primarily art. Having already begun writing accomplished poetry in his youth, Yeats decided not to follow the family tradition of attending Trinity College, Dublin, but instead enrolled in Dublin's Metropolitan School of Art. At this time, Yeats's interest in the occult flowered into the formation, with his friend George Russell, of the Dublin Hermetic Society. Yeats's passionate study of spiritualism and mysticism persisted throughout his life, culminating in the creation of the elaborate and cryptic cosmogony explained in his philosophical book, *A Vision* (1926).

In 1885, Yeats met the Irish nationalist John O'Leary, who turned Yeats's attention to the Gaelic revival and the Celtic nationalist movement then developing in Ireland. Irish folklore and heritage became yet another integral element of Yeats's writings and poetry from this time onward. Yeats's first book, a short play titled *Mosada*, was published in 1886. (In time, he would write twenty-five verse plays, including *The Player Queen* in 1922 and *Purgatory* in 1939.) In 1889, O'Leary introduced Yeats to Maud Gonne, a fiery and beautiful Irish nationalist. Repeatedly refusing his marriage proposals, Gonne was to remain the unattained ideal throughout Yeats's life. Also in 1889, Yeats published *The Wanderings of Oisin,* his first book of lyric poetry.

Yeats developed a friendship with Ezra Pound and drew inspiration from him from 1910 onward. In 1917, after one last rejected proposal to Maud Gonne, Yeats married Georgie Hyde-Lees, an educated and unconventional woman from London who, on their honeymoon, began to communicate with the spirit world by means of automatic writing. Yeats was fifty-two years old when he wed Georgie, who was only twenty-five at the time, and began the restoration of Thoor Ballylee, a tower in County Galway not far from Coole Park. Although they lived in the tower only briefly, it would occupy a prominent place in his personal symbology. In 1919, Yeats published *The Wild Swans at Coole,* a book of poems whose title refers to Coole Park, the home of Lady Gregory and site where Yeats passed many of his summers. Yeats's relationship with Georgie inspired some of his greatest love poems and also introduced a vital turning point in his writing career. Following their marriage, Yeats wrote monumental books of poetry, including *Michael Robartes and the Dancer* (1921), *The Tower* (1928), and *The Winding Stair and Other Poems* (1933). The couple had two children together, a daughter, Anne Butler Yeats, born in 1919, and a son, Michael Butler Yeats, born in 1921.

Yeats won the Nobel Prize for Literature in 1923. With the establishment of the Irish Free State, Yeats was given a seat in the new Irish Senate in 1922, but due to failing health, was compelled to step down from the position in 1928. He devoted the rest of his life to poetry and died of heart failure on January 28, 1939, on the French Riviera. Although buried in France, his remains were moved to his beloved County Sligo in 1948, where his tombstone is engraved with the unforgettable epitaph which he himself composed: "Cast a cold Eye / On Life, on Death. / Horseman, pass by!"

Seamus Heaney on William Butler Yeats

Opinions are divided about W.B. Yeats's way of reading his poems. There are those who like the elevated chant and approve of the distinction it creates between formal verse and informal conversation; and there are those who dislike it because they want the low-key give-and-take of ordinary speech to be retained when poetry is spoken aloud.

I have no doubt about which side I am on: I think Yeats's semi-liturgical utterance is both right and revealing. Once you hear the heightened voice and the sustained syntax, the held line and the pointed rhyme, you understand that for him the poem was first and foremost a bodying forth of sound. Robert Frost spoke of "the sound of sense" as an important element in his poetics, but in Yeats's case what we are dealing with is a hefted shape. In a silent reading of his work, your inner ear does indeed respond to the emphatic, metrical pace of the writing, but when he performs, the sound-pitch and the sense-push are inescapable, and you almost want to stand up and mime in accompaniment. To listen to the old poet give passionate utterance, line by articulated line, to the second from last stanza of "Coole Park and Ballylee, 1931" is to experience physically the sense of a famous statement he would make a few years later in "A General Introduction to My Work":

I sometimes compare myself with the mad old slum women I hear denouncing and remembering; "How dare you," I heard one say of some imaginary suitor, "and you without health or home!" If I spoke my thoughts aloud they might be as angry and as wild. It was a long time before I had made a language to my liking; I began to make it when I discovered twenty years ago that I must seek, not as Wordsworth thought, words in common use, but a powerful and passionate syntax, and a complete coincidence between period and stanza. Because I need a passionate syntax for passionate subject matter I compel myself to accept those traditional metres that have developed with the language.

Listen to the way Yeats amplifies the rhyme-words "sound" and "bound" at the end of the first and third lines of the fourth stanza of "Coole Park and Ballylee, 1931," and the way he gives a cutting edge to the vowels in "chair" and "everywhere" at the end of the second and fourth. The music of "remembering" resonates in the former case, the music of "denouncing," of an "angry and wild" response to old age, in the latter. And from the beginning to the end of the spoken stanza, that feeling of a man "compelling himself to accept…traditional metres" is present in the held tension, the sustained pitch, the voice braced to carry another line and yet another until the gathered force of the appositional phrases winds down to the full stop—an aural as well as a visual full stop—after "came."

In one of his soliloquies, Hamlet speaks contemptuously of himself because he "unpacks his heart in words," and thereby slackens and expends his power and spirit. With Yeats, it is otherwise. In his words, the heart is always packed, the spirit cresting.

Yeats included this poem, "Those Images," in a handwritten letter to Edith Shackleton Heald.

The Lake Isle of Innisfree

I will arise and go now, and go to Innisfree,
And a small cabin build there, of clay and wattles made:
Nine bean-rows will I have there, a hive for the honey-bee,
And live alone in the bee-loud glade.

And I shall have some peace there, for peace comes dropping slow,
Dropping from the veils of the morning to where the cricket sings;
There midnight's all a glimmer, and noon a purple glow,
And evening full of the linnet's wings.

I will arise and go now, for always night and day
I hear lake water lapping with low sounds by the shore;
While I stand on the roadway, or on the pavements grey,
I hear it in the deep heart's core.

[1890]

Adam's Curse

We sat together at one summer's end,
That beautiful mild woman, your close friend,
And you and I, and talked of poetry.
I said, "A line will take us hours maybe;
Yet if it does not seem a moment's thought,
Our stitching and unstitching has been naught.
Better go down upon your marrow-bones
And scrub a kitchen pavement, or break stones
Like an old pauper, in all kinds of weather;
For to articulate sweet sounds together
Is to work harder than all these, and yet
Be thought an idler by the noisy set
Of bankers, schoolmasters, and clergymen
The martyrs call the world."

And thereupon
That beautiful mild woman for whose sake
There's many a one shall find out all heartache
On finding that her voice is sweet and low
Replied, "To be born woman is to know—
Although they do not talk of it at school—
That we must labour to be beautiful."

I said, "It's certain there is no fine thing
Since Adam's fall but needs much labouring.
There have been lovers who thought love should be
So much compounded of high courtesy
That they would sigh and quote with learned looks
Precedents out of beautiful old books;
Yet now it seems an idle trade enough."

We sat grown quiet at the name of love;
We saw the last embers of daylight die,
And in the trembling blue-green of the sky
A moon, worn as if it had been a shell
Washed by time's waters as they rose and fell
About the stars and broke in days and years.

I had a thought for no one's but your ears:
That you were beautiful, and that I strove
To love you in the old high way of love;
That it had all seemed happy, and yet we'd grown
As weary-hearted as that hollow moon.

[1902]

The Second Coming

Turning and turning in the widening gyre
The falcon cannot hear the falconer;
Things fall apart; the centre cannot hold;
Mere anarchy is loosed upon the world,
The blood-dimmed tide is loosed, and everywhere
The ceremony of innocence is drowned;
The best lack all conviction, while the worst
Are full of passionate intensity.

Surely some revelation is at hand;
Surely the Second Coming is at hand.
The Second Coming! Hardly are those words out
When a vast image out of *Spiritus Mundi*
Troubles my sight: somewhere in sands of the desert
A shape with lion body and the head of a man,
A gaze blank and pitiless as the sun,
Is moving its slow thighs, while all about it
Reel shadows of the indignant desert birds.
The darkness drops again; but now I know
That twenty centuries of stony sleep
Were vexed to nightmare by a rocking cradle,
And what rough beast, its hour come round at last,
Slouches towards Bethlehem to be born?

[1920]

Among School Children

I

I walk through the long schoolroom questioning;
A kind old nun in a white hood replies;
The children learn to cipher and to sing,
To study reading-books and history,
To cut and sew, be neat in everything
In the best modern way—the children's eyes
In momentary wonder stare upon
A sixty-year-old smiling public man.

II

I dream of a Ledaean body, bent
Above a sinking fire, a tale that she
Told of a harsh reproof, or trivial event
That changed some childish day to tragedy—
Told, and it seemed that our two natures blent
Into a sphere from youthful sympathy,
Or else, to alter Plato's parable,
Into the yolk and white of the one shell.

III

And thinking of that fit of grief or rage
I look upon one child or t'other there
And wonder if she stood so at that age—
For even daughters of the swan can share
Something of every paddler's heritage—
And had that colour upon cheek or hair,
And thereupon my heart is driven wild:
She stands before me as a living child.

IV

Her present image floats into the mind—
Did Quattrocento finger fashion it
Hollow of cheek as though it drank the wind
And took a mess of shadows for its meat?
And I though never of Ledaean kind
Had pretty plumage once—enough of that,
Better to smile on all that smile, and show
There is a comfortable kind of old scarecrow.

V

What youthful mother, a shape upon her lap
Honey of generation had betrayed,
And that must sleep, shriek, struggle to escape
As recollection or the drug decide,
Would think her son, did she but see that shape
With sixty or more winters on its head,
A compensation for the pang of his birth,
Or the uncertainty of his setting forth?

VI

Plato thought nature but a spume that plays
Upon a ghostly paradigm of things;
Solider Aristotle played the taws
Upon the bottom of a king of kings;
World-famous golden-thighed Pythagoras
Fingered upon a fiddle-stick or strings
What a star sang and careless Muses heard:
Old clothes upon old sticks to scare a bird.

VII

Both nuns and mothers worship images,
But those the candles light are not as those
That animate a mother's reveries,
But keep a marble or a bronze repose.
And yet they too break hearts—O Presences
That passion, piety or affection knows,
And that all heavenly glory symbolise—
O self-born mockers of man's enterprise;

VIII

Labour is blossoming or dancing where
The body is not bruised to pleasure soul,
Nor beauty born out of its own despair,
Nor blear-eyed wisdom out of midnight oil.
O chestnut tree, great rooted blossomer,
Are you the leaf, the blossom or the bole?
O body swayed to music, O brightening glance,
How can we know the dancer from the dance?

[1927]

Sailing to Byzantium

I

That is no country for old men. The young
In one another's arms, birds in the trees
—Those dying generations—at their song,
The salmon-falls, the mackerel-crowded seas,
Fish, flesh, or fowl, commend all summer long
Whatever is begotten, born, and dies.
Caught in that sensual music all neglect
Monuments of unageing intellect.

II

An aged man is but a paltry thing,
A tattered coat upon a stick, unless
Soul clap its hands and sing, and louder sing
For every tatter in its mortal dress,
Nor is there singing school but studying
Monuments of its own magnificence;
And therefore I have sailed the seas and come
To the holy city of Byzantium.

III

O sages standing in God's holy fire
As in the gold mosaic of a wall,
Come from the holy fire, perne in a gyre,
And be the singing-masters of my soul.
Consume my heart away; sick with desire
And fastened to a dying animal
It knows not what is is; and gather me
Into the artifice of eternity.

IV

Once out of nature I shall never take
My bodily form from any natural thing,
But such a form as Grecian goldsmiths make
Of hammered gold and gold enamelling
To keep a drowsy Emperor awake;
Or set upon a golden bough to sing
To lords and ladies of Byzantium
Of what is past, or passing, or to come.

[1927]

Crazy Jane on the Day of Judgment

"Love is all
Unsatisfied
That cannot take the whole
Body and soul";
And that is what Jane said.

"Take the sour
If you take me,
I can scoff and lour
And scold for an hour."
"That's certainly the case," said he.

"Naked I lay
The grass my bed;
Naked and hidden away,
That black day";
And that is what Jane said.

"What can be shown?
What true love be?
All could be known or shown
If Time were but gone."
"That's certainly the case," said he.

[1933]

Coole Park and Ballylee, 1931

Under my window-ledge the waters race,
Otters below and moor-hens on the top,
Run for a mile undimmed in Heaven's face
Then darkening through "dark" Raftery's "cellar" drop,
Run underground, rise in a rocky place
In Coole demesne, and there to finish up
Spread to a lake and drop into a hole.
What's water but the generated soul?

Upon the border of that lake's a wood
Now all dry sticks under a wintry sun,
And in a copse of beeches there I stood,
For Nature's pulled her tragic buskin on
And all the rant's a mirror of my mood:
At sudden thunder of the mounting swan
I turned about and looked where branches break
The glittering reaches of the flooded lake.

Another emblem there! That stormy white
But seems a concentration of the sky;
And, like the soul, it sails into the sight
And in the morning's gone, no man knows why;
And is so lovely that it sets to right
What knowledge or its lack had set awry,
So arrogantly pure, a child might think
It can be murdered with a spot of ink.

Sound of a stick upon the floor, a sound
From somebody that toils from chair to chair;
Beloved books that famous hands have bound,
Old marble heads, old pictures everywhere;
Great rooms where travelled men and children found
Content or joy; a last inheritor
Where none has reigned that lacked a name and fame
Or out of folly into folly came.

A spot whereon the founders lived and died
Seemed once more dear than life; ancestral trees
Or gardens rich in memory glorified
Marriages, alliances and families,
And every bride's ambition satisfied.
Where fashion or mere fantasy decrees
Man shifts about—all that great glory spent—
Like some poor Arab tribesman and his tent.

We were the last romantics—chose for theme
Traditional sanctity and loveliness;
Whatever's written in what poets name
The book of the people; whatever most can bless
The mind of man or elevate a rhyme;
But all is changed, that high horse riderless,
Though mounted in that saddle Homer rode
Where the swan drifts upon a darkening flood.

[1933]

Gertrude Stein

(1874–1946) b. Allegheny, Pennsylvania, United States

Disc 1

Tracks 13–15

Gertrude Stein was born in Allegheny, Pennsylvania, on February 3, 1874. The daughter of affluent parents, her father relocated the family to Vienna and Paris for four years before settling in Oakland, California. Following her parents' deaths, Stein moved east in 1893 and enrolled in what would later be known as Radcliffe College. There she studied psychology under the philosopher William James, whom Stein would cite as a great influence on her later writing. Perhaps intending to follow in James's footsteps, Stein enrolled in The Johns Hopkins Medical School to continue studying psychology after graduating from Radcliffe. It was here, as she would later recall, that Stein began her first romantic relationships with other women. In 1903, she moved with her brother Leo to Paris, the city that she would come to call home, and in which she would build her literary reputation.

In Paris, Stein's own artistic and literary wit, together with her brother's known skills as an art critic, drew a circle of fine artists and writers into the salon that had begun meeting in their apartment. Picasso, Matisse, Apollinaire, and Hemingway were but a few of the many illustrious figures who visited the Steins's salon. A great promoter of Modernist experimentalism, Stein made her own literary debut in 1909 with a novel titled *Three Lives*. In 1906, Stein met another American, Alice B. Toklas, with whom she fell in love. Leo moved out when Alice moved in, and Toklas became Stein's secretary as well as lifelong companion. Stein's poetic debut followed in 1914, with the publication of *Tender Buttons*, a book-length sequence of prose poems highly influenced by Cubism. Eschewing traditional, exhausted notions of syntax and composition, the book is a testament to Stein's profoundly unique sensibility and genius. Several other books of poetry followed, but none gained the wide acclaim and notoriety that this first volume did.

Stein is perhaps better known for the two novels that were to follow, *The Making of Americans* (1925), which chronicles the story of humanity in that of a single family, and *The Autobiography of Alice B. Toklas* (1933), which is actually the story of Stein's own life. While writing *Alice B. Toklas*, Stein also wrote *Stanzas in Meditation*, a difficult lyric sequence that remained unpublished long after her death but is now widely considered a masterpiece. Though both were Jewish and homosexual, Stein and Toklas remained in France throughout the Nazi occupation, and Stein later published a memoir of the experience. Stein continued to stay abreast of the literary and poetic worlds until her death from cancer on July 27, 1946, in France.

C. D. Wright on Gertrude Stein

C. D. Wright on Gertrude Stein

Gertrude Stein was born in 1874, as was Robert Frost. Rimbaud was twenty then (all done with writing), and Whitman (whose beard was famous and reported to attract butterflies) was fifty-four. English was Stein's third language. Though born in a Pittsburgh suburb, the youngest of five, she lived in Austria and France before returning to the States to grow up in Oakland. She attended Radcliffe College (then Harvard Annex; recently re-annexed but currently referred to as "merged"), and Johns Hopkins before dropping (all but flunking) out of medical school and joining her brother Leo in Paris in 1903—essentially for the duration of her life. Her relationship with France would endure, her relationship to Leo would not. Though her brother introduced her to Cezanne and Picasso among other artists, once Leo dismissed her writings as those of a kook, their days together were numbered. After their split, Stein was reported to have acknowledged her brother with a nod (bow) from her automobile; silence otherwise scored the encounter.

In 1906, she met her match in the person of Alice B. Toklas. Stein's earliest work, titled *Q.E.D.*, wasn't published until four years after her death. Indeed, most of the corpus of her genre-bending books were either published posthumously or privately—a Picasso was even unloaded to finance the publication of *Lucy Church Amiably*. Notwithstanding publishing obstacles, at the age of fifty-nine, she penned *The Autobiography of Alice B. Toklas* in six weeks and it became a bestseller. In 1934, *Four Saints in Three Acts* would open on Broadway. At the time, she was also giving lectures in America. She was a celebrity. She was a lion. She was historical, exactly as she wanted to be from "a baby on." Gertrude Stein died under anesthesia in 1946, seven years after the death of Yeats, almost a decade before Stevens, nearly two before Frost.

"She used words," Laura (Riding) Jackson would say of her, "as if they had no experience." A reconstructed Riding would say that self-same usage came to naught. Edmund Wilson would put her on a par with Proust, Joyce, and Yeats. No one stayed neutral about her or her writing. She knew *everybody*; everybody knew her. She expressed annoyance that people seemed more interested in her than her writing, but the writing itself was much discussed by writers, critics, and the public in her own time. Even now, it continues to be much discussed. Few can yet claim neutrality with

Stein appeared on the cover of *Time* magazine on September 11, 1933.

respect to Stein. Her influence surges, submerges, resurges. Her "violent devotion to the new" remains unsettling to a majority of readers and writers, and to some constitutes a vulgar preoccupation from the get-go. Even as an undergraduate, her professor, the poet William Vaughn Moody would scribble in her paper's margin, "Your vehemence runs away with your syntax." To find reinforcement for her way of deploying the language, she would have to look toward visual art—cubism in particular—not literature. She developed her own methods in poetry, which she treated as a plastic art—words as objects, not fixed units of meaning. However, the actual sense of the word, in "Steinese," stands clear.

Stein's signature is a vigorous application of repetition. Beginning, middle, and ending are foresworn for the loop, the continuous present, a technique she considered cinematic. Certainly with respect to the printed word, time would never be the same after Stein. "There's joy in repetition," moans singer/songwriter Prince. "I'm not a fool," Stein insisted, "I know in daily life people don't go around saying a rose is a rose is a rose, but in that line the rose is red for the first time in English poetry in one hundred years." She has a point. A noun "caressed and addressed" by Stein stimulates the senses and rewards the alert reader.

Stein's vocabulary is childishly simple and literal. Her tone is naïve. She merely verbalizes what she sees. But exposure of method is not disclosure of being. Behind the simple façade is a lion that never sleeps. And behind the lion is yet another façade. There is a boggling level of inclusiveness in Stein, made all the more so given her method of composition, the ceaseless reiteration of which, medically speaking, might qualify as a syndrome. Out of this reiteration comes an intensity, and from this inclusiveness, a democracy in word, phrase, and sentence structure which combined to vitalize poetry in a late age. No one has equaled her exaggerated melodies, and not until an admirer of the visual arts, Frank O'Hara, took to the streets of New York in the 1950s, would there be another American poet offering the era such immediacy, excitement, and an altogether rare literary streak of optimism.

Gertrude Stein was a merrily errant writer. Her unfailing ear, radical syntax, and, perhaps more than any other quality, her comfort with her own procedures, set her texts securely in the foreground of American experimentalists. If her aims can be said to begin the language all over again, she made a grand beginning.

Christian Berard

Eating is her subject.

While eating is her subject.

Where eating is her subject.

Withdraw whether it is eating which is her subject. Literally while she ate eating is her subject. Afterwards too and in between. This is an introduction to what she ate.

She ate a pigeon and a soufflé.

That was on one day.

She ate a thin ham and its sauce.

That was on another day.

She ate desserts.

That had been on one day.

She had fish grouse and little cakes that was before that day.

She had breaded veal and grapes that was on that day.

After that she ate every day.

Very little but very good.

She ate very well that day.

What is the difference between steaming and roasting, she ate it cold because of Saturday.

Remembering potatoes because of preparation for part of the day.

There is a difference in preparation of cray-fish which makes a change in their fish for instance.

What was it besides bread.

Why is eating her subject.

There are reasons why eating is her subject.

Because.

Help Helena.

With whether a pound.

Everybody who comes has been with whether we mean ours allowed.

Tea rose snuff box tea rose.

Willed him well will till well.

By higher but tire by cry my tie for her.

Meeting with with said.

Gain may be hours.

There there their softness.

By my buy high.

By my softness.

There with their willow with without out outmost lain in out.

Has she had her tooth without a telegram.

Nothing surprises Edith. Her sister made it once for all.

Chair met alongside.

Paved picnic with gratitude.

He is strong and sturdy.

Pile with a pretty boy.

Having tired of some one.

Tire try.

Imagine how they felt when they were invited.

Preamble to restitution.

Tire and indifferent.

Narratives with pistache.

A partly boiled.

Next sentence.

Now or not nightly.

A sentence it is a whether wither intended.

A sentence text. Taxed.

A sampler with ingredients may be unmixed with their accounts how does it look like. If in way around. Like lightning.

Apprehension is why they help to do what is in amount what is an amount.

A sentence felt way laid.

A sentence without a horse.

It is a mend that to distribute with send.

A sentence is in a letter ladder latter.

Birth with birth.

If any thinks about what is made for the sake they will manage to place taking take may.

How are browns.

How are browns.

Got to go away.

Anybody can be taught to love whatever whatever they like better.

Taught of butter.

Whatever they like better.

[1934]

The story of how she bowed to her brother.

Who has whom as his.

Did she bow to her brother. When she saw him.

Any long story. Of how she bowed to her brother.

Sometimes not.

She bowed to her brother. Accidentally. When she saw him.

Often as well. As not.

She did not. Bow to her brother. When she. Saw him.

This could happen. Without. Him.

Everybody finds in it a sentence that pleases them.

This is the story included in. How she bowed to her brother.

Could another brother have a grand daughter.

No. But. He could have a grandson.

This has nothing to do with the other brother of whom it is said that we read she bowed to her brother.

There could be a union between reading and learning.

And now everybody. Reads. She bowed. To her brother.

And no one. Thinks.

Thinks that it is clearly. Startling.

She started. By not bowing. To her brother.

And this was not the beginning.

She has forgotten.

How she bowed. To her brother.

And. In mentioning. She did mention. That this was. A recollection.

For fortunately. In detail. Details are given.

Made an expression. Of recollection.

Does whether. They gather. That they heard. Whether. They bowed. To each other. Or not.

If in. They made it. Doubtful. Or double. Of their holding it. A momentary after. That she was never. Readily made rather. That they were. Whether. She asked her. Was she doing anything. Either.

In all this there lay. No description. And so. Whether. They could come to be nearly. More. Than more. Or rather. Did she. Bow to her brother.

PART II

They were a few. And they knew. Not that. She had bowed. To her brother. There were not. A few. Who knew. That she. Had. Bowed to her brother. Because if they knew. They would say. That a few. Knew. That she. Had bowed to her brother. But necessarily. Not a few. Knew. They did. Not know. Because they. Were not there. There are not a few. Who are there. Because. Nobody. Was there. Nor did. She know. That she was there. To help to share. And they can. Be there. To tell. Them. So. That. They know. She bowed. To her brother. More. There. Than. There.

III

It might be easily pointed out. By the chance. Of a. Wish. No wish.

He might. Not wish. Not to. Be easily. Pointed out. By no. Wish.

Which they. Might easily.

Not be pointed. Out. As. A and not. The wish.

It is not. To be. Pointed out. That. There. Is. No wish.

Not. A wish.

She bowed to her brother. Was not easily. Pointed out. And. No wish.

Which it. And easily. Pointed out. And. No. Wish.

She and. No wish. Which is. Not easily pointed out. And. So which. They. And. No wish. Which. And not. Easily pointed out. She bowed to her brother. And no wish. And not. Easily pointed out. And not. Wish.

For them. Which. To wish. Not. Which. Easily.

Pointed out. And. No wish. Which. She. No wish. Easily pointed out.

Which. She easily pointed out. Which. She bowed to her brother. And. Which.

If she had been likely to restate that doors which relate an advantage to their advancing. And not at all. As a coincidence.

She bowed to her brother. This was a chance. That might have happened. Minutely.

To interrupt a white dog. Who can occasionally.

In instance

No one counts alike

She bowed to her brother. For. And. Counts alike.

She bowed. To her brother. Could be lost. By their leaving. It as lost. By. The time. In which. They feel. They will. It is. Indebted. That able. Presence. As very much. And idle. If she were walking along. She would be. She would not. Bow to her brother. If she were riding. Along. She would. Be. She would. Be. Not as bowing. To her. Brother.

As she rode along. Easily. By driving. As she rode. Along. She. Bowed. To her brother.

It is. True. As. She drove. Along. She. Bowed. To her brother.

Just like that.

She bowed. To her brother.

They were. There. That is to say. They were. Passing there. They were passing there. But not. On that day. And with this. To say. It was said. She bowed. To her brother. Which was. A fact.

If she bowed. To her brother. Which was. A fact. That is. If she bowed. Which. If she bowed. Which she did. She bowed to her brother.

Which she did. She bowed to her brother. Or rather. Which she did. She bowed to her brother. Or rather which she did she bowed to her brother.

She could think. Of how she was. No better. Than when. They could say. Not. How do you do. To-day.

Because. It is an accident. In suddenness. When there is. No stress. On their. Address. They do not address you. By saying. Rather. That they went by. And came again. Not. As. Or. Why.

It is. What is. Even. Not always occurred. Just by the time. That it. Can happen. To be curious. She bowed. To her brother. And why. Again. In there. Should have been. Not more. Than. That. Which. She bowed. To her brother.

By which. It is. In tendency. To more. By which. It is. In tendency to not. Have had. She in the. Three. She bowed. To her brother.

Would it be. In a way. Not they. Would. Not. They. Be in a way that is. To say. She. Is to say. Did. She bow. To her brother. In. Which way. Did. She come to say. It was. That way.

She bowed to her brother.

It it was. Separately. Not. To separate. Separately. Won. Is there. But three. Was it. With them. As perhaps. Portions. For three. Which. In which. She bowed to her brother.

Not. After. In intention. The same. As mention. She did not mention. Nor was there. Intention. That she. Bowed to her brother.

She bowed to her brother.

[1934]

If I Told Him
A Completed Portrait of Picasso

If I told him would he like it. Would he like it if I told him.

Would he like it would Napoleon would Napoleon would would he like it.

If Napoleon if I told him if I told him if Napoleon. Would he like it if I told him if I told him if Napoleon. Would he like it if Napoleon if Napoleon if I told him. If I told him if Napoleon if Napoleon if I told him. If I told him would he like it would he like it if I told him.

Now.

Not now.

And now.

Now.

Exactly as as kings.

Feeling full for it.

Exactitude as kings.

So to beseech you as full as for it.

Exactly or as kings.

Shutters shut and open so do queens. Shutters shut and shutters and so shutters shut and shutters and so and so shutters and so shutters shut and so shutters shut and shutters and so. And so shutters shut and so and also. And also and so and so and also.

Exact resemblance to exact resemblance the exact resemblance as exact as a resemblance, exactly as resembling, exactly resembling, exactly in resemblance exactly a resemblance, exactly and resemblance. For this is so. Because.

Now actively repeat at all, now actively repeat at all, now actively repeat at all.

Have hold and hear, actively repeat at all.

I judge judge.

As a resemblance to him.

Who comes first. Napoleon the first.

Who comes too coming coming too, who goes there, as they go they share, who shares all, all is as all as as yet or as yet.

Now to date now to date. Now and now and date and the date.

Who came first Napoleon at first. Who came first Napoleon the first. Who came first, Napoleon first.

Presently.

Exactly do they do.

First exactly.

Exactly do they do too.

First exactly.

And first exactly.

Exactly do they do.

And first exactly and exactly.

And do they do.

At first exactly and first exactly and do they do.

The first exactly.

And do they do.

The first exactly.

At first exactly.

First as exactly.

At first as exactly.

Presently.

As presently.

As as presently.

He he he he and he and he and and he and he and he and and as and as he and as he and he. He is and as he is, and as he is and he is, he is and as he and he and as he is and he and he and and he and he.

Can curls rob can curls quote, quotable.
As presently.
As exactitude.
As trains.
Has trains.
Has trains.
As trains.
As trains.
Presently.
Proportions.
Presently.
As proportions as presently.
Father and farther.
Was the king or room.
Farther and whether.
Was there was there was there what was there was there what was there was there there was there.
Whether and in there.
As even say so.
One.
I land.
Two.
I land.
Three.
The land.
Three.
The land.
Three.
The land.
Two.
I land.
Two.
I land.
One.

I land.
Two.
I land.
As a so.
They cannot.
A note.
They cannot.
A float.
They cannot.
They dote.
They cannot.
They as denote.
Miracles play.
Play fairly.
Play fairly well.
A well.
As well.
As or as presently.
Let me recite what history teaches. History teaches.

[1934]

Robert Frost

(1874–1963) b. San Francisco, California, United States

Disc 1
Tracks 16–21

Considering Robert Frost's long-standing association with New England, it is perhaps surprising that he hails from San Francisco, where he was born on March 26, 1874. Frost lived there for his first eleven years until his father, a journalist and politician, died of tuberculosis. His family then moved to Lawrence, Massachusetts, where Frost attended high school. He published his first poems in the high school's *Bulletin* and graduated co-valedictorian with Elinor White, whom he later married. In 1892, Frost enrolled at Dartmouth, but quit after only a semester; five years later, he enrolled in Harvard, but again quit before completion. He never earned a college degree, but instead worked odd jobs at mills and grammar schools and operated a farm. Although he wrote many poems during this period, he published few. His only notable success was the publication of the poem "My Butterfly: An Elegy" in the New York literary magazine *The Independent*.

In 1912, perhaps frustrated by the lack of poetic success, Frost uprooted and moved to England. He was quickly encompassed into a literary circle that included Ezra Pound (whom Frost appears not to have admired very much), Robert Graves, T.E. Hulme, and Edward Thomas, a young critic who became one of Frost's closest friends and critics. In England, Frost's first book of poetry, *A Boy's Will* (1913), was published relatively quickly and met with great success; and his second volume, *North of Boston* (1914), is frequently acknowledged as the finest of all Frost's collections.

With his success as a poet secured, Frost and his family returned to the United States where they purchased a New Hampshire farm in 1915. His next book of poetry, *Mountain Interval* (1916), only increased his renown in America and brought with it a long series of poetry readings, lectures, and university affiliations. The collection *New Hampshire*, published in 1923, brought Frost the first of his four Pulitzer Prizes, which accompany an astonishing number of other awards and accolades. He continued to write poetry for the rest of his life, and in 1961, he became the first poet ever to read at a presidential inauguration when he was invited to recite his poem "The Gift Outright" for John F. Kennedy.

Robert Frost died in Boston on January 29, 1963. Rejecting the more fashionable poetical experimentalism of his day, Frost was an unequalled master of verse forms and metrics. Suffused with a dark and unmistakably modern psychology, his work overturns the very category of quaint, regional poetry into which it is too often placed. His image as the New England farmer-poet belies the timeless, universal concepts and tensions found in his work.

Richard Wilbur on Robert Frost

There is a singer everyone has heard,
Loud, a mid-summer and a mid-wood bird,
Who makes the solid tree trunks sound again.
He says that leaves are old and that for flowers
Mid-summer is to spring as one to ten.
He says the early petal-fall is past
When pear and cherry bloom went down in showers
On sunny days a moment overcast;
And comes that other fall we name the fall.
He says the highway dust is over all.
The bird would cease and be as other birds
But that he knows in singing not to sing.
The question that he frames in all but words
Is what to make of a diminished thing.

The oven bird, which Frost celebrates in that irregular sonnet, is a woods-dwelling warbler whose mid-summer song is "Teacher! Teacher! Teacher!" repeated ten or a dozen times. That might make one think of some school child, with raised hand, who is eager to ask a question; and the poem does end by asking a question—"what to make of a diminished thing?" We might, and should, take that question to reflect the diminishment of the bird's world, the loss of spring with its flowers and mating-cries, and the coming of fall. One of Frost's great virtues is that any poem of his is fully satisfying on a literal level. Yet by what Frost called a "displacement," we might also take this poem to be about that other kind of "singer," the poet. In that case, the question would mean, "How shall a poet keep on writing when his youthful fervor and inspiration have declined?" Finally, in a further resonance, the poem might be asking what poetry—with its inclination to psalm and transport and vision—should do with itself in the doubtful twentieth century?

As anyone who has read Frost in quantity knows, all of those understandings—the literal one and the two suggested ones—are legitimate. The poet himself did not like to hear his hints and overtones expounded, but they are there.

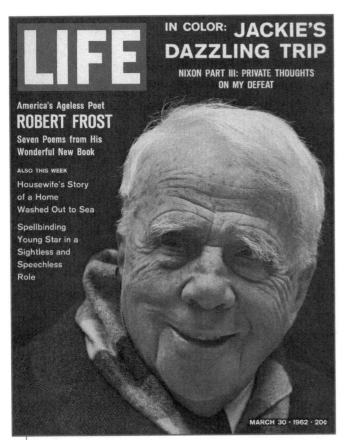

Life magazine celebrated the eighty-eight-year-old Frost's new book with a cover story in the March 30, 1962, issue.

Frost writes a skeptical, considering poetry, which includes some reticent but real acknowledgments of the Creator. There is strong human love in it, and strong love for an unanswering Nature. A persistent theme, often embodied in wall-symbolism, is that of human limitations: there are negative limits (to our knowledge, for instance, or our charity) but there are also benign limits (boundaries, traditions) within which coherence and character are sustained. Frost's poetry begins by choosing certain limits for itself; it takes its initial stand in the local, the rural, the particular, and the colloquial. And, having said this, we may take a moment to glance at what it means—in terms of music—for the oven bird to "know in singing not to sing."

In a famous early letter to a friend, Frost distinguished between his own practice and that of Swinburnian poets for whom "the music of words was a matter of harmonized vowels and consonants." For Frost, the earthier objective was "to make music out of what I may call the sound of sense"—which meant that the sounds and rhythms of his poems were to echo or evoke the natural intonations of animated speech. There are times, in Frost, when he seems to be asking that we read him with a Yankee accent; but he is far from being a dialect poet, and any English-speaking reader will hear in his lines the live, familiar tones and emphases of a conversing voice.

In his turning away from abstract musicality, and in his basing of poetry in everyday speech, Frost was one of the great invigorators of modern verse. When he gave what is now called a "poetry reading," it bore no resemblance to a concert; it was not a sequence of performances interspersed with hushes and applause. What it consisted of was a rambling and engaging monologue, in the course of which the poet would be reminded of this poem or that, and would recite it from memory—often interrupting the poem to add something parenthetical. In such a format, Frost might at times slight the exquisiteness of a poem like "Spring Pools," or the grimness of some other; yet many of his poems were magnificently said. Listening to them in isolation, as they happen on Disc One, it is well to remember Frost's reading practice and to imagine them as rising out of a flow of great talk. As indeed they did.

The Oven Bird

DISC 1, TRACK 17

There is a singer everyone has heard,
Loud, a mid-summer and a mid-wood bird,
Who makes the solid tree trunks sound again.
He says that leaves are old and that for flowers
Mid-summer is to spring as one to ten.
He says the early petal-fall is past,
When pear and cherry bloom went down in showers
On sunny days a moment overcast;
And comes that other fall we name the fall.
He says the highway dust is over all.
The bird would cease and be as other birds
But that he knows in singing not to sing.
The question that he frames in all but words
Is what to make of a diminished thing.

[1916]

The Road Not Taken

DISC 1, TRACK 18

Two roads diverged in a yellow wood,
And sorry I could not travel both
And be one traveler, long I stood
And looked down one as far as I could
To where it bent in the undergrowth;

Then took the other, as just as fair,
And having perhaps the better claim,
Because it was grassy and wanted wear;
Though as for that, the passing there
Had worn them really about the same,

And both that morning equally lay
In leaves no step had trodden black.
Oh, I kept the first for another day!
Yet knowing how way leads on to way,
I doubted if I should ever come back.

I shall be telling this with a sigh
Somewhere ages and ages hence:
Two roads diverged in a wood, and I—
I took the one less traveled by,
And that has made all the difference.

[1916]

Stopping by Woods on a Snowy Evening

DISC 1, TRACK 19

Whose woods these are I think I know.
His house is in the village, though;
He will not see me stopping here
To watch his woods fill up with snow.

My little horse must think it queer
To stop without a farmhouse near
Between the woods and frozen lake
The darkest evening of the year.

He gives his harness bells a shake
To ask if there is some mistake.
The only other sound's the sweep
Of easy wind and downy flake.

The woods are lovely, dark, and deep,
But I have promises to keep,
And miles to go before I sleep,
And miles to go before I sleep.

[1923]

Nothing Gold Can Stay

DISC 1, TRACK 20

Nature's first green is gold,
Her hardest hue to hold.
Her early leaf's a flower;
But only so an hour.
Then leaf subsides to leaf.
So Eden sank to grief,
So dawn goes down to day.
Nothing gold can stay.

[1923]

To Earthward

Love at the lips was touch
As sweet as I could bear;
And once that seemed too much;
I lived on air

That crossed me from sweet things
The flow of—was it musk
From hidden grapevine springs
Down hill at dusk?

I had the swirl and ache
From sprays of honeysuckle
That when they're gathered shake
Dew on the knuckle.

I craved strong sweets, but those
Seemed strong when I was young;
The petal of the rose
It was that stung.

Now no joy but lacks salt
That is not dashed with pain
And weariness and fault;
I crave the stain

Of tears, the aftermark
Of almost too much love,
The sweet of bitter bark
And burning clove.

When stiff and sore and scarred
I take away my hand
From leaning on it hard
In grass and sand,

The hurt is not enough:
I long for weight and strength
To feel the earth as rough
To all my length.

[1923]

The Silken Tent

She is as in a field a silken tent
At midday when a sunny summer breeze
Has dried the dew and all its ropes relent,
So that in guys it gently sways at ease,
And its supporting central cedar pole,
That is its pinnacle to heavenward
And signifies the sureness of the soul,
Seems to owe naught to any single cord,
But strictly held by none, is loosely bound
By countless silken ties of love and thought
To everything on earth the compass round,
And only by one's going slightly taut
In the capriciousness of summer air
Is of the slightest bondage made aware.

[1942]

Come In

As I came to the edge of the woods,
Thrush music—hark!
Now if it was dusk outside,
Inside it was dark.

Too dark in the woods for a bird
By sleight of wing
To better its perch for the night,
Though it still could sing.

The last of the light of the sun
That had died in the west
Still lived for one song more
In a thrush's breast.

Far in the pillared dark
Thrush music went—
Almost like a call to come in
To the dark and lament.

But no, I was out for stars:
I would not come in.
I meant not even if asked,
And I hadn't been.

[1942]

Carl Sandburg

(1878–1967) b. Galesburg, Illinois, United States

Disc 1
Tracks 22-25

Born on January 6, 1878, in Galesburg, Illinois, Carl Sandburg showed little poetic or literary inclination early in his life. His parents, August and Clara Sandburg, were Swedish immigrants, and Sandburg grew up with Swedish as his first language. Some scholars have argued that Sandburg's radical metrics and poetic rhythm may be accounted for in part by his not having been a native speaker of English. At the age of thirteen, Carl left school to become a day laborer in order to help support the family. He briefly traveled west to Kansas by hopping freight trains, but then elected to serve in the Spanish-American War, during which he was stationed in Puerto Rico.

Returning home to Galesburg, Sandburg attended Lombard College for four years but never completed his degree. While there, his first volume of poems was published in 1904 with the help of his professor, Philip Wright. Titled *Reckless Ecstasy*, it was completely overlooked by both critics and the public. Leaving Illinois, Sandburg settled in Milwaukee, where his leftist political views and Socialist sympathies became apparent. He actively worked for the Social-Democrat Party, and from 1910 to 1912, he served as the secretary for Milwaukee's Socialist mayor. Before moving to Chicago in 1913, he married Lillian Steichen, a schoolteacher and sister of the celebrated photographer Edward Steichen, and began to submit poems and articles to various magazines.

In Chicago, Sandburg worked as an editorial writer for the *Daily News*. In less than a year, he won the Levinson Prize for his well-known poem "Chicago," and became recognized as a member of the Chicago literary renaissance, which also included such figures as Theodore Dreiser and Edgar Lee Masters. In 1916, his reputation as a poet skyrocketed with the publication of *Chicago Poems*. Celebrating both agricultural and urban America, he was quickly acknowledged as one of the leading poets of the day. More volumes quickly followed, including *Cornhuskers* (1918) and *Smoke and Steel* (1920), which further enhanced his reputation.

Though he continued to write and publish poetry until his death, Sandburg is also widely recognized for his other works, including a meticulously researched six-volume biography of Abraham Lincoln. The second part of this labor of love, *Abraham Lincoln: The War Years* (1939), was awarded the Pulitzer Prize. He is also remembered as a folk singer and songwriter, the author of several children's stories, and as a novelist (his *Remembrance Rock* was published in 1948). His later volumes of poetry, including *Complete Poems* (1950), which won him a second Pulitzer, and *Honey and Salt* (1963), continued his unblushing celebration of America in rich, earthy language. In 1962, Sandburg was designated Illinois' first Poet Laureate, and in 1964, he received the Medal of Freedom from President Lyndon Johnson. Sandburg died on July 22, 1967, in North Carolina, where he was living at the time. His ashes were buried beneath a "Remembrance Rock" installed in the garden behind the family's first home in Galesburg.

Rosellen Brown
Carl Sandburg

Rosellen Brown on Carl Sandburg

Carl Sandburg was an icon in his time, the kind of public poet—both humble and exalted bearer of a nation's best vision of itself—that we haven't had for many years and may never have again, given our current cynicism about public figures. Sandburg was the ruggedly handsome, burning-eyed Midwestern son of Swedish parents, one literate, the other distinctly not, whose shock of forward-falling white hair made him recognizable from a thousand feet. He won two Pulitzer prizes, one in 1940 for his biography of Lincoln in the war years, the other in 1951 for his *Complete Poems*. A charismatic reader of his work who mesmerized audiences with his guitar and a demeanor that combined just-folks humility with oracular enunciation, he was lionized by institutions as various as the NAACP and the *Ed Sullivan Show*; he addressed Congress, he advised Hollywood producers; his craggy face was featured on the cover of *Life*. Although he was born in Galesburg, Illinois, and spent most of his later years in North Carolina, Sandburg's reputation remains nothing less than heroic in Chicago: in a number of books beginning with *Chicago Poems*, he combined an unintimidating and accessible language and a loose, often prose-like line that accommodated the city's contradictions and complexity and gave shape and dignity to its roughest qualities. Every contemporary anthology included his salute to the "Hog Butcher for the World" which still refers to itself as the City of the Big Shoulders, and every child (myself included) learned by heart his haiku-like "Fog," whose imagistic paint-stroke colors many of his gentler poems. A few bridge the extremes, such as "Harbor," in which the glorious shock of the sight of Lake Michigan breaks halfway into a depressing litany of urban miseries. Sandburg's true genius lies between these two poles—between the generic, celebratory, Whitmanesque yawp ("great men, pageants of war and labor, soldiers and workers, mothers lifting their children") and the softer, painterly watercolors ("the bashful mornings hurl mist on the stripes of sunrise") in countless portraits of individual Americans, some named, some nameless, most of them so individualized one could almost identify them in a grainy wide-angled photograph or a WPA-decade painting.

Neither as complex as Whitman nor as subtle as Frost, that other white-haired sweetheart of the people, Sandburg brought a blunt, honest, documentary anger to

Life magazine cover of Sandburg from February 21, 1938

his vision of impoverished workers, neglected children, the overworked, and the underpaid. As a young journalist he had been an earnest socialist, and he never tired of punching out his casually cadenced free verse indictments of the plutocrats, industrialists, religious hucksters, and crooked politicians who feast on the flesh of the poor. ("The lawyers—tell me why a hearse horse snickers hauling a lawyer's bones.") In nearly two hundred pages of *The People, Yes*, he constructed a precise and compassionate monument to the diversity of democracy that is, finally, both wearing and magnificent. Sometimes sentimental but just as often acute and bitter in its populist cynicism about where economic and political power lie, what finally prevails is his admiration for the patience with which the powerless wear the yoke of their oppression. It's been a long time since Carl Sandburg has been taken seriously by the critics, who love to patronize him for his aesthetic deficiencies and heavy-handed sympathies, but it's only consistent that his ambition, frankly acknowledged, was to be read by the kind of people who populated his poems. The endless paradox of co-optation, of course, shows in how easily Sandburg's outraged indictments of the comfortable and the powerful went down with the well-shod prize-givers of his day—so much for the dangers of literary fury. He accepted his popularity with grace and gratitude, whatever sense of irony he felt kept securely in check, and performed as a homey elder statesman of the arts until his death in 1967. The best of his poetry has sharp teeth but his victims seem to have felt he was only dispensing love-bites and never felt injury. Or perhaps his exhaustiveness—the honor he paid a thousand characters—confused them: no matter what the editorialist may be saying, nothing, apparently, is as flattering as being included in the picture.

"Chicago" handwritten and signed by the author

Chicago

Hog Butcher for the World,
Tool Maker, Stacker of Wheat,
Player with Railroads and the Nation's Freight
    Handler;
Stormy, husky, brawling,
City of the Big Shoulders:

They tell me you are wicked and I believe them, for I
    have seen your painted women under the gas
    lamps luring the farm boys.
And they tell me you are crooked and I answer: Yes, it
    is true I have seen the gunman kill and go free to
    kill again.
And they tell me you are brutal and my reply is: On
    the faces of women and children I have seen the
    marks of wanton hunger.
And having answered so I turn once more to those
    who sneer at this my city, and I give them back
    the sneer and say to them:
Come and show me another city with lifted head
    singing so proud to be alive and coarse and strong
    and cunning.
Flinging magnetic curses amid the toil of piling job
    on job, here is a tall bold slugger set vivid against
    the little soft cities;

Fierce as a dog with tongue lapping for action,
    cunning as a savage pitted against the wilderness.
        Bareheaded,
        Shoveling,
        Wrecking,
        Planning,
        Building, breaking, rebuilding,
Under the smoke, dust all over his mouth, laughing
    with white teeth,
Under the terrible burden of destiny laughing as a
    young man laughs,
Laughing even as an ignorant fighter laughs who has
    never lost a battle,
Bragging and laughing that under his wrist is the
    pulse, and under his ribs the heart of the people,
        Laughing!
Laughing the stormy, husky, brawling laughter of
    Youth, half-naked, sweating, proud to be Hog
    Butcher, Tool Maker, Stacker of Wheat, Player
    with Railroads and Freight Handler to the Nation.

[1916]

Fog

The fog comes
on little cat feet.

It sits looking
over harbor and city
on silent haunches
and then moves on.

[1916]

Grass

DISC 1, TRACK 23

Pile the bodies high at Austerlitz and Waterloo.
Shovel them under and let me work—
              I am the grass; I cover all.

And pile them high at Gettysburg
And pile them high at Ypres and Verdun.
Shovel them under and let me work.
Two years, ten years, and passengers ask the conductor:
              What place is this?
              Where are we now?

              I am the grass.
              Let me work.

[1918]

Cool Tombs

When Abraham Lincoln was shoveled into the tombs,
    he forgot the copperheads and the assassin...in
    the dust, in the cool tombs.

And Ulysses Grant lost all thought of con men and
    Wall Street, cash and collateral turned ashes...in
    the dust, in the cool tombs.

Pocahontas' body, lovely as a poplar, sweet as a red
    haw in November or a pawpaw in May, did she
    wonder? does she remember?...in the dust, in the
    cool tombs?

Take any streetful of people buying clothes and
    groceries, cheering a hero or throwing confetti
    and blowing tin horns...tell me if the lovers are
    losers...tell me if any get more than the lovers...in
    the dust...in the cool tombs.

[1918]

107
from The People, Yes

    The people will live on.
The learning and blundering people will live on.
    They will be tricked and sold and again sold
And go back to the nourishing earth for rootholds,
    The people so peculiar in renewal and comeback,
    You can't laugh off their capacity to take it.
The mammoth rests between his cyclonic dramas.

The people so often sleepy, weary, enigmatic,
is a vast huddle with many units saying:
    "I earn my living.
    I make enough to get by
    and it takes all my time.
    If I had more time
    I could do more for myself
    and maybe for others.
    I could read and study
    and talk things over
    and find out about things.
    It takes time.
    I wish I had the time."
    The people is a tragic and comic two-face:
    hero and hoodlum: phantom and gorilla
    twisting to moan with a gargoyle mouth:
    "They buy me and sell me...it's a game...
    sometime I'll break loose..."

Once having marched
Over the margins of animal necessity,
Over the grim line of sheer subsistence
    Then man came
To the deeper rituals of his bones,
To the lights lighter than any bones,
To the time for thinking things over,
To the dance, the song, the story,
Or the hours given over to dreaming,
        Once having so marched.

Between the finite limitations of the five senses
and the endless yearnings of man for the beyond
the people hold to the humdrum bidding of work and food
while reaching out when it comes their way
for lights beyond the prisms of the five senses,
for keepsakes lasting beyond any hunger or death.
    This reaching is alive.
The panderers and liars have violated and smutted it.
    Yet this reaching is alive yet
    for lights and keepsakes.

    The people know the salt of the sea
    and the strength of the winds
    lashing the corners of the earth.
    The people take the earth
    as a tomb of rest and a cradle of hope.
    Who else speaks for the Family of Man?
    They are in tune and step
    with constellations of universal law.

The people is a polychrome,
a spectrum and a prism
held in a moving monolith,
a console organ of changing themes,
a clavilux of color poems
wherein the sea offers fog
and the fog moves off in rain
and the labrador sunset shortens
to a nocturne of clear stars
serene over the shot spray
of northern lights.

The steel mill sky is alive.
The fire breaks white and zigzag
Shot on a gun-metal gloaming.
Man is a long time coming.
Man will yet win.
Brother may yet line up with brother:

This old anvil laughs at many broken hammers.
    There are men who can't be bought.
    The fireborn are at home in fire.
    The stars make no noise.
    You can't hinder the wind from blowing.
    Time is a great teacher.
    Who can live without hope?

In the darkness with a great bundle of grief
    the people march.
In the night, and overhead a shovel of stars for
    keeps, the people march:
                    "Where to? what next?"

                        [1936]

Wallace Stevens

(1879–1955) b. Reading, Pennsylvania, United States

Disc 1

Tracks 26–28

Wallace Stevens was born in Reading, Pennsylvania, on October 2, 1879. He attended the local high school before attending Harvard University from 1897 to 1900. While at Harvard, he wrote for and edited the *Harvard Advocate*, and began a long friendship with the philosopher George Santayana. Although he never received his degree from Harvard, Stevens was awarded a degree from the New York Law School in 1903 and a year later was admitted to the New York bar. That same year, a mutual acquaintance introduced him to Elsie Kachel, a young woman who worked in a store playing the piano in the sheet music department. Stevens and Kachel married in 1908. During this period, Stevens led essentially two lives, as he would for the remainder of his days. In one life, he pursued a successful law career; in the other, he wrote exquisite lyric poetry. In time he would find success in both. While in his mid-thirties, he began publishing poems in magazines, but his first collection, *Harmonium*, wouldn't appear until Stevens was forty-four. Published in 1923, *Harmonium* was received warmly by many critics, including the poet Marianne Moore. However, the book sold poorly. Stevens's law career was more successful at this point in his life; after having been associated with the Hartford Accident and Indemnity Company since 1916, he became vice president of the firm in 1934. Stevens never considered giving up law to focus solely on poetry. He believed pursuing the two in combination gave his life character.

The mediocre response to *Harmonium* appears to have discouraged Stevens initially, but he finally produced a second volume, *Ideas of Order*, in 1935. Like its predecessor, this book also received mixed reviews, but this time Stevens refused to be discouraged and quickly produced another volume, *The Man with the Blue Guitar*, in 1937. Gradually, the sumptuousness and brilliance of Stevens's work received wider appreciation and his volumes were progressively better received. Influenced by the Symbolists, his poetry concerns itself largely with the power and dynamics of the imagination and always showcases Stevens's remarkable ability to embody meditations in language both mellifluous and image-rich. He also began publishing prose and essays, most notably the fascinating book of essays on the role of poetry, *The Necessary Angel* (1951).

Working his office job by day and creating poetry by night, Stevens continued to publish new volumes of poetry up until 1947, when his final full volume, *The Auroras of Autumn*, was published. Showing emerging elements of Ezra Pound's Imagism, it continued to demonstrate the same basic ideals Stevens had revealed in his first volume. It was only now, in the 1950s, that he began receiving recognition as one of the seminal and most important poets of the twentieth century. In 1950, he received the prestigious Bollingen Prize in Poetry and, in 1955, received both the National Book Award and a Pulitzer Prize for *The Collected Poems of Wallace Stevens*. His poetry continued to rise in popularity after his death that year, and he is now regarded as one of the most influential and important poets of the modern era, contributing an imaginative and elemental form of poetry never before experienced and as yet unrepeated.

Mark Strand on Wallace Stevens

Wallace Stevens, one of the most admired American poets of the twentieth century, is also perhaps the least understood. At first, readers may be puzzled by his language, which includes nonsense syllables and unusual words, frequently in close juxtaposition, or by arguments that seem obscure and difficult to follow. But after several readings, the poems become familiar. Their syntactical peculiarities, their propensity for elaboration and digression become sources of delight.

Although "Bantams in Pine-Woods" is probably the most extreme and amusing example of Stevens's wordplay with its endearing mixture of stridency and boastfulness, it is another poem in this selection I wish to call special attention to. Less flamboyant in its wordplay than "Bantams in Pine-Woods," "Fabliau of Florida" is every bit as surprising. That is, its wordplay may not be immediately recognized, but once it is, the poem, which at first seemed little more than a description of a boat on a beach at night, begins to be about something else. Once we discover that its first word is a pun on "bark," the change is initiated. "Barque of phosphor" ceases to be simply a boat shining in moonlight. It becomes a luminous cry, and represents the transformation of raw utterance into polished speech. The transformation continues in the second stanza where the barque is not urged to move outward to sea, but rather toward heaven, an odd destination for a boat, though not for a poem whose author has high hopes for himself as a poet. "Fabliau of Florida" enacts a doubling of intentions, one having to do with a magically evocative beach scene, the other with the poet's dedication to poetry and, more specifically, to the making of poems. Thus, the shore and the study are metaphorically bound. And each, in turn, is a place where new opposites are juxtaposed—the sea and the land in the case of the shoreline, imagination and reality in the case of the study. The last stanza of "Fabliau of Florida" tells us that the sound of the surf will continue forever, but since "surf" is a pun on "serf," it tells us simultaneously that the sound of the serf will also continue. At this point, it is clear that the serf is the poet who both serves and serves up poetry. That he drones may be disconcerting at first, but the fact is, many poets drone as they press the sound of syllables into sense. Stevens himself describes doing this. Finally, "Fabliau of Florida," far from being the simple poem it might have been

And for what, except for you, do I feel love?
Do I press the extremest book of the wisest man
Close to me, hidden in me day and night?
In the uncertain light of single, certain truth,
Equal in living changingness to the light
In which I met you, in which we sit at rest,
For a moment in the central of our being,
The vivid transparence that you bring is peace.

without its bracketing puns, is instead a moving testament of a poet's profound attachment to the art he serves.

Any successful reading of the poems of Wallace Stevens demands that attention be paid to even the slightest suggestion of wordplay. What at first seems like a frivolous intellectual exercise becomes a powerful emotional statement. Again and again in his poems, Stevens honors poetry's central place in the shaping of human feeling.

First stanza of "Notes Toward a Supreme Fiction" handwritten by Stevens

A typescript letter from Stevens to William Carlos Williams, dated January 22, 1942

PAUL RUTHERFORD, PRESIDENT

Hartford Accident and Indemnity Company
HOME OFFICE—HARTFORD, CONNECTICUT

WALLACE STEVENS
VICE-PRESIDENT

R. W. MULLEN
ASSISTANT SECRETARY

January 22, 1942.

Mr. W. C. Williams
9 Ridge Road
Rutherford, New Jersey

Dear Bill:

Thanks for your postcard. I am just getting under way. Twenty or thirty years from now I expect to be really well oiled. Don't worry about my gray hair. Whenever I ring for a stenographer she comes in with a pistol strapped around her belt.

Best regards young feller and best wishes,

Fabliau of Florida

Barque of phosphor
On the palmy beach,

Move outward into heaven,
Into the alabasters
And night blues.

Foam and cloud are one.
Sultry moon-monsters
Are dissolving.

Fill your black hull
With white moonlight.

There will never be an end
To this droning of the surf.

[1923]

Bantams in Pine-Woods

Chieftain Iffucan of Azcan in caftan
Of tan with henna hackles, halt!

Damned universal cock, as if the sun
Was blackamoor to bear your blazing tail.

Fat! Fat! Fat! Fat! I am the personal.
Your world is you. I am my world.

You ten-foot poet among inchlings. Fat!
Begone! An inchling bristles in these pines,

Bristles, and points their Appalachian tangs,
And fears not portly Azcan nor his hoos.

[1923]

Thirteen Ways of Looking at a Blackbird

I

Among twenty snowy mountains,
The only moving thing
Was the eye of the black bird.

II

I was of three minds,
Like a tree
In which there are three blackbirds.

III

The blackbird whirled in the autumn winds.
It was a small part of the pantomime.

IV

A man and a woman
Are one.
A man and a woman and a blackbird
Are one.

V

I do not know which to prefer,
The beauty of inflections
Or the beauty of innuendoes,
The blackbird whistling
Or just after.

VI

Icicles filled the long window
With barbaric glass.
The shadow of the blackbird
Crossed it, to and fro.
The mood
Traced in the shadow
An indecipherable cause.

VII

O thin men of Haddam,
Who do you imagine golden birds?
Do you not see how the blackbird
Walks around the feet
Of the women about you?

VIII

I know noble accents
And lucid, inescapable rhythms;
But I know, too,
That the blackbird is involved
In what I know.

IX

When the blackbird flew out of sight,
It marked the edge
Of one of many circles.

X

At the sight of blackbirds
Flying in a green light,
Even the bawds of euphony
Would cry out sharply.

XI

He rode over Connecticut
In a glass coach.
Once, a fear pierced him,
In that he mistook
The shadow of his equipage
For blackbirds.

XII

The river is moving.
The blackbird must be flying.

XIII

It was evening all afternoon.
It was snowing
And it was going to snow.
The blackbird sat
In the cedar-limbs.

[1923]

The Idea of Order at Key West

She sang beyond the genius of the sea.
The water never formed to mind or voice,
Like a body wholly body, fluttering
Its empty sleeves; and yet its mimic motion
Made constant cry, caused constantly a cry,
That was not ours although we understood,
Inhuman, of the veritable ocean.

The sea was not a mask. No more was she.
The song and water were not medleyed sound
Even if what she sang was what she heard,
Since what she sang was uttered word by word.
It may be that in all her phrases stirred
The grinding water and the gasping wind;
But it was she and not the sea we heard.

For she was the maker of the song she sang.
The ever-hooded, tragic-gestured sea
Was merely a place by which she walked to sing.
Whose spirit is this? we said, because we knew
It was the spirit that we sought and knew
That we should ask this often as she sang.

If it was only the dark voice of the sea
That rose, or even colored by many waves;
If it was only the outer voice of sky
And cloud, of the sunken coral water-walled,
However clear, it would have been deep air,
The heaving speech of air, a summer sound
Repeated in a summer without end
And sound alone. But it was more than that,
More even than her voice, and ours, among
The meaningless plungings of water and the wind,
Theatrical distances, bronze shadows heaped
On high horizons, mountainous atmospheres
Of sky and sea.
                    It was her voice that made
The sky acutest as its vanishing.
She measured to the hour its solitude.
She was the single artificer of the world
In which she sang. And when she sang, the sea,
Whatever self it had, became the self
That was her song, for she was the maker. Then we,
As we beheld her striding there alone,
Knew that there never was a world for her
Except the one she sang and, singing, made.

Ramon Fernandez, tell me, if you know,
Why, when the singing ended and we turned
Toward the town, tell why the glassy lights,
The lights in the fishing boats at anchor there,
As the night descended, tilting in the air,
Mastered the night and portioned out the sea,
Fixing emblazoned zones and fiery poles,
Arranging, deepening, enchanting night.

Oh! Blessed rage for order, pale Ramon,
The maker's rage to order words of the sea,
Words of the fragrant portals, dimly-starred,
And of ourselves and of our origins,
In ghostlier demarcations, keener sounds.

[1936]

So-And-So Reclining on Her Couch

On her side, reclining on her elbow.
This mechanism, this apparition,
Suppose we call it Projection A.

She floats in air at the level of
The eye, completely anonymous,
Born, as she was, at twenty-one,

Without lineage or language, only
The curving of her hip, as motionless gesture,
Eyes dripping blue, so much to learn.

If just above her head there hung,
Suspended in air, the slightest crown
Of Gothic prong and practick bright,

The suspension, as in solid space,
The suspending hand withdrawn, would be
An invisible gesture. Let this be called

Projection B. To get at the thing
Without gestures is to get at it as
Idea. She floats in the contention, the flux

Between the thing as idea and
The idea as thing. She is half who made her.
This is the final Projection, C.

The arrangement contains the desire of
The artist. But one confides in what has no
Concealed creator. One walks easily

The unpainted shore, accepts the world
As anything but sculpture. Good-bye
Mrs. Pappadopoulos, and thanks.

[1947]

Not Ideas About the Thing But the Thing Itself

At the earliest ending of winter,
In March, a scrawny cry from outside
Seemed like a sound in his mind.

He knew that he heard it,
A bird's cry, at daylight or before,
In the early March wind.

The sun was rising at six,
No longer a battered panache above snow...
It would have been outside.

It was not from the vast ventriloquism
Of sleep's faded papier-mâché...
The sun was coming from outside.

That scrawny cry—it was
A chorister whose c preceded the choir.
It was part of the colossal sun,

Surrounded by its choral rings,
Still far away. It was like
A new knowledge of reality.

[1954]

James Joyce

(1882-1941) b. Ireland

Disc 1

Track 29-30

The oldest of eight surviving children, James Joyce was born on February 2, 1882 in a comfortable suburb of Dublin. His father was a fairly prosperous merchant, but apparently also a heavy drinker who was imprudent with his money. In 1888, Joyce was sent to school at the Jesuit-run Clongowes Wood College where he was a successful student despite the emotional and intellectual difficulties he encountered in the school's harshly disciplined environment. Joyce later drew upon these difficulties when writing his semi-autobiographical first novel, *A Portrait of the Artist as a Young Man*. In 1898 he enrolled at University College, Dublin, where he earned his degree in Romance Languages. By his graduation in 1902, he was already an aspiring writer, encouraged by the success of the Irish literary renaissance spearheaded by W. B. Yeats. However, Joyce's few poems and first works of prose were far from earning him the literary reputation he would one day know.

In 1903 Joyce briefly returned to Dublin to see his mother, who died the next year. That same year, Joyce married Nora Barnacle, and moved to Trieste, where he dedicated himself to writing. Before leaving Dublin, he had given a small volume of tightly wound lyric poems entitled *Chamber Music* to a publisher, and it later appeared as Joyce's first published work in 1907. Thereafter he focused his creative energies on writing the prose works that would ultimately secure his literary reputation. In 1914 he published *Dubliners*, a collection of short stories containing the much-anthologized "Araby" and "The Dead." The collection's success brought Joyce the attention of the literary world, including that of Ezra Pound, who helped him publish *Portrait*, his next major work, in 1916. In the following year, Joyce contracted glaucoma, and he would suffer periods of near-blindness and undergo painful operations for the remainder of his life.

Joyce and Nora moved to Paris in 1920 as a result of World War I. Undoubtedly, the outbreak of the war had, in some measure, contributed to the writing of his massive and groundbreaking novel *Ulysses*, published in 1922. The work was heralded as a masterpiece by critics as diverse as T. S. Eliot and Ernest Hemingway, and is today considered by many to be the finest novel of the twentieth century. It brought Joyce international fame on an almost unprecedented level. In 1927, he published his second and last small volume of poetry, *Pomes Pennyeach*. In many ways a tribute to Ireland's Gaelic culture, this second volume of poems was stylistically very similar to his first. Unfortunately, it went largely unnoticed in the wake of the tremendous success of *Ulysses*. Joyce spent the rest of his life working on the experimental prose piece *Finnegans Wake*, which somewhat bridges the gap between poetry and fiction in its dedication to language over narrative. However, these were again difficult years for Joyce, due in part to the deteriorating mental condition of his daughter, Lucia Anna, who was ultimately institutionalized. In 1939, after the publication of *Finnegans Wake*, Joyce left Paris for Zurich to escape the turmoil of World War II. He died there in 1941. Remembered more as a fiction writer than a poet, his body of work has nonetheless proven profoundly important in the evolution of twentieth-century poetry.

Paul Muldoon on James Joyce

We don't usually think of James Joyce as a poet, yet he began and ended as just that. Among his earliest writings is "The Holy Office" (1904) with its unholy rant against the leaders of the Irish literary elite, including W.B. Yeats:

> *That they may dream their dreamy dreams*
> *I carry off their filthy streams*

Joyce's sense of himself as a purgative or—to borrow a term used much later in the 20th century—a "dirty realist," seems to extend through the scatological pun in the title of *Chamber Music* (1907), his first publication, though the feel of the poems is much like those written by the very revivalists he reviled:

> *The grey winds, the cold winds are blowing*
> *Where I go.*
> *I hear the noise of many waters*
> *Far below.*
> *All day, all night, I hear them flowing*
> *To and fro.*

Joyce's next book of verse, *Pomes Pennyeach*, appeared twenty years later, in 1927, and included the haunting "She Weeps Over Rahoon":

> *Love, hear thou*
> *How soft, how sad his voice is ever calling,*
> *Ever unanswered and the dark rain falling,*
> *Then as now.*

James Joyce wrote "Ecce Puer" upon the birth of his grandson, Stephen James Joyce, shown here with Joyce in a 1934 photo.

In terms of both its tone and content, this poem is reminiscent of the scene in Joyce's great short story, "The Dead," published in *Dubliners* (1914), in which Gretta Conroy remembers Michael Furey, the boy who died for love of her in Galway. Joyce followed up his other prose master-piece, *Ulysses* (1922), with what may be most use-fully thought of as a return to poetry. For, as Harry Levin wrote of *Finnegans Wake* (1939):

Its texture is so close, its structure so organic, that it cannot yet be considered readable in the sense of an ordinary novel. Indeed, it begins with the latter part of a sentence, the beginning of which is found on the last page. The circular con-struction, which carries out Vico's philosophy of history, invites us to plunge in almost anywhere.

That invitation "to plunge in" is rarely taken up, alas, even by otherwise strong swimmers, who tend to run their eyes over the surface of the text and determine that they'll be quite simply out of their depth. It's an understandable response, one that I continue to have myself as I'm faced by six hundred pages of dense writing. Yet what comes across quite powerfully from having had the privilege of hearing Joyce himself read the conclusion of the Anna Livia section of *Finnegans Wake,* is just how musical this writing is and, more to the point, just how meaningful. Once we give ourselves over to the force of Anna Livia Plurabelle (a manifestation of the river Liffey which flows through dear dirty Dublin, or "Dear Dirty Dumpling" as it appears here) we begin to make sense of this part of the great "collideroscape" which, as Joyce made clear in a letter, features "two washerwomen who as night falls become a tree and a stone." That's why one speaker announces "My ho head halls," a reference to the sleeping giant, Finn MacCool, who's associated with "Howth Head," just outside Dublin, and whose name forms the first part of Finnegan. Since circularity ("Finn<u>again</u>") is the mode of *Finnegans Wake*, it's only fitting that the title of Joyce's last book should send us back to the "streams" and "dreamy dreams" of 'The Holy Office,' that we be exhorted to awake from the nightmare, or dream, of history, that we might stand out-side time. As Samuel Beckett puts it:

You complain that this stuff is not written in English. It is not written at all. It is not to be read—or rather it is not only to be read. It is to be looked at and listened to. His writing is not about something; it is that something itself.

II
(Chamber Music #2)

The twilight turns from amethyst
　To deep and deeper blue,
The lamp fills with a pale green glow
　The trees of the avenue.

The old piano plays an air,
　Sedate and slow and gay;
She bends upon the yellow keys,
　Her head inclines this way.

Shy thoughts and grave wide eyes and hands
　That wander as they list—
The twilight turns to darker blue
　With lights of amethyst.

[1907]

X
(Chamber Music #10)

Bright cap and streamers,
　He sings in the hollow:
　Come follow, come follow,
　　All you that love.
Leave dreams to the dreamers
　That will not after,
　That song and laughter
　　Do nothing move.

With ribbons streaming
　He sings the bolder;
　In troop at his shoulder
　　The wild bees hum.
And the time of dreaming
　Dreams is over—
　As lover to lover,
　　Sweetheart, I come.

[1907]

XVIII

(Chamber Music #18)

O Sweetheart, hear you
  Your lover's tale,
A man shall have sorrow
  When friends him fail.

For he shall know then
  Friends be untrue
And a little ashes
  Their words come to.

But one unto him
  Will softly move
And softly woo him
  In ways of love.

His hand is under
  Her smooth round breast.
So he who has sorrow
  Shall have rest.

[1907]

She Weeps Over Rahoon

Rain on Rahoon falls softly, softly falling,
Where my dark lover lies.
Sad is his voice that calls me, sadly calling,
At grey moonrise.

Love, hear thou
How soft, how sad his voice is ever calling,
Ever unanswered and the dark rain falling,
Then as now.

Dark too our hearts, O love, shall lie and cold
As his sad heart has lain
Under the moongrey nettles, the black mould
And muttering rain.

[1913]

Ecce Puer

Of the dark past
A boy is born
With joy and grief
My heart is torn

Calm in his cradle
The living lies.
May love and mercy
Unclose his eyes!

Young life is breathed
On the glass;
The world that was not
Comes to pass.

A child is sleeping:
An old man gone.
O, father forsaken,
Forgive your son!

[1932]

Well, you know or don't you kennet or haven't I told you every telling has a taling and that's the he and the she of it. Look, look, the dusk is growing! My branches lofty are taking root. And my cold cher's gone ashley. Fieluhr? Filou! What age is at? It saon is late. 'Tis endless now senne eye or erewone last saw Waterhouse's clogh. They took it asunder, I hurd thum sigh. When will they reassemble it? O, my back, my back, my bach! I'd want to go to Aches-les-Pains. Pingpong! There's the Belle for Sexaloitez! And Concepta de Send-us-pray! Pang! Wring out the clothes! Wring in the dew! Godavari, vert the showers! And grant thaya grace! Aman. Will we spread them here now? Ay, we will. Flip! Spread on your bank and I'll spread mine on mine. Flep! It's what I'm doing. Spread! It's churning chill. Der went is rising. I'll lay a few stones on the hostel sheets. A man and his bride embraced between them. Else I'd have sprinkled and folded them only. And I'll tie my butcher's apron here. It's suety yet. The strollers will pass it by. Six shifts, ten kerchiefs, nine to hold to the fire and this for the code, the convent napkins, twelve, one baby's shawl. Good mother Jossiph knows, she said. Whose head? Mutter snores? Deataceas! Wharnow are alle her childer, say? In kingdome gone or power to come or gloria be to them farther? Allalivial, allalluvial! Some here, more no more, more again lost alla stranger. I've heard tell that same brooch of the Shannons was married into a family in Spain. And all the Dunders de Dunnes in Markland's Vineland beyond Brendan's herring pool takes number nine in yangsee's hats. And one of Biddy's beads went bobbing till she rounded up lost histereve with a marigold and a cobbler's candle in a side strain of a main drain of a manzinahurries off Bachelor's Walk. But all that's left to the last of the Meaghers in the loup of the years prefixed and between is one kneebuckle and two hooks in the front. Do you tell me that now? I do in troth. Orara por Orbe and poor Las Animas! Ussa, Ulla, we're umbas all! Mezha, didn't you hear it a deluge of times, ufer and ufer, respund to spond? You deed, you deed! I need, I need! It's that irrawaddyng I've stoke in my aars. It all but husheth the lethest zswound. Oronoko! What's your trouble? Is that the great Finnleader himself in his joakimono on his statue riding the high horse there forehengist? Father of Otters, it is himself! Yonne there! Isset that? On Fallareen Common? You're thinking of Astley's Amphitheayter where the bobby restrained you making sugarstuck pouts to the ghostwhite horse of the Peppers. Throw the cobwebs from your eyes, woman, and spread your washing proper! It's well I know your sort of slop. Flap! Ireland sober is Ireland stiff. Lord help you, Maria, full of grease, the load is with me! Your prayers. I sonht zo! Madammangut! Were you lifting your elbow, tell us, glazy cheeks, in Conway's Carrigacurra canteen? Was I what, hobbledyhips? Flop! Your rere gait's creakorheuman bitts your butts disagrees. Amn't I up since the damp dawn, marthared mary allacook, with Corrigan's pulse and varicoarse veins, my pramaxle smashed, Alice Jane in decline and my oneeyed mongrel twice run over, soaking and bleaching boiler rags, and sweating cold, a widow like me, for to deck my tennis champion son, the laundryman with

the lavandier flannels? You won your limpopo limp from the husky hussars when Collars and Cuffs was heir to the town and your slur gave the stink to Carlow. Holy Scamander, I sar it again! Near the golden falls. Icis on us! Seints of light! Zezere! Subdue your noise, you hamble creature! What is it but a blackburry growth or the dwyergray ass them four old codgers owns. Are you meanam Tarpey and Lyons and Gregory? I meyne now, thank all, the four of them, and the roar of them, that draves that stray in the mist and old Johnny MacDougal along with them. Is that the Poolbeg flasher beyant, pharphar, or a fireboat coasting nyar the Kishtna or a glow I behold within a hedge or my Garry come back from the Indes? Wait till the honeying of the lune, love! Die eve, little eve, die! We see that wonder in your eye. We'll meet again, we'll part once more. The spot I'll seek if the hour you'll find. My chart shines high where the blue milk's upset. Forgivemequick, I'm going! Bubye! And you, pluck your watch, forgetmenot. Your evenlode. So save to jurna's end! My sights are swimming thicker on me by the shadows to this place. I sow home slowly now by own way, moyvalley way. Towy I too, rathmine.

Ah, but she was the queer old skeowsha anyhow, Anna Livia, trinkettoes! And sure he was the quare old buntz too, Dear Dirty Dumpling, foostherfather of fingalls and dotthergills. Gammer and gaffer we're all their gangsters. Hadn't he seven dams to wive him? And every dam had her seven crutches. And every crutch had its seven hues. And each hue had a differing cry. Sudds for me and supper for you and the doctor's bill for Joe John. Befor! Bifur! He married his markets, cheap by foul, I know, like any Etrurian Catholic Heathen, in their pinky limony creamy birnies and their turkiss indienne mauves. But at milkidmass who was the spouse? Then all that was was fair. Tys Elvenland! Teems of times and happy returns. The seim anew. Ordovico or viricordo. Anna was, Livia is, Plurabelle's to be. Northmen's thing made southfolk's place but howmulty plurators made eachone in person? Latin me that, my trinity scholar, out of eure sanscreed into oure eryan! *Hircus Civis Eblanensis!* He had buckgoat paps on him, soft ones for orphans. Ho, Lord! Twins of his bosom. Lord save us! And ho! Hey? What all men. Hot? His tittering daughters of. Whawk?

Can't hear with the waters of. The chittering waters of. Flittering bats, fieldmice bawk talk. Ho! Are you not gone ahome? What Thom Malone? Can't hear with bawk of bats, all thim liffeying waters of. Ho, talk save us! My foos won't moos. I feel as old as yonder elm. A tale told of Shaun or Shem? All Livia's daughtersons. Dark hawks hear us. Night! Night! My ho head halls. I feel as heavy as yonder stone. Tell me John or Shaun? Who were Shem and Shaun the living sons or daughters of? Night now! Tell me, tell me, tell me, elm! Night night! Telmetale of stem or stone. Beside the rivering waters of, hitherandthithering waters of. Night!

[1939]

William Carlos Williams

(1883–1963) b. Rutherford, New Jersey, United States

Disc 1

Tracks 31–34

William Carlos Williams was born on September 17, 1883, in Rutherford, New Jersey, where he would spend most of his life. He attended high school at Horace Mann, where he began experimenting with poetry. Although his parents were both admirers of literature and art, they encouraged Williams to pursue a career in medicine. Ultimately, Williams decided to follow both paths: he enrolled in the University of Pennsylvania's medical program while continuing to write poetry in his free time. At university, Williams befriended Ezra Pound, whose Imagism was to have great influence on Williams's early work. Through Pound, he met several other poets, including H.D. (Hilda Doolittle), and in 1913, Pound helped arrange to have Williams's first volume of poetry, *The Tempers*, published.

With the completion of his medical degree, Williams proved that he could dedicate himself to both medicine and poetry. In fact, many people have seen a connection between his medical practice and his poetic work—from the necessity of honing technical skills to the importance of establishing interpersonal relationships. He studied pediatrics briefly in Germany and returned to Rutherford. There he opened a private practice that he would sustain for the next forty years and embarked on a prolific career as poet, novelist, playwright, and essayist. He soon advanced to the forefront of the emerging Imagist movement, championed by Pound and T.S. Eliot, although he found himself increasingly disenchanted with the movement's valorization of European culture and traditions. In his *In the American Grain* (1925), Williams explored American character and culture through essays on key figures from New World history and continued to seek out a uniquely American poetic. In this regard, he diverged from Pound and Eliot, and this split may have been responsible, in part, for Williams's small audience throughout the 1920s and '30s despite his popularity among critics and other poets.

In 1946, Williams published the first of his *Paterson* volumes. Published in five serial volumes (and part of a sixth) between 1946 and 1963, these long poetic works analyzed and celebrated modern American cultural identity and brought Williams increasing attention and respect from the public as well as the poetic world. Newly emerging poets, most notably Allen Ginsberg and the other Beat writers, began to look to Williams as a source of inspiration due to his willingness to break away from traditional forms and techniques. It was perhaps only at this late point in Williams's career that full understanding of the significance of his work emerged. He remained prolific in his later years, but as early as 1948, his health had begun to decline following a heart attack. After a series of increasingly difficult strokes, he died on March 4, 1963, shortly after winning his first and only Pulitzer Prize for his last book of poems, *Pictures from Brueghel and Other Poems*.

Robert Pinsky on William Carlos Williams

William Carlos Williams still sets a standard of art for making poetry in an American way. He brings unsurpassed intensity to free verse, to our spoken language, to seemingly dirt-plain words and ideas like "car" or "field" or "crazy."

Yes, he exemplifies the art of the eye, as the stereotype of his work has it, but what makes his poems persist is the art of ear and mind, the extraordinary sentences and rhythms he made. Like music, his poems execute a shape in time.

When Williams sets vowels and consonants echoing and varying one another, the design is subtle and cannot be separated from the way he uses an image—say, the most common of New Jersey field-weeds. The plant in "Queen-Anne's-Lace" is his occasion for dismantling and supercharging the traditional invocation of flowers and ladies:

> *Her body is not so white as*
> *anemone petals nor so smooth—nor*
> *so remote a thing. It is a field*
> *of the wild carrot taking*
> *the field by force; the grass*
> *does not raise above it.*

The formal grammar of the first sentence—and Williams's ability to use gravely formal constructions, like his power with abstractions, is so deft it can go unnoticed—makes a fine contrast with the more direct second sentence. The play of repeated sounds and words is erotic and sensual as the sixteenth-century Englishman Campion is sensual, but with an American rhythm, and Williams's own way of noticing how each flowerhead resembles the field. The poem ends:

Robert Pinsky On William Carlos Williams

...Each part
is a blossom under his touch
to which the fibres of her being
stem one by one, each to its end,
until the whole field is a
white desire, empty, a single stem,
a cluster, flower by flower,
a pious wish to whiteness gone over—
or nothing.

This is harmonious and rich in sound as few poems in careful end-rhyme are rich. And its syntax makes a free, comely, exhilarating shape that few "experimental," fragmentary poems can equal.

As "Queen-Anne's-Lace" plays happily with the boundaries of the love-lyric, other poems refresh and tease other expectations. The ending of "To Elsie," as part XVIII of "Spring and All" has come to be known, concludes with a daring but natural twentieth-century, New Jersey monosyllable that rings like a cymbal-clash: ———

It is only in isolate flecks that
something
is given off

No one
to witness
and adjust, no one to drive the car

The bent arpeggio of consonant and vowel running through "only in isolate flecks that / something is given off" resembles some elegant invention of Charlie Parker or Dizzy Gillespie. The loftiness of "isolate flecks" and the plainness of "drive the car" make another kind of far-out chord, the meditative quality of mind and the alert, direct observation, realized in nature and in the second nature of "car." This is the sound in language of original thought, a reminder that Williams's work is far more than a photo album of images. Even his much-quoted slogan "no ideas but in things," after all, knows that it is an idea, a proposition couched in abstract terms. Like everything Williams wrote, it also embodies an interesting, unique grammatical and acoustical contour.

Handwritten notes by Williams on his prescription pad regarding Ezra Pound

Queen-Anne's-Lace

Her body is not so white as
anemone petals nor so smooth—nor
so remote a thing. It is a field
of the wild carrot taking
the field by force; the grass
does not raise above it.
Here is no question of whiteness,
white as can be, with a purple mole
at the center of each flower.
Each flower is a hand's span
of her whiteness. Wherever
his hand has lain there is
a tiny purple blemish. Each part
is a blossom under his touch
to which the fibres of her being
stem one by one, each to its end,
until the whole field is a
white desire, empty, a single stem,
a cluster, flower by flower,
a pious wish to whiteness gone over—
or nothing.

[1921]

Spring and All

By the road to the contagious hospital
under the surge of the blue
mottled clouds driven from the
northeast—a cold wind. Beyond, the
waste of broad, muddy fields
brown with dried weeds, standing and fallen

patches of standing water
the scattering of tall trees

All along the road the reddish
purplish, forked, upstanding, twiggy
stuff of bushes and small trees
with dead, brown leaves under them
leafless vines—

Lifeless in appearance, sluggish
dazed spring approaches—

They enter the new world naked,
cold, uncertain of all
save that they enter. All about them
the cold, familiar wind—

Now the grass, tomorrow
the stiff curl of wildcarrot leaf
One by one objects are defined—
It quickens: clarity, outline of leaf

But now the stark dignity of
entrance—Still, the profound change
has come upon them: rooted, they
grip down and begin to awaken

[1923]

To Elsie

The pure products of America
go crazy—
mountain folk from Kentucky

or the ribbed north end of
Jersey
with its isolate lakes and

valleys, its deaf-mutes, thieves
old names
and promiscuity between

devil-may-care men who have taken
to railroading
out of sheer lust of adventure—

and young slatterns, bathed
in filth
from Monday to Saturday

to be tricked out that night
with gauds
from imaginations which have no

peasant traditions to give them
character
but flutter and flaunt

sheer rags—succumbing without
emotion
save numbed terror

under some hedge of choke-cherry
or viburnum—
which they cannot express—

Unless it be that marriage
perhaps
with a dash of Indian blood

will throw up a girl so desolate
so hemmed round
with disease or murder

that she'll be rescued by an
agent—
reared by the state and

sent out at fifteen to work in
some hard-pressed
house in the suburbs—

some doctor's family, some Elsie—
voluptuous water
expressing with broken

brain the truth about us—
her great
ungainly hips and flopping breasts

addressed to cheap
jewelry
and rich young men with fine eyes

as if the earth under our feet
were
an excrement of some sky

and we degraded prisoners
destined
to hunger until we eat filth

while the imagination strains
after deer
going by fields of goldenrod in

the stifling heat of September
Somehow
it seems to destroy us

It is only in isolate flecks that
something
is given off

No one
to witness
and adjust, no one to drive the car

[1923]

The Red Wheelbarrow

DISC 1, TRACK 34

so much depends
upon

a red wheel
barrow

glazed with rain
water

beside the white
chickens.

[1923]

A Sort of a Song

Let the snake wait under
his weed
and the writing
be of words, slow and quick, sharp
to strike, quiet to wait,
sleepless.

—through metaphor to reconcile
the people and the stones.
Compose. (No ideas
but in things) Invent!
Saxifrage is my flower that splits
the rocks.

[1944]

To a Poor Old Woman

munching a plum on
the street a paper bag
of them in her hand

They taste good to her
They taste good
to her. They taste
good to her

You can see it by
the way she gives herself
to the one half
sucked out in her hand

Comforted
a solace of ripe plums
seeming to fill the air
They taste good to her

[1935]

Ezra Pound

(1885–1972) b. Hailey, Idaho, United States

Disc 1
Tracks 35–38

Ezra Pound was born in Hailey, Idaho, on October 30, 1885, but his family moved to Pennsylvania in 1889, where he spent most of his childhood and received most of his education. He earned his degree from Hamilton College in 1905 after spending two years studying at the University of Pennsylvania, where he had befriended William Carlos Williams. He taught Romance languages at Wabash College for a brief time, after which he left for Europe in 1908. He traveled to Venice, where his first volume of poetry, *A Lume Spento*, was published in 1908, and then on to London, where he settled.

By 1911, he had already published six volumes of verse and had established himself as a central literary figure in London, where he believed a new literary renaissance was about to occur. During this time, he met and befriended his idol, W.B. Yeats; he also developed a burgeoning interest in Chinese and Japanese poetry, which contributed to the anti-Romantic style he was to create and disseminate: Imagism. In his famous manifesto "A Retrospect," Pound defined Imagism as a poetry that eschewed superfluity and abstraction and that embodied a "direct treatment of the 'thing.'" One of the first major Modernist movements, Imagism thrived for several years to come, and its principles are exemplified in Pound's poem "In a Station of the Metro" and H.D.'s "Oread."

Pound's literary fame rests not only on his poetry, but also on his promotion of and influence on many of his contemporaries' literary careers. Almost as if determined to ensure that the renaissance he desired would come to be, he sought out new and promising literary talents and assisted in the writing, editing, and publication of their work. Among the major figures he cultivated are Williams, Marianne Moore, H.D. (to whom he was once engaged), James Joyce, Ernest Hemingway, and T.S. Eliot. Pound even assisted Yeats in finding his later style.

In 1919, sections of what is now widely considered his first major poetic accomplishment, "Homage to Sextus Propertius," appeared in *Poetry* magazine. The following year, Pound left London and moved to Paris for almost five years before settling in Rapallo, Italy. Pound's masterpiece, *The Cantos*, now consumed much of his time; he published the first volume in 1925 to tremendous acclaim. *The Cantos*, a long lyrical sequence weaving together fragments of mythology, history, and social commentary, addresses the evils of usury and unchecked capitalism, at the same time it reveals unmistakably pro-fascist and anti-Semitic sentiments. The second volume, *XXX Cantos*, followed in 1930 and moves on to discuss early American history through the use of Ulysses's travels. During the late 1930s, he began to endorse fascism and even gave pro-fascist, anti-Semitic radio broadcasts, an act that brought about his arrest by Italian partisans who brought him to FBI agents in Genoa in 1945. Before being returned to the U.S., he was imprisoned near Pisa, where he completed the next volume of cantos, *The Pisan Cantos* (1948). He was charged with treason, but ruled unfit to stand trial. Pound was placed in a mental hospital instead.

At the appeal of numerous writers and followers, including Archibald MacLeish, T.S. Eliot, Ernest Hemingway, and Robert Frost, Pound was released from the hospital in 1958 and returned to Italy, where he lived a largely solitary life until his death in Venice on November 1, 1972. While his fascist politics are impossible to overlook, Pound's significant contributions to modern poetry have earned him unending respect as a poet, critic, and patron of the arts.

Charles Bernstein on Ezra Pound

Ezra Pound was one of the most ambitious, influential, and innovative poets of the Modernist period of the first half of the twentieth century. Pound made significant contributions to American poetry not only as a poet but also as a translator, editor, polemicist, and essayist.

Pound's poetics had a profound influence on both the poets and readers of his generation. He was a primary proponent of other Modernist writers, including Yeats (who served as a model for him), Eliot (with whom he edited *The Waste Land*), James Joyce, William Carlos Williams, and H.D., as well as poets of the next generation, such as Louis Zukofsky and Basil Bunting. Pound strenuously attacked the prevailing verse styles of his time, which he found flabby and vague. Such verse, he said, had lost its musicality because of its lock-step adherence to metrical structures that substituted the regularity of the metronome for the intricate patterning of composition by ear. As a leading proponent of what came to be known, somewhat problematically, as "free verse," Pound said that poetry could be divided according to three essential elements: *phanopoeia*, *melopoeia*, and *logopoeia*—the play of image, music, and meaning. In his manifestos for Imagism and Vorticism, he advanced a poetry stripped of all nonessential elements, where every word makes a necessary contribution to the poem, "which presents an intellectual and emotional complex in an instant of time."

Pound's "In a Station of the Metro" (1916), exemplary of the condensation and obliqueness of the Imagist aesthetic, also reflects the influence of classical Chinese poetry:

The apparition of these faces in the crowd;
Petals on a wet, black bough.

A second approach that Pound took to poetry, early in his career, was the use of masks or personae (*Personae* is the title he gave to his collection of shorter poems). Rather than the poem representing the voice of the author, as in much lyric poetry, the speaker in Pound's persona poems is a made-up character with whom Pound does not completely identify. This allows Pound to be satiric, even sarcastic, not only about the subject of the poems but about their speaker, although he sometimes appears to share the sentiments of the poem's persona, making for an interesting ambiguity. Section II of "Hugh Selwyn Mauberley" lampoons what "the age" (the period just before World War I) "demanded"—the superficial hit of "plaster" rather than the richer pleasures of "alabaster." Section V is a bitter (and anti-patriotic) comment on the futility of World War I, in which so many young men died for a "botched civilization."

"Cantico Del Sole" is a particularly funny example of Pound's critique of contemporary American culture's rejection of art. The poem is based on a judge's ruling that obscenity is okay in the classics because the audience for the classics is so small. In his poem, Pound mockingly repeats a sentiment that might be said by the advocates of censorship, but he substitutes "classics" for "pornography": "The thought of what America would be like / If the Classics had a wide circulation / Troubles my sleep." Hearing Pound draw out "America" and "wide circulation" adds a strikingly performative element to his send-up.

The third, and most important, approach Pound took to poetic composition is reflected in his "epic" poem *The Cantos*, a series of long poems on which he worked from his mid-thirties until the end of his life. Pound defined an epic as a "poem including history." By calling his poem an "epic," Pound brings to mind such works as Homer's *Odyssey*, Dante's *Divine Comedy*, and Virgil's *Aenead*. Unlike these narrative poems, however, *The Cantos* uses collage or what now might be called "sampling"—the juxtaposition of quotations from a carefully selected range of eastern and western cultures, including a fair amount of American history and current events. Quoted material forms only a small part of the overall text, however, since the entire poem is shot through with Pound's own interventions, interpolations, and compositional extensions. Pound's quotations are often in Chinese, Italian, French, and other languages and he usually leaves them untranslated. This is because Pound was interested in an opaque texture for the poem; he once commented that if you didn't understand something you should just push on. In the later *Cantos*, Pound organizes the words spatially on the page, decisively breaking with the flush-left orientation of much Western poetry up until that time while following the lead of Stéphane Mallarmé's *Un Coup de Dés*. The result is a poem of immense sweep, often gorgeous lyricism, with a sometimes baffling range of references and many infuriatingly didactic passages. For this poetry of ideas, Pound maximizes discontinuity or what some would call fragmentation. At the same time, he tries to maintain strong authorial control over the intended meaning to be derived from the juxtaposition of what he called "luminous details."

Over the course of *The Cantos*, and in his essays, Pound becomes increasingly obsessed with economics and, in particular, his belief that charging interest on money lent—in other words, the whole system of monetary credit—was destroying Western civilization. In Canto XLV, he attacks "usury"—lending money at exorbitant interest rates, which for Pound was any interest rate. Pound believed interest eroded the rock-solid value of things.

Pound's economic views became increasingly rabid over time. He associated Jews with money-lending and usury (a common stereotype with genocidal implications), insisting that Jews, not being grounded in the land they own, contributed to a waste-land of modern fragmentation (an unintentionally ironic view for one of the greatest progenitors of modernist fragmentation in poetry and one who lived most of his life in exile). During World War II, while living in Italy, Pound sided with the fascist cause, writing poems and speeches extolling Mussolini and excoriating Roosevelt.

Pound's troubling politics are interwoven throughout his work with his poetics and aesthetics, making for a useful, albeit sometimes distasteful, study of the unavoidable relation of poetry to politics. Pound's work reflects, like much of the century in which he wrote, both the best and worst of Western civilization.

Handwritten manuscript draft by Pound of "XLV," or "Usura," from *The Cantos*

The River-Merchant's Wife: A Letter

While my hair was still cut straight across my forehead
I played about the front gate, pulling flowers.
You came by on bamboo stilts, playing horse,
You walked about my seat, playing with blue plums.
And we went on living in the village of Chokan:
Two small people, without dislike or suspicion.

At fourteen I married My Lord you.
I never laughed, being bashful.
Lowering my head, I looked at the wall.
Called to, a thousand times, I never looked back.

At fifteen I stopped scowling,
I desired my dust to be mingled with yours
Forever and forever and forever.
Why should I climb the look out?

At sixteen you departed,
You went into far Ku-to-en, by the river of swirling eddies,
And you have been gone five months.
The monkeys make sorrowful noise overhead.

You dragged your feet when you went out.
By the gate now, the moss is grown, the different mosses,
Too deep to clear them away!
The leaves fall early this autumn, in wind.
The paired butterflies are already yellow with August
Over the grass in the West garden;
They hurt me. I grow older.
If you are coming down through the narrows of the river
   Kiang,
Please let me know beforehand,
And I will come out to meet you
       As far as Cho-fu-Sa.
—*Rihaku (Li T'ai Po), eighth century A.D.*

[1915]

Cantico Del Sole

from Instigations

DISC 1, TRACK 36

The thought of what America would be like
If the Classics had a wide circulation
    Troubles my sleep,
The thought of what America,
The thought of what America,
The thought of what America would be like
If the Classics had a wide circulation
    Troubles my sleep.
Nunc dimittis, now lettest thou thy servant,
Now lettest thou thy servant
    Depart in peace.
The thought of what America,
The thought of what America,
The thought of what America would be like
If the Classics had a wide circulation…
    Oh well!
    It troubles my sleep.

[1915]

In a Station of the Metro

The apparition of these faces in the crowd;
Petals on a wet, black bough.

[1916]

Hugh Selwyn Mauberley

DISC 1, TRACK 37

E. P. Ode Pour L'Election de son Sépulchre

For three years, out of key with his time,
He strove to resuscitate the dead art
Of poetry; to maintain "the sublime"
In the old sense. Wrong from the start—

No, hardly, but seeing he had been born
In a half savage country, out of date;
Bent resolutely on wringing lilies from the acorn;
Capaneus; trout for factitious bait;

Ἴδμεν γάρ τοι πάνθ᾽, ὄσ᾽ ἐνὶ Τροίη
Caught in the unstopped ear;
Giving the rocks small lee-way
The chopped seas held him, therefore, that year.

His true Penelope was Flaubert,
He fished by obstinate isles;
Observed the elegance of Circe's hair
Rather than the mottoes on sun-dials.

Unaffected by "the march of events,"
He passed from men's memory in *l'an trentuniesme*
De son eage; the case presents
No adjunct to the Muses' diadem.

II
The age demanded an image
Of its accelerated grimace,
Something for the modern stage,
Not, at any rate, an Attic grace;

Not, not certainly, the obscure reveries
Of the inward gaze;
Better mendacities
Than the classics in paraphrase!

The "age demanded" chiefly a mould in plaster,
Made with no loss of time,
A prose kinema, not, not assuredly, alabaster
Or the "sculpture" of rhyme.

III
The tea-rose tea-gown, etc.
Supplants the mousseline of Cos,
The pianola "replaces"
Sappho's barbitos.

Christ follows Dionysus,
Phallic and ambrosial
Made way for macerations;
Caliban casts out Ariel.

All things are a flowing,
Sage Heracleitus says;
But a tawdry cheapness
Shall outlast our days.

Even the Christian beauty
Defects—after Samothrace;
We see τὸ καλόν
Decreed in the market place.

Faun's flesh is not to us,
Nor the saint's vision.
We have the press for wafer;
Franchise for circumcision.

All men, in law, are equals.
Free of Pisistratus,
We choose a knave or an eunuch
To rule over us.

O bright Apollo,
τίν' ἄνδρα, τίν' ἥρωα, τινα θεόν,
What god, man, or hero
Shall I place a tin wreath upon!

IV
These fought in any case,
and some believing,
                  pro domo, in any case…

Some quick to arm,
some for adventure,
some from fear of weakness,
some from fear of censure,
some for love of slaughter, in imagination,
learning later…
some in fear, learning love of slaughter;

Died some, pro patria,
                  non "dulce" non "et decor"…
walked eye-deep in hell
believing in old men's lies, then unbelieving
came home, home to a lie,
home to many deceits,
home to old lies and new infamy;
usury age-old and age-thick
and liars in public places.

Daring as never before, wastage as never before.
Young blood and high blood,
fair cheeks, and fine bodies;

fortitude as never before

frankness as never before,
disillusions as never told in the old days,
hysterias, trench confessions,
laughter out of dead bellies.

V
There died a myriad,
And of the best, among them,
For an old bitch gone in the teeth,
For a botched civilization,

Charm, smiling at the good mouth,
Quick eyes gone under earth's lid,

For two gross of broken statues,
For a few thousand battered books.

[1920]

XLV

from The Cantos

DISC 1, TRACK 38

With Usura

With usura hath no man a house of good stone
each block cut smooth and well fitting
that design might cover their face,
with usura
hath no man a painted paradise on his church wall
harpes et luz
or where virgin receiveth message
and halo projects from incision,
with usura
seeth no man Gonzaga his heirs and his concubines
no picture is made to endure nor to live with
but it is made to sell and sell quickly
with usura, sin against nature,
is thy bread ever more of stale rags
is thy bread dry as paper,
with no mountain wheat, no strong flour
with usura the line grows thick
with usura is no clear demarcation
and no man can find site for his dwelling.
Stonecutter is kept from his stone
weaver is kept from his loom
WITH USURA
wool comes not to market
sheep bringeth no gain with usura
Usura is a murrain, usura
blunteth the needle in the maid's hand

and stoppeth the spinner's cunning. Pietro Lombardo
came not by usura
Duccio came not by usura
nor Pier della Francesca; Zuan Bellin' not by usura
nor was "La Calunnia" painted.
Came not by usura Angelico; came not Ambrogio Praedis,
Came no church of cut stone signed: *Adamo me fecit.*
Not by usura St Trophime
Not by usura Saint Hilaire,
Usura rusteth the chisel
It rusteth the craft and the craftsman
It gnaweth the thread in the loom
None learneth to weave gold in her pattern;
Azure hath a canker by usura; cramoisi is unbroidered
Emerald findeth no Memling
Usura slayeth the child in the womb
It stayeth the young man's courting
It hath brought palsey to bed, lyeth
between the young bride and her bridegroom
                    CONTRA NATURAM
They have brought whores for Eleusis
Corpses are set to banquet
at behest of usura.

[1937]

H.D.
(1886–1961) b. Bethlehem, Pennsylvania, United States

Disc 1
Tracks 39–40

H.D. was born Hilda Doolittle on September 10, 1886, in the auspiciously named town of Bethlehem, Pennsylvania. The daughter of a Moravian music teacher and an astronomer, her early life appears to have been dominated and determined primarily by her relationships with both her immediate and her extended family. In 1904, she entered Bryn Mawr College, where her poetic life began in earnest. There she befriended fellow poet Marianne Moore, and even more importantly, Ezra Pound, who was a graduate student at the University of Pennsylvania at the time. Pound's impact on Doolittle, poetically and personally, cannot be underestimated; at one time they were engaged to be married, and it was Pound who suggested the two-letter pen name by which she is more commonly remembered. Although H.D. was not yet publishing poetry while in college, she was writing it, and Pound drew her into the emerging Imagist movement.

H.D. left school after only two years, apparently due to poor grades. In 1911, she traveled to London, where Ezra Pound had established his circle of literary figures. What was meant to be a summer vacation became a permanent residency; she quickly merged into Pound's group of Imagists and never returned to America. Two years later, her first poems were published in *Poetry* with Pound's help. That same year, she married another in Pound's circle, Richard Aldington, whose infidelities drew the marriage's happiness to a close. Thereafter, H.D. grew increasingly involved in a remarkable friendship with D.H. Lawrence, who introduced her to Cecil Gray, the future father of her daughter. Her marriage to Aldington ended in 1919. That same year, she became intimately involved with Annie Winifred Ellerman, a British poet, novelist, and critic who published under the name Bryher. H.D.'s collections of poems from this period include *Sea Garden* (1916), and *The God* (1917).

H.D. traveled to Europe with Bryher, publishing such volumes as *Hymen* (1921), *Heliodora and Other Poems* (1924), *Collected Poems* (1925), and *Red Roses for Bronze* (1931) along the way. She spent the years 1933 to 1934 in Vienna where she studied under and was psychoanalyzed by Sigmund Freud, experiences commemorated in the semi-fictional memoir *Tribute to Freud*. She continued to write and publish poetry throughout her life, though she gained little acknowledgment or acclaim. To some extent, this can be attributed to the fact that her later poetry, such as the long narrative poem *Helen in Egypt* (1961), began to strain the boundaries of Imagism. Moreover, she had begun to write from a feminist perspective in a time when feminism was little accepted. H.D. died on September 21, 1961, having suffered a stroke while on the phone with one of her closest friends. She has come to be recognized as one of the leading voices of Modernist poetry.

Rafael Campo
H.D.
Rafael Campo on H.D.

Rafael Campo on H.D.

Friend to many of the best-known poets of the Modernist movement, such as Ezra Pound and William Carlos Williams, H.D., as she abbreviated herself to readers, was ironically perhaps the most valuably "modern" of all her peers, although some critics have maintained that she remained relatively obscure because of her early and strong association with the Imagists, whose public appeal never matched the ambitions of their leaders. I have always wondered whether other more insidious forces kept her marginalized. Here was a woman writer who dared to live openly with another woman for most of her adult life, one whose strongly feminist ideas, which found resounding expression in her brilliant poems, were far more revolutionary than anything else Modernism espoused. H.D. was the true visionary of her moment, who disputed not only the elitism of a literary world that averted its genteel eyes from the horrors and wonders of the advancing technology of the time, but also challenged those in her own circles who did confront these changes to go even further and address the most radical issue of all, namely the possibility of real human equality—even across gender and sexuality. To H.D., Modernism meant much more than perceiving purely the unadorned object, or "only the thing." In her uniquely modern imagination, she also discerns human relationships contextualized in their starkly new and sometimes alienating surroundings, thus speaking to the critical necessity of empathy.

What better an arena to explore such fundamentally humane issues than that of classical mythology, one of the central stories of which H.D. had the audacity to rewrite in perhaps her most compelling work, the book-length poem *Helen in Egypt*. The ambition of this project, especially for a woman of rather humble origins writing in the early twentieth century, cannot be overstated. This stunning book also increased her distance from her secure origins as a poet, when under the cacophonous influence of Pound she had produced her justly famous lapidary poems, made almost entirely of arresting images. For H.D., writing about Helen must have come to feel almost autobiographical, in the sense that she, like Helen, spent so much of her life in exile, and was so often "spoken for." H.D. left the United States for Europe during her youth, and, after a failed marriage, never returned.

Helen in Egypt gives us a parallel version of the classical tale, one in which Helen is transported not to Troy but instead mysteriously to Egypt. Immediately the familiar story is complicated, echoing the "displacement" of the Modernist era, while H.D. goes on to make her astutely ironic comment on the futility of war, which in her narrative is fought over only a phantom beauty, while the real Helen observes from a foreign land. (Published in the wake of another of the world's greatest wars, all the more destructive for its new fangled sciences of killing, H.D.'s themes were then all the more painfully cogent.) She also ingeniously critiques the sometimes brutishness of male heterosexual desire by allowing Helen, who is reviled, passive, and silenced in nearly every recounting of the story, to speak freely and eloquently; though through most of the poem she wears a mask, which is as much a shield against possession by men as it is a disguise; she is clearly a liberated woman. Rather than the daughter of a violent rape become a wanton adulteress who inspires enmity and genocide, H.D.'s Helen is conceived in love, and is presented, outside of the lens of male heterosexual desire, as a strong figure who is both pure of purpose (if not exactly chaste) and who inspires Achilles' admiration. The plain music and structural concision of the poem that mark it as Modern are evident throughout. H.D.'s further innovations, of linking Modernist aesthetics and concerns with feminism and ultimately empathy, yield a masterpiece that is not exceeded by any poem we have from her more renowned contemporaries.

H.D. died in 1961, never knowing the kind of acclaim she belatedly has begun to receive four decades later. When we listen to her voice now, quavering slightly yet utterly courageous, it is difficult to imagine just how far she had come in her own life, and in a fast-changing world that still was not quite ready to hear all that she had to say. Even the great and nearly unthinkable idea of rescuing Helen from millennia of hatred and domination seems in comparison only the slightest of approximations.

A typed draft of *Helen in Egypt* corrected by H.D., with a letter at the bottom signed and dated September 23 (year unknown)

Helen in Egypt

I

Do not despair, the hosts
surging beneath the Walls,
(not more than I) are ghosts;
  do not bewail the Fall,
  the scene is empty and I am a
  yet in this Amen-temple,

I hear their voices,
there is no veil between us,
only space and leisure

and long corridors of lotus-bud
furled on the pillars,
and the lotus-flower unfurled,

with reed of the papyrus;
Amen (or Zeus we called him)
brought me here;

fear nothing of the future or the past,
He, God will guide you,
bring you to this place,

as he brought me, his daughter,
twin-sister of twin-brothers
and Clytemnestra, shadow of us all;

the old enchantment holds,
here there is peace
for Helena, Helen hated of all Greece.

- - - - - - - - September 23 - - - - - - - -

Dear Norman,
You asked for some poems. I have written nothing for five years, but somehow suddenly, this Helen in Egypt began; I have just finished 8 of these sections in 3 days. I will send on the other 4. Then, I feel that I can go on and on, if the spirit moves, for this you will see, is again the old motive. Maybe a short note might be indicated. According to the old myth, Helen was never at Troy at all, Euripides wrote this play on the theme, Helen in Egypt. It is the "phantasmagora " or unreality of war as against the reality of the eternal and of Love.

II

The potion is not poison,
it is not Lethe and forgetfulness
but everlasting memory,

the glory and the beauty of the ships,
the wave that bore them onward
and the shock of hidden shoal,

the peril of the rocks,
the weary fall of sail,
the rope drawn taut,

the breathing and breath-taking
climb and fall, mountain and valley
challenging, the coast

drawn near, drawn far,
the helmsman's bitter oath
to see the goal receding

in the night; everlasting, everlasting
nothingness and lethargy of waiting;
O Helen, Helen, Daemon that thou art,

we will be done forever
with this charm, this evil philtre,
this curse of Aphrodite;

so they fought, forgetting women,
hero to hero, sworn brother and lover,
and cursing Helen through eternity.

- - - - - - - - - - - - - - - - - - - -

This theme presents endless possibilities- and I have been really so happy. It is in a way, a synthesis of my Walls and the general theme of the "true tale" in Sword and Rose. I hope you will like this. I think Bryher and the little birthday house-party was very good for me, and the long summer rest for I could not work in that heat. I bless it all now- and dear Perdita's visit. Thank you again for greetings and the little good-luck fish- you see what a charm it has proved? Bless you and thank you. I will type out the rest, later. Gratefully, ...

Garden

I

You are clear
O rose, cut in rock,
hard as the descent of hail.

I could scrape the colour
from the petals
like spilt dye from a rock.

If I could break you
I could break a tree.

If I could stir
I could break a tree—
I could break you.

II

O wind, rend open the heat,
cut apart the heat,
rend it to tatters.

Fruit cannot drop
through this thick air—
fruit cannot fall into heat
that presses up and blunts
the points of pears
and rounds the grapes.

Cut the heat—
plough through it,
turning it on either side
of your path.

[1916]

Orchard

I saw the first pear
as it fell—
the honey-seeking, golden-banded,
the yellow swarm
was not more fleet than I,
(spare us from loveliness)
and I fell prostrate
crying:
you have flayed us
with your blossoms,
spare us the beauty
of fruit-trees.

The honey-seeking
paused not,
the air thundered their song,
and I alone was prostrate.

O rough-hewn
god of the orchard,
I bring you an offering—
do you, alone unbeautiful,
son of the god,
spare us from loveliness:

these fallen hazel-nuts,
stripped late of their green sheaths,
grapes, red-purple,
their berries
dripping with wine,
pomegranates already broken,
and shrunken figs
and quinces untouched,
I bring you as offering.

[1916]

Helen

All Greece hates
the still eyes in the white face,
the lustre as of olives
where she stands,
and the white hands.

All Greece reviles
the wan face when she smiles,
hating it deeper still
when it grows wan and white,
remembering past enchantments
and past ills.

Greece sees unmoved,
God's daughter, born of love,
the beauty of cool feet
and slenderest knees,
could love indeed the maid,
only if she were laid,
white ash amid funereal cypresses.

[1924]

Oread

Whirl up, sea—
whirl your pointed pines,
splash your great pines
on our rocks,
hurl your green over us,
cover us with your pools of fir.

[1924]

from Helen in Egypt

Book One

3

…

few were the words we said,
nor knew each other,
nor asked, are you Spirit?

are you sister? are you brother?
are you alive?
are you dead?

the harpers will sing forever
of how Achilles met Helen
among the shades,

but we were not, we are not shadows;
as we walk, heel and sole
leave our sandal-prints in the sand,

though the wounded heel treads lightly
and more lightly follow,
the purple sandals.

…

8

How could I hide my eyes?
how could I veil my face?
with ash or charcoal from the embers?

I drew out a blackened stick,
but he snatched it,
he flung it back,

"what sort of enchantment is this?
what art will you wield with a fagot?
are you Hecate? are you a witch?

a vulture, a hieroglyph,
the sign or the name of a goddess?
what sort of goddess is this?

where are we? who are you?
where is this desolate coast?
who am I?   am I a ghost?"

"you are living, O child of Thetis,
as you never lived before,"
then he caught at my wrist,

"Helena, cursed of Greece,
I have seen you upon the ramparts,
no art is beneath your power,

you stole the chosen, the flower
of all-time, of all-history,
my children, my legions;

for you were the ships burnt,
O cursèd, O envious Isis,
you—you—a vulture, a hieroglyph";

"Zeus be my witness," I said,
"it was he, Amen dreamed of all this
phantasmagoria of Troy,

it was dream and a phantasy";
O Thetis, O sea-mother,
I prayed, as he clutched my throat

with his fingers' remorseless steel,
let me go out, let me forget,
let me be lost…….

O Thetis, O sea-mother, I prayed under his cloak,
let me remember, let me remember,
forever, this Star in the night.

[1961]

Robinson Jeffers

(1887–1962) b. Pittsburgh, Pennsylvania, United States

Disc 1
Tracks 41–43

John Robinson Jeffers was born on January 10, 1887, in Pittsburgh, the son of the Reverend Dr. William Hamilton Jeffers, a professor of Old Testament literature and exegesis at the Western Theological Seminary, and Annie Robinson Tuttle, a church organist. His father quickly immersed Jeffers in a rigorous classical education of Greek, Latin, and Presbyterian doctrine. Jeffers spent much of his childhood in Europe with his family, where he attended boarding schools in Geneva, Lausanne, Zurich, Leipzig, and Vevey. In 1902, at the age of fifteen, Jeffers enrolled as a sophomore in the University of Western Pennsylvania (now the University of Pittsburgh), already fluent in Greek, Latin, French, Italian, and German. When the family moved to Los Angeles the following year, Jeffers transferred to Occidental College, where he became an editor of the school's literary magazine. Graduating from Occidental in 1905, he soon began graduate studies in literature at the University of Southern California, taking courses in philosophy, Old English, Dante, and Roman Imperial history, among others. In a class on Faust, he met and began an affair with Una Call Kuster, who was married to a prominent Los Angeles attorney. In 1907, he entered the medical school at USC and stayed in that program until 1910, when he left to study forestry at the University of Washington for one year. He returned to California in 1911 and published his first volume of poetry, *Flagons and Apples*, in 1912. The next year, Una Kuster divorced her husband. She married Jeffers on August 2, 1913.

Jeffers's plans to move to England with Una were disrupted by the outbreak of World War I. The couple instead relocated to the California coast village of Carmel where they would live for the rest of their lives. In Una, Jeffers had found his muse, an emotionally and intellectually compatible partner. In the rugged Carmel coast, the young poet found an endlessly inspiring landscape. Una gave birth in 1914 to a daughter who died in infancy, but in 1916 delivered twin sons—the same year Jeffers published his second volume of poetry, *Californians*. Jeffers began construction on Tor House, a stone cottage for his family, and in 1919, built the forty-foot Hawk Tower with his own hands. *Tamar and Other Poems*, released in 1924, was a breakthrough for Jeffers. Although published by an obscure press, *Tamar* was soon discovered by a number of critics who compared Jeffers to the great Greek tragedians. This led to an expanded reissue called *Roan Stallion, Tamar, and Other Poems*, which was a critical and popular success. It was in these poems that Jeffers first began to express the ideas that he would later call "Inhumanism"—the assertion that mankind was too egocentric, too unmoved by the "astonishing beauty of things." He published numerous poetry collections throughout the rest of the '20s and '30s.

Jeffers's imagery was at once beautiful in its descriptions of the natural world and disturbing—using taboo themes such as incest to symbolize our "turned-inwardness." Classical Greek tragedy often inspired his poetry and, in 1946, led him to the theater. Jeffers's Broadway adaptation of Euripides' *Medea* marked the poet's greatest popular success. However, in 1948, Jeffers published his most controversial collection of poetry, *The Double Axe*, in which he formally defined Inhumanism but also criticized the Allies' role in World War II, putting Roosevelt and Churchill on the same moral level as Hitler and Mussolini (prompting his publisher, Random House, to include a disclaimer). Shortly thereafter, Jeffers's dearest Una fell ill with cancer and died in 1950. *Hungerfield and Other Poems* (1954), Jeffers's last volume of poetry, contains a moving eulogy to Una. Jeffers died in 1962 at Tor House.

Robert Hass

Robinson Jeffers

Robert Hass on Robinson Jeffers

Robinson Jeffers found his peculiar strength sometime in the early 1920s. He had moved from Los Angeles to Carmel, California, in 1914, at the outbreak of World War I, a young man just married and intending to write poetry. The verse he was publishing in 1917 sounds like this:

> *Was it lovely to lie among violets a blossom in the valleys of love*
> *   on the breast of the south?*
> *It was lovely but lovelier now*
> *To behold the calm head of the dancer we dreaded, his curls are*
> *   as tendrils of the vineyard, O Death.*

By 1924, in a poem called "Continent's End," he was writing like this:

> *At the equinox when the earth was veiled in a late rain,*
> *   wreathed with wet poppies, waiting spring,*
> *The ocean swelled for a far storm and beat its boundary,*
> *   the ground-swell shook the beds of granite.*

He is aiming for sobriety and strength, a sound that has some of the objective feel of narrative prose, as if he wants to diminish the lyrical interference of his own presence as a writer and let the world be present in his work on something like its own terms. The style he forges, with its long line, its suppleness and somber beauty, its sense of power and hardness and prophetic edge is—once you've heard it—unmistakable.

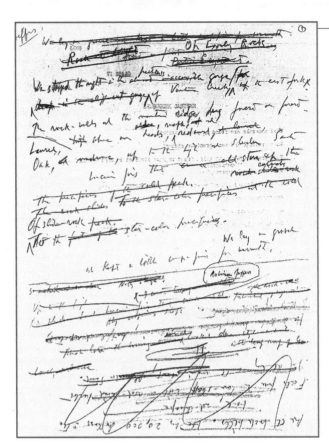

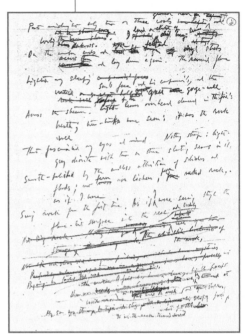

Handwritten manuscript by Jeffers of "Oh, Lovely Rock"

There are many moments in his work when this style seems the perfect instrument for rendering the grand movements of the natural world he liked so much to observe. In these lines from "The Cycle," for example:

The clapping blackness of the wings of pointed cormorants, the great indolent planes
Of autumn pelicans nine or a dozen strung shorelong,
But chiefly the gulls, the cloud-calligraphers of windy spirals before a storm
Cruise north and south over the sea-rocks and over
That bluish enormous opal.

Sometimes, the pleasure of reading his lines is that they seem—such is the force of the descriptions—a practical equivalent to the immensity and harsh beauty of the coast itself. You can see the birds; you can almost smell the salt:

The fierce musical cries of a couple of sparrowhawks hunting on the headland,
Hovering and darting, their heads northwestward,
Prick like silver arrows shot through a curtain the noise of the ocean
Trampling its granite; their red backs gleam
Under my windows around the stone corners, nothing gracefuller, nothing
Nimbler in the wind.

FIFTEEN CENTS (CANADA, 21)   April 4, 1932

TIME

The Weekly Newsmagazine

ROBINSON JEFFERS
"A romantic
"Human feeling here could do anything . . ."
(See Books)

Volume XIX   Number 14

Jeffers appeared on the cover of the April 4, 1932, issue of *Time* magazine.

Jeffers loved the idea of an art that had the strength of the world outside his window. "Death's a fierce meadowlark," he writes in "Wise Men in their Bad Hours," thinking about how much humans are like summer grasshoppers,

> *but to die having made*
> *Something more equal to the centuries*
> *Than muscle and bone, is mostly to shed weakness.*

"To shed weakness." It's an idea that some art, by imitating nature, will outlive most human beings, will outlive the whole turbulence of human feeling. Look how he puts it at the end of the poem:

> *The mountains are dead stone, the people*
> *Admire or hate their stature, their insolent quietness,*
> *The mountains are not softened or troubled*
> *And a few dead men's thoughts have the same temper.*

In the 1920s, when Jeffers wrote these lines, readers seemed to have mostly noticed their force and assurance. In the 1930s, during a world depression and in the midst of the rise of fascism, his contempt for what was soft and troubling began to sound to people a little differently. It began to sound differently to Jeffers himself, and his view shifts from the birds outside his window to the movements of history. In 1935, in a poem called "Rearmament":

> *I would burn my right hand in a slow fire*
> *To change the future...I should do foolishly. The beauty of modern*
> *Man is not in the persons but in the*
> *Disastrous rhythm, the heavy and mobile masses, the dance of the*
> *Dream-led masses down the dark mountain.*

It's hard to know if he could have written exactly these lines if he had really known the future. This is the Jeffers who troubled his contemporaries and can still trouble us today. One doesn't want to argue with him so much as point him in the direction of the "mobile masses" and see if he would still be inclined to tell the victims of the gas chambers, the families in which parents and children watched each other being shot and tossed into ditches, the women raped in internment camps, the men who raped them, the children made swollen and then arthritic from famine that their beauty consists in the part they played in the rhythm of the twentieth century.

There was a level at which Jeffers simply thought that human evolution was not a successful experiment, that human culture was so destructive and so out of control that it would be just as well when the experiment finally ended and, from the point of view of the rest of the species on earth, the sooner the better. He was, in this rather grim way, an early environmentalist, perhaps the first American poet to grasp the devastating extent of the changes human technologies and populations were wreaking on the rest of the earth's biological life. He came to think that the one hope for human beings was detachment from desire—which he thought it very unlikely that humans would be capable of—and contemplation of the beauty of the world, and an honoring of it —all of it—including its cruelties. He called this set of ideas "Inhumanism," and he preached it in his long narrative poems as well as his short lyrics:

Flowers wither, grass fades, trees wilt,
The forest is burnt;
The rock is not burnt.

The deer starve, the winter birds
Die on their twigs and lie
In the blue dawns in the snow.

Men suffer want and become
Curiously ignoble; as prosperity
Makes them curiously vile.

But look how noble the world is,
the lonely-flowing waters, the secret—
Keeping stones, the flowing sky.

Many readers come to Jeffers simply for the strength and beauty of his descriptions of the natural world, and don't worry too much about the strange sexual violence of his mythic narratives and the pessimism of his diagnosis of human culture. Others come to him for that diagnosis and the spirit that informs it. He lost his popular readership in the 1940s because of the unpopularity of his political views, and then regained it in the 1960s and '70s because of his vision of the environment. Forty years after his death, the descriptive power of his poems seems undiminished. His ideas seem, if anything, more relevant. They are hard to get around, and they are meant to trouble us.

Hurt Hawks

I

The broken pillar of the wing jags from the clotted shoulder,
The wing trails like a banner in defeat,
No more to use the sky forever but live with famine
And pain a few days: cat nor coyote
Will shorten the week of waiting for death, there is game without talons.
He stands under the oak-bush and waits
The lame feet of salvation; at night he remembers freedom
And flies in a dream, the dawns ruin it.
He is strong and pain is worse to the strong, incapacity is worse.
The curs of the day come and torment him
At distance, no one but death the redeemer will humble that head,
The intrepid readiness, the terrible eyes.
The wild God of the world is sometimes merciful to those
That ask mercy, not often to the arrogant.
You do not know him, you communal people, or you have forgotten him;
Intemperate and savage, the hawk remembers him;
Beautiful and wild, the hawks, and men that are dying, remember him.

II

I'd sooner, except the penalties, kill a man than a hawk; but the great redtail
Had nothing left but unable misery
From the bones too shattered for mending, the wing that trailed under his talons when he moved.
We had fed him six weeks, I gave him freedom,
He wandered over the foreland hill and returned in the evening, asking for death,
Not like a beggar, still eyed with the old
Implacable arrogance. I gave him the lead gift in the twilight. What fell was relaxed,
Owl-downy, soft feminine feathers; but what
Soared: the fierce rush: the night-herons by the flooded river cried fear at its rising
Before it was quite unsheathed from reality.

[1928]

The Purse-Seine

Our sardine fishermen work at night in the dark of the moon; daylight or moonlight
They could not tell where to spread the net, unable to see the phosphorescence of the shoals of fish.
They work northward from Monterey, coasting Santa Cruz; off New Year's Point or off Pigeon Point
The look-out man will see some lakes of milk-color light on the sea's night-purple; he points, and the helmsman
Turns the dark prow, the motorboat circles the gleaming shoal and drifts out her seine-net. They close the circle
And purse the bottom of the net, then with great labor haul it in.

                     I cannot tell you
How beautiful the scene is, and a little terrible, then, when the crowded fish
Know they are caught, and wildly beat from one wall to the other of their closing destiny the phosphorescent
Water to a pool of flame, each beautiful slender body sheeted with flame, like a live rocket
A comet's tail wake of clear yellow flame; while outside the narrowing
Floats and cordage of the net great sea-lions come up to watch, sighing in the dark; the vast walls of night
Stand erect to the stars.

                     Lately I was looking from a night mountain-top
On a wide city, the colored splendor, galaxies of light: how could I help but recall the seine-net
Gathering the luminous fish? I cannot tell you how beautiful the city appeared, and a little terrible.
I thought, We have geared the machines and locked all together into interdependence; we have built the great cities; now
There is no escape. We have gathered vast populations incapable of free survival, insulated
From the strong earth, each person in himself helpless, on all dependent. The circle is closed, and the net
Is being hauled in. They hardly feel the cords drawing, yet they shine already. The inevitable mass-disasters
Will not come in our time nor in our children's, but we and our children
Must watch the net draw narrower, government take all powers—or revolution, and the new government
Take more than all, add to kept bodies kept souls—or anarchy, the mass-disasters.

                     These things are Progress;
Do you marvel our verse is troubled or frowning, while it keeps its reason? Or it lets go, lets the mood flow
In the manner of the recent young men into mere hysteria, splintered gleams, crackled laughter. But they are quite wrong.
There is no reason for amazement: surely one always knew that cultures decay, and life's end is death.

                                             [1937]

The Day Is a Poem

(September 19, 1939)

DISC 1, TRACK 42

This morning Hitler spoke in Danzig, we hear his voice.

A man of genius: that is, of amazing

Ability, courage, devotion, cored on a sick child's soul,

Heard clearly through the dog wrath, a sick child

Wailing in Danzig; invoking destruction and wailing at it.

Here, the day was extremely hot; about noon

A south wind like a blast from hell's mouth spilled a slight rain

On the parched land, and at five a light earthquake

Danced the house, no harm done. Tonight I have been amusing myself

Watching the blood-red moon droop slowly

Into black sea through bursts of dry lightning and distant thunder.

Well: the day is a poem: but too much

Like one of Jeffers's, crusted with blood and barbaric omens,

Painful to excess, inhuman as a hawk's cry.

[1941]

Oh, Lovely Rock

DISC 1, TRACK 43

We stayed the night in the pathless gorge of Ventana
    Creek, up the east fork.
The rock walls and the mountain ridges hung forest on
    forest above our heads, maple and redwood,
Laurel, oak, madrone, up to the high and slender Santa
    Lucian firs that stare up the cataracts
Of slide-rock to the star-color precipices.

                    We lay on gravel and
    kept a little camp-fire for warmth.
Past midnight only two or three coals glowed red in the
    cooling darkness; I laid a clutch of dead
    bay-leaves

On the ember ends and felted dry sticks across them
    and lay down again. The revived flame
Lighted my sleeping son's face and his companion's,
    and the vertical face of the great gorge-wall
Across the stream. Light leaves overhead danced in the
    fire's breath, tree-trunks were seen: it was the rock
    wall
That fascinated my eyes and mind. Nothing strange:
    light-gray diorite with two or three slanting seams in
    it,
Smooth-polished by the endless attrition of slides and
    floods; no fern nor lichen, pure naked rock…as if I
    were
Seeing rock for the first time. As if I were seeing
    through the flame-lit surface into the real and bodily
And living rock. Nothing strange…I cannot
Tell you how strange: the silent passion, the deep
    nobility and childlike loveliness: this fate going on
Outside our fates. It is here in the mountain like a
    grave smiling child. I shall die, and my boys
Will live and die, our world will go on through its rapid
    agonies of change and discovery; this age will die,
And wolves have howled in the snow around a new
    Bethlehem: this rock will be here, grave, earnest,
    not passive: the energies
That are its atoms will still be bearing the whole
    mountain above: and I, many packed centuries ago,
Felt its intense reality with love and wonder, this lonely
    rock.

[1947]

Carmel Point

The extraordinary patience of things!
This beautiful place defaced with a crop of suburban
    houses—
How beautiful when we first beheld it,
Unbroken field of poppy and lupin walled with clean
    cliffs;
No intrusion but two or three horses pasturing,
Or a few milch cows rubbing their flanks on the
    outcrop rock-heads—
Now the spoiler has come: does it care?
Not faintly. It has all time. It knows the people are a
    tide
That swells and in time will ebb, and all
Their works dissolve. Meanwhile the image of the
    pristine beauty
Lives in the very grain of the granite,
Safe as the endless ocean that climbs our cliff.
    —As for us:
We must uncenter our minds from ourselves;
We must unhumanize our views a little, and become
    confident
As the rock and ocean that we were made from.

[1954]

John Crowe Ransom

(1888–1974) b. Pulaski, Tennessee, United States

Disc 1

Tracks 44–46

John Crowe Ransom was born on April 30, 1888. The son of Methodist minister John James Ransom and his wife Ella Crowe, Ransom grew up in a deeply religious household in Pulaski, Tennessee. Precocious, Ransom enrolled in Nashville's Vanderbilt University at the age of fifteen; after his graduation in 1909, he studied classics as a Rhodes Scholar at Oxford. Ransom accepted a position in Vanderbilt's English Department in 1914. In 1920, he married Robb Reavill, a native of Colorado and graduate of Vassar College, and together they had three children. Except for some time spent in military service during World War I, he taught at Vanderbilt until 1937, when he departed for Kenyon College. Here he became the founding editor of *The Kenyon Review*.

Ransom's first academic interest was philosophy, but his persistent interest in aesthetic issues—as well as his involvement with the literary group known as "The Fugitives"—inspired him to write poetry. He was to become the guiding member and leading theorist of The Fugitives, who also counted poets Robert Penn Warren, Allen Tate, and Donald Davidson among their members. Besides offering criticism of one another's poems and publishing the magazine *The Fugitive*, the group discussed the intellectual and artistic problems of the modern world and sought to escape what they considered Romanticism's plague-like influence. During the 1920s, the group advocated forms of southern nationalism, and southern landscapes, history, and customs began to dominate their work. By the '30s, they argued that the agrarian society in the South should stand as a bastion against industrial materialism and communism, as seen in their 1930 symposium titled *I'll Take My Stand: The South and the Agrarian Tradition*.

Ransom produced no more than three slim volumes of lyrics, namely, *Poems about God* (1919), *Chills and Fever* (1924), and *Two Gentlemen in Bonds* (1927). Notorious for his lifelong dedication to reworking his poetry after its publication, he is generally thought to have printed his definitive work in *The Fugitive* between 1922 and 1925. Although he wanted passionately to make a lasting contribution to the poetic tradition, Ransom determined that he had depleted his poetic themes and stopped writing poetry in 1927, and it is perhaps in his role as critic that Ransom made his most significant impact. The critical method he espoused and refined—known as The New Criticism after Ransom's 1941 book-length study of the same name—had an enormous influence on the way poems were read and taught for generations to come. The New Criticism focused on the "organic unity" of the work of art, encouraging analytical readings divorced from historical contexts and authors' biographies. A friend to many poets of his own generation, Ransom was also teacher and mentor to many younger poets as well, including Randall Jarrell and Robert Lowell. Although he had not written a poem for nearly a quarter of a century, Ransom received the Bollingen Prize in 1951 and the National Book Award for his *Selected Poems* in 1964. Following his retirement from Kenyon, he continued to write criticism, lecture, and collect honors for his work until his death on July 3, 1974.

John Hollander on John Crowe Ransom

John Crowe Ransom was already an extremely important poet for the generation preceding mine, some of whom had been his students, and writers of my age who had encountered anthology pieces of his like the cautionary "Blue Girls"—a quintessential American teacher's poem—as early as in high school. He was famous, not only as a poet but as a literary critic and theorist as well as the editor of *The Kenyon Review*, one of the outstanding quarterlies of its day. He was also celebrated as a teacher of literature to writers. Before the days of the ubiquitous poetry workshop, writers in colleges taught prospective writers, along with other good readers, literature. The whole point of this was that by going through great or exemplary works with a writer and critic, rather than with a philologically tracked "professional" academic scholar, one could learn to teach oneself how to get better as a writer, as writers in English from Chaucer through Ransom's own generation had done. In this he was akin to Yvor Winters, Allen Tate, Mark Van Doren, R.P. Blackmur, William Empson, and other poets, many of whose students became poets of note in successive decades.

We value Ransom's poems particularly highly for their totally original angle of vision, for their extremely modernist use of iambic metrical forms, and for their complementary diction, which moves from neo-classic power to a characteristic quirkiness, as in some of his elegies and epitaphs—"Bells for John Whiteside's Daughter," for example, where the poet contemplates the dead girl's "brown study" and remembers how she

...took arms against her shadow
Or harried into the pond

The lazy geese, like a snow cloud
Dripping their snow on the green grass,
Tricking and stopping, sleepy and proud,
Who cried in goose, Alas...

—or "Dead Boy" (a poem for "a boy not beautiful, nor good, nor clever"):

The little cousin is dead, by foul subtraction,
A green bough from Virginia's aged tree,
And none of the country kin like the transaction,
Nor some of the world of outer dark, like me.

or in the charming "Janet Waking" where the deceased is a small girl's pet hen:

It was a transmogrifying bee
Came droning down on Chucky's old bald head
And sat and put the poison.

I remember an evening fifty years ago when, with a small group of Columbia undergraduates, John Berryman reacted magnificently to a challenge by a young poet among them who had protested that there could be no good modern sonnets, simply by reciting, without a word of commentary, John Crowe Ransom's absolutely perfect "Piazza Piece" which opens with the importuning of "a gentleman in a dust coat, trying" to make a "lovely lady" hear his pleas; the sestet of the sonnet "a lady young in beauty waiting" but not for him. Whether or not, as has been suggested, the gentleman here is Death, Ransom's poetry always speaks in a characteristically rhythmic voice, which Berryman caught perfectly, as I would discover a few years later after hearing him read and playing croquet with him (he was a ruthless conqueror at that elegantly slow-paced game). Ransom's "Captain Carpenter" is a mock-heroic ballad about a quixotic soldier being consumed bit by bit in his successive vainglorious encounters, for example, in fighting with "the wife of Satan":

Their strokes and counters whistled in the wind
I wish he had delivered half his blows
But where she should have made off like a hind
The bitch bit off his arms at the elbows.

Ransom recited this aloud, confirming what the knowledgeable reader had heard in his or her head to begin with—the *bitch bit* off his *arms* at the *el-bows* giving a splendidly fake archaic sound to the word. The stately pentameter quatrains replacing the usual ballad-stanzas help frame the almost unique tone of this celebrated poem. "Captain Carpenter" is, among other things, a grotesquely comical tale in lieu of a dirge, not for the Old South, but for an allegorical figure thereof propounded by the rhetoric about itself which in turn is propounded by its residues. All the writers I knew when young knew its last quatrain: "The curse of hell upon the sleek upstart" (again, the meter demands *up-start*)

> *That got the Captain finally on his back*
> *And took the red red vitals of his heart*
> *And made the kites to whet their beaks clack clack.*

Ransom was always strongly and gently deconstructing heroic fictions, as in "Necrological," "Philomela," "Armageddon" and others; but one hardly thinks of Ransom as a poet of love. "Spectral Lovers" and the wonderful "The Equilibrists," one of his very finest poems (the term is an older name for acrobats) that prefigures the trope of Stephen Sondheim's "Send in the Clowns," wryly consider heroic and modern love with a unique distancing, yet without the darkness of impassioned contemplation.

Ransom never attempted a large or comprehensive piece of poetic mythmaking; instead, he left us a good number of exemplary masterpieces. I suppose that my very favorite poem of his remains his uncharacteristically somewhat difficult "Painted Head," which contemplates how "the extravagant device of art / Unhousing by abstraction this once head / Was capital irony" (and note the puns on "capital") and moves back at the end to a celebration of how what is absent from the painting gives vividness to its rendering of blue eyes, facial plains, and hair:

> *...Beauty is of body.*
> *The flesh contouring shallowly on a head*
> *Is a rock-garden needing body's love*
> *And best bodiness to colorify*
>
> *The big blue birds sitting and sea-shell flats*
> *And caves, and on the iron acropolis*
> *To spread the hyacinthine hair and rear*
> *The olive garden for the nightingales.*

Captain Carpenter

Captain Carpenter rose up in his prime
Put on his pistols and went riding out
But had got wellnigh nowhere at that time
Till he fell in with ladies in a rout.

It was a pretty lady and all her train
That played with him so sweetly but before
An hour she'd taken a sword with all her main
And twined him of his nose for evermore.

Captain Carpenter mounted up one day
And rose straightway into a stranger rogue
That looked unchristian but be that as may
The Captain did not wait upon prologue.

But drew upon him out of his great heart
The other swung against him with a club
And cracked his two legs at the shinny part
And let him roll and stick like any tub.

Captain Carpenter rode many a time
From male and female took he sundry harms
He met the wife of Satan crying "I'm
The she-wolf bids you shall bear no more arms."

Their strokes and counters whistled in the wind
I wish he had delivered half his blows
But where she should have made off like a hind
The bitch bit off his arms at the elbows.

And Captain Carpenter parted with his ears
To a black devil that used him in this wise
O Jesus ere his threescore and ten years
Another had plucked out his sweet blue eyes.

Captain Carpenter got up on his roan
And sallied from the gate in hell's despite
I heard him asking in the grimmest tone
If any enemy yet there was to fight?

"To any adversary it is fame
If he risk to be wounded by my tongue
Or burnt in two beneath my red heart's flame
Such are the perils he is cast among.

"But if he can he has a pretty choice
From an anatomy with little to lose
Whether he cut my tongue and take my voice
Or whether it be my round red heart he choose."

It was the neatest knave that ever was seen
Stepping in perfume from his lady's bower
Who at this word put in his merry mien
And fell on Captain Carpenter like a tower.

I would not knock old fellows in the dust
But there lay Captain Carpenter on his back
His weapons were the old heart in his bust
And a blade shook between rotten teeth alack.

The rogue in scarlet and grey soon knew his mind
He wished to get his trophy and depart
With gentle apology and touch refined
He pierced him and produced the Captain's heart.

God's mercy rest on Captain Carpenter now
I thought him Sirs an honest gentleman
Citizen husband soldier and scholar enow
Let jangling kites eat of him if they can.

But God's deep curses follow after those
That shore him of his goodly nose and ears
His legs and strong arms at the two elbows
And eyes that had not watered seventy years.

The curse of hell upon the sleek upstart
That got the Captain finally on his back
And took the red vitals of his heart
And made the kites to whet their beaks clack clack.

[1924]

Bells for John Whiteside's Daughter

DISC 1, TRACK 46

There was such speed in her little body,
And such lightness in her footfall,
It is no wonder her brown study
Astonishes us all.

Her wars were bruited in our high window.
We looked among orchard trees and beyond,
Where she took arms against her shadow,
Or harried unto the pond

The lazy geese, like a snow cloud
Dripping their snow on the green grass,
Tricking and stopping, sleepy and proud,
Who cried in goose, Alas,

For tireless heart within the little
Lady with rod that made them rise
From their noon apple dreams, and scuttle
Goose-fashion under the skies!

But now go the bells, and we are ready;
In one house we are sternly stopped
To say we are vexed at her brown study,
Lying so primly propped.

[1924]

Painted Head

By dark severance the apparition head
Smiles from the air a capital on no
Column or a Platonic perhaps head
On a canvas sky depending from nothing;

Stirs up an old illusion of grandeur
By tickling the instinct of heads to be
Absolute and to try decapitation
And to play truant from the body bush;

But too happy and beautiful for those sorts
Of head (homekeeping heads are happiest)
Discovers maybe thirty unwidowed years
Of not dishonoring the faithful stem;

Is nameless and has authored for the evil
Historian headhunters neither book
Nor state and is therefore distinct from tart
Heads with crowns and guilty gallery heads;

So that the extravagant device of art
Unhousing by abstraction this once head
Was capital irony by a loving hand
That knew the no treason of a head like this;

Makes repentance in an unlovely head
For having vinegarly traduced the flesh
Till, the hurt flesh recusing, the hard egg
Is shrunken to its own deathlike surface;

And an image thus. The body bears the head
(So hardly one they terribly are two)
Feeds and obeys and unto please what end?
Not to the glory of tyrant head but to

The increase of body. Beauty is of body.
The flesh contouring shallowly on a head
Is a rock-garden needing body's love
And best bodiness to colorify

The big blue birds sitting and sea-shell flats
And caves, and on the iron acropolis
To spread the hyacinthine hair and rear
The olive garden for the nightingales.

[1924]

The Equilibrists

Full of her long white arms and milky skin
He had a thousand times remembered sin.
Alone in the press of people travelled he,
Minding her jacinth and myrrh and ivory.

Mouth he remembered: the quaint orifice
From which came heat that flamed upon the kiss,
Till cold words came down spiral from the head,
Grey doves from the officious tower illsped.

Body: it was a white field ready for love.
On her body's field, with the gaunt tower above,
The lilies grew, beseeching him to take,
If he would pluck and wear them, bruise and break.

Eyes talking: Never mind the cruel words,
Embrace my flowers but not embrace the swords.
But what they said, the doves came straightway flying
And unsaid: Honor, Honor, they came crying.

Importunate her doves. Too pure, too wise,
Clambering on his shoulder, saying, Arise,
Leave me now, and never let us meet,
Eternal distance now command thy feet.

Predicament indeed, which thus discovers
Honor among thieves, Honor between lovers.
O such a little word is Honor, they feel!
But the grey word is between them cold as steel.

At length I saw these lovers fully were come
Into their torture of equilibrium:
Dreadfully had forsworn each other, and yet
They were bound each to each, and they did not forget.

And rigid as two painful stars, and twirled
About the clustered night their prison world,
They burned with fierce love always to come near,
But Honor beat them back and kept them clear.

Ah, the strict lovers, they are ruined now!
I cried in anger. But with puddled brow
Devising for those gibbeted and brave
Came I descanting: Man, what would you have?

For spin your period out, and draw your breath,
A kinder saeculum begins with Death.
Would you ascend to Heaven and bodiless dwell?
Or take your bodies honorless to Hell?

In Heaven you have heard no marriage is,
No white flesh tinder to your lecheries,
Your male and female tissue sweetly shaped
Sublimed away, and furious blood escaped.

Great lovers lie in Hell, the stubborn ones
Infatuate of the flesh upon the bones;
Stuprate, they rend each other when they kiss,
The pieces kiss again—no end to this.

But still I watched them spinning, orbited nice.
Their flames were not more radiant than their ice.
I dug in the quiet earth and wrought the tomb
And made these lines to memorize their doom:—

Equilibrists lie here; stranger, tread light;
Close, but untouching in each other's sight;
Mouldered the lips and ashy the tall skull,
Let them lie perilous and beautiful.

[1927]

Dead Boy

The little cousin is dead, by foul subtraction,
A green bough from Virginia's aged tree,
And none of the county kin like the transaction,
Nor some of the world of outer dark, like me.

A boy not beautiful, nor good, nor clever,
A black cloud full of storms too hot for keeping,
A sword beneath his mother's heart—yet never
Woman bewept her babe as this is weeping.

A pig with a pasty face, so I had said,
Squealing for cookies, kinned by poor pretense
With a noble house. But the little man quite dead,
I see the forbears' antique lineaments.

The elder men have strode by the box of death
To the wide flag porch, and muttering low send round
The bruit of the day. O friendly waste of breath!
Their hearts are hurt with a deep dynastic wound.

He was pale and little, the foolish neighbors say;
The first-fruits, saith the Preacher, the Lord hath taken;
But this was the old tree's late branch wrenched away,
Grieving the sapless limbs, the shorn and shaken.

[1927]

T. S. Eliot

(1888–1965) b. St. Louis, Missouri, United States

Disc 1

Tracks 47–49

Thomas Stearns Eliot was born in St. Louis, Missouri, on September 26, 1888. Among the prominent individuals in his family's history were Reverend William Eliot, who founded Washington College in St. Louis, and Isaac Stearns, one of the original settlers of the Massachusetts Bay Colony. An excellent student, Eliot was educated at the Smith Academy in St. Louis and then moved on to Harvard University in 1906. There he wrote for *The Harvard Advocate* and studied French literature and philosophy. Arthur Symons's *The Symbolist Movement in Literature*, an influential book that introduced Rimbaud, Verlaine, and the Symbolists to many English readers, held particular importance for Eliot who began writing his own symbolist poems at this time, mainly in the manner of Jules Laforgue. Graduating in 1910 with both an undergraduate and a master's degree, Eliot traveled to Paris and studied at the Sorbonne. After a year in France, he returned to Harvard and began work towards a doctorate in philosophy, but ultimately moved back to Europe, settling in London in 1914.

In London, Eliot worked briefly as a teacher and then more extensively as a bank clerk at Lloyd's. In 1915, he published several poems—including "The Love Song of J. Alfred Prufrock" in *Poetry*—with the assistance of Ezra Pound, the leading literary promoter of the day. That same year, Eliot married his first wife, Vivien Haigh-Wood, an Englishwoman. Problems between them led to their separation almost two decades later. Again with Pound's help and connections, Eliot's first full volume of poetry, *Prufrock and Other Observations*, appeared in 1917. The book quickly placed Eliot at the forefront of the avant-garde. During this time Eliot also helped edit the Imagist magazine, *The Egoist*. He followed *Prufrock* with *Poems* (originally published as *Ara Vos Prec*) in 1919, and *The Sacred Wood*, a collection of literary essays, in 1920. While receiving treatment for a nervous breakdown in a Swiss sanitarium, Eliot finished the long poem *The Waste Land*, which was published in 1922, and instantly gained landmark status.

Reflecting contemporary cultural disillusionment and confusion, *The Waste Land* struck a chord with an enormous audience and elevated Eliot's reputation to almost unprecedented levels. Following it with additional volumes of poetry, critical essays, and plays, Eliot became a dominant voice in the literary world throughout the West. He also founded a famous literary magazine in 1922, *The Criterion*, which, before it stopped publication in 1939, would publish such writers as Yeats, Pound, Woolf, and Proust. In 1925, he became associated with the publishing firm that would become Faber and Faber. Two years later, Eliot became a British citizen and converted to Anglicanism, a development that would have a significant effect on his poetry. Eliot's work from this period on through to his final volume, *Four Quartets* (1943), exhibits an increasingly pronounced streak of orthodoxy and conservatism. However, the narrowing of Eliot's political and social views failed to diminish the broad appeal and power of his literary work. He was awarded the Nobel Prize in 1948.

In 1956, ten years after the death of his first wife, Eliot married Valerie Fletcher, his thirty-year-old secretary at Faber and Faber. He wrote little poetry during these final years, and the emergence of "confessional" and more romantic, subjective strains of poetry conspired to diminish his earlier popularity. Despite this change in literary fashion and persistent criticism of his work's emotional detachment, Eliot continues to be recognized as one of the greatest poets of the Modern era. He died in London in 1965.

Agha Shahid Ali

T.S. Eliot

Agha Shahid Ali on T. S. Eliot

Written in 1910, "The Love Song of J. Alfred Prufrock," Eliot's first published poem (Harriet Monroe of *Poetry* had rejected it but then published it in 1915 on Ezra Pound's insistence), remains the best introduction to Eliot the poet. It contains not only all the Modernist strategies that would later be found in *The Waste Land* and become associated with the poet, but also, in active practice, the critical principles Eliot had advanced in his most famous essay, "Tradition and the Individual Talent" (1919).

One issue preoccupying him in that essay is that of the poet who is eccentric, that is, one who searches for novelty. Eliot asserts, the "business of the poet is not to find new emotions, but to use the ordinary ones and, in working them up into poetry, to express feelings which are not in actual emotions at all." Poetry is an "escape from personality." For someone like Eliot, who believed that literature "has a simultaneous existence and composes a simultaneous order," a poet must obtain tradition by "great labor," because tradition cannot be inherited. The essay has the European poet very much in mind as its audience, something that becomes clear when Eliot goes on to say that the "mind of Europe" is far more important than the poet's own mind.

While Eliot's project became the recovery of tradition (from the Bible down to anything else including—in departures from the mind of Europe—Sanskrit and Pali texts), he adopted various Modernist strategies to preserve and express it, strategies that draw attention to themselves as manifestations of style: epigraphs, quotes, echoes, and allusions. Out of the blue (it would have seemed to Eliot's first readers), a line from Dante or Shakespeare confronts the reader. And though he was against the search for novelty, there certainly was novelty in his techniques, some of them adopted from films— jump-cuts, absent transitions, many voices in one voice, a collage of voices. Prufrock has no problem moving from theme to image to wherever his mind is taking him:

Oh, do not ask, "What is it?"
Let us go and make our visit.

So how does Eliot escape from personality here? Well, the poem is clearly not autobiographical. Eliot was only twenty-two when he wrote it, whereas the protagonist wearily says:

> *I grow old...I grow old...*
> *I shall wear the bottoms of my trousers rolled.*

We cannot look to the poem for biography—it is clearly in the tradition of the dramatic monologue—as we can't, quite remarkably, even in an out-and-out lyrical poem such as "La Figlia Che Piange." In it we never learn who the "he" or "she" is. Is the speaker Eliot himself? Evocative and sensuous, the poem lives in its own world and escapes biography. Nothing outside the poem—not even the poet's own life—can come between the reader and the poem. What the reader finds helpful is brushing up his sense of tradition. As Prufrock reveals his inability to reveal himself, he uses tradition as his marvelous mask: Hamlet, Michelangelo, Lazarus, and St. John the Baptist. All the literary echoes buried in the poem demonstrate the strategy by which the poet could express tradition—through echoes and sometimes outright "thefts"—as in one way or the other almost all his poems do. One is again and again dazzled by the voice that contains so many voices. Out of the blue, it seems, the reader is confronted with a line or passage from Dante or Shakespeare or Webster or Marvell and is compelled by their incorporation into the poem's fabric.

In "Journey of the Magi," also, Eliot escapes personality, autobiography, and "confession." The speaker is one of the Magi in his old age, dictating his memoir,

> *but set down*
> *This set down*
> *This: were we led all*
> *that way for*
> *Birth or Death?*

and trying to make sense of the entire experience of seeing Christ.

Always interested in philosophical and religious issues, such as the ones dealt with in "Journey of the Magi," Eliot was to use *Four Quartets* as the place for his grandest meditation. By the time he wrote "Burnt Norton," the first quartet, Modernist strategies had so settled inside him that he did not have to practice style ostentatiously. Rather, he adopts a philosophic style, deals directly with abstract issues:

> *If all time is eternally present,*
> *All time is unredeemable.*

A close study of Eliot reveals the constant paradox of a poet who is absolutely revolutionary in his aesthetic practice but very conservative in his political, cultural, and literary views: he was a "classicist in literature, royalist in politics, and Anglo-Catholic in religion." He asserted this in England, where he settled, in 1914–15, to turn himself—one can confidently say—into a European as only an American can.

W.B. Yeats and Eliot talk to one another during a luncheon in 1925. It was their first meeting in the U.S.

The Love Song of J. Alfred Prufrock

DISC 1, TRACK 48

S'io credessi che mia risposta fosse
A persona che mai tornasse al mondo,
Questa fiamma staria senza più scosse.
Ma per ciò che giammai di questo fondo
Non tornò vivo alcun, s'i'odo il vero,
Senza tema d'infamia ti rispondo.

Let us go then, you and I,
When the evening is spread out against the sky
Like a patient etherised upon a table;
Let us go, through certain half-deserted streets,
The muttering retreats
Of restless nights in one-night cheap hotels
And sawdust restaurants with oyster-shells:
Streets that follow like a tedious argument
Of insidious intent
To lead you to an overwhelming question…
Oh, do not ask, "What is it?"
Let us go and make our visit.

    In the room the women come and go
Talking of Michelangelo.

    The yellow fog that rubs its back upon the
        window-panes,
The yellow smoke that rubs its muzzle on the
        window-panes
Licked its tongue into the corners of the evening,
Lingered upon the pools that stand in drains,
Let fall upon its back the soot that falls from
        chimneys,
Slipped by the terrace, made a sudden leap,
And seeing that it was a soft October night,
Curled once about the house, and fell asleep.

    And indeed there will be a time
For the yellow smoke that slides along the street
Rubbing its back upon the window-panes;

There will be time, there will be time
To prepare a face to meet the faces that you meet;
There will be time to murder and create,
And time for all the works and days of hands
That lift and drop a question on your plate;
Time for you and time for me,
And time yet for a hundred indecisions,
And for a hundred visions and revisions,
Before the taking of a toast and tea.

    In the room the women come and go
Talking of Michelangelo.

    And indeed there will be time
To wonder, "Do I dare?" and, "Do I dare?"
Time to turn back and descend the stair,
With a bald spot in the middle of my hair—
[They will say: "How his hair is growing thin!"]
My morning coat, my collar mounting firmly to the chin,
My necktie rich and modest, but asserted by a
        simple pin—
[They will say: "But how his arms and legs are thin!"]
Do I dare
Disturb the universe?
In a minute there is time
For decisions and revisions which a minute will reverse.

    For I have known them all already, known them all—
Have known the evenings, mornings, afternoons,
I have measured out my life with coffee spoons;
I know the voices dying with a dying fall
Beneath the music from a farther room.
    So how should I presume?

    And I have known the eyes already, known them all—
The eyes that fix you in a formulated phrase,
And when I am formulated, sprawling on a pin,
When I am pinned and wriggling on the wall,
Then how should I begin
To spit out all the butt-ends of my days and ways?
    And how should I presume?

    And I have known the arms already, known them all—
Arms that are braceleted and white and bare
[But in the lamplight, downed with light brown hair!]

Is it perfume from a dress
That makes me so digress?
Arms that lie along a table, or wrap about a shawl.
    And should I then presume?
    And how should I begin?

                    . . . . .

Shall I say, I have gone at dusk through narrow streets
And watched the smoke that rises from the pipes
Of lonely men in shirt-sleeves, leaning out of
        windows?…

    I should have been a pair of ragged claws
Scuttling across the floors of silent seas.

                    . . . . .

And the afternoon, the evening, sleeps so peacefully!
Smoothed by long fingers,
Asleep…tired…or it malingers,
Stretched on the floor, here beside you and me.
Should I, after tea and cakes and ices,
Have the strength to force the moment to its crisis?
But though I have wept and fasted, wept and prayed,
Though I have seen my head [grown slightly bald]
        brought in upon a platter,
I am no prophet—and here's no great matter;
I have seen the moment of my greatness flicker,
And I have seen the eternal Footman hold my coat, and
        snicker,
And in short, I was afraid.

    And would it have been worth it, after all.
After the cups, the marmalade, the tea,
Among the porcelain, among some talk of you and me,
Would it have been worth while,
To have bitten off the matter with a smile,
To have squeezed the universe into a ball
To roll it toward some overwhelming question,
To say: "I am Lazarus, come from the dead,
Come back to tell you all, I shall tell you all"—
If one, settling a pillow by her head,
    Should say: "That is not what I meant at all.
    That is not it, at all."
    And would it have been worth it, after all,
Would it have been worth while,
After the sunsets and the dooryards and the sprinkled
        streets,

After the novels, after the teacups, after the skirts
        that trail along the floor—
And this, and so much more?—
It is impossible to say just what I mean!
But as if a magic lantern threw the nerves in
        patterns on a screen:
Would it have been worth while
If one, settling a pillow or throwing off a shawl,
And turning toward the window, should say:
    "That is not it at all,
    That is not what I meant, at all."

                    . . . . .

No! I am not Prince Hamlet, nor was meant to be;
Am an attendant lord, one that will do
To swell a progress, start a scene or two,
Advise the prince; no doubt, an easy tool,
Deferential, glad to be of use,
Politic, cautious, and meticulous;
Full of high sentence, but a bit obtuse;
At times, indeed, almost ridiculous—
Almost, at times, the Fool.

    I grow old…I grow old…
I shall wear the bottoms of my trousers rolled.

    Shall I part my hair behind? Do I dare to eat a
        peach?
I shall wear white flannel trousers, and walk upon
        the beach.
I have heard the mermaids singing, each to each.

    I do not think that they will sing to me.

    I have seen them riding seaward on the waves
Combing the white hair of the waves blown back
When the wind blows the water white and black.

    We have lingered in the chambers of the sea
By sea-girls wreathed with seaweed red and brown
Till human voices wake us, and we drown.

                                    [1917]

La Figlia Che Piange

Stand on the highest pavement of the stair—
Lean on a garden urn—
Weave, weave the sunlight in your hair—
Clasp your flowers to you with a pained surprise—
Fling them to the ground and turn
With a fugitive resentment in your eyes:
But weave, weave the sunlight in your hair.

So I would have had him leave,
So I would have had her stand and grieve,
So he would have left
As the soul leaves the body torn and bruised,
As the mind deserts the body it has used.
I should find
Some way incomparably light and deft,
Some way we both should understand,
Simple and faithless as a smile and shake of the hand.

She turned away, but with the autumn weather
Compelled my imagination many days,
Many days and many hours:
Her hair over her arms and her arms full of flowers.
And I wonder how they should have been together!
I should have lost a gesture and a pose.
Sometimes these cogitations still amaze
The troubled midnight and the noon's repose.

[1917]

Journey of the Magi

"A cold coming we had of it,
Just the worst time of the year
For a journey, and such a long journey:
The ways deep and the weather sharp,
The very dead of winter."
And the camels galled, sore-footed, refractory,
Lying down in the melting snow.
There were times we regretted
The summer palaces on slopes, the terraces,
And the silken girls bringing sherbet.
Then the camel men cursing and grumbling
And running away, and wanting their liquor and women,
And the night-fires going out, and the lack of shelters,
And the cities hostile and the towns unfriendly
And the villages dirty and charging high prices:
A hard time we had of it.
At the end we preferred to travel all night,
Sleeping in snatches,
With the voices singing in our ears, saying
That this was all folly.

    Then at dawn we came down to a temperate valley,
Wet, below the snow line, smelling of vegetation;
With a running stream and a water-mill beating the darkness,
And three trees on the low sky,
And an old white horse galloped away in the meadow.
Then we came to a tavern with vine-leaves over the lintel,
Six hands at an open door dicing for pieces of silver,
And feet kicking the empty wine-skins.
But there was no information, and so we continued
And arrived at evening, not a moment too soon
Finding the place; it was (you may say) satisfactory.

    All this was a long time ago, I remember,
And I would do it again, but set down
This set down
This: were we led all that way for
Birth or Death? There was a Birth, certainly,
We had evidence and no doubt. I had seen birth and death,

But had thought they were different; this Birth was
Hard and bitter agony for us, like Death, our death.
We returned to our places, these Kingdoms,
But no longer at ease here, in the old dispensation,
With an alien people clutching their gods.
I should be glad of another death.

[1927]

Burnt Norton
from Four Quartets

τοῦ λόγου δ'ἐόντος ξυνοῦ ζώουσιν
οἱ πολλοὶ ὡς ἰδίαν ἔχοντες φρόνησιν.
                                        I. p. 77. Fr. 2.

ὁδὸς ἄνω κάτω μία καὶ ὡυτή.
                                        I. p. 89. Fr. 60.

Diels: *Die Fragmente der Vorsokratiker*
                        (Herakleitos).

I

Time present and time past
Are both perhaps present in time future,
And time future contained in time past.
If all time is eternally present
All time is unredeemable.
What might have been is an abstraction
Remaining a perpetual possibility
Only in a world of speculation.
What might have been and what has been
Point to one end, which is always present.
Footfalls echo in the memory
Down the passage which we did not take
Towards the door we never opened
Into the rose-garden. My words echo
Thus, in your mind.
                        But to what purpose
Disturbing the dust on a bowl of rose-leaves
I do not know.
                        Other echoes
Inhabit the garden. Shall we follow?
Quick, said the bird, find them, find them,
Round the corner. Through the first gate,
Into our first world, shall we follow
The deception of the thrush? Into our first world.
There they were, dignified, invisible,
Moving without pressure, over the dead leaves,

In the autumn heat, through the vibrant air,
And the bird called, in response to
The unheard music hidden in the shrubbery,
And the unseen eyebeam crossed, for the roses
Had the look of flowers that are looked at.
There they were as our guests, accepted and accepting.
So we moved, and they, in a formal pattern,
Along the empty alley, into the box circle,
To look down into the drained pool.
Dry the pool, dry concrete, brown edged,
And the pool was filled with water out of sunlight,
And the lotos rose, quietly, quietly,
The surface glittered out of heart of light,
And they were behind us, reflected in the pool.
Then a cloud passed, and the pool was empty.
Go, said the bird, for the leaves were full of children,
Hidden excitedly, containing laughter.
Go, go, go, said the bird: human kind
Cannot bear very much reality.
Time past and time future
What might have been and what has been
Point to one end, which is always present.

II

Garlic and sapphires in the mud
Clot the bedded axle-tree.
The trilling wire in the blood
Sings below inveterate scars
And reconciles forgotten wars.
The dance along the artery
The circulation of the lymph
Are figured in the drift of stars
Ascend to summer in the tree
We move above the moving tree
In light upon the figured leaf
And hear upon the sodden floor
Below, the boarhound and the boar
Pursue their pattern as before
But reconciled among the stars.

At the still point of the turning world. Neither flesh
    nor fleshless;
Neither from nor towards; at the still point, there the
    dance is,
But neither arrest nor movement. And do not call it
    fixity,
Where past and future are gathered. Neither movement
    from nor towards,
Neither ascent nor decline. Except for the point, the
    still point,
There would be no dance, and there is only the dance.
I can only say, *there* we have been: but I cannot say
    where.
And I cannot say, how long, for that is to place it in
    time.

The inner freedom from the practical desire,
The release from action and suffering, release from
    the inner
And the outer compulsion, yet surrounded
By a grace of sense, a white light still and moving,
Erhebung without motion, concentration
Without elimination, both a new world
And the old made explicit, understood
In the completion of its partial ecstasy,
The resolution of its partial horror.
Yet the enchainment of past and future
Woven in the weakness of the changing body,
Protects mankind from heaven and damnation
Which flesh cannot endure.
                              Time past and time future
Allow but a little consciousness.
To be conscious is not to be in time
But only in time can the moment in the rose-garden,
The moment in the arbour where the rain beat,
The moment in the draughty church at smokefall
Be remembered; involved with past and future.
Only through time time is conquered.

III

Here is a place of disaffection
Time before and time after
In a dim light: neither daylight
Investing form with lucid stillness
Turning shadow into transient beauty
With slow rotation suggesting permanence
Nor darkness to purify the soul
Emptying the sensual with deprivation
Cleansing affection from the temporal.
Neither plenitude nor vacancy. Only a flicker
Over the strained time-ridden faces
Distracted from distraction by distraction
Filled with fancies and empty of meaning
Tumid apathy with no concentration
Men and bits of paper, whirled by the cold wind
That blows before and after time,
Wind in and out of unwholesome lungs
Time before and time after.
Eructation of unhealthy souls
Into the faded air, the torpid
Driven on the wind that sweeps the gloomy hills of
    London,
Hampstead and Clerkenwell, Campden and Putney,
Highgate, Primrose and Ludgate. Not here
Not here the darkness, in this twittering world.

Descend lower, descend only
Into the world of perpetual solitude,
World not world, but that which is not world,
Internal darkness, deprivation
And destitution of all property,
Desiccation of the world of sense,
Evacuation of the world of fancy,
Inoperancy of the world of spirit;
This is the one way, and the other
Is the same, not in movement
But abstention from movement; while the world moves
In appetency, on its metalled ways
Of time past and time future.

IV

Time and the bell have buried the day,
The black cloud carries the sun away.
Will the sunflower turn to us, will the clematis
Stray down, bend to us; tendril and spray
Clutch and cling?
Chill
Fingers of yew be curled
Down on us? After the kingfisher's wing
Has answered light to light, and is silent, the light is
   still
At the still point of the turning world.

V

Words move, music moves
Only in time; but that which is only living
Can only die. Words, after speech, reach
Into the silence. Only by the form, the pattern,
Can words or music reach
The stillness, as a Chinese jar still
Moves perpetually in its stillness.
Not the stillness of the violin, while the note lasts,
Not that only, but the co-existence,
Or say that the end precedes the beginning,
And the end and the beginning were always there
Before the beginning and after the end.
And all is always now. Words strain,
Crack and sometimes break, under the burden,
Under the tension, slip, slide, perish,
Decay with imprecision, will not stay in place,
Will not stay still. Shrieking voices
Scolding, mocking, or merely chattering,
Always assail them. The Word in the desert
Is most attacked by voices of temptation,
The crying shadow in the funeral dance,
The loud lament of the disconsolate chimera.

The detail of the pattern is movement,
As in the figure of the ten stairs.
Desire itself is movement
Not in itself desirable;
Love is itself unmoving,
Only the cause and end of movement,
Timeless, and undesiring
Except in the aspect of time
Caught in the form of limitation
Between un-being and being.
Sudden in a shaft of sunlight
Even while the dust moves
There rises the hidden laughter
Of children in the foliage
Quick now, here, now, always—
Ridiculous the waste sad time
Stretching before and after.

[1936]

Edna St. Vincent Millay

(1892–1950) b. Rockland, Maine, United States

Disc 2
Tracks 1–4

Edna St. Vincent Millay was born in Rockland, Maine, on February 22, 1892. Her parents, Cora Lounella and Henry Tolman Millay, divorced when Millay was eight years old. After the breakup, her mother moved Edna and her sisters to Camden, Maine, and raised them on her own. Millay's mother provided for her family by nursing, and by most accounts, she soundly encouraged her daughters' ambitions and ensured for them strong literary and musical backgrounds. In high school, Millay concentrated on literature and theater, and in 1912, she made her literary debut. Encouraged by her mother, Millay entered a poetry contest sponsored by the literary magazine *The Lyric Year*, and her long, mystical poem "The Renaissance" instantly caught the eye of Ferdinand Earle, one of the contest's judges. Earle persuaded Millay to change the poem's title to "Renascence," and although it only ranked fourth overall, the poem was published in *The Lyric Year* that November. The poem earned Millay a scholarship to Vassar as well as acclaim from many prominent literary figures, including Witter Bynner.

At Vassar, Millay (whom close friends called "Vincent") continued to write and publish poetry and remained active in theater. In 1917, the year of her graduation, she published her first book of poetry, *Renascence and Other Poems*. Also while at Vassar, Millay began having intimate relationships with several women, including the English actress Wynne Matthison, and from this point forward would live more or less openly bisexual. Her second book of poetry, *A Few Figs from Thistles* (1920), dealt uninhibitedly with feminist issues and lesbian sentiments, as did the first of her three lyric plays, *The Lamp and the Bell*, which was commissioned by Vassar and published in 1921. With college behind her, Millay placed herself in the center of New York City's bohemian neighborhood, Greenwich Village. She continued both her poetry and drama writing and was heralded as the voice of her generation. *The Harp Weaver and Other Poems*, her fourth book of poetry, was published in 1923 and won the Pulitzer Prize, the first to be awarded to a woman for poetry. She also began seeing a number of male lovers at this time, including a man named Floyd Dell, who tried unsuccessfully to quell her lesbian tendencies and obtain her hand in marriage. In 1923, she did marry—but not to Dell. After returning from two years in Europe as a correspondent for *Vanity Fair*, Millay wed a man named Eugen Jan Boissevain.

Many surmise that Boissevain's successful turn at publicizing Millay's poetry may have been one motivation for their sexually open marriage, and Boissevain continued to manage Millay's career until his death in 1949. Millay died one year later in her home in Austerlitz, New York. In later years, a political awareness and a mature, tender tone replaced the fashionably cynical touch of Millay's early lyrics, but she will always be remembered as the prototypical reckless, self-determined, romantic "New Woman."

Molly Peacock on Edna St. Vincent Millay

One of Edna St. Vincent Millay's favorite girlhood dinners was fudge. In 1900, her mother had boldly divorced her father, earning a living as a practical nurse in their small town, often away from home on cases with her patients. This left twelve-year-old Vincent, as her family and friends called her—shortened from St. Vincent, her middle name—in charge of her two younger sisters. Passionate about poetry and music, she spent the bit of household money her mother left her not on food but on books, crayons, sheet music, and paper. She and her sisters scoured the pantry, turning up with flour, sugar, eggs, and chocolate for dinner. I cannot think of a more ideal childhood day than reading, writing, drawing, singing, playing the piano, and chasing your sisters up and down the stairs while the fudge sets.

Mrs. Millay would come home to enter her girls' world, suggesting verse for them to read and memorize, urging Vincent not only to write poems (she wrote her first at the age of five) but to submit them to contests. When Vincent was twenty, her mother hurried her home from her father's sickbed to submit her poem "Renascence" to a national contest, creating a controversy when she failed to win first prize. The letters in her favor launched her into a literary spotlight which each year became more intense until, at the age of thirty, she became the first woman to win the Pulitzer Prize in poetry.

She was a spellbinding reader of her poetry, drawing at the height of her reputation thousands of fans. You might call her the first performance poet, the original hair-tosser, a sexy, elfin redhead. Though Millay was in Paris at the same time as Gertrude Stein, Ernest Hemingway, and F. Scott Fitzgerald, she had little interest in the avant-garde. Her aesthetic, formed in her childhood both by a love of the rules of traditional verse and an intrinsically rule-less bohemian home life, allowed her to claim the sonnet as a poetic safe house for her great subject: the lawless behavior of love. In this she was allied to her friend, the poet and socialite renegade Elinor Wylie.

Millay became a diva of the sonnet, publishing some of the sexiest, wisest, most passionate, and most feminist poetry of the twentieth century, each a rhythmical, sometimes whimsical, sometimes savagely intense fourteen lines. "Love Is Not All," from her sonnet sequence "Fatal Interview," is a testament to the vitality of an extramarital affair, published while she lived comfortably at "Steepletop," the berry farm she shared with her husband, Eugen Jan Boissevain. It is a mature love poem, granting to the lover all that is humanly possible in a world that Millay laces with images of hunger, death, and betrayal.

As knowing as she became, her poetry maintained a freshness of voice throughout her life. You can hear the ebullience in "Childhood Is the Kingdom Where Nobody Dies," a free verse poem in which Millay constructs a ghostly loneliness from bits of conversation and domestic life.

Always politically involved, from protesting the Sacco and Vanzetti case to urging the U.S. to enter World War II to rescue European victims of the Nazis, Millay read "The Pioneer," which was later titled "Sonnet to Inez Milholland," at the unveiling of the statues of leaders in the cause of equal rights for women, Lucretia Mott, Susan B. Anthony, and Elizabeth Cady Stanton. The last line, "Take up the song; forget the epitaph," is inscribed in stone in the Poets' Corner of the Cathedral of St. John the Divine in New York City.

Millay made what some would call a minor art—that is, she reinvigorated a traditional verse form, the sonnet, reclaiming it for a woman's voice—about the major lyric themes of love and death. She was as uncompromising in her devotion to the rules of verse as she was in her flaunting of social rules. My guess is that Millay would not have held these two ideas as contradictions, but only as the opposition of forces that create from the energy of the lived life, an art driven by that life's energy.

First Fig

My candle burns at both ends;
    It will not last the night;
But ah, my foes, and oh, my friends—
    It gives a lovely light!

[1920]

Recuerdo

DISC 2, TRACK 2

We were very tired, we were very merry—
We had gone back and forth all night on the ferry.
It was bare and bright, and smelled like a stable—
But we looked into a fire, we leaned across a table,
We lay on a hill-top underneath the moon;
And the whistles kept blowing, and the dawn came soon.

We were very tired, we were very merry—
We had gone back and forth all night on the ferry;
And you ate an apple, and I ate a pear,
From a dozen of each we had bought somewhere;
And the sky went wan, and the wind came cold,
And the sun rose dripping, a bucketful of gold.

We were very tired, we were very merry,
We had gone back and forth all night on the ferry.
We hailed, "Good morrow, mother!" to a shawl-covered head,
And bought a morning paper, which neither of us read;

And she wept, "God bless you!" for the apples and pears,
And we gave her all our money but our subway fares.

[1920]

Love Is Not All: It Is Not Meat nor Drink

Love is not all: it is not meat nor drink
Nor slumber nor a roof against the rain;
Nor yet a floating spar to men that sink
And rise and sink and rise and sink again;
Love can not fill the thickened lung with breath,
Nor clean the blood, nor set the fractured bone;
Yet many a man is making friends with death
Even as I speak, for lack of love alone.
It well may be that in a difficult hour,
Pinned down by pain and moaning for release,
Or nagged by want past resolution's power,
I might be driven to sell your love for peace,
Or trade the memory of this night for food.
It well may be. I do not think I would.

[1926]

I Shall Forget You Presently, My Dear

DISC 2, TRACK 3

I shall forget you presently, my dear,
So make the most of this, your little day,
Your little month, your little half a year,
Ere I forget, or die, or move away,
And we are done forever; by and by
I shall forget you, as I said, but now,
If you entreat me with your loveliest lie
I will protest you with my favorite vow.
I would indeed that love were longer-lived,
And vows were not so brittle as they are,
But so it is, and nature has contrived
To struggle on without a break thus far,—
Whether or not we find what we are seeking
Is idle, biologically speaking.

[1934]

Childhood Is the Kingdom Where Nobody Dies

Childhood is not from birth to a certain age and at a
    certain age
The child is grown, and puts away childish things.
Childhood is the kingdom where nobody dies.

Nobody that matters, that is. Distant relatives of
    course
Die, whom one never has seen or has seen for an hour,
And they gave one candy in a pink-and-green stripéd
    bag, or a jack-knife,
And went away, and cannot really be said to have lived
    at all.

And cats die. They lie on the floor and lash their tails,
And their reticent fur is suddenly all in motion
With fleas that one never knew were there,
Polished and brown, knowing all there is to know,
Trekking off into the living world.
You fetch a shoe-box, but it's much too small, because
    she won't curl up now:
So you find a bigger box, and bury her in the yard, and
    weep.

But you do not wake up a month from then, two
    months,
A year from then, two years, in the middle of the night
And weep, with your knuckles in your mouth, and say
    Oh, God! Oh, God!
Childhood is the kingdom where nobody dies that
    matters,—mothers and fathers don't die.

And if you have said, "For heaven's sake, must you
    always be kissing a person?"
Or, "I do wish to gracious you'd stop tapping on the
    window with your thimble!"

Tomorrow, or even the day after tomorrow if you're
    busy having fun,
Is plenty of time to say, "I'm sorry, mother."

To be grown up is to sit at the table with people who
    have died, who neither listen nor speak;
Who do not drink their tea, though they always said
Tea was such a comfort.

Run down into the cellar and bring up the last jar of
    raspberries; they are not tempted.
Flatter them, ask them what was it they said exactly
That time, to the bishop, or to the overseer, or to
    Mrs. Mason;
They are not taken in.
Shout at them, get red in the face, rise,
Drag them up out of their chairs by their stiff
    shoulders and shake them and yell at them;
They are not startled, they are not even embarrassed;
    they slide back into their chairs.

Your tea is cold now.
You drink it standing up,
And leave the house.

[1934]

Dorothy Parker

(1893–1967) b. West End, New Jersey, United States

Disc 2
Tracks 5–8

Born on August 22, 1893, Dorothy Rothschild is remembered today as Dorothy Parker, having taken the surname of her first husband, Edwin Pond Parker II. Her mother Annie died when Parker was four years old, and her father Jacob remarried shortly thereafter. Parker was educated at Miss Dana's School in Morristown, New Jersey, and the Blessed Sacrament Academy, a school contained in a New York City convent. Surprisingly, Parker, one of America's most celebrated and quick-minded witticists, never received a high school diploma. She entered the workforce at an early age, helping to provide financial assistance to her father, whose once-successful garment business had begun to decline. In 1913, her father died, and Parker, on her own at this point, supported herself as a dance instructor until her literary and intellectual career began in 1914.

In that year, Parker sold her first poem, "Any Porch," to *Vanity Fair*, whose editor then helped her secure a job with the editorial staff of *Vogue*. She later joined the editorial staff of *Vanity Fair*, eventually becoming their chief drama critic, and her associations at the magazine brought her into contact with the Northeast's cultural and intellectual elite. In 1917, she married Parker, a successful Wall Street broker. Shortly thereafter, while her husband was away on military service, Parker's literary career took off. Although she was fired from *Vanity Fair* in 1920 after writing an unfavorable review of an actress who turned out to be married to one of the magazine's major advertisers, she quickly rebounded by writing reviews for various other magazines, including *Ainslee's* and, later in the '20s, *The New Yorker*. The Algonquin Hotel's famous Round Table—of which Parker was a key member—formed during this time, bringing together such literary figures as Robert Benchley and Robert Sherwood, both of whom became good friends of Parker. Very much in tune with America's emerging "Jazz Age," Parker's sharp wit guaranteed her popularity at the various clubs and speakeasies she was known to frequent. After returning home, Parker's husband appears to have remained an outsider from her literary circle, and this put a strain on their marriage. Parker had an abortion and attempted suicide in 1923; she and her husband began drinking heavily and grew further apart, finally divorcing in 1928. Having received largely favorable reviews for her first volume of poetry, *Enough Rope* (1926), Parker, along with Edna St. Vincent Millay, came to personify the "New Woman" of the 1920s.

The beginning of the Great Depression in the 1930s brought another marked change in Parker's life and poetry. The Jazz Age in which she had participated so enthusiastically was essentially over; writing in reaction to fascism, her poetry took on a more political turn. In addition to poetry and reviews, Parker also wrote short stories, publishing the collections *Laments for the Living* in 1930 and *After Such Pleasures* in 1933. That same year, Parker married Alan Campbell, and the couple moved to Hollywood to write screenplays together. Possibly their greatest success was 1937's *A Star is Born*. Her poetry continued to shift from the witty, light-hearted style of the '20s to a more serious, introspective style, as shown in her 1936 volume *Collected Poems: Deep as a Well*. This trend continued, and in the 1940s, Parker endorsed and supported several radical causes, including communism. She continued to publish poetry and endorse emerging activist movements, Civil Rights and feminism chief among them, until her death on June 7, 1967.

Susan Hahn on Dorothy Parker

In reading through Dorothy Parker's poetry, it is not so much the witty, terrifically bitter, pithy lines that are easy to remember and provoke an edgy smile, but rather it is the collected despair of her work that lingers, nags, and haunts.

Dorothy Parker was a brilliant, strong, and paradoxically sad, vulnerable woman, if one reads autobiography into a poet's work, which in her case I think is appropriate. She was a "confessional" poet, but she definitely did it *her way*. As strung-out emotionally as Stevie Smith (with all her wit and melancholy) and Sylvia Plath (with all her fury and melancholy), Parker was as clever as clever *can be* with language and with melancholy—almost to the point of frustration. Often, she would suddenly, and with great agility, tie up a poem with a dazzling ribbon of distraction. For example, the poem "Well-Worn Story" has the sway and song of Emily Dickinson until the last stanza where she cuts herself off from the intense emotion of the earlier lines:

I wore my heart like a wet, red stain
On the breast of a velvet gown.

The poem ends:

Now what should I do in this place
But sit and count the chimes,
And splash cold water on my face
And spoil a page with rhymes?

I wish she had stayed with the passionate emotion instead of becoming so deftly pen-to-paper aware. And yet—*and yet*—in some poems like "Afternoon," with its yearning for both the lived and unlived life, and "Résumé," wit and pain marry into a strong union.

Razors pain you;
Rivers are damp;
Acids stain you;
And drugs cause cramp.
Guns aren't lawful;
Nooses give;
Gas smells awful;
You might as well live.

Here she tells the reader she's been to *that side of town*. But in doing so she doesn't splatter herself onto the page. There's nothing to clean up. The merging of despondency and humor are sculpted into rock—solid. The poem evokes a quiet, uncomfortable smile or, when read aloud to a group, a quiet, nervous laugh. A quiet, nervous *yes*.

In all her writings—poetry, short stories, plays, criticism—Dorothy Parker was consistently amusing, poignant, biting, desperate, and desperately memorable, as in "Cherry White"—quick with Dickinson's dashes, Smith's slyness, and Plath's pathos. But it is clearly Parker's pessimism all the way—tragic and lightly dismissive, mindbending, and heart-breaking.

I never see that prettiest thing—
A cherry bough gone white with Spring—
But what I think, "How gay 'twould be
To hang me from a flowering tree."

One Perfect Rose

DISC 2, TRACK 6

A single flow'r he sent me, since we met.
    All tenderly his messenger he chose;
Deep-hearted, pure, with scented dew still wet—
    One perfect rose.

I knew the language of the floweret;
    "My fragile leaves," it said, "his heart enclose."
Love long has taken for his amulet
    One perfect rose.

Why is it no one ever sent me yet
    One perfect limousine, do you suppose?
Ah no, it's always just my luck to get
    One perfect rose.

[1926]

Résumé

DISC 2, TRACK 7

Razors pain you;
Rivers are damp;
Acids stain you;
And drugs cause cramp.
Guns aren't lawful;
Nooses give;
Gas smells awful;
You might as well live.

[1926]

News Item

Men seldom make passes
At girls who wear glasses.

[1926]

Afternoon

DISC 2, TRACK 8

When I am old, and comforted,
    And done with this desire,
With Memory to share my bed
    And Peace to share my fire,

I'll comb my hair in scalloped bands
    Beneath my laundered cap,
And watch my cool and fragile hands
    Lie light upon my lap.

And I will have a spriggèd gown
    With lace to kiss my throat;
I'll draw my curtain to the town,
    And hum a purring note.

And I'll forget the way of tears,
    And rock, and stir my tea.
But oh, I wish those blessed years
    Were further than they be!

[1928]

A Pig's-Eye View of Literature

The Lives and Times of John Keats, Percy Bysshe Shelley, and George Gordon Noel, Lord Byron

Byron and Shelley and Keats
Were a trio of lyrical treats.
The forehead of Shelley was cluttered with curls,
And Keats never was a descendant of earls,
And Byron walked out with a number of girls,
    But it didn't impair the poetical feats
        Of Byron and Shelley,
        Of Byron and Shelley,
    Of Byron and Shelley and Keats.

Oscar Wilde
If, with the literate, I am
Impelled to try an epigram,
I never seek to take the credit;
We all assume that Oscar said it.

Harriet Beecher Stowe
The pure and worthy Mrs. Stowe
Is one we all are proud to know
As mother, wife, and authoress,—
Thank God I am content with less!

D.G. Rossetti
Dante Gabriel Rossetti
Buried all of his *libretti*,
Thought the matter over,—then
Went and dug them up again.

Thomas Carlyle
Carlyle combined the lit'ry life
With throwing teacups at his wife,
Remarking, rather testily,
"Oh, stop your dodging, Mrs. C.!"

Charles Dickens
Who call him spurious and shoddy
Shall do it o'er my lifeless body.
I heartily invite such birds
To come outside and say those words!

Alexandre Dumas and His Son
Although I work, and seldom cease,
At Dumas *père* and Dumas *fils*,
Alas, I cannot make me care
For Dumas *fils* and Dumas *père*.

Alfred Lord Tennyson
Should Heaven send me any son,
I hope he's not like Tennyson.
I'd rather have him play a fiddle
Than rise and bow and speak an idyll.

George Gissing
When I admit neglect of Gissing,
They say I don't know what I'm missing.
Until their arguments are subtler,
I think I'll stick to Samuel Butler.

Walter Savage Landor
Upon the work of Walter Landor
I am unfit to write with candor.
If you can read it, well and good;
But as for me, I never could.

George Sand
What time the gifted lady took
Away from paper, pen, and book,
She spent in amorous dalliance
(They do those things so well in France).

[1928]

The Lady's Reward

Lady, lady, never start
Conversation toward your heart;
Keep your pretty words serene;
Never murmur what you mean.
Show yourself, by word and look,
Swift and shallow as a brook.
Be as cool and quick to go
As a drop of April snow;
Be as delicate and gay
As a cherry flower in May.
Lady, lady, never speak
Of the tears that burn your cheek—
She will never win him, whose
Words had shown she feared to lose.
Be you wise and never sad,
You will get your lovely lad.
Never serious be, nor true,
And your wish will come to you—
And if that makes you happy, kid,
You'll be the first it ever did.

[1931]

E. E. Cummings

(1894–1962) b. Cambridge, Massachusetts, United States

Disc 2

Tracks 9–11

Edward Estlin Cummings was born on October 14, 1894, in Cambridge, Massachusetts. Having completed his secondary education at Cambridge High and the Latin School in 1911, Cummings enrolled at Harvard University, where his father had held a teaching position before becoming a Unitarian minister. While at Harvard, he befriended novelist John Dos Passos. With Dos Passos encouraging his artistic leanings, Cummings became a believer in the science of aesthetics and embarked upon a life of painting and writing. He graduated magna cum laude with a B.A. in English and classics in 1915 and delivered the commencement address, which centered on his own theories of art; a year later he received his master's degree, also from Harvard. He worked odd jobs for a year before volunteering for a French ambulance service during World War I. While in France, the letters written home by Cummings and his friend William Slater Brown angered French censors with their critical commentary on the war. The two were arrested and imprisoned for three months in a camp at La Ferte-Mace; Cummings's experiences at the camp inspired his novel *The Enormous Room*, published in 1922.

Released from the camp late in 1917, Cummings went to Paris to study art and pursue his writing. In 1923, his first solo volume of poetry (he had earlier appeared in a compilation volume entitled *Eight Harvard Poets*) was published with the help of Dos Passos. Titled *Tulips and Chimneys*, the book received wide popular acclaim in the U.S. with readers praising the excitability of the book's syntax and punctuation as well as the peculiar sharpness of its imagery. These two features have become inextricably associated with Cummings's work, although he clearly adapted them from the verse experiments of Gertrude Stein and Amy Lowell, respectively. For most of the 1920s, Cummings traveled between New York and Paris, using a roving assignment from *Vanity Fair* to support himself. In 1924, he married Elaine Orr, the former wife of critic Schofield Thayer, having been romantically involved with her since 1918. The couple had already produced a daughter, Nancy, in 1919. Two months after their marriage, Cummings's wife left him for another man, and they quickly divorced, estranging Cummings from his beloved daughter. Cummings would later marry and divorce another woman, Anne Barton, before marrying fashion model and photographer Marion Morehouse in 1932.

Throughout this period, Cummings's work showed strong jazz and slang influences, beginning with *XLI Poems* and *&* in 1925. In 1931, he published a book of artwork called *CIOPW* (the title referred to the artwork's media: charcoal, ink, oil, pencil, watercolor). That same year, Cummings toured Russia, and later transformed his experiences there into the prose work *Eimi* (1933), in which he equated his travels through Russia to those of Dante among the lost souls of Hell. Cummings continued to write poetry for the remainder of his life, and although his critical reception never quite matched his wide and enduring public appeal, he did win several awards, including a special National Book Award citation and the Bollingen Prize. He spent a year as professor at Harvard from 1952 to 1953, and his lectures from that time are published in the well-known volume *i: six nonlectures*. Among his later volumes of poetry the most notable is perhaps *XAIPE* (1950), which recounts his travels through Spain, Italy, and Greece. Cummings died on September 3, 1962.

Brad Leithauser on E. E. Cummings

The longest poem E.E. Cummings ever wrote (the early, short-lined "Puella Mea") fills only seven of the more than one thousand pages in his *Complete Poems: 1904–1962*. Not for him the extended, balanced argument, the branching narrative, the steady, measured march across a spacious terrain. He was a sprinter, not a distance man—someone who, throughout a long and often bumpy career, remained devoted to the tight, intense, demanding challenges of the brief lyric poem.

This consistency helped to anchor an artist whose life embraced all sorts of irregularities and contradictions. Born in 1894 in Cambridge, Massachusetts, Edward Estlin Cummings was a Unitarian minister's son who laced his verses with alcohol, prostitutes, and profanity; a scion of the Eastern establishment who advocated communism as a young man and McCarthyism in his middle age; a defiantly proud individualist who subsisted for most of his adult life on a parental "allowance"; a literary guerrilla who composed some of the most unorthodox, weird-looking poems ever written by an American, while remaining unwaveringly loyal to that hoariest of poetic forms, the sonnet.

Cummings's poems often present a dense and difficult—occasionally impenetrable-looking—surface. Especially in his opening lines, he can appear ferociously inhospitable:

(as that named Fred
-someBody:hippopotamus,scratch-
ing,one,knee with,its,

Or:

weazened Irrefutable unastonished
two,countenances seated in arranging;sunlight
with-ered unspea-king:tWeNtY,f i n g e r s,large

A drawing made by Cummings dated October 18, 1904, when he was ten years old.

Yet the emotions underpinning his poems are often "pure": powerful upwellings of some undiluted emotion. For all the polyphony in his poems (the layering of voices, the parentheses buried within parentheses), Cummings isn't, by and large, a poet of emotional qualifications, of a nuanced contending of feelings. Hence, it is no surprise that he is commonly perceived as a poet of two polar modes: the satiric and the lyrical. In his satirical poems, the reader meets a notably unmixed hostility, often for the trappings of modern life (mechanization, commercialization, the impersonality of party politics), and often, in its virulence, verging on indiscriminate misanthropy. In his lyrical mode, we're likely to meet a stainless joy, often for the pleasures of romantic love (after two disastrous marriages, Cummings found enduring happiness with his third wife, the beautiful Marion Morehouse), and often, in its giddiness, bordering on cloying sentimentality. It is both Cummings's burden and his blessing that his feelings frequently seem to get the better of him.

He is often at his considerable best in poems and passages where his eccentric locutions suggest a linguistic organization tighter and more concise than that governing everyday speech. Such moments abound in "anyone lived in a pretty how town," surely one of the great short lyrics of our time. It's the story of a pair of all but anonymous villagers, called anyone and noone, whose passage through life (in a mere thirty-six lines, they fall in love, marry, age, and die) is enacted alongside the rotations of the seasons, the yawning caverns of the heavens. A phrase like "anyone's any was all to her" might be rephrased in a variety of ways ("whatever mattered at all to him mattered greatly to her," perhaps, or "his least desire was everything in the world to her"), but never more tersely, or more appealingly.

Or take the final phrase of one of the loveliest lyrics in *XAIPE*: "for also then's until"—which might be paraphrased as "because winter is likewise transitory and will give way to spring." But whatever rephrasing you come up with, it would almost certainly lack the original's compactness. In Cummings's best moments, you suspect not merely that there is method in his madness; you stand convinced that he speaks more directly—even more logically—than other poets do. Oddity reveals itself as sanity. The world is, happily, upended. Here is poetry that partakes of one of literature's largest and most satisfying paradoxes: the pleasure we derive from language that pares down language, from words that eliminate words.

in Just–

in Just-
spring   when the world is mud-
luscious the little
lame balloonman

whistles   far   and wee

and eddieandbill come
running from marbles and
piracies and it's
spring

when the world is puddle-wonderful

the queer
old balloonman whistles
far   and   wee
and bettyandisbel come dancing

from hop-scotch and jump-rope and
it's
spring
and
    the

        goat-footed

balloonMan   whistles
far
and
wee

[1923]

love is a place

love is a place
& through this place of
love move
(with brightness of peace)
all places

yes is a world
& in this world of
yes live
(skilfully curled)
all worlds

[1935]

may i feel said he

may i feel said he
(i'll squeal said she
just once said he)
it's fun said she

(may i touch said he
how much said she
a lot said he)
why not said she

(let's go said he
not too far said she
what's too far said he
where you are said she)

may i stay said he
(which way said she
like this said he
if you kiss said she

may i move said he
is it love said she)
if you're willing said he
(but you're killing said she

but it's life said he
but your wife said she
now said he)
ow said she

(tiptop said he
don't stop said she
oh no said he)
go slow said she

(cccome?said he
ummm said she)
you're divine!said he
(you are Mine said she)

[1935]

anyone lived in a pretty how town

DISC 2, TRACK 10

anyone lived in a pretty how town
(with up so floating many bells down)
spring summer autumn winter
he sang his didn't he danced his did.

Women and men(both little and small)
cared for anyone not at all
they sowed their isn't they reaped their same
sun moon stars rain

children guessed(but only a few
and down they forgot as up they grew
autumn winter spring summer)
that noone loved him more by more

when by now and tree by leaf
she laughed his joy she cried his grief
bird by snow and stir by still
anyone's any was all to her

someones married their everyones
laughed their cryings and did their dance
(sleep wake hope and then) they
said their nevers they slept their dream

stars rain sun moon
(and only the snow can begin to explain
how children are apt to forget to remember
with up so floating many bells down)

one day anyone died i guess
(and noone stooped to kiss his face)
busy folk buried them side by side
little by little and was by was

all by all and deep by deep
and more by more they dream their sleep
noone and anyone earth by april
wish by spirit and if by yes.

Women and men(both dong and ding)
summer autumn winter spring
reaped their sowing and went their came
sun moon stars rain

[1940]

as freedom is a breakfastfood

as freedom is a breakfastfood
or truth can live with right and wrong
or molehills are from mountains made
—long enough and just so long
will being pay the rent of seem
and genius please the talentgang
and water most encourage flame

as hatracks into peachtrees grow
or hopes dance best on bald men's hair
and every finger is a toe
and any courage is a fear
—long enough and just so long
will the impure think all things pure
and hornets wail by children stung

or as the seeing are the blind
and robins never welcome spring
nor flatfolk prove their world is round
nor dingsters die at break of dong
and common's rare and millstones float
—long enough and just so long
tomorrow will not be too late

worms are the words but joy's the voice
down shall go which and up come who
breasts will be breasts thighs will be thighs
deeds cannot dream what dreams can do
—time is a tree(this life one leaf)
but love is the sky and i am for you
just so long and long enough

[1940]

pity this busy monster

pity this busy monster,manunkind,

not. Progress is a comfortable disease:
your victim(death and life safely beyond)

plays with the bigness of his littleness
—electrons deify one razorblade
into a mountainrange;lenses extend

unwish through curving wherewhen till unwish
returns on its unself.
                         A world of made
is not a world of born—pity poor flesh

and trees,poor stars and stones, but never this
fine specimen of hypermagical

ultraomnipotence. We doctors know

a hopeless case if—listen:there's a hell
of a good universe next door;let's go

[1944]

Robert Graves
(1895-1985) b. Wimbledon, England

Disc 2
Track 12-15

Robert Graves was born on July 24 (or July 26—there is disagreement about the two dates) to Albert Percival Graves, an Irish poet and Gaelic scholar, and Amalie von Ranke Graves, grandniece of the distinguished German historian Leopold von Ranke. After the outbreak of World War I, he joined the Royal Welch Fusiliers, and served three tours of combat duty in France. Upon his return to England, he entered St. John's College, Oxford, graduating with a B. Litt. degree in 1926. He married Nancy Nicholson, a painter, in 1918, and during the brief period of time he spent as a professor at the University of Cairo, he was accompanied not only by his wife and children but also by the American poet Laura Riding. The turbulent *ménage à trois* lasted until 1927, when he and his wife separated. They had had four children.

Graves moved with Riding to Deya, Majorca, where they remained together until she left him in 1939. Shortly afterwards, he began a new relationship with Beryl Hodge, who became his wife and with whom he fathered four more children. He attracted international attention, and Deya was known chiefly as Graves' village. He became an inspiration to many writers: In 1950, for example, the young American poet W.S. Merwin, influenced by the elegant formalism that Graves practiced as well as by his interest in myth, lived in Deya as tutor to his son. And in 1962 and 1963, Kingsley Amis visited Graves in Deya.

Graves thought of himself primarily as a poet, and had published more than a dozen books of poetry by 1929. But his prose works—novels, several mythological studies, and *Goodbye to All That,* a memoir of his military life and a denunciation of war —were the source of his income and the works by which he was, and still is, chiefly known. All were controversial: *Goodbye to All That* because it alienated some wartime comrades, including the poet Siegfried Sassoon; the historical/mythological works because they rewrote the conventional interpretations of their subjects. The works, though displaying great erudition and historical expertise, are best understood as imaginative meditations. *I, Claudius* (1934), for example, and its sequel *Claudius the God* the following year, play freely with conventional historiography. And, most strikingly, *The White Goddess* (1948) is no less than an imaginative theory of poetic inspiration, in which the muse/goddess is a female counterpart to Eros. It is more than likely that Graves's experience with Laura Riding informs his theory. The book was, and still is, enormously influential; it was important, as one instance, to the poetry of Ted Hughes. Riding was also central to his major ideas about poetry. As he wrote in the foreword to one of his ever-changing *Collected Poems*: "In 1925 I first became acquainted with the poems and critical work of Laura Riding, and in 1926 with herself; and slowly began to revise my whole attitude to poetry." That revision entailed a departure from the conventional notions of formalism that characterize his earlier work and an increasing sense of the importance of the sort of mythos that he espoused in *The White Goddess.*

In 1967 Graves published a collaborative translation (with Omar Ali-Shah, a Sufi poet) of *The Rubaiyat of Omar Khayyam,* which had previously been known through the Victorian rendition of Edward Fitzgerald. Once again he was a target, this time of professional Orientalists, not only because he abandoned the prosodic form that Fitzgerald had adhered to as incompatible with modern English, but also as a result of the charge that the twelfth-century manuscript from which he had worked was a forgery.

Following a decade of mental debility, Graves died in 1985 at the age of ninety. The magnitude of his legacy—an estimated 140 books—is sufficient reason for an overdue revaluation.

W. S. Merwin on Robert Graves

On 'To Juan At The Winter Solstice'

For me, this is the most telling, resonant, and memorable of Robert Graves's poems. He must have been about fifty when he wrote it, some time around the end of World War II. Graves was born in 1895, and Juan was the younger son of his second marriage. After World War II, Graves and his wife Beryl moved from England back to the house on Majorca that he had built before the war with earnings from his extremely successful memoir, *Goodbye to All That,* and his historical novel *I, Claudius.* He wrote at least one detailed account of his return to his Majorcan house (which he had named Canellun, "house of the moon"). His neighbors there, in the nearby village of Deya, had taken such good care of it that he found his old straw hat still on the table where he had left it, years earlier. But although he and Beryl both spoke some Spanish, Juan's name was always pronounced in the English way: "Joo-an," with the accent on the first syllable. That was something I did not know when I first came upon the poem, in a small bookshop, when I was in college. It was included in a slim, red volume that had just been published: *Poems 1938-1945,* representing the war years, when he was living in the country, in England.

When I first read the poem, Graves had just finished, or was just bringing to completion, *The White Goddess,* the book that is the keystone of his life's work, containing all that is most original, seminal, and provocative in his attitude and matured approach to life and poetry. It also includes a fairly representative sampling of his weaknesses and flaws, his cantankerous, autocratic views and dogmatic obsessions, set forth in his clear, precise, unequivocal prose. When that book was published in 1948, it seemed to be a kind of revelation to many poets of my generation (I was twenty). The subtitle characterized the book as "A Historic Grammar of Poetic Myth," and the mythology upon which Graves drew for his rich lexicon was Celtic as well as classical—in fact he treated them as aspects of the "one story" that is the theme of his poem to his infant son, Juan. The scope and detail of Graves's learning in that work, the idiosyncrasies of his views, the daring and rashness of his argument, were presented with an authority that was startling and appealing in the relatively stuffy Anglo-American academic-literary world of the 1940s. The book is romantic in every sense—the White Goddess is the moon goddess of lust and fear—and it would be a while before many of us would manage to put some of its doctrines into perspective and distinguish what was reliable there from what was merely Graves's hobby-horse. When I first read the book I did not realize that Graves was not presenting his "Grammar" as a vast, luminous metaphor, a means of expression, but that he took it literally. He was, in effect, a fundamentalist preaching an unfamiliar faith.

Yet I think that if we are wary of its wishful scholarship and its artfully skewed deductions and pronouncements, *The White Goddess* remains vividly suggestive and stimulating, a repository of travelers' tales from a wild and partly fanciful landscape, a huge, intricate, historic fiction. And the poem that Graves wrote to his young son in the full excitement of finishing his crucial work is a bardic summary of the panorama and passions, the views, the insights and fantasies presented in this "Grammar of Poetic Myth," which must have occupied him with growing intensity for a long time.

The poem begins with a statement of oracular force unequalled elsewhere in Graves's poetry, as though he had had to compile the whole of *The White Goddess* to arrive at this concise dictum. "There is one story and one story only/That will prove worth your telling . . ." For the "one story and one story only" is, of course, the tale and testimony of the manifestations of the great Mother Goddess in the cycles of the turning universe and in the cells, trees, beasts, and passions of the living world, "from woman back to woman." In the "re-enactments of that story, poet and king, generation after generation, in the service of the goddess "barter life for love." Then the poem, like the book, proceeds to enumerate the "true" myths of the transformations in that tale, and arrives at two of the most deeply felt lines in his poetry: "Fear in your heart cries to the loving-cup:/ Sorrow to sorrow as the sparks fly upward."

If Graves were to be represented by one poem only, I think it should be this one.

The Castle

CD 2 / TRACK 13

Walls, mounds, enclosing corrugations
Of darkness, moonlight on dry grass.
Walking this courtyard, sleepless, in fever;
Planning to use—but by definition
There's no way out, no way out—
Rope-ladders, baulks of timber, pulleys,
A rocket whizzing over the walls and moat—
Machines easy to improvise.

          No escape,
No such thing; to dream of new dimensions,
Cheating checkmate by painting the king's robe
So that he slides like a queen;
Or to cry, "Nightmare, nightmare!"
Like a corpse in the cholera-pit
Under a load of corpses;
Or to run the head against these blind walls,
Enter the dungeon, torment the eyes
With apparitions chained two and two,
And go frantic with fear—
To die and wake up sweating in moonlight
In the same courtyard, sleepless as before.

[1929]

Ulysses

To the much-tossed Ulysses, never done
    With woman whether gowned as wife or whore,
Penelope and Circe seemed as one:
She like a whore made his lewd fancies run,
    And wifely she a hero to him bore.

Their counter-changings terrified his way:
    They were the clashing rocks, Symplegades,
Scylla and Charybdis too were they;
Now angry storms frosting the sea with spray
    And now the lotus island's drunken ease.

They multiplied into the Sirens' throng,
    Forewarned by fear of whom he stood bound fast
Hand and foot helpless to the vessel's mast,
Yet would not stop his ears: daring their song
    He groaned and sweated til that shore was past.

One, two and many: flesh had made him blind,
    Flesh had one pleasure only in the act,
Flesh set one purpose only in the mind—
Triumph of flesh and afterwards to find
    Still those same terrors wherewith flesh was
     racked.

His wiles were witty and his fame far known,
Every king's daughter sought him for her own,
    Yet he was nothing to be won or lost.
    All lands to him were Ithaca: love-tossed
He loathed the fraud, yet would not bed alone.

[1933]

To Juan at the Winter Solstice

There is one story and one story only
That will prove worth your telling,
Whether as learned bard or gifted child;
To it all lines or lesser gauds belong
That startle with their shining
Such common stories as they stray into.

Is it of trees you tell, their months and virtues,
Or strange beasts that beset you,
Of birds that croak at you the Triple will?
Or of the Zodiac and how slow it turns
Below the Boreal Crown,
Prison of all true kings that ever reigned?

Water to water, ark again to ark,
From woman back to woman:
So each new victim treads unfalteringly
The never altered circuit of his fate,
Bringing twelve peers as witness
Both to his starry rise and starry fall.

Or is it of the Virgin's silver beauty,
All fish below the thighs?
She in her left hand bears a leafy quince;
When with her right she crooks a finger, smiling,
How may the King hold back?
Royally then he barters life for love.

Or of the undying snake from chaos hatched,
Whose coils contain the ocean,
Into whose chops with naked sword he springs,
Then in black water, tangled by the reeds,
Battles three days and nights,
To be spewed up beside her scalloped shore?

Much snow is falling, winds roar hollowly,
The owl hoots from the elder,
Fear in your heart cries to the loving-cup:
Sorrow to sorrow as the sparks fly upward.
The log groans and confesses:
There is one story and one story only.

Dwell on her graciousness, dwell on her smiling,
Do not forget what flowers
The great boar trampled down in ivy time.
Her brow was creamy as the crested wave,
Her sea-grey eyes were wild
But nothing promised that is not performed.

[1946]

Return of the Goddess

Under your Milky Way
 And slow-revolving Bear
Frogs from the alder thicket pray
In terror of your judgement day,
 Loud with repentance there.

The log they crowned as king
 Grew sodden, lurched and sank;
An owl floats by on silent wing
Dark water bubbles from the spring;
 They invoke you from each bank.

At dawn you shall appear,
 A gaunt red-leggèd crane,
You whom they know too well for fear,
Lunging your beak down like a spear
 To fetch them home again.

> *Sufficiunt*
> *Tecum,*
> *Caryatis,*
> *Domnia*
> *Quina.*

[1948]

Amergin's Charm

[The text restored from mediaeval Irish and Welsh variants.]

I am a stag: *of seven tines,*
I am a flood: *across a plain,*
I am a wind: *on a deep lake,*
I am a tear: *the Sun lets fall,*
I am a hawk: *above the cliff,*
I am a thorn: *beneath the nail,*
I am a wonder: *among flowers,*
I am a wizard: *who but I*
Sets the cool head aflame with smoke?

I am a spear: *that roars for blood,*
I am a salmon: *in a pool,*
I am a lure: *from paradise,*
I am a hill: *where poets walk,*
I am a boar: *renowned and red,*
I am a breaker: *threatening doom,*
I am a tide: *that drags to death,*
I am an infant: *who but I*
Peeps from the unhewn dolmen arch?

I am the womb: *of every holt,*
I am the blaze: *on every hill,*
I am the queen: *of every hive,*
I am the shield: *for every head,*
I am the grave: *of every hope.*

[1948]

The Blue-Fly

Five summer days, five summer nights,
The ignorant, loutish, giddy blue-fly
Hung without motion on the cling peach,
Humming occasionally: "O my love, my fair one!"
    As in the *Canticles*.

Magnified one thousand times, the insect
Looks farcically human; laugh if you will!
Bald head, stage-fairy wings, blear eyes,
A caved-in chest, hairy black mandibles,
    Long spindly thighs.

The crime was detected on the sixth day.
What then could be said or done? By anyone?
It would have been vindictive, mean and what-not
To swat that fly for being a blue-fly,
    For debauch of a peach.

Is it fair, either, to bring a microscope
To bear on the case, even in search of truth?
Nature, doubtless, has some compelling cause
To glut the carriers of her epidemics—
    Nor did the peach complain.

[1953]

With Her Lips Only

This honest wife, challenged at dusk
At the garden gate, under a moon perhaps,
In scent of honeysuckle, dared to deny
Love to an urgent lover: with her lips only,
Not with her heart. It was no assignation;
Taken aback, what could she say else?
For the children's sake, the lie was venial;
"For the children's sake," she argued with her conscience.

Yet a mortal lie must follow before dawn:
Challenged as usual in her own bed,
She protests love to an urgent husband,
Not with her heart but with her lips only;
"For the children's sake," she argues with her conscience,
"For the children"—turning suddenly cold towards them.

[1953]

A Time of Waiting

The moment comes when my sound senses
Warn me to keep the pot at a quiet simmer,
Conclude no rash decisions, enter into
No random friendships, check the runaway tongue
And fix my mind in a close caul of doubt—
Which is more difficult, maybe, than to face
Night-long assaults of lurking furies.

The pool lies almost empty; I watch it nursed
By a thin stream. Such idle intervals
Are from waning moon to the new—a moon always
Holds the cords of my heart. Then patience, hands;
Dabble your nerveless fingers in the shallows;
A time shall come when she has need of them.

[1964]

Louise Bogan

(1897–1970) b. Livermore Falls, Maine, United States

Disc 2
Tracks 16–18

Louise Bogan was born in Livermore Falls, Maine, on August 11, 1897. Bogan was alienated from her father, a clerk at a paper company; her mother, an erratic woman dissatisfied with her marriage, frequently took her daughter on extended trips. Bogan received her early education at Mount St. Mary's Academy and then at the Girls' Latin School in Boston, where classical instruction encouraged her poetic aspirations. In 1915, Bogan enrolled in Boston University but dropped out a year later and married Curt Alexander, a lieutenant in the army. In 1920, Alexander died of pneumonia, leaving Bogan with a daughter to raise on her own. During the time just prior to her husband's death, Bogan had been associating with a rather bohemian group of literary friends in New York, including William Carlos Williams, Malcolm Cowley, Marianne Moore, and most importantly, her mentor Edmund Wilson. By 1921, her poems were appearing in such prestigious magazines as *The New Republic, The Measure*, and *Vanity Fair*, and with Wilson's encouragement, she began earning money writing reviews. After a brief stay in Vienna, she returned to New York and published her first full collection of poems in 1923, *Body of This Death*. Comprised chiefly of short, formally rigorous lyrics, the book failed to establish immediately the reputation she would achieve over time, but it was well-received by critics.

In 1925, Bogan remarried, this time to a fellow poet named Raymond Holden, and the couple began a turbulent life together drifting from New York to Boston to New Mexico and back. She continued to publish poems in various literary magazines and journals, and her second volume, *Dark Summer*, was published in 1929. More than any other, this volume established Bogan as one of the prominent poets of her day. In 1931, Bogan began publishing poetry reviews in *The New Yorker*, and her association with that magazine would develop into a thirty-eight–year career for Bogan, whose reviews were considered highly fair, accessible, and always insightful. At the time, W.H. Auden proclaimed her America's best poetry critic; today she is as equally respected for her criticism as for her poetry. During the 1930s and '40s, Bogan enjoyed the benefits of her poetic reputation, accepting various teaching positions and receiving many awards, including a Guggenheim Fellowship and an induction into the American Academy of Arts and Letters.

Later in life, Bogan supplemented her poetry with other works, including a critical survey of poetry titled *Achievement in American Poetry 1900–1950* (1951), a book of critical essays titled *Selected Criticism* (1955), and numerous translations. Her collected poems, *The Blue Estuaries Poems 1923–1968*, appeared in 1968, followed after her death by *A Poet's Alphabet*, a collection of articles and reviews culled primarily from her years at *The New Yorker*. Respected as one of the most skilled crafters of poetry of her age, Louise Bogan died on February 4, 1970, in New York City.

Richard Howard on
Louise Bogan

Richard Howard on Louise Bogan

The pronouncement that Louise Bogan was the best American woman poet between Dickinson and Bishop would not have pleased her, for she disliked—fastidious and detached spirit that she was—all such headings and herdings; I make it merely to call attention to the signal merit of her narrowly focused but passionate verse, most of which was written in the first half of her life, much anthologized but, compacted as it was in the charged stanzas of the seventeenth-century poets she so admired, never won "popularity" in the heart-on-the-sleeve manner of her contemporary Edna St. Vincent Millay.

Bogan was, of course, the author of six books of lyric verse, much sifted to produce, in *The Blue Estuaries* of 1968, a life's work of 110 poems; her several volumes of criticism, too (she served for nearly forty years as poetry critic for *The New Yorker*, though she discussed much more than poetry in those pages), were posthumously winnowed down to one big book, "Reflections on the Literary Art and Vocation" and appropriately titled by her editors *A Poet's Alphabet*. Though the landscapes of her poetry were always American (New England and the Atlantic seaboard), there was nothing provincial about her criticism, which achieved a trenchant accounting of Gide and Rilke, of Dinesen and Lorca, of Yeats and Colette, as well as a characteristically stringent response to American classics such as Hawthorne and Dickinson, Whitman and James. Nor is it surprising that her prose carried her further into a sort of autobiographical meditation assembled by her literary executor from journals, memoirs, stories, and letters: *Journey Around My Room* is a great American document of ironic self-appraisal.

Yet it is the poetry which shines brightest, and will endure as the great lyric achievement of her time, the line of truth exactly superimposed on the line of feeling. The implications of her verse are best stated by Marianne Moore, who remarked in a review of her work as early as 1941, that "it is a fact as well as a mystery that weakness is power, that handicap is proficiency, that the scar is a credential, that indignation is no adversary for gratitude, or heroism for joy. There are medicines." That shrewdly accounts for the moral sense of Louise Bogan's poems, a triumph not shared, as I began by saying, by any American woman poet since Dickinson.

Medusa

I had come to the house, in a cave of trees,
Facing a sheer sky.
Everything moved,—a bell hung ready to strike,
Sun and reflection wheeled by.

When the bare eyes were before me
And the hissing hair,
Held up at a window, seen through a door.
The stiff bald eyes, the serpents on the forehead
Formed in the air.

This is a dead scene forever now.
Nothing will ever stir.
The end will never brighten it more than this,
Nor the rain blur.

The water will always fall, and will not fall,
And the tipped bell make no sound.
The grass will always be growing for hay
Deep on the ground.

And I shall stand here like a shadow
Under the great balanced day,
My eyes on the yellow dust, that was lifting in the wind,
And does not drift away.

[1923]

The Daemon

Must I tell again
In the words I know
For the ears of men
The flesh, the blow?

Must I show outright
The bruise in the side,
The halt in the night,
And how death cried?

Must I speak to the lot
Who little bore?
It said *Why not?*
It said *Once more*.

[1929]

The Sleeping Fury

You are here now,
Who were so loud and feared, in a symbol before me,
Alone and asleep, and I at last look long upon you.

Your hair fallen on your cheek, no longer in the semblance of serpents,
Lifted in the gale; your mouth, that shrieked so, silent.
You, my scourge, my sister, lie asleep, like a child,
Who, after rage, for an hour quiet, sleeps out its tears.

The days close to winter
Rough with strong sound. We hear the sea and the forest,
And the flames of your torches fly, lit by others,
Ripped by the wind, in the night. The black sheep for sacrifice
Huddle together. The milk is cold in the jars.

All to no purpose, as before, the knife whetted and plunged,
The shout raised, to match the clamor you have given them.
You alone turn away, not appeased; unaltered, avenger.

Hands full of scourges, wreathed with your flames and adders,
You alone turned away, but did not move from my side,
Under the broken light, when the soft nights took the torches.

At thin morning you showed, thick and wrong in that calm,
The ignoble dream and the mask, sly, with slits at the eyes,
Pretence and half-sorrow, beneath which a coward's hope trembled.

You uncovered at night, in the locked stillness of houses,
False love due the child's heart, the kissed-out lie, the embraces,
Made by the two who for peace tenderly turned to each other.

You who know what we love, but drive us to know it;
You with your whips and shrieks, bearer of truth and of solitude;
You who give, unlike men, to expiation your mercy.

Dropping the scourge when at last the scourged advances to meet it,
You, when the hunted turns, no longer remain the hunter
But stand silent and wait, at last returning his gaze.

Beautiful now as a child whose hair, wet with rage and tears
Clings to its face. And now I may look upon you,
Having once met your eyes. You lie in sleep and forget me.
Alone and strong in my peace, I look upon you in yours.

[1937]

The Dream

O God, in the dream the terrible horse began
To paw at the air, and make for me with his blows.
Fear kept for thirty-five years poured through his mane,
And retribution equally old, or nearly, breathed through
    his nose.

Coward complete, I lay and wept on the ground
When some strong creature appeared, and leapt for the
    rein.
Another woman, as I lay half in a swound,
Leapt in the air, and clutched at the leather and chain.

Give him, she said, something of yours as a charm.
Throw him, she said, some poor thing you alone claim.
No, no, I cried, he hates me; he's out for harm,
And whether I yield or not, it is all the same.

But, like a lion in a legend, when I flung the glove
Pulled from my sweating, my cold right hand,
The terrible beast, that no one may understand,
Came to my side, and put down his head in love.

[1941]

Song for the Last Act

Now that I have your face by heart, I look
Less at its features than its darkening frame
Where quince and melon, yellow as young flame,
Lie with quilled dahlias and the shepherd's crook.
Beyond, a garden. There, in insolent ease
The lead and marble figures watch the show
Of yet another summer loath to go
Although the scythes hang in the apple trees.

Now that I have your face by heart, I look.

Now that I have your voice by heart, I read
In the black chords upon a dulling page
Music that is not meant for music's cage,
Whose emblems mix with words that shake and bleed.
The staves are shuttled over with a stark
Unprinted silence. In a double dream
I must spell out the storm, the running stream.
The beat's too swift. The notes shift in the dark.

Now that I have your voice by heart, I read.

Now that I have your heart by heart, I see
The wharves with their great ships and architraves;
The rigging and the cargo and the slaves
On a strange beach under a broken sky.
O not departure, but a voyage done!
The bales stand on the stone; the anchor weeps
Its red rust downward, and the long vine creeps
Beside the salt herb, in the lengthening sun.

Now that I have your heart by heart, I see.

[1949]

Melvin B. Tolson

(1898–1966) b. Moberly, Missouri, United States

Disc 2
Tracks 19–21

Melvin Beaunorus Tolson was born on February 6, 1898, in Moberly, Missouri. Throughout his childhood, Tolson's family seldom lived in the same town for very long; his father, a Methodist minister, frequently received new assignments to congregations in small towns in northern Missouri and central Iowa. An ambitious, intellectual, and self-disciplined man who taught himself Greek and Latin, Tolson's father was an enormous influence on the poet. Similarly self-motivated, Tolson published his first poem (an elegy on the sinking of the *Titanic*) in an Oskaloosa, Iowa, newspaper at the age of fourteen. In 1916, Tolson's family moved to Kansas City, where he finished junior and senior high school; in 1918, he enrolled in Fisk University. Shortly thereafter he transferred to Pennsylvania's Lincoln University. In his junior year at Lincoln, he attended a fraternity dance where he met Ruth Southall, a native of Virginia who was visiting relatives at the time.

Having won several debate and public-speaking awards, Tolson graduated from Lincoln with honors and began teaching English at Wiley College in Marshall, Texas. In 1922, he married Southall, with whom he had four children. A major turning point in Tolson's career took place in 1930, when he took leave from his teaching position to spend a year working on a master's in comparative literature at Columbia. His thesis project centered on the Harlem Renaissance and brought him into professional and personal contact with Harlem literary figures, inspiring his collection of short narrative poems, *A Gallery of Harlem Portraits*. Though a few poems from the book were published from 1937 to 1939, the collection was published in its entirety only after Tolson's death.

In 1939, Tolson began writing a column for *The Washington Tribune* and would continue to do so through 1944. Also in 1939, his poem "Dark Symphony" won a national poetry contest sponsored by the American Negro Exposition in Chicago, and its publication in the *Atlantic Monthly* two years later led to the publication of his first book of poems, *Rendezvous with America*, in 1944. *Rendezvous* celebrates the historic contributions of black Americans while dramatizing their struggle to achieve recognition for their achievements; it was received widely and well, earning the praise of such literary figures as Langston Hughes, Richard Wright, and Margaret Walker. In 1947, Tolson left Wiley College and began teaching at Langston University in Oklahoma; later that year, he was named Poet Laureate of Liberia and commissioned to write a poem in honor of the republic's centenary, which he completed in 1953. *The Libretto for the Republic of Liberia* earned him admittance to the Liberian Knighthood of the Order of the Star of Africa.

Tolson published his last book, *Harlem Gallery*, the same year the American Academy of Arts and Letters presented him with its annual poetry award, and shortly before his death in Dallas on August 29, 1966, he received an award from the Rockefeller Foundation. Tolson's influence and poetic scope continue to be debated in academic circles; while some early white critics such as Allan Tate praised his assimilation of the Anglo-American tradition, many of his African-American contemporaries during the period of the Black Arts Movement of the 1960s and '70s attacked or dismissed him for the same reason.

Rita Dove on Melvin B. Tolson

Melvin B. Tolson's first book, *Rendezvous with America*, is both a promise and a warning. Its centerpiece, the long poem "Dark Symphony," offers a sweeping review of black American history, with each of its six sections assigned a musical signature. *Allegro Moderato* (blacks in the Revolutionary War), *Lento Grave* (the horrors of slavery), *Andante Sostenuto* (Emancipation and sharecropping), *Tempo Primo* (Harlem Renaissance), *Larghetto* (the Great Depression), and the final section *Tempo di Marcia*, which proclaims the determination of Black Americans to advance "Out of the dead ends of Poverty" and "Across barricades of Jim Crowism" to a better world. A precocious, almost brash book, *Rendezvous with America* is a bravura showcase for Tolson's catholic curiosity and keen morality, tempered by an ironic grace.

Libretto for the Republic of Liberia was written in honor of the centennial of the founding of that country. With its litany of African/Asian/European heroes, its great rhapsody and telescoped aeons, *Libretto* rises above the circumstances of its genesis. The melodrama of man's ambitions is swirled across a canvas that begins with prehistoric glaciers and tumbles into the *Futureafrique*—pageantry and intrigue abreast on a tide of high-fidelity language.

Harlem Gallery, Book I: The Curator, Tolson's projected epic poem, appeared in 1965. Whereas many mainstream literati greeted it with enthusiasm, proclaiming it as the lyrical successor of *The Waste Land*, *The Bridge*, and *Paterson*, proponents of the rapidly solidifying Black Aesthetic—who had rejected "white" literary standards—were less impressed. Divided into twenty-four sections corresponding to the letters in the Greek alphabet, "Harlem Gallery" contains allusions to Vedic gods, Tintoretto, and Pre-Cambrian pottery, as well as snippets in Latin and French. Spliced into this highly stylized ode are little stories—dramatic monologues, vignettes—which serve to illustrate the philosophical stance of the more discursive parts, and Tolson uses a host of other characteristics typical of the African-American oral tradition: mimicry, exaggerated language, spontaneity, braggery, using rhythm and inflection to carry the implication of a statement. The author's extravagant verbiage pays homage to a variety of dictions; irony and pathos, slapstick and pontification maneuver side-by-side. Yet this dazzling array of allusions betrays no favoritism for any social or cultural group; if anything, Tolson deliberately complicates our preconceived notions of cultural—and, by further comparison, existential—order. *Harlem Gallery* is composed according to Tolson's "S-Trinity of Parnassus"—the melding of sound, sight, and sense. Sound refers to the oral nature of the poem; Tolson intended his lines to be read aloud. Sight is engaged through the visual impact of the centered lines, which contributes to the forward thrust that a lively oral recitation would possess. "Sense" refers to both meaning and the sensory aspect of language.

The first part of a proposed five-part epos delineating the odyssey of blacks in America, *Harlem Gallery* muses on the predicament of being black and an artist in America. The narrator, a mulatto of "afroirishjewish origins," serves as curator of a posh art gallery, where he has ample opportunity to observe the shenanigans of the black bourgeoisie, as well as the strivings of the artists they feed upon. "O Tempora, / *what* is man?" the Curator asks; "O Mores, / what *manner* of man is this?" In an attempt to answer this question, *Harlem Gallery* charts the lives of three black artists. First we meet John Laugart, a half-blind, destitute painter who refuses to compromise his art in order to pay the rent. The consequences? "He was robbed and murdered in his flat, / and the only witness was a Hamletian rat." But John Laugart's tragic fate is eclipsed by the underworld glimmer of the Zulu Club, where Hideho Heights, the "poet laureate of Harlem," is reciting his jocular, rather militant version of the John Henry ballad. Boisterous and irreverent, Hideho nevertheless hides his more ambitious writing from the public. The third Harlem artist is Mister Starks, conductor of the Harlem Symphony orchestra. Starks has compromised his talents by writing boogie-woogie records when he should have been pursuing the excellence of his one triumph, the *Black Orchid Suite*.

Harlem Gallery is not merely a showcase for Tolson's linguistic and lyrical virtuosity; neither is it a hodgepodge of anecdotes and small lives set like cameos in the heavy silver of philosophical discourse. Rather, the lives of John Laugart, Hideho Heights, and Mister Starks offer illustrations of three alternatives for the black artist. One can embrace the "Bitch-Goddess of Success"—"My talent was an Uptown whore," says Mister Starks, "my wit a Downtown pimp"—or, like Laugart, remain uncompromising and be spurned. Or one can lead the double life of Hideho, producing crowd-pleasers while creating in secret the works one hopes will last.

Where does Melvin Tolson place himself in this panoply? Certainly not with Mister Starks, although he is sympathetic to Starks's weakness. And though he admired Hideho's flair, Tolson did not hide his "difficult" poems from the public.

Paradoxically, it is John Laugart, the artist given least space in *Harlem Gallery*, who most exemplifies Tolson's own sense of artistic responsibility. Although Tolson did not die destitute and anonymous (in fact, a few months before his death from cancer in 1966, he received the annual poetry award of the American Academy of Arts and Letters), he was misunderstood by those to whom he dedicated his energies in the creation of his last work—the black *literati*. In an interview, he once stated: "…I, as a black poet, have absorbed the Great Ideas of the Great White World, and interpreted them in the melting-pot idiom of my people. My roots are in Africa, Europe, and America." Melvin Tolson contained multitudes and did not shy away from the paradoxes of that melting-pot—indeed, he was able to refine from that cruel matrix a golden, ostentatious lyricism, drenched in the pain and beauty of the blues.

An Ex-Judge at the Bar

Bartender, make it straight and make it two—
One for the you in me and the me in you.
Now let us put our heads together: one
Is half enough for malice, sense, or fun.

I know, Bartender, yes, I know when the Law
Should wag its tail or rip with fang and claw.
When Pilate washed his hands, that neat event
Set for us judges a Caesarean precedent.

What I shall tell you now, as man is man,
You'll find in neither Bible nor Koran.
It happened after my return from France
At the bar in Tony's Lady of Romance.

We boys drank pros and cons, sang *Dixie*; and then,
The bar a Sahara, we pledged to meet again.
But lo, on the bar there stood in naked scorn
The Goddess Justice, like September Morn.

Who blindfolds Justice on the courthouse roof
While the lawyers weave the sleight-of-hand of proof?
I listened, Bartender, with my heart and head,
As the Goddess Justice unbandaged her eyes and said:

"To make the world safe for Democracy,
You lost a leg in Flanders fields—*oui, oui*?
To gain the judge's seat, you twined the noose
That swung the Negro higher than a goose."

Bartender, who has dotted every *i*?
Crossed every *t*? Put legs on every *y*?
Therefore, I challenged her: "Lay on, Macduff,
And damned be him who first cries, 'Hold, enough!'"

The boys guffawed, and Justice began to laugh
Like a maniac on a broken phonograph.
Bartender, make it straight and make it three—
One for the Negro...one for you and me.

[1944]

Dark Symphony

I

Allegro Moderato
Black Crispus Attucks taught
                    Us how to die
Before white Patrick Henry's bugle breath
Uttered the vertical
                    Transmitting cry:
"Yea, give me liberty or give me death."

Waifs of the auction block,
                    Men black and strong
The juggernauts of despotism withstood,
Loin-girt with faith that worms
                    Equate the wrong
And dust is purged to create brotherhood.

No Banquo's ghost can rise
                    Against us now,
Aver we hobnailed Man beneath the brute,
Squeezed down the thorns of greed
                    On Labor's brow,
Garroted lands and carted off the loot.

II

Lento Grave
The centuries-old pathos in our voices
Saddens the great white world,
And the wizardry of our dusky rhythms
Conjures up shadow-shapes of ante-bellum years:

Black slaves singing *One More River to Cross*
In the torture tombs of slave-ships,
Black slaves singing *Steal Away to Jesus*
In jungle swamps,
Black slaves singing *The Crucifixion*
In slave-pens at midnight,
Black slaves singing *Swing Low, Sweet Chariot*
In cabins of death,
Black slaves singing *Go Down, Moses*
In the canebrakes of the Southern Pharaohs.

III

Andante Sostenuto
They tell us to forget
The Golgotha we tread…
We who are scourged with hate,
A price upon our head.
They who have shackled us
Require of us a song,
They who have wasted us
Bid us condone the wrong.

They tell us to forget
Democracy is spurned.
They tell us to forget
The Bill of Rights is burned.
Three hundred years we slaved,
We slave and suffer yet:
Though flesh and bone rebel,
They tell us to forget!

Oh, how can we forget
Our human rights denied?
Oh, how can we forget
Our manhood crucified?
When Justice is profaned
And plea with curse is met,
When Freedom's gates are barred,
Oh, how can we forget?

IV

Tempo Primo
The New Negro strides upon the continent
In seven-league boots…
The New Negro
Who sprang form the vigor-stout loins
Of Nat Turner, gallows-martyr for Freedom,
Of Joseph Cinquez, Black Moses of the Amistad
    Mutiny,
Of Frederick Douglass, oracle of the Catholic Man,
Of Sojourner Truth, eye and ear of Lincoln's legions,
Of Harriet Tubman, Saint Bernard of the Underground
    Railroad.

The New Negro
Breaks the icons of his detractors,
Wipes out the conspiracy of silence,
Speaks to *his* America:
"My history-moulding ancestors
Planted the first crops of wheat on these shores,
Built ships to conquer the seven seas,
Erected the Cotton Empire,
Flung railroads across a hemisphere,
Disemboweled the earth's iron and coal,
Tunneled the mountains and bridged rivers,
Harvested the grain and hewed forests,
Sentineled the Thirteen Colonies,
Unfurled Old Glory at the North Pole,
Fought a hundred battles for the Republic."

The New Negro:
His giant hands fling murals upon high chambers,
His drama teaches a world to laugh and weep,
His music leads continents captive,
His voice thunders the Brotherhood of Labor,
His science creates seven wonders,
His Republic of Letters challenges the Negro-baiters.

The New Negro,
Hard muscled, Fascist-hating, Democracy-ensouled,
Strides in seven-league boots
Along the Highway of Today
Toward the Promised Land of Tomorrow!

V

Larghetto
None in the Land can say
To us black men Today:
You send the tractors on their bloody path,
And create Okies for The *Grapes of Wrath*.
You breed the slum that breeds a *Native Son*
To damn the good earth Pilgrim Fathers won.

None in the Land can say
To us black men Today:
You dupe the poor with rags-to-riches tales,
And leave the workers empty dinner pails.
You stuff the ballot box, and honest men
Are muzzled by your demagogic din.

None in the Land can say
To us black men Today:
You smash stock markets with your coined blitzkriegs,
And make a hundred million guinea pigs.
You counterfeit our Christianity,
And bring contempt upon Democracy.

None in the Land can say
To us black men Today:
You prowl when citizens are fast asleep,
And hatch Fifth Column plots to blast the deep
Foundation of the State and leave the Land
A vast Sahara with a Fascist brand.

VI
Tempo di Marcia
Out of abysses of Illiteracy,
Through labyrinths of Lies,
Across waste lands of Disease…
We advance!

Out of dead-ends of Poverty,
Through wildernesses of Superstition,
Across barricades of Jim Crowism…
We advance!

With the Peoples of the World…
We advance!

[1944]

Lambda

From the mouth of the Harlem Gallery
came a voice like a
ferry horn in a river fog:

"Hey, man, when you gonna close this dump?
Fetch highbrow stuff from the middlebrows who
don't give a damn and the lowbrows who ain't hip!
Think you're a little high-yellow Jesus?"

No longer was I a boxer with a brain bruised
against its walls by Tyche's fists,
as I welcomed Hideho Heights,
the vagabond bard of Lenox Avenue,
whose satyric legends adhered like beggar's-lice.

"Sorry, Curator, I got here late:
my black ma birthed me in the Whites' bottom drawer,
and the Reds forgot to fish me out!"

His belly laughed and quaked
the Blakean tigers and lambs on the walls.
Haw-Haw's whale of a forefinger mocked
Max Donachie's revolutionary hero, Crispus Attucks,
in the Harlem Gallery and on Boston Commons.
"In the beginning was the Word,"
he challenged, "not the Brush!"
The scorn in the eyes that raked the gallery
was the scorn of an Ozymandias.

The metal smelted from the ore of ideas,
his grin revealed all the gold he had stored away.
"Just came from a jam session
at the Daddy-O Club," he said.
"I'm just one step from heaven
with the blues a-percolating in my head.
You should've heard old Satchmo blow his horn!
The Lord God A'mighty made no mistake
the day that cat was born!"

Like a bridegroom unloosing a virgin knot,
from an inner pocket he coaxed a manuscript.
"Just given Satchmo a one-way ticket
to Immortality," he said. "Pure inspiration!"
His lips folded about the neck of a whiskey bottle
whose label belied its white-heat hooch.
I heard a gurgle, a gurgle—a death rattle.
His eyes as bright as a parachute light,
he began to rhetorize in the grand style
of a Doctor Faustus in the dilapidated Harlem Opera House:

King Oliver of New Orleans
has kicked the bucket, but he left behind
old Satchmo with his red-hot horn
to syncopate the heart and mind.
The honky-tonks in Storyville
have turned to ashes, have turned to dust,
but old Satchmo is still around
like Uncle Sam's IN GOD WE TRUST.

Where, oh, where is Bessie Smith
with her heart as big as the blues of truth?
Where, oh, where is Mister Jelly Roll
with his Cadillac and diamond tooth?
Where, oh, where is Papa Handy
with his blue notes a-dragging from bar to bar?
Where, oh, where is bulletproof Leadbelly
with his tall tales and 12-string guitar?

Old Hip Cats,
when you sang and played the blues
the night Satchmo was born,
did you know hypodermic needles in Rome
couldn't hoodoo him away from his horn?
Wyatt Earp's legend, John Henry's, too,
is a dare and a bet to old Satchmo
when his groovy blues put headlines in the news
from the Gold Coast to cold Moscow.

Old Satchmo's
gravelly voice and tapping foot and crazy notes
set my soul on fire.
If I climbed
the seventy-seven steps of the Seventh
Heaven, Satchmo's high C would carry me higher!
Are you hip to this, Harlem? Are you hip?
On Judgment Day, Gabriel will say
after he blows his horn:
"I'd be the greatest trumpeter in the Universe,
if old Satchmo had never been born!"

[1965]

Laura (Riding) Jackson

(1901–1991) b. New York, New York, United States

Disc 2

Tracks 22-24

Laura (Riding) Jackson was born Laura Reichenthal in New York City on January 16, 1901. Her mother's invalidism and her father's inability to find steady work cast a pall over Riding's childhood; as she grew, she eventually came to resent her father's Marxist politics and blamed him for much of the family's misfortune. Subsequently, she renounced politics in favor of poetry. In 1914, the Reichenthals moved from a tenement on Manhattan's East Side to an apartment in the Bedford-Stuyvesant neighborhood of Brooklyn. In 1918, Riding was admitted to Cornell University on a scholarship, and in 1920, she married Louis Gottschalk, a history instructor at Cornell, and moved with him as he found teaching positions in Urbana, Illinois, and then Louisville, Kentucky. In a bold and decidedly feminist gesture, she asked her new husband to take her name, and he became Louis Reichenthal Gottschalk. In 1923, she changed her own name to Laura Riding Gottschalk.

Although Riding continued to take classes in varied fields of interest, she never completed a degree. Time was better spent writing poetry. In 1923, she submitted her work to the literary magazine published by The Fugitives, a group of poet-scholars that included John Crowe Ransom, Allen Tate, and Robert Penn Warren. Surprisingly, Riding, a Jewish girl from New York City, eventually became allied with this decidedly southern group of gentlemen; her anti-romanticism, originality, intelligence, and irony appealed to them well enough for them to publish twenty-one of her poems between 1923 and 1925. In 1924, they even awarded her the magazine's Nashville Prize for the year's best poem published in their pages. As her career as a poet began to take off, her new vocation strained her relationship with Louis. In 1925, they divorced.

In 1926, Riding's book *The Close Chaplet* was published, its name derived from a poem by Robert Graves. That same year, she accepted an invitation from Graves to join him and his wife, Nancy, and their two children in England. This began Riding's famous fourteen-year association with Graves. Together they founded Seizin Press and cowrote *A Survey of Modernist Poetry*. In addition, she wrote *A Pamphlet against Anthologies*, and *A Survey of Contemporaries and Snobs*, which elaborated upon her conception of poetry, incorporating new linguistic approaches in her criticism. In 1927, she formally changed her name to Laura Riding. Although her time in England was for the most part non-turbulent, she threw herself from a window and fractured her spine in 1929. It appears that Riding's suicide attempt was in part an attempt to escape from her complex emotional entanglement in the Graves's household. After a full recovery, she relocated later that year to Mallorca with Graves, who had separated from his wife.

Riding published many collections of poems throughout the late 1920s and '30s, including *Love as Love, Death as Death*; *Poems: A Joking Word*; *Twenty Poems Less*; and *Collected Poems* (1938). Toward the end of the decade, however, she began to feel betrayed by language's rampant ambiguity. In 1939, the year her relationship with Graves ended, she denounced poetry, which she saw as a hindrance to words' ability to convey truth. In June 1941, Riding married writer Schuyler B. Jackson in Elkton, Maryland. In 1943, the couple moved to a rundown bungalow in Wabasso, Florida, and together worked on a number of lexicographical treatises, including *Rational Meaning: A New Foundation for the Definition of Words*, which they completed in 1974. In 1980, a revised edition of Riding's *Collected Poems* appeared, and in 1991, she received the Bollingen Prize for her lifetime contribution to poetry. She died in Wabasso, Florida, on September 2, 1991.

Forrest Gander on Laura (Riding) Jackson

While she was still in her thirties, Laura Riding renounced poetry. It wasn't, she asserted later, a capable vehicle for arriving at truth. Turning from the literary world, she moved with her soon-to-be husband to Florida where they lived in relative poverty. She published nothing for more than twenty years and then, in 1962, ended her withdrawal with a broadcast talk explaining her renunciation of poetry. After that, she published a varied body of post-poetic work during the last thirty years of her life.

Riding remains, unequivocally, one of the most fascinating literary figures of the twentieth century. In her short career as a poet, she was associated with many significant writers on either side of the Atlantic. In the 1920s, she was celebrated by The Fugitives, an assembly of southern formalist poets. She moved to New York for a few months and befriended a coterie of artists and writers including Hart Crane. In England in the 1930s, she was admired by young poets in Oxford and Cambridge, and in London she was championed by Leonard and Virginia Woolf, whose Hogarth Press published two of her books. W.H. Auden (before she accused him of stealing her rhythms) called her our "only living philosophical poet." She made friends in Paris with Gertrude Stein whose work Riding both reviewed and published. A feminist of sorts, intent on purging Western consciousness of patriarchal assumptions, Riding presided for several years over an expatriate literary community in Mallorca, Spain. Meanwhile, her criticism, cowritten with Robert Graves, served to inspire The New Critics whose literary sensibilities dominated the 1940s and 1950s. Despite the astonishing variety of her works and her literary connections, she is chiefly remembered today as a Modernist poet who cultivated an original style of spare, assertive language.

Born in 1901 to political, nonreligious Jewish parents, Laura Reichenthal grew up in Brooklyn. Perhaps her father's ardent socialism served to inspire Laura's idealism. In any case, she gradually abandoned her father's politics in order to apprentice herself to something grander which she came to call "truth." In 1922, while attending Cornell University, she married her college professor Louis Gottschalk and began writing poems under the name Laura Riding Gottschalk. The marriage didn't last long. Within a few years, she was living in England with Robert Graves and his wife, Nancy, in a ménage à trois from which Nancy—and her children with Robert—was gradually weaned into separate quarters. Meanwhile, words and ideas poured from Riding and Graves as from two open faucets.

Riding began her *Collected Poems* with "Forgotten Girlhood" which ends: "And only perfection matters." The words "beauty," "pure," "essence," "eternal," "true," "love," and "death" occur in the poems as talismans of Riding's concern for absolutes. A few of her poems have an affinity with Stein's. They proceed by repetitions of—and incremental variations on—syntactically simple, declarative statements. As her work matured, she purged her poems of conventions such as imagery, sensual details, and sentiment. Her writing became increasingly didactic and oracular, enacting her own intellectual presence, the strict and peculiar music of her mind.

In her poem "Death as Death," Riding asserts that someone might choose to die, "to conceive death as death," in an instant easily enough. But if one survives that instant, survives "the quick cold hand" of death, then life reasserts itself with a roar and life's hellishness becomes apparent all over again. Paradise, which death might have brought near, distances itself from the survivor. Then, Riding claims, the body feels how it is truly alive and this feeling is incomparable—"like nothing else"—because likening life to something else would only lessen life, cut in half its unique value. Paradoxically, "Death as Death" is a celebration of the intensity of being alive.

In "Death as Death," we see Riding's affinity for the verb "is," a verb conducive to establishing equations and definitions. And we see her build up the poem in sequential clauses characterized by parallelism and paradox. Throughout the poem, Riding develops dialectical tensions between difficulty and ease, paradise and hell, blindness and vision, death and life. The first stanza consists of two long sentences on either side of the short declaration, with its quirky, inverted subject and verb, "So is it come by easily / for one instant." In the first line the word "death" is repeated. In the second, "difficulty" is balanced against "easily." In the next two lines, "blankness" and "understanding" oppose each other. And in the following lines, the two adjectives modifying a noun in "quick cold hand" are mirrored in "hot slow head." At the poem's conclusion, Riding offsets "foresight," a sense of the future, with "actuality," a sense of the present. She finds that neither foresight nor prophecy is equal to the experience of the "plain" present. At any moment, the gift of life is wholly original, beyond compare, beyond even words of gratitude.

After several rich, tumultuous years with Robert Graves, during one of which she famously jumped from a third-story window, Laura Riding isolated herself in Florida with Schuyler Jackson, a charismatic writer she met when she moved back to the United States from Spain. Jackson left his wife and children in Pennsylvania. In 1941, he and Laura Riding married and they worked together, until his death, on a substantial book called *Rational Meaning: A New Foundation for the Definition of Words*, published at long last in 1997. It was intended to clarify the relation between human goodness and diction.

O Vocables of Love

O vocables of love,
O zones of dreamt responses
Where wing on wing folds in
The negro centuries of sleep
And the thick lips compress
Compendiums of silence—

Throats claw the mirror of blind triumph,
Eyes pursue sight into the heart of terror.
Call within call
Succumbs to the indistinguishable
Wall within wall
Embracing the last crushed vocable,
The spoken unity of efforts.

O vocables of love,
The end of an end is an echo,
A last cry follows a last cry.
Finality of finality
Is perfection's touch of folly.
Ruin unfolds from ruin.
A remnant breeds a universe of fragment.
Horizons spread intelligibility
And once more it is yesterday.

[1927]

Death as Death

DISC 2, TRACK 23

To conceive death as death
Is difficulty come by easily,
A blankness fallen among
Images of understanding,
Death like a quick cold hand
On the hot slow head of suicide.
So is it come by easily
For one instant. Then again furnaces
Roar in the ears, then again hell revolves,
And the elastic eye holds paradise
At visible length from blindness,
And dazedly the body echoes
"Like this, like this, like nothing else."

Like nothing—a similarity
Without resemblance. The prophetic eye,
Closing upon difficulty,
Opens upon comparison,
Halving the actuality
As a gift too plain, for which
Gratitude has no language,
Foresight no vision.

[1928]

Nothing So Far

Nothing so far but moonlight
Where the mind is;
Nothing in that place, this hold,
To hold;
Only their faceless shadows to announce
Perhaps they come—
Nor even do they know
Whereto they cast them.

Yet here, all that remains
When each has been the universe:
No universe, but each, or nothing.
Here is the future swell curved round
To all that was.

What were we, then,
Before the being of ourselves began?
Nothing so far but strangeness
Where the moments of the mind return.
Nearly, the place was lost
In that we went to stranger places.

Nothing so far but nearly
The long familiar pang
Of never having gone;
And words below a whisper which
If tended as the graves of live men should be
May bring their names and faces home.

It makes a loving promise to itself,
Womanly, that there
More presences are promised
Than by the difficult light appear.
Nothing appears but moonlight's morning—
By which to count were as to strew
The look of day with last night's rid of moths.

[1937]

Take Hands

Take hands.
There is no love now.
But there are hands.
There is no joining now,
But a joining has been
Of the fastening of fingers
And their opening.
More than the clasp even, the kiss
Speaks loneliness,
How we dwell apart,
And how love triumphs in this.

[1938]

Langston Hughes

(1902–1967) b. Joplin, Missouri, United States

Disc 2
Tracks 25–29

Langston Hughes, widely considered the quintessential poet of the Harlem Renaissance, was born in Joplin, Missouri, on February 1, 1902. His parents separated shortly after Langston's birth. His father, businessman and lawyer James Nathaniel Hughes, moved to Cuba and eventually settled in Mexico; Hughes remained with his mother, teacher Carrie Mercer (Langston) Hughes, who relocated from city to city, before moving in with his maternal grandmother. In 1914, he returned to live with his mother and stepfather in Lincoln, Illinois, where his graduating class at elementary school named him Class Poet. Hughes attended Cleveland's Central High School, where he excelled in athletics and seemed to be heading toward a promising career as a writer. During a yearlong visit to Mexico, his father encouraged him to pursue a more practical career, agreeing to pay his tuition as long as he studied engineering. Hughes began taking engineering classes at Columbia in 1921, but it wasn't meant to be—he dropped out of the program after his first year. However, within that year, he had published his first poem, "The Negro Speaks of Rivers," in the leading Negro publication of the day, *The Crisis*. After Columbia, he began a period of working odd jobs in various locations, including Rotterdam and Paris, but most importantly, Harlem. He continued to write poetry while working in Harlem, and his name began circulating in local literary circles. In 1925, at an awards dinner for another Negro magazine, *Opportunity*, Hughes was sought out by Carl Van Vechten, a white photographer and novelist interested in the Harlem Renaissance. Van Vetchen recommended Hughes's manuscript of poems to his own publisher, Alfred A. Knopf, and shortly thereafter the prestigious firm published *The Weary Blues* (1926).

In that same year, Hughes received a scholarship to Lincoln University, where he earned his undergraduate degree in 1929. His second book of poetry, *Fine Clothes to the Jew*, came out in 1927, but was met with mixed reviews. Many readers preferred more decorous and dressed-up representations of black life to the frank and gritty portrayals Hughes offered in this book, the title of which refers to the practice of selling one's wardrobe to a pawnbroker in times of need. During the 1930s, Hughes traveled extensively, most notably to the Soviet Union; his politics took a leftist turn and he became highly interested in socialism. Throughout his early years, Hughes worked a number of odd jobs to make ends meet, but during this period he supported himself as a writer and lecturer, making him the first African-American to be able do so. By the 1940s, Hughes's literary output was comprehensive and vast, encompassing novels, short stories, plays, and reminiscences in addition to poetry. Much of these works reflected Hughes's lifelong love of music, particularly jazz. Of his later poetic works, 1951's *Montage of a Dream Deferred* has proven the most important and the most popular.

Hughes is also well known for his "Simple" stories, a widely acclaimed and provocative series of prose pieces that depict a character named Jesse B. Semple (or "Simple"), a native Virginian now living in Harlem and confronting racial segregation and other brutalities. Hughes filled five volumes with these stories, and in 1957 they served as the basis of a popular musical production, *Simply Heaven*. He died on May 22, 1967, having continued to write and publish right up to the very end of his life. Hughes never married, while his personal warmth and gentleness of spirit are legendary, he seems to have spent the greater part of his life alone, writing.

Al Young on Langston Hughes

Al Young on Langston Hughes

At his great-grandparents' flat a couple of years ago, a little boy born in 1990 tugged me to the sofa.

"Mr. Young," he said, "guess what?"

"What's that, Brandon?"

"You know in the old days, in the really old days…?"

"Yes?"

Snickering, he said, "They used to call us Negroes."

"Hmm, I think I do remember that."

Brandon broke into a big smile, then laughed. "Don't you think that's funny?" he said again, fascinated with this new word he had just learned, "*Knee-grows*…That is *funny*."

Funny or sad, I couldn't help but think Langston Hughes would have loved this story. After all, *The First Book of Negroes* was among the many books he wrote for children; for curious boys and girls like Brandon. One of the most prolific and translated of American authors, Langston Hughes published books of poetry, short stories, essays, memoirs, biographies, anthologies, translations, and plays. But it was as a poet that he is mostly remembered. "The Negro Speaks of Rivers," "I, Too," and "The Weary Blues" are his signature poems. Encoded in the song-like lines of these three dramatic monologues are most of the subjects and themes that Hughes would take up, in one form or another, again and again. These subjects include: the burdensome shame and waste of America's color prejudice, the ironies of Jim Crow, the dignity and nobility of his African heritage, a celebration of African-American culture (the performing arts in general and jazz in particular, but also oratory, history, storytelling, myth), and the essential human need for freedom and social justice.

Born in 1902 in Joplin, Missouri, Langston Hughes's life moved right along with the twentieth century. After his parents separated and his father moved to Mexico, he was raised by his maternal grandmother. From summer-long visits to his father's large Mexican estate, Hughes learned Spanish. When he composed "The Negro Speaks of Rivers," he was running track for his high school in Cleveland, Ohio. At a time when the poetry of American expatriates Ezra Pound and T.S. Eliot was

I've known rivers:
I've known rivers ancient as the world
and older than the flow of human blood
in human veins.
  My soul has grown deep like the rivers.
I bathed in the Euphrates when dawns
              were young.
I built my hut beside the Congo and
       it lulled me to sleep.
I looked upon the Nile and raised the
    pyramids above it.
I heard the singing of the Mississippi
    when Abe Lincoln went down
       to New Orleans,
and I've seen its muddy bosom
    turn all golden in the sunset.
I've known rivers:
ancient, dusky rivers.
My soul has grown deep
    like the rivers.
          From memory to read
on radio show —
              Langston Hughes

Hughes wrote down his poem
"The Negro Speaks of Rivers"
from memory to read on a radio
program.

shaping the challenging look and sound of cutting-edge literary Modernism, the home-grown Langston Hughes—like Carl Sandburg, Vachel Lindsay, and Marianne Moore, among others—was inventing and perfecting a powerful populist modernism.

Beginning with the socially hip Miz Chapman's second-grade class at the Kingston School for Colored back in Laurel, Mississippi, I was regularly required to learn and recite poems by heart. Long before the Harlem Renaissance, as we now call it, had been packaged and all but locked up and franchised, Miz Chapman had us reading and memorizing Paul Laurence Dunbar, James Weldon Johnson, Claude McKay, and Countee Cullen. While recordings of poets reading their work were not widely available, my classmates and I understood that poems did not live on the page; they only camped there. From church and family gatherings, where someone could always be counted upon to break out into song or rhyme, we knew poems lived in the body. The words to "The Weary Blues," "I, Too," or "The Negro Speaks of Rivers" sound fresh and new each time I either say them myself or listen to a likeness of their master's voice, the voice of the poet who composed them.

First-rate composers—Anton Dvorak, Bela Bartok, Cole Porter, Mary Lou Williams, Duke Ellington, and Thelonious Monk come to mind—build their music from everything they hear going on around them, from the formalized to the vernacular and the colloquial. Langston Hughes, who loved the blues with its two-faced trickster aspects of sorrow and abandon, could also translate meaningfully the death-fixated poems of Chile's Gabriela Mistral as well as the rhythm-driven, socially engaged poetry of Cuba's Nicolás Guillén.

Call it colored, call it Negro, call it Afro- or African-American—the poetry of Langston Hughes, alive with clues to the origins of the blues, continues to quiver as it goes on delivering its news from an America whose rivers could do with some deep, soulful loving.

The Negro Speaks of Rivers

DISC 2, TRACK 26

(To W.E.B. DuBois)

I've known rivers:
I've known rivers ancient as the world and older than
    the flow of human blood in human veins.

My soul has grown deep like the rivers.

I bathed in the Euphrates when dawns were young.
I built my hut near the Congo and it lulled me to sleep.
I looked upon the Nile and raised the pyramids above
    it.
I heard the singing of the Mississippi when Abe Lincoln
    went down to New Orleans, and I've seen its muddy
    bosom turn all golden in the sunset.

I've known rivers:
Ancient, dusky rivers.

My soul has grown deep like the rivers.

[1920]

Mother to Son

DISC 2, TRACK 27

Well, son, I'll tell you:
Life for me ain't been no crystal stair.
It's had tacks in it,
And splinters,
And boards torn up,
And places with no carpet on the floor—
Bare.
But all the time
I'se been a-climbin' on,
And reachin' landin's,
And turnin' corners,
And sometimes goin' in the dark
Where there ain't been no light.
So boy, don't you turn back.
Don't you set down on the steps
'Cause you finds it's kinder hard.
Don't you fall now—
For I'se still goin', honey,
I'se still climbin',
And life for me ain't been no crystal stair.

[1926]

The Weary Blues

DISC 2, TRACK 28

Droning a drowsy syncopated tune,
Rocking back and forth to a mellow croon,
    I heard a Negro play.
Down on Lenox Avenue the other night
By the pale dull pallor of an old gas light
    He did a lazy sway....
    He did a lazy sway....
To the tune o' those Weary Blues.
With his ebony hands on each ivory key
He made that poor piano moan with melody.
    O Blues!
Swaying to and fro on his rickety stool
He played that sad raggy tune like a musical fool.
    Sweet Blues!
Coming from a black man's soul.
    O Blues!
In a deep song voice with a melancholy tone
I hear that Negro sing, that old piano moan—
    "Ain't got nobody in all this world,
        Ain't got nobody but ma self.
        I's gwine to quit ma frownin'
        And put ma troubles on the shelf."

Thump, thump, thump, went his foot on the floor.
He played a few chords then he sang some more—
    "I got the Weary Blues
        And I can't be satisfied.
        Got the Weary Blues
        And can't be satisfied—
        I ain't happy no mo'
        And I wish that I had died."
And far into the night he crooned that tune.
The stars went out and so did the moon.
The singer stopped playing and went to bed
While the Weary Blues echoed through his head.
He slept like a rock or a man that's dead.

[1926]

I, Too

I, too, sing America.

I am the darker brother.
They send me to eat in the kitchen
When company comes,
But I laugh,
And eat well,
And grow strong.

Tomorrow,
I'll sit at the table
When company comes.
Nobody'll dare
Say to me,
"Eat in the kitchen,"
Then.

Besides,
They'll see how beautiful I am
And be ashamed—

I, too, am America.

[1926]

Good Morning

Good morning, daddy!
I was born here, he said,
watched Harlem grow
until colored folks spread
from river to river
across the middle of Manhattan
out of Penn Station
dark tenth of a nation,
planes from Puerto Rico,
and holds of boats, chico,
up from Cuba Haiti Jamaica,
in buses marked New York
from Georgia Florida Louisiana
to Harlem Brooklyn the Bronx

[1951]

Harlem [2]

DISC 2, TRACK 29

What happens to a dream deferred?

Does it dry up
like a raisin in the sun?
Or fester like a sore—
And then run?
Does it stink like rotten meat?
Or crust and sugar over—
like a syrupy sweet?

Maybe it just sags
like a heavy load.

Or does it explode?

[1958]

Luck

Sometimes a crumb falls
From the tables of joy,
Sometimes a bone
Is flung.

To some people
Love is given,
To others
Only heaven.

[1959]

Ogden Nash

(1902–1971) b. Savannah, Georgia, United States

Disc 2
Tracks 30–32

Ogden Nash was born into a prominent Southern family on August 19, 1902. Originally from Savannah, Georgia, Nash relocated throughout his childhood as his father tracked business opportunities from city to city. After attending St. George's secondary school in Newport, Rhode Island, he enrolled at Harvard University in 1920 but was forced to drop out after one year for financial reasons. (Nash was always quick to remind people that he was not kicked out.) He drifted through several jobs before becoming a publicist for the publishing house Doubleday Page; while maintaining this job, he also began to write poetry seriously, and in 1925, he published his first children's story, *The Cricket of Carador*. In 1929, Nash was hired by *The New Yorker*, where he later published his first poem, "Spring Comes to Murray Hill." Many other quick and amusing poems followed, and Nash's first collection of poems, *Hard Lines*, appeared in 1931. Not surprisingly, it was largely ignored by the academic and literary worlds, while finding great popularity among the public.

In 1931, Nash published his second collection, *Free Wheeling*, and married Frances Rider Leonard, a Vassar graduate he met at a dinner dance in Baltimore in 1928. After the sharp, almost cynical pieces of his first books, Nash shifted to a wiser, gentler tone as his roles as husband and father began to shape his poetry. Nash's books of poems appeared with great regularity during this period, as they would throughout the remainder of his career: *Happy Days* in 1933, *The Primrose Path* in 1935, *I'm a Stranger Here Myself* in 1938, and *The Face is Familiar* in 1940. All in all, he published nineteen collections of poetry in his lifetime. In 1936, Nash uprooted and moved to Hollywood with his family and took a job writing screenplays for MGM Studios. A surprising move for Nash, this career change failed to bring him much fame or repute, and none of his screenplays produced very successful movies. In 1942, he decided to return with his family to the East Coast. While he had proved unsuccessful in the movie business, he did cowrite the Broadway play *One Touch of Venus* in 1943, which became enormously popular when it hit the stage.

Nash continued to publish poetry throughout the 1950s and '60s, including several volumes for children, such as *Parents Keep Out: Elderly Poems for Young Readers* (1951). He also entered the lecture circuit in both the U.S. and England and appeared frequently on radio comedy shows, conscientiously maintaining all these activities until his death in Baltimore on May 19, 1971. Always a popular poet with the public, in recent years critics have begun examining his work more closely. Uncovering the carefully crafted poetic elements embedded in the brilliant surfaces of his irresistible wit, some have even placed him alongside such great satirists as Jonathan Swift and other classic comedic writers such as Lewis Carroll.

Billy Collins on Ogden Nash

During the middle decades of the twentieth century, Ogden Nash was the most widely read and openly enjoyed poet in America. The wisdom of his decision to quit teaching (he said he lost his "entire nervous system carving lamb for a table of fourteen-year-olds") and later to give up a staff job at *The New Yorker* is confirmed by his long, successful career as a freelance writer of short, witty poems. The sales of his nineteen books of poetry were steady. His humorous, ingeniously rhymed verses appeared regularly in the pages of such popular magazines as *Cosmopolitan*, *Esquire*, *Harper's*, *Vogue*, *Ladies' Home Journal*, *Look*, *McCall's*, and the *Saturday Evening Post*. Some of his epigrammatic rhymes ("Candy / Is dandy, / But liquor / Is quicker") even became part of the country's repertoire of folk slogans. Nash and other writers of short comic verse such as Richard Armour pleased wide audiences of readers, but, not surprisingly, received no critical attention. Consigned to that subgenre of poetry, "light verse," they were taken less than seriously because of their jokiness and their comical rhymes—the very qualities that endear them to their readers. Today, humor has regained its footing in poetry, but given Nash's reputation, it is still no small wonder that we find him standing here in this collection shoulder to shoulder with Langston Hughes and W.H. Auden. This inclusion is hardly a sign of a Nash Revival (although his *Saturday Evening Post* counterpart in painting, Norman Rockwell, is now enjoying a favorable reassessment), but a closer look at Nash's writing might serve to illustrate what is unique about his work and to clarify the boundaries of the term "light verse." Listening to and reading his poems might even restimulate the delight his poems have conveyed to so many.

The trouble with light verse, according to William Matthews, is that instead of achieving a humorous slant on experience, it "sets out to be funny." Nash fits this assessment perfectly in that his strength and his weakness both arise from the fact that his poems want to amuse us from beginning to end. He does not use humor as a path to the serious, nor do his poems take unexpectedly humorous turns. Rather, the poems are saturated with witty rhymes and other kinds of verbal high jinks right from the start. Even the standard joke can keep a straight face until the punch line, but Nash's language puts on a comic performance at every point: ———————

June means weddings in everyone's lexicon,
Wedding in Swedish, wedding in Mexican.
Breezes play Mendelssohn, treeses play Youmans,
Birds wed birds, and humans wed humans.
All year long the gentlemen woo,
But the ladies dream of a June "I do."
Ladies grown loony, and gentlemen loonier;
This year's June is next year's Junior.
("Here Usually Comes the Bride")

The result is a monochromatic tone—spirited, wry, charmingly playful, but always the same. As we move from line to line, we know exactly what to expect: more humor, more silliness, more verbal folly. Nash is not for everyone, and a little of him—it must be said—goes a long way.

Nash's dominant humor derives from two sources: the gentle bite of his social satire and his delightful butchering of conventional spelling and syllabification for the sake of rhyme. His obsessive subject, in Nash's own words, is always "the minor idiocies of humanity." His satirical targets include politicians and clerics, doctors and editors, as well as the nosy, the oafish, the snobbish, and the chronically late. Sometimes he sprays his shots:

The doctor gets you when you're born,
The preacher, when you marry,
And the lawyer lurks with costly clerks
If too much on you carry...

Other times, he pinpoints his victim:

Like an art lover looking at the Mona Lisa in the Louvre
Is the New York Herald Tribune *looking at Mr. Herbert Houvre.*

Like James Thurber, Nash is an avid examiner of marriage, a subject largely excluded from serious poetry and left to the novel since the Romantics. He said he found families interesting because only there "do we find the battle of the sexes raging concurrently with the battle between the generations." He called himself a "student husband" even after thirty years of marriage, an institution he defined as "a legal and religious alliance entered into by a man who can't sleep with the window shut and a woman who can't sleep with the window open." Both husbands (who snore and forget birthdays) and wives (who are gabby and wear too much lipstick) are derided in equal measure. Perhaps the poem that best sums up Nash's view of the gender wars is "The Trouble with Women Is Men," which opens with these typically long-winded lines:

175 / Ogden Nash

> *A husband is a man who two minutes after his head touches the pillow is snoring like an overloaded omnibus,*
> *Particularly on those occasions when between the humidity and the mosquitoes your own bed is no longer a bed but an insomnibus...*

That Nash could coin "insomnibus" to go with "omnibus" shows that he would go to any lengths to forge a rhyme even if it meant making up words, twisting existing words into new shapes, or pushing a poem to the brink of nonsense. In English poetry, few besides Byron (who can rhyme "intellectual" with "hen-pecked you all") can compete with Nash in the field of rhyming ingenuity, or, some would say, rhyming dementia.

Nash on a television quiz show panel, circa 1955

Robert Frost said that whenever he read a poem that rhymed, he always looked down the right side of the page to see who had won, the poet or the rhyme scheme. Usually we want the poet to win by controlling the rhymes; bad poetry is the place where rhymes tend to dominate. But much of the surprise and joy in Nash's poems comes from the poet's willingness to allow the rhymes to win. Nash habitually surrenders to the strange network of echoes within the language, rhyming "chatting wittily" with "Little Italy," "boomerang" with "meringue," and "carrots" with "parrots"; or—bold as Joyce—he invents new words for the occasion, coupling "linoleum" with "melancholium," "prowess" with "wowess," and "matricide" with "Cleopatricide." The rhymes take charge; the tail comically wags the dog.

Boosting the level of mirth is Nash's habit of radically varying the length of his lines, mixing short with absurdly long lines, for example:

> *There is one form of life to which I unconditionally surrender,*
> *Which is the feminine gender...*
> *I think there must be some great difference in the way men and women are built,*
> *Because women walk around all day wearing shoes that a man would break his neck the first step he took in them because where a man's shoe has a heel a woman's shoe has a stilt.*

The breathless jumble of words would not be so funny if we did not hear in the background the tetrameter or pentameter line that our poetry-attuned ears have been trained on and that Nash is writing against.

Nash occasionally wrote serious poems, some of which give us a glimpse of a darker side, but he usually stays in his favorite poetic gear: the short, playfully rhymed, humorous lyric. His verses are a home for whimsy and goofiness when such impulses were excluded from serious Modernist poetry. And few poets spread poetic enjoyment so widely as he does, creating a delight that reminds us of the connection between poetry and the childhood pleasures of clapping and rhyming. Light and light-footed as his verse may be, Nash's wild rhymes, his cavalier mishandling of prosody, and his tireless inventiveness reveal the most essential of a poet's credentials—a crazed affection for the language.

The Trouble with Women Is Men

A husband is a man who two minutes after his head
touches the pillow is snoring like an overloaded
omnibus,
Particularly on those occasions when between the
humidity and the mosquitoes your own bed is no
longer a bed, but an insomnibus,
And if you turn on the light for a little reading he is
sensitive to the faintest gleam,
But if by any chance you are asleep and he wakeful, he
is not slow to rouse you with the complaint that he
can't close his eyes, what about slipping downstairs
and freezing him a cooling dish of pistachio ice
cream.
His touch with a bottle opener is sure,
But he cannot help you get a tight dress over your head
without catching three hooks and a button in your
coiffure.
Nor can he so much as wash his ears without leaving an
inch of water on the bathroom linoleum,
But if you mention it you evoke not a promise to splash
no more but a mood of deep melancholium.
Indeed, each time he transgresses your chance of
correcting his faults grows lesser,
Because he produces either a maddeningly logical
explanation or a look of martyrdom which leaves you
instead of him feeling the remorse of the
transgressor.
Such are husbandly foibles, but there are moments
when a foible ceases to be a foible.
Next time you ask for a glass of water and when he
brings it you have a needle almost threaded and
instead of setting it down he stands there holding it
out to you, just kick him fairly hard in the stomach,
you will find it thoroughly enjoible.

[1942]

Portrait of the Artist as a Prematurely Old Man

It is common knowledge to every schoolboy and even
every Bachelor of Arts,
That all sin is divided into two parts.
One kind of sin is called a sin of commission, and that
is very important,
And it is what you are doing when you are doing
something you ortant,
And the other kind of sin is just the opposite and is
called a sin of omission and is equally bad in the eyes
of all right-thinking people, from Billy Sunday to
Buddha,
And it consists of not having done something you
shuddha.
Well, there are more ways than one to kill a cat,
And offhand you'd think there were more kinds of sin
than that,
But I suppose that once upon a time there was
somebody somewhere who just wouldn't be pacified
Until they got sin classified,
So now even if you are a combination of Casanova and
Bluebeard and Jesse James and Benedict Arnold and
an oriental magician
Still, the only kind of sin you can pull out of the hat is a
sin either of om- or com-mission.
I might as well give you my opinion of these two kinds
of sin as long as, in a way, against each other we are
pitting them,
And that is, don't bother your head about sins of
commission because however sinful, they must at
least be fun or else you wouldn't be committing
them.
It is the sin of omission, the second kind of sin,
That lays eggs under your skin.
The way you get really painfully bitten
Is by the insurance you haven't taken out and the
checks you haven't added up the stubs of and the
appointments you haven't kept and the bills you
haven't paid and the letters you haven't written,

And they start piling up and up and up on top of you,

Till you are so bowed down that unless you get up on
a ladder the bald spot of a midget standing on its
head in a cellar is about the only thing of which
you can get a proper view.

Also, about sins of omission there is one particularly
painful lack of beauty,

Namely, it isn't as though it has been a riotous red
letter day or night every time you neglected to do
your duty;

You didn't get a wicked forbidden thrill

Every time you let a policy lapse or forgot to pay a bill;

You didn't slap the lads in the tavern on the back and
loudly cry Whee,

Let's all fail to write just one more letter before we go
home, and this round of unwritten letters is on me.

No, you never get any fun

Out of the things you haven't done,

But they are the things that I do not like to be amid,

Because the suitable things you didn't do give you a lot
more trouble than the unsuitable things you did.

The moral is that it is probably better not to sin at all,
but if some kind of sin you must be pursuing,

Well, remember to do it by doing rather than by not
doing.

[1945]

DISC 2, TRACK 31

I Do, I Will, I Have

How wise I am to have instructed the butler to instruct
the first footman to instruct the second footman to
instruct the doorman to order my carriage;

I am about to volunteer a definition of marriage.

Just as I know that there are two Hagens, Walter and
Copen,

I know that marriage is a legal and religious alliance
entered into by a man who can't sleep with the
window shut and a woman who can't sleep with the
window open.

Moreover, just as I am unsure of the difference between
flora and fauna and flotsam and jetsam,

I am quite sure that marriage is the alliance of two
people one of whom never remembers birthdays and
the other never forgetsam,

And he refuses to believe there is a leak in the water
pipe or the gas pipe and she is convinced she is
about to asphyxiate or drown,

And she says Quick get up and get my hairbrushes off
the windowsill, it's raining in, and he replies Oh
they're all right, it's only raining straight down.

That is why marriage is so much more interesting than
divorce,

Because it's the only known example of the happy
meeting of the immovable object and the irresistible
force.

So I hope husbands and wives will continue to debate
and combat over everything debatable and
combatable,

Because I believe a little incompatibility is the spice of
life, particularly if he has income and she is pattable.

[1949]

I Must Tell You About My Novel

DISC 2, TRACK 32

My grandpa wasn't salty,
No hero he of fable,
His English wasn't faulty,
He wore a coat at table.
His character lacked the color
Of either saint or satyr,
His life was rather duller
Than that of Walter Pater.

Look at Grandpa, take a look!
How can I write a book!

His temper wasn't crusty,
He shone not forth majestic
For barroom exploits lusty,
Or tyranny domestic.
He swung not on the gallows
But went to his salvation
While toasting stale marshmallows,
His only dissipation.

Look at Grandpa, take a look!
How can I write a book!

My Uncle John was cautious,
He never slipped his anchor,
His probity was nauseous,
In fact he was a banker.
He hubbed no hubba hubbas,
And buckled he no swashes,
He wore a pair of rubbers
Inside of his galoshes.

Look at my uncle, take a look!
How can I write a book!

My other uncle, Herbie,
Just once enlarged his orbit,
The day he crushed his derby
While cheering James J. Corbett.
No toper he, or wencher,
He backed nor horse nor houri,
His raciest adventure
A summons to the jury.

Look at my uncles, take a look!
How can I write a book!

Round my ancestral menfolk
There hangs no spicy aura,
I have no racy kinfolk
From Rome or Gloccamora.
Not nitwits, not Napoleons,
The mill they were the run of,
My family weren't Mongolians;
Then whom can I make fun of?

Look!
No book!

[1949]

Laments for a Dying Language

What's the monster of this week?
"Mystique"—
A noun that in its current arcane use leaves me frigid,
Since it is not to be found in either the O.E.D. or
    Webster's Unabridgèd.
It is primarily the invention of the mystagogues of
    esoteric criticism, so it means whatever they choose,
But I will give you an example of what I think they
    think it means, only from the domain of a different
    muse.
I recently heard on the air a song in which the lover
    states that the loved one is his idea
Of a band of angels singing "Ave Maria."
This is not only a metaphor unique,
It is also an example of the songwriter's mystique at its
    peak.

II

Someone comes up with a linguistic gimmick,
And thousands flock to mimic.
This noisy age, when big loud bangs give way to bangs
    louder and bigger still,
And admirals, congressmen, and minor government
    officials pop off at will,
Gives us two gimmicks that reflect our minds' corrosion:
"Crash program" and "explosion."
See here the population explosion, the freedom
    explosion, the Broadway and off-Broadway incest-
    theme explosion, the explosion of British secretaries
    in offices of grandiose pretensions,
And there the crash program for defense, for space
    exploration, for a third major league, for nominating
    the candidates previous to the conventions.
With each successive bang my hopes grow limper
That the world's end will be a simple whimper.

III

In the nice-minded Department of Prunes and Prisms,
It's I for you
And euphemisms.
Hence the phrase I would eagerly jettison:
"Senior citizen."
Shall we retranslate
Joel 2, 28?
To the sociologist squeamish
The words "Your old men shall dream dreams" are less
    than beamish,
So "Your senior citizens shall dream dreams" it shall
    henceforth be,
Along with Hemingway's "The Senior Citizen and the
    Sea."
I, though no Joel, prophesy that someday while the
    senior citizens are projecting the image of an age-
    adjusted social group,
The old men will rise up and knock them for a loop.

IV

Those authors I can never love
Who write, "It fit him like a glove."
Though baseballs may be hit, not "hitted,"
The past of "fit" is always "fitted."
The sole exception worth a *haricot*
Is "Joshua fit de battle ob Jericho."

V

Coin brassy words at will, debase the coinage;
We're in an if-you-cannot-lick-them-join age,
A slovenliness-provides-its-own-excuse age,
Where usage overnight condones misusage.
Farewell, farewell to my beloved language,
Once English, now a vile orangutanguage.

[1951]

W. H. Auden

(1907–1973) b. York, England

Disc 2
Tracks 33–36

Born in York on February 21, 1907, Wystan Hugh Auden attended St. Edmund's School in Hindhead. There he met Christopher Isherwood, who became a lifelong friend and frequent collaborator. After St. Edmund's, Auden moved on to Gresham's School in Norfolk, where he began to write poetry. He read widely at Gresham's, becoming a great admirer of Robert Frost, Thomas Hardy, and William Blake. In 1922, his poem "Dawn" appeared in *The Gresham*, the school's magazine.

In 1925, Auden entered Christ Church College of Oxford, where he initially studied the natural sciences. Here a friend, Stephen Spender, helped him to publish a small volume of verse in 1928. Auden moved to Berlin for a year after completing his undergraduate work, and was joined by Isherwood, whose famous *Berlin Stories* reflect their time there. Returning to England in 1930, Auden took various teaching jobs and published his first book of poems. Published by Faber and Faber while T.S. Eliot was an editor there, the poems in Auden's debut collection (entitled simply *Poems*) addressed England's depressed social and economic conditions. Auden's debut established him as a leading voice in a new generation of young leftist poets that included Louis MacNeice, Stephen Spender, and C. Day Lewis. This reputation was reinforced by his next two books, *The Orators* (1932), and *The Dance of Death* (1933), a verse drama. Throughout the '30s, Auden's sense of political responsibility gave direction to his art and motivated much of his behavior, including marrying Erika Mann, the daughter of Thomas Mann, so that she could get a British passport and leave Nazi Germany, despite his own homosexuality.

In 1939, Auden left England for America. He was accompanied by Isherwood, but they settled in different parts of the country. While some maintain that Auden's expatriation was an act of cowardice in the face of impending war with Germany, what led Auden to leave England was his wish to remove himself from London's stifling literary scene. Shortly after settling in New York City, Auden met the young American Chester Kallman. The two quickly became lovers, and despite the difficulty and inconstancy of their romantic attachment, theirs was a lasting companionship. A talented writer himself, Kallman collaborated with Auden on several *opera libretti*, including that for composer Igor Stravinsky's *The Rake's Progress*. In 1940, Auden published *Another Time*, a collection that includes some of his most popular lyrics, such as "Lullaby," "In Memory of W.B. Yeats," "Funeral Blues," and "Musée des Beaux Arts." During World War II, Auden's political and artistic ideals underwent notable changes. He abandoned the Marxist and Freudian tendencies of his earlier years and embraced Anglo-Catholicism; his poetry, increasingly Christian in content, became comprised largely of longer pieces, including *The Double Man* (1941), *The Sea and the Mirror* (1944), and *For the Time Being* (1944), a Christmas oratorio. In 1946, Auden became an American citizen. A year later, he published the Pulitzer Prize–winning *The Age of Anxiety*, a long philosophical dialogue written in Anglo-Saxon measures. He also became a noted essayist and editor during this period.

After releasing 1955's *The Shield of Achilles*, Auden returned to England to accept a professorship at Oxford in 1956. From 1958 on, he alternately lived in Austria, New York, and Oxford while continuing to publish his poetry. He died in Vienna in his sleep on the night of September 28, 1973, a few hours after having given his final poetry reading.

Dana Gioia
W. H. Auden on

Dana Gioia on W. H. Auden

The writers who affect us most deeply are usually the ones we discover early—often in adolescence. We read differently then, with more passionate curiosity, because we are caught in the process of discovering who we are and what we might become.

I first read W.H. Auden's poetry at sixteen. My sophomore anthology contained a few of his poems. They struck me so powerfully that I tracked down a copy of his *Collected Poetry* at the local department store. There was no paperback edition available, so I had to buy the book in hardback—for $5.95—a luxury I had never before allowed myself. As I first paged through the thick, handsome volume stopping at random among the many poems, I experienced almost immediately that clarifying moment of recognition that a reader has only a few times in life. Here was a book that summoned and spoke to all of me.

At this distance of time I cannot pretend to understand the full nature of my younger self's response, but at least three things first drew me to Auden's poetry—its music, its intelligence, and its great sense of fun. For me, poetry is primarily an auditory art, and no modern poet has a better ear than Auden. Great lyric poems cast a spell—a heightened state of attention and receptivity. The first time I read "Lay Your Sleeping Head, My Love" or "As I Walked Out One Evening," I was genuinely enchanted. Back then, it had never occurred to me that I would grow up to be a poet. I intended to be a composer, and I was delighted and intrigued both by the strange beauty and the variety of Auden's verbal music. My earliest interest in prosody came from trying to work out the rhythms of particular poems:

> "O where are you going?" said reader to rider,
> "That valley is fatal when furnaces burn,
> Yonder's the midden whose odours will madden
> That gap is the grave where the tall return."

Intelligence has a dubious reputation in poetry—probably for a good reason since it so often gets in the way of intuition, feeling, and imagination. But in his best

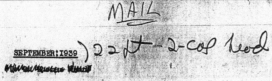

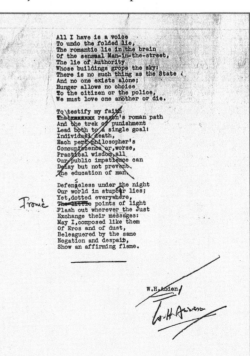

Typescript draft of "September 1, 1939" by Auden

poems, Auden's extraordinary intelligence never detaches itself from his emotions. He analyzes what he feels—which are often contradictory impulses—with imaginative brilliance and penetrating candor. That honesty is sometimes astonishing. Another poet might well begin a love poem by saying, "Lay your sleeping head, my love," but who else but Auden would follow with the second line, "Human on my faithless arm?" In that magnificent poem, as in so many of his best lyrics, the lines unfold as a passionate dance of intellect and emotion.

Finally, Auden's poems were such fun—to read, to recite, to remember, to imitate, to emulate. Sometimes the fun was on the surface as in the witty social satire, "The Unknown Citizen," which was probably the first poem of his that I read. But more often, Auden reminded me of Robert Frost's maxim that, "All the fun is in how you say a thing." Auden's poems were a delight to wrap one's tongue around. Even serious works, like "In Memory of W.B. Yeats" or "September 1, 1939," seemed suffused with the physical pleasure essential to poetry.

My attachment to Auden was not only immediate and profound. It also proved enduring. There has never been a period of my life when I have not found reading his poetry or prose rewarding, although different works have attracted me at different times. Auden claimed famously that "Poetry makes nothing happen." In the larger political sense he intended, he was probably right. But in terms of shaping the individual imagination, his poetry certainly changed my life—enlarging my sense of the world, language, and the human heart.

O Where Are You Going?

"O where are you going?" said reader to rider,
"That valley is fatal where furnaces burn,
Yonder's the midden whose odours will madden,
That gap is the grave where the tall return."

"O do you imagine," said fearer to farer,
"That dusk will delay on your path to the pass,
Your diligent looking discover the lacking,
Your footsteps feel from granite to grass?"

"O what was that bird," said horror to hearer,
"Did you see that shape in the twisted trees?
Behind you swiftly the figure comes softly,
The spot on your skin is a shocking disease."

"Out of this house"—said rider to reader,
"Yours never will"—said farer to fearer,
"They're looking for you"—said hearer to horror,
As he left them there, as he left them there.

[1931]

Funeral Blues

Stop all the clocks, cut off the telephone,
Prevent the dog from barking with a juicy bone,
Silence the pianos and with muffled drum
Bring out the coffin, let the mourners come.

Let aeroplanes circle moaning overhead
Scribbling on the sky the message He Is Dead,
Put crêpe bows round the white necks of the public doves,
Let the traffic policemen wear black cotton gloves.

He was my North, my South, my East and West,
My working week and my Sunday rest,
My noon, my midnight, my talk, my song;
I thought that love would last for ever: I was wrong.

The stars are not wanted now: put out every one;
Pack up the moon and dismantle the sun;
Pour away the ocean and sweep up the wood;
For nothing now can ever come to any good.

[1936]

As I Walked Out One Evening

As I walked out one evening,
    Walking down Bristol Street,
The crowds upon the pavement
    Were fields of harvest wheat.

And down by the brimming river
    I heard a lover sing
Under an arch of the railway:
    "Love has no ending.

"I'll love you, dear, I'll love you
    Till China and Africa meet,
And the river jumps over the mountain
    And the salmon sing in the street,

"I'll love you till the ocean
    Is folded and hung up to dry
And the seven stars go squawking
    Like geese about the sky.

The years shall run like rabbits,
    For in my arms I hold
The Flower of the Ages,
    And the first love of the world."

But all the clocks in the city
    Began to whirr and chime:
"O let not Time deceive you,
    You cannot conquer Time.

"In the burrows of the Nightmare
    Where Justice naked is,
Time watches from the shadow
    And coughs when you would kiss.

"In headaches and in worry
    Vaguely life leaks away,
And Time will have his fancy
    To-morrow or to-day.

"Into many a green valley
    Drifts the appalling snow;
Time breaks the threaded dances
    And the diver's brilliant bow.

"O plunge your hands in water,
    Plunge them in up to the wrist;
Stare, stare in the basin
    And wonder what you've missed.

"The glacier knocks in the cupboard,
    The desert sighs in the bed,
And the crack in the tea-cup opens
    A lane to the land of the dead.

"Where the beggars raffle the banknotes
    And the Giant is enchanting to Jack,
And the Lily-white Boy is a Roarer,
    And Jill goes down on her back.

"O look, look in the mirror,
    O look in your distress;
Life remains a blessing
    Although you cannot bless.

"O stand, stand at the window
    As the tears scald and start;
You shall love your crooked neighbour
    With your crooked heart."

It was late, late in the evening,
    The lovers they were gone;
The clocks had ceased their chiming,
    And the deep river ran on.

[1937]

In Memory of W. B. Yeats

(d. Jan. 1939)

DISC 2, TRACK 34

I

He disappeared in the dead of winter:
The brooks were frozen, the airports almost deserted,
And snow disfigured the public statues;
The mercury sank in the mouth of the dying day.
What instruments we have agree
The day of his death was a dark cold day.

Far from his illness
The wolves ran on through the evergreen forests,
The peasant river was untempted by the fashionable quays;
By mourning tongues
The death of the poet was kept from his poems.

But for him it was his last afternoon as himself,
An afternoon of nurses and rumours;
The provinces of his body revolted,
The squares of his mind were empty,
Silence invaded the suburbs,
The current of his feeling failed; he became his admirers.

Now he is scattered among a hundred cities
And wholly given over to unfamiliar affections,
To find his happiness in another kind of wood
And be punished under a foreign code of conscience.
The words of a dead man
Are modified in the guts of the living.

But in the importance and noise of to-morrow
When the brokers are roaring like beasts on the floor of the Bourse,
And the poor have the sufferings to which they are fairly accustomed,
And each in the cell of himself is almost convinced of his freedom,
A few thousand will think of this day
As one thinks of a day when one did something slightly unusual.
What instruments we have agree
The day of his death was a dark cold day.

II

You were silly like us; your gift survived it all:
The parish of rich women, physical decay,
Yourself. Mad Ireland hurt you into poetry.
Now Ireland has her madness and her weather still,
For poetry makes nothing happen: it survives
In the valley of its making where executives
Would never want to tamper, flows on south
From ranches of isolation and the busy griefs,
Raw towns that we believe and die in; it survives,
A way of happening, a mouth.

III

Earth, receive an honoured guest:
William Yeats is laid to rest.
Let the Irish vessel lie
Emptied of its poetry.

In the nightmare of the dark
All the dogs of Europe bark,
And the living nations wait,
Each sequestered in its hate;

Intellectual disgrace
Stares from every human face,
And the seas of pity lie
Locked and frozen in each eye.

Follow, poet, follow right
To the bottom of the night,
With your unconstraining voice
Still persuade us to rejoice;

With the farming of a verse
Make a vineyard of the curse,
Sing of human unsuccess
In a rapture of distress;

In the deserts of the heart
Let the healing fountain start,
In the prison of his days
Teach the free man how to praise.

[1940]

Musée des Beaux Arts

DISC 2, TRACK 35

About suffering they were never wrong,
The Old Masters: how well they understood
Its human position; how it takes place
While someone else is eating or opening a window or
    just walking dully along;
How, when the aged are reverently, passionately
    waiting
For the miraculous birth, there always must be
Children who did not specially want it to happen,
    skating
On a pond at the edge of the wood:
They never forgot
That even the dreadful martyrdom must run its
    course
Anyhow in a corner, some untidy spot
Where the dogs go on with their doggy life and the
    torturer's horse
Scratches its innocent behind on a tree.

In Brueghel's *Icarus*, for instance: how everything
    turns away
Quite leisurely from the disaster; the ploughman may
Have heard the splash, the forsaken cry,
But for him it was not an important failure; the sun
    shone
As it had to on the white legs disappearing into the
    green
Water; and the expensive delicate ship that must have
    seen
Something amazing, a boy falling out of the sky,
Had somewhere to get to and sailed calmly on.

[1940]

If I Could Tell You

DISC 2, TRACK 36

Time will say nothing but I told you so,
Time only knows the price we have to pay;
If I could tell you I would let you know.

If we should weep when clowns put on their show,
If we should stumble when musicians play,
Time will say nothing but I told you so.

There are no fortunes to be told, although,
Because I love you more than I can say,
If I could tell you I would let you know.

The winds must come from somewhere when they blow,
There must be reasons why the leaves decay;
Time will say nothing but I told you so.

Perhaps the roses really want to grow,
The vision seriously intends to stay;
If I could tell you I would let you know.

Suppose the lions all get up and go,
And all the brooks and soldiers run away;
Will Time say nothing but I told you so?
If I could tell you I would let you know.

[1940]

Louis MacNeice

(1907–1963) b. Belfast, Ireland

Disc 2
Tracks 37–39

Louis MacNeice was born in 1907 in Belfast, Ireland, and spent most of his childhood in the more rural harbor town of Carrickfergus. His father was a brooding clergyman in the Church of Ireland and eventually became a bishop; his mother was beset by chronic depression and died of tuberculosis when MacNeice was six years old. It appears that his siblings and various nannies and governesses dominated his early years; in time, MacNeice left home to attend Sherborne Preparatory School in Dorset. His academic achievements there helped earn him a classics scholarship to Marlborough College, a boy's public school in Wiltshire. Here he befriended art historian Anthony Blunt, perhaps most famous for being exposed as a Soviet agent in 1979. While at Marlborough, MacNeice's interest in poetry blossomed, and it was as a poet, scholar, athlete, and artist that he entered Merton College, Oxford, in 1926.

MacNeice studied classics and philosophy at Oxford, alongside his contemporary, W.H. Auden, though it appears that the two did not actually meet while at Oxford. In 1929, MacNeice published his first book of poetry, *Blind Fireworks*, and although it attracted little attention at the time, it has been praised in retrospect as a sharp, skillful, and intelligent collection. On the last day of his term at Oxford, MacNeice married Giovanna Marie Therese Babette Ezra, the stepdaughter of an Oxford scholar, and the couple moved to Birmingham. Here MacNeice taught classics at Birmingham University and befriended W.H. Auden, who introduced him to a newly formed local theater group. MacNeice would eventually become a notable playwright as well as poet. Showing Auden's influence, MacNeice's second volume, *Poems*, appeared in 1935, and it was at Auden's urging that MacNeice undertook to translate Aeschylus' *Agamemnon*. Published in 1936, MacNeice's version of the Greek tragedy received high praise from the drama community and its stage production was very popular; today it is considered among the era's best poetic translations of any Greek drama. In 1937, MacNeice and Auden coauthored and published *Letters from Iceland*, a collection of prose and verse, and in the following year MacNeice published his second book of poems, *The Earth Compels*. These works continued to enhance his reputation, but it was his 1939 volume, *Autumn Journal*, bringing together history, politics, and autobiography, that truly established MacNeice as an important literary figure.

After the breakup of his marriage, MacNeice moved to London in the late '30s and America in 1940, perhaps wishing to follow Auden there. He left America and returned to London in 1941, and there he began working for the BBC doing radio broadcasts, which he would continue to do until his death. His last volumes of poetry, *Solstices* (1961) and *The Burning Perch* (1963), testify to his enduring skill, exuberance, and poetic wit. He died in 1963, only days after the publication of *The Burning Perch*. Long overlooked in favor of the more visible W.H. Auden, critics have reassessed MacNeice's status since the 1970s, and he is now recognized as an important figure in modern literature's development, particularly in that of modern Irish literature in English.

Peter McDonald on Louis MacNeice

One of Louis MacNeice's early poems begins by stating that "I meet you in an evil time." This was in the 1930s, when "evil" was certainly in the air. Yet the poem itself refuses to let the pressures of its time call the shots; war and terror may loom, but so does the "beauty narcotic and deciduous" of a modern city, where "On all the traffic-islands stand white globes like moons"; so does the theater where "pink thighs flash like the spokes of a wheel," and so do "the bare and high / Places of England," where "the sheep like grey stones / Humble my human pretensions"; so, even, looms a briefly glimpsed figure of "The commercial traveller joking in the urinal." The poem ends with a prayer to "let all these so ephemeral things / Be somehow permanent like the swallow's tangent wings." Of all the poets of his time, MacNeice is the one most acutely attuned to the ways in which verse—and the voice that informs the movement of verse—can be charged by the "ephemeral," and can flash this into poetry's often apparently tangential utterance, an utterance which may be, at the same time, "somehow permanent."

The permanence of MacNeice's achievement as a poet is now in little doubt. Partly, this is a matter of posterity: without MacNeice's voice and example there would be no Philip Larkin, Derek Mahon, Michael Longley, or Paul Muldoon—to name just four—in the shape that we know them. Yet MacNeice, as is the way with really important writers, contrives to remain something much more than anybody's predecessor. Nearly forty years after his death, he continues to exert the force and stimulate the excitement of a living presence for many readers. Much that obscured MacNeice's reputation during his lifetime is now gone. His great contemporary, W.H. Auden, can be seen as a different kind of poet—a companion, but not a rival. The Ireland that effectively disowned him as too English has developed a less bigoted sense of its cultural wealth; and, perhaps most important, the fetish of Modernist style has lessened its appeal, allowing MacNeice's wonderfully various and capacious poetic forms and registers to be celebrated as true expressions—though not untrue to the dissonance of their century—of the singing line in English poetry.

The history MacNeice lived through was important, but this most alert and attentive of observers understood something that weaker poets forget: even history is, in the end, a matter of "ephemeral things." His astonishing long poem of 1938, *Autumn Journal*, watches London prepare for war all the more provocatively for keeping an eye on the oddities and bafflements of life then and there, and allowing memories and desires—Ireland and its conflicts, a finished love-affair, schooldays, the grind of the day job—to flood the scenes. The London of *Autumn Journal*, where newspapers are full of the Munich Crisis and the fall of Barcelona while engineers build gun emplacements on Primrose Hill, is also a city "littered with remembered kisses." To be faithful to the particular detail is more than just a point of style in poetry. MacNeice is constant in his fascination with and relish for the difference and otherness of a world "crazier and more of it than we think, / Incorrigibly plural," in which "Ordinary people are peculiar too," with "Swear-words like roses in their talk."

This apparent, and still, maybe, unfashionable, humility is part of MacNeice's deep and abiding artistic strength. If he wrote few poems that are not properly demanding of the reader's intelligence, he wrote none that is wilfully or self-consciously difficult. If his poetry shies away from making a cult of his own person-ality, it speaks still with a completely original and authentic voice that is both of, and beyond, its particular time. MacNeice seems to me—as increasingly he does to others—the most important and rewarding Irish and British poet since W.B. Yeats. Like the very best poets, the time his writing so stylishly and faithfully keeps turns out to be ours as well as his own.

Bagpipe Music

It's no go the merrygoround, it's no go the rickshaw,
All we want is a limousine and a ticket for the peepshow.
Their knickers are made of crêpe-de-chine, their shoes are made of python,
Their halls are lined with tiger rugs and their walls with heads of bison.

John MacDonald found a corpse, put it under the sofa,
Waited till it came to life and hit it with a poker,
Sold its eyes for souvenirs, sold its blood for whisky,
Kept its bones for dumb-bells to use when he was fifty.

It's no go the Yogi-Man, it's no go Blavatsky,
All we want is a bank balance and a bit of skirt in a taxi.

Annie MacDougall went to milk, caught her foot in the heather,
Woke to hear a dance record playing of Old Vienna.
It's no go your maidenheads, it's no go your culture,
All we want is a Dunlop tyre and the devil mend the puncture.

The Laird o' Phelps spent Hogmanay declaring he was sober,
Counted his feet to prove the fact and found he had one foot over.
Mrs. Carmichael had her fifth, looked at the job with repulsion,
Said to the midwife "Take it away; I'm through with over production."

It's no go the gossip column, it's no go the ceilidh,
All we want is a mother's help and a sugar-stick for the baby.

Willie Murray cut his thumb, couldn't count the damage,
Took the hide of an Ayrshire cow and used it for a bandage.
His brother caught three hundred cran when the seas were lavish,
Threw the bleeders back in the sea and went upon the parish.

It's no go the Herring Board, it's no go the Bible,
All we want is a packet of fags when our hands are idle.

It's no go the picture palace, it's no go the stadium,
It's no go the country cot with a pot of pink geraniums,
It's no go the Government grants, it's no go the elections,
Sit on your arse for fifty years and hang your hat on a pension.

It's no go my honey love, it's no go my poppet;
Work your hands from day to day, the winds will blow the profit.
The glass is falling hour by hour, the glass will fall for ever,
But if you break the bloody glass you won't hold up the weather.

[1937]

Conversation

DISC 2, TRACK 38

Ordinary people are peculiar too:
Watch the vagrant in their eyes
Who sneaks away while they are talking with you
Into some black wood behind the skull,
Following un-, or other, realities,
Fishing for shadows in a pool.

But sometimes the vagrant comes the other way
Out of their eyes and into yours
Having mistaken you perhaps for yesterday
Or for tomorrow night, a wood in which
He may pick up among the pine-needles and burrs
The lost purse, the dropped stitch.

Vagrancy however is forbidden; ordinary men
Soon come back to normal, look you straight
In the eyes as if to say 'It will not happen again',
Put up a barrage of common sense to baulk
Intimacy but by mistake interpolate
Swear-words like roses in their talk.

[1941]

Meeting Point

DISC 2, TRACK 39

Time was away and somewhere else,
There were two glasses and two chairs
And two people with the one pulse
(Somebody stopped the moving stairs):
Time was away and somewhere else.

And they were neither up nor down,
The stream's music did not stop
Flowing through heather, limpid brown,
Although they sat in a coffee shop
And they were neither up nor down.

The bell was silent in the air
Holding its inverted poise—
Between the clang and clang a flower,
A brazen calyx of no noise:
The bell was silent in the air.

The camels crossed the miles of sand
That stretched around the cups and plates;
The desert was their own, they planned
To portion out the stars and dates:
The camels crossed the miles of sand.

Time was away and somewhere else.
The waiter did not come, the clock
Forgot them and the radio waltz
Came out like water from a rock:
Time was away and somewhere else.

Her fingers flicked away the ash
That bloomed again in tropic trees:
Not caring if the markets crash
When they had forests such as these,
Her fingers flicked away the ash.

God or whatever means the Good
Be praised that time can stop like this,
That what the heart has understood
Can verify in the body's peace
God or whatever means the Good.

Time was away and she was here
And life no longer what it was,
The bell was silent in the air
And all the room a glow because
Time was away and she was here.

[1941]

The British Museum Reading Room

Under the hive-like dome the stooping haunted readers
Go up and down the alleys, tap the cells of knowledge—
    Honey and wax, the accumulation of years—
Some on commission, some for the love of learning,
Some because they have nothing better to do
Or because they hope these walls of books will deaden
    The drumming of the demon in their ears.

Cranks, hacks, poverty-stricken scholars,
In pince-nez, period hats or romantic beards
    And cherishing their hobby or their doom
Some are too much alive and some are asleep
Hanging like bats in a world of inverted values,
Folded up in themselves in a world which is safe and silent:
    This is the British Museum Reading Room.

Out on the steps in the sun the pigeons are courting,
Puffing their ruffs and sweeping their tails or taking
    A sun-bath at their ease
And under the totem poles—the ancient terror—
Between the enormous fluted Ionic columns
There seeps from heavily jowled or hawk-like foreign faces
    The guttural sorrow of the refugees.

[1941]

Star-gazer

Forty-two years ago (to me if to no one else
The number is of some interest) it was a brilliant starry night
And the westward train was empty and had no corridors
So darting from side to side I could catch the unwonted sight
Of those almost intolerably bright
Holes, punched in the sky, which excited me partly because
Of their Latin names and partly because I had read in the textbooks
How very far off they were, it seemed their light
Had left them (some at least) long years before I was.

And this remembering now I mark that what
Light was leaving some of them at least then,
Forty-two years ago, will never arrive
In time for me to catch it, which light when
It does get here may find that there is not
Anyone left alive
To run from side to side in a late night train
Admiring it and adding noughts in vain.

[1963]

Theodore Roethke

(1908–1963) b. Saginaw, Michigan, United States

Disc 2
Tracks 40-43

Theodore Roethke was born in Saginaw, Michigan, in 1908. As a child, Roethke spent countless hours in his father's greenhouse, which he would eventually immortalize in a number of well-known poems. His father died while Roethke was still young, and the trauma of that loss surfaces in Roethke's powerfully ambivalent poetic images of his father. Roethke enrolled in the University of Michigan in 1925 and graduated magna cum laude in 1929, after which he took graduate courses at both the University of Michigan and at Harvard University. The Great Depression forced Roethke to leave Harvard, and he took a teaching position at Lafayette College in 1931, followed by another at Michigan State in 1935. During this time he worked seriously on his own poetry and befriended such poets as Stanley Kunitz, Louise Bogan, and William Carlos Williams. When he moved to Penn State University to teach in 1936, his poetry had begun appearing in such respected journals as *Poetry* and *The Saturday Review*. In 1941, he published his first volume of poetry, *Open House*. The book won the acclaim of many critics, most prominently that of W. H. Auden.

After the publication of *Open House*, Roethke left Penn State and taught at Bennington College. His next volume, published in 1948, is widely considered not only Roethke's best, but a watershed in American poetry as well. Titled *The Lost Son and Other Poems*, the sensuous, fertile imagery recollected from Roethke's early days in the greenhouse evokes an organic world suffused with spiritual energy. Owing much to poets such as W. B. Yeats and Dylan Thomas, the volume set the tone and style for much of Roethke's poetry to come. At this stage in his career, Roethke began teaching at the University of Washington, where he would instruct a number of students of poetry who went on to prominent careers of their own, including Richard Hugo, Carolyn Kizer, David Wagoner, and James Wright. Roethke's friends and family had come to think of him as a confirmed bachelor, but in 1953 he married Beatrice Heath O'Connell, a former student of his at Bennington in the 1930s. The ceremony was small, with Auden and poet Louise Bogan serving as best man and matron of honor.

Throughout the 1950s, Roethke taught, wrote, and garnered many awards, including a Pulitzer Prize for *The Waking: Poems 1933–1953*, a Guggenheim Fellowship, a Fulbright Fellowship, and a National Book Award for *Words for the Wind* (1957). This second collection comprised two long poems, "Dying Man" and "Meditations of an Old Woman," poems on the natural world, love poems (including the well-known "I Knew a Woman"), and a suite of poems for children. However, Roethke's growing success was interrupted by frequent and severe bouts of depression, and although he claimed that weathering emotional turmoil brought him new poetic insight, he often found himself hospitalized during this time.

By 1960, Roethke was recognized as one of the top poets of the day. His poetic accomplishments continued unabated until he suffered a fatal heart attack while visiting friends in 1963. Many of his late poems were published posthumously in such volumes as *The Far Field* (1964), which won Roethke a second National Book Award. His intensely lyrical, sensuous, and often visionary work greatly influenced a number of prominent poets, including Robert Bly, James Dickey, Ted Hughes, and perhaps most notably, Sylvia Plath.

Joy Harjo on Theodore Roethke

I first heard *The Waking* years ago in an undergraduate poetry class at the University of New Mexico. Other poems had coaxed me to begin writing—poems by Simon Ortiz, Adrienne Rich, Galway Kinnell, and Pablo Neruda. It was John Coltrane's horn as well, and the singing that went on until late through the night in Indian country all over the country. And then Roethke showed up with an irreverent reverence, with a sideways manner of speaking. He reminded me of the best singers, because in my tribal traditions poems are sung, not spoken. In any tradition, there are some poems that never leave you, no matter where you travel or the manner in which you travel. *The Waking* by Theodore Roethke is one of these:

> *I wake to sleep, and take my waking slow.*
> *I feel my fate in what I cannot fear.*
> *I learn by going where I have to go.*

Some poems wind through your sleep, up through your marrow into the hard stuff. They have hooks like songs, mnemonic devices so that the singer in the poet will always find a place to live.

> *We think by feeling. What is there to know?*
> *I hear my being dance from ear to ear.*
> *I wake to sleep, and take my waking slow.*

Each poem is constructed of lines, of rhythms, and words that are sounds. Each poem is a field of energy. There's form and there's shape, like a house or a jukebox. Some forms are of contemporary design, like free verse. *The Waking* is in an old French form, the villanelle. The form has to fit the content. The content needs a place to live.

Of those so close beside me, which are you?
God bless the Ground! I shall walk softly there,
And learn by going where I have to go.

The lines of this poem make a ladder, a road on which the human soul can walk with dignity into the consciousness that makes the sky and earth, into the awareness that constructs dreams. The poem then can be an intermediary as we travel between waking and sleeping, towards the light of sky.

Light takes the Tree; but who can tell us how?
The lowly worm climbs up a winding stair;
I wake to sleep, and take my waking slow.

Here comes the repeating line again and it is sunrise, or is it dusk and suddenly we are aware of the fragility of life as the sun takes a turn. Absolutely everything matters, each step through the up and down of it. I want to take my shoes off and stay awhile but I must keep going.

Great Nature has another thing to do
To you and me; so take the lively air,
And, lovely, learn by going where to go.

If a poem is constructed well it illuminates sacred land, imagines a perfect place in which to contemplate how to move from here to there. For any construction, whether it be a manner of thinking or a house, there must be a solid foundation, mathematics, appropriate materials, a path for the wind, and an aesthetics of how to live.

This shaking keeps me steady. I should know.
What falls away is always. And is near.
I wake to sleep, and take my waking slow.
I learn by going where I have to go.

The walking triplet lines now have made a foundation of four. The poem has made a house or a field of meaning. There's a spirit who lives here, who continues to sing no matter that the poet has gone on to another poem, another world.

My Papa's Waltz

The whiskey on your breath
Could make a small boy dizzy;
But I hung on like death:
Such waltzing was not easy.

We romped until the pans
Slid from the kitchen shelf;
My mother's countenance
Could not unfrown itself.

The hand that held my wrist
Was battered on one knuckle;
At every step you missed
My right ear scraped a buckle.

You beat time on my head
With a palm caked hard by dirt,
Then waltzed me off to bed
Still clinging to your shirt.

[1948]

The Waking

I wake to sleep, and take my waking slow.
I feel my fate in what I cannot fear.
I learn by going where I have to go.

We think by feeling. What is there to know?
I hear my being dance from ear to ear.
I wake to sleep, and take my waking slow.

Of those so close beside me, which are you?
God bless the Ground! I shall walk softly there,
And learn by going where I have to go.

Light takes the Tree; but who can tell us how?
The lowly worm climbs up a winding stair;
I wake to sleep, and take my waking slow.

Great Nature has another thing to do
To you and me; so take the lively air,
And, lovely, learn by going where to go.

This shaking keeps me steady. I should know.
What falls away is always. And is near.
I wake to sleep, and take my waking slow.
I learn by going where I have to go.

[1953]

I Knew a Woman

I knew a woman, lovely in her bones,
When small birds sighed, she would sigh back at them;
Ah, when she moved, she moved more ways than one:
The shapes a bright container can contain!
Of her choice virtues only gods should speak,
Or English poets who grew up on Greek
(I'd have them sing in chorus, cheek to cheek).

How well her wishes went! She stroked my chin,
She taught me Turn, and Counter-turn, and Stand;
She taught me Touch, that undulant white skin;
I nibbled meekly from her proffered hand;
She was the sickle; I, poor I, the rake,
Coming behind her for her pretty sake
(But what prodigious mowing we did make).

Love likes a gander, and adores a goose:
Her full lips pursed, the errant note to seize;
She played it quick, she played it light and loose;
My eyes, they dazzled at her flowing knees;
Her several parts could keep a pure repose,
Or one hip quiver with a mobile nose
(She moved in circles, and those circles moved).

Let seed be grass, and grass turn into hay:
I'm martyr to a motion not my own;
What's freedom for? To know eternity.
I swear she cast a shadow white as stone.
But who would count eternity in days?
These old bones live to learn her wanton ways:
(I measure time by how a body sways).

[1958]

The Sloth

In moving-slow he has no Peer.
You ask him something in his Ear,
He thinks about it for a Year;

And, then, before he says a Word
There, upside down (unlike a Bird),
He will assume that you have Heard—

A most Ex-as-per-at-ing Lug.
But should you call his manner Smug,
He'll sigh and give his Branch a Hug;

Then off again to Sleep he goes,
Still swaying gently by his Toes,
And you just *know* he knows he knows.

[1958]

In a Dark Time

In a dark time, the eye begins to see,
I meet my shadow in the deepening shade;
I hear my echo in the echoing wood—
A lord of nature weeping to a tree.
I live between the heron and the wren,
Beasts of the hill and serpents of the den.

What's madness but nobility of soul
At odds with circumstance? The day's on fire!
I know the purity of pure despair,
My shadow pinned against a sweating wall.
That place among the rocks—is it a cave,
Or winding path? The edge is what I have.

A steady storm of correspondences!
A night flowing with birds, a ragged moon,
And in broad day the midnight come again!
A man goes far to find out what he is—
Death of the self in a long, tearless night,
All natural shapes blazing unnatural light.

Dark, dark my light, and darker my desire.
My soul, like some heat-maddened summer fly,
Keeps buzzing at the sill. Which I is *I*?
A fallen man, I climb out of my fear.
The mind enters itself, and God the mind,
And one is One, free in the tearing wind.

[1964]

Elizabeth Bishop

(1911–1979) b. Worcester, Massachusetts, United States

Disc 2
Tracks 44–46

Born on February 8, 1911, Elizabeth Bishop weathered an extremely unstable childhood. Her father died when she was less than a year old, and her mother suffered a number of nervous collapses before being committed permanently to a mental asylum when Bishop was five. Bishop was then sent to Nova Scotia to stay with her maternal grandparents, and then to Worcester, Massachusetts, to live with her aunt and uncle on her father's side. From 1927 to 1930, she attended Walnut Hill School outside Boston and then enrolled in Vassar College. She graduated from Vassar in May 1934, but not before meeting the poet Marianne Moore in March of that year. Despite their age difference (Moore was twenty-four years her senior) the two became quick friends, and Moore met Bishop's poetry with instrumental encouragement and guidance. In 1936, an anthology titled *Trial Balances* included a number of Bishop's poems and an introduction by Moore. This was Bishop's first major appearance in print; her poems had appeared previously only in the Vassar undergraduate magazine that she cofounded.

After Vassar, Bishop spent a few years traveling—over the course of which she befriended poets Randall Jarrell and Robert Lowell—before buying a home in Key West, Florida, in 1938. *North and South*, her first book of poems, proved difficult to sell to a publisher, but when it finally appeared in 1946, it won praise from many respected critics and poets of the day. She received several awards for it, including an appointment as the Consultant in Poetry for the Library of Congress (later renamed Poet Laureate). In 1951, making a dramatic change of life, Bishop moved to Brazil to live with her lover, a woman named Lota de Macedo Soares, the daughter of a wealthy Brazilian aristocrat. Although Bishop published little new work during this period, living in South America with Soares provided Bishop with much needed companionship and stability. In 1955, *North and South* was reprinted with many new poems, under the title *Poems: North and South—A Cold Spring*. Again, the volume received wide acclaim, and despite a few negative reviews, it won Bishop a Pulitzer Prize. It wasn't until 1965 that another full volume of new poetry was produced, *Questions of Travel*.

During the late '60s, the problems that had plagued Bishop's early years began to reappear. Her health again became fragile and her relationship with Soares started to strain; they both entered a period of depression. In 1966, Bishop took her first-ever teaching position at the University of Washington in Seattle and began to wean herself away from Brazil. A year later, Bishop took a trip to New York and met Soares there. That night, as Bishop slept, Soares swallowed an overdose of tranquilizers in their hotel room and collapsed into a coma that eventually proved fatal. Bishop spent the next few years disentangling herself from her life in Brazil and eventually assumed a permanent position at Harvard University. Bishop's final collection of poems, 1976's *Geography III*, contains some of her best-loved poems, including "In the Waiting Room," "The Moose," and the unforgettable villanelle, "One Art." Bishop died in Boston on October 6, 1979. Apart from her translations from the Portuguese, Spanish, and French, her *Complete Poems: 1927–1979* comprises little more than one hundred poems. Nonetheless, the impact made by this small body of work continues to be felt. Known as a "poet's poet" in her lifetime, Bishop's reputation has grown in recent years to include a wider audience, a dedicated following of those who appreciate her work's exacting craftsmanship and passionate attention to detail.

Jorie Graham on Elizabeth Bishop

Elizabeth Bishop was a remarkably original poet whom it would be difficult to place in any particular school. She is connected to American modernist poetry by her concern with the mechanics of the imagination, with what is "real" and how that reality is "invented." In this regard, she is sometimes linked with Wallace Stevens, for example (though she herself most loved George Herbert and Edward Lear).

That is why, more than in their apparent thematic situations—catching a fish and letting it go, describing a map, making a list of things one has lost, sitting in a dentist's waiting room reading the *National Geographic*—the heart of Elizabeth Bishop's extraordinary poems tends to be in the activity one has to engage in to read them.

A Bishop poem typically takes place on a border. We are journeying from one place to another, that journey being one towards knowledge and self-knowledge. "Place" becomes, in her poems, a notion, even a sensation, loaded with particular freight: it is, for example, in "The Map," simultaneously made of land, of history, of paper and ink, of fantasy and imagination. The state of just *being*, and the state of *imagining*, and the work of imagination involved in *reading*, become a way of reproducing what we, as humans, do when we create belief-systems: how we find the sacred in the mundane, the spiritual in the domestic, our pilgrim's "Journey" in the little tourist journey. One kind of reality doesn't "stand for" the other in Bishop's world. They are the same activity, but seen from different points of view. In her destabilizing of clear-cut boundaries between different kinds of "reality," Bishop asks us to feel our participation in the activity of imaginative reading. One can see this as a secular version of certain aspects of sacred rituals. Reimagining represented things comes close to resurrecting something in our very own selves—in our minds and bodies—which feels at once sacred and profane, mortal and immortal, made of time and at the same time quite deeply outside of time. She categorizes these simultaneous but conflicting states of being as many things, but most prominently as things in "geography" (not in time) and things in "history" (made of time).

So that just what a *place* is—a site called "here," felt by a spirit and a body to be sufficiently solid to hold us still, to hold us to a governed sense of "self"—and

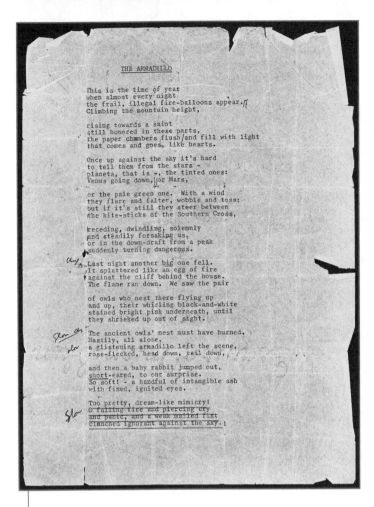

THE ARMADILLO

This is the time of year
when almost every night
the frail, illegal fire-balloons appear.
Climbing the mountain height,

rising towards a saint
still honored in these parts,
the paper chambers flush and fill with light
that comes and goes, like hearts.

Once up against the sky it's hard
to tell them from the stars -
planets, that is -, the tinted ones:
Venus going down, or Mars,

or the pale green one. With a wind
they flare and falter, wobble and toss;
but if it's still they steer between
the kite-sticks of the Southern Cross,

receding, dwindling, solemnly
and steadily forsaking us,
or in the down-draft from a peak
suddenly turning dangerous.

Last night another big one fell.
It splattered like an egg of fire
against the cliff behind the house.
The flame ran down. We saw the pair

of owls who nest there flying up
and up, their whirling black-and-white
stained bright pink underneath, until
they shrieked up out of sight.

The ancient owls' nest must have burned.
Hastily, all alone,
a glistening armadillo left the scene,
rose-flecked, head down, tail down,

and then a baby rabbit jumped out,
short-eared, to our surprise.
So soft! - a handful of intangible ash
with fixed, ignited eyes.

Too pretty, dream-like mimicry!
O falling fire and piercing cry
and panic, and a weak mailed fist
clenched ignorant against the sky.

Typescript with revisions of Bishop's "The Armadillo," which first appeared in *The New Yorker* in 1957, and which Robert Lowell considered the inspiration for his "Skunk Hour"

subsequently what that stillness, or stilling, of our multiplicity (an arrival of sorts) would entail, is the question. And it is a question usually posed with an explanatory sense of the other kind of "place," not ours, not us, not still. So her poems occur on: quais, shores, boatdecks, jungle-rims; at the edges of the natural world (gazing upon its landscapes, seascapes, birds, fish, mythic creatures, emissaries of all kinds). They occur at the border of wilderness of spirit and the domesticated self (where a *scream* cracks open a dentist's waiting room, or where one's "self" feels itself to be both an unknowable vortex called "I" and an artificially stilled "Elizabeth"). Sometimes the border is that between the made and what it represents, and one finds oneself peering from this moment of history into another, via a book, a fable, a mechanical toy, a science magazine. Sometimes one is thrown down at the border of all kinds of other "realms": biblical scene, oil painting of seascape, etching of imagined scene. In her early work, the borders she most often straddles are those of the real and the surreal, the real and the supernatural, the actual and the versions of the actual as represented by memory or imagination.

Increasingly urgently, in Bishop's work, we are made to feel we exist—we take form—(and *make* form)—in that conflagration called *here*, and that the passage of time will take us, inexorably, to some place or condition called *there*. Our destination? A reality that can hold not merely perception but also disappointment and grief and disbelief within bounds that render it (albeit barely) endurable.

Because we both *take* this journey, and *are* this journey, we need a very particular kind of map: a Bishop poem is that map. As with all maps, it attempts to locate us in *relation* to place—a location whose initial effect may be one of *dis*location.

Looking at *The Map*, we are made to feel the strange-god's eye view any map represents, showing us all place by the same means, at the same remove. It invites us to find where we are in such all-inclusiveness, what ground (or point of view) we hold at our eerily mental distance. Are we strangers, nationals, tourists, pilgrims, angels, conquerors?

In addition, this mysterious map (as it moves—via our interpretation, musing, curiosity—from its apparent objectivity into our subjectivity) begins to make us feel the slippages between where we are to go, where we *might* go—perhaps, even where we actually *should* go. It suggests, with great understatement, the large moral, and even political, anxieties representation can awaken, as the world, in this strangely mediated, apparently unemotional version of itself, crosses over from one level of visibility—there, colored paper, in our hands—to a strange invisibility (what on earth is *in* that pink zone?) (or *behind* that city name?) (or *meant* by that cartoon-like resemblance)—and then on to new, more complicated and more "whole" levels of visibility: the child-like imagination of place; the description of it; and eventually the actual encounter with it where it is, in effect, invented—meaning by that, "made real."

What aspect of imagination carries one to any of these destinations? And why—given *that* going—*go* at all, why enter the temporal realm of becoming, when one can, in essence, by not going, *be* everywhere? This is the problem of incarnation of course, the tragedy—and eventual grace—of the limits of individuality, the fall into division choice enacts, body dictates, and knowledge requires.

There is a peculiar brilliant possibility always implied in such a dilemma: to go and not go at once, to be here and there at once, to be divided—fragmented even—into subjective and objective sensations of self and world, and then to be doubled, as it were, by "travel" out of the single point-of-view, into a wholeness. Such complex constructions of self (and soul) are what Bishop is after.

To read a Bishop poem is to experience dizzying shifts of mental activity. In *The Map*, for example, we are asked to "read" both "lies" and "shadowed" as simultaneously the actions of *actual* land against water at land's end, *actual* shadowings of water in water, *and* the images of the land's edge represented by the map maker's "laying" of its outline and "shadowing" of it by map-coloration. There is no final resolution. It is her genius that both "readings" are true. By this trilling *between* realities—from the enormity of land to the rendering of it on a map—she helps us experience the spiritually enlarging sensation that both the more temporally stained one (real land, real passage of light occasioning shadowing) and the more radically atemporal one (pattern on paper representing that land) are equally present dimensions by which consciousness apprehends reality.

Also prominent are her acts of self-revision. "Shadows, or are they shallows" stresses simultaneously the piercing need for precision in the act-of-looking, and the equally urgent act of looking via words, not just via eyes. The verb "showing" leaves us squarely in that doubleness, referring us both to the actual place and the mapmaker's. The "edges/ledges" rhyme reemphasizes this telescopic doubleness. Weeds are "real" (i.e., they live and die in time). The "hanging down" is, too, real—we don't see weeds on a map, they are "imagined." The "simple blue" tugs us back towards the mapmaker's two-dimensionality.

The Vermeer-like calm of Bishop's apparently simple-spoken surfaces establishes other even subtler sensations, or regions, of reality, each with its own relative duration: the childlike, fabulistic tone of the two "surreal" questions; the mild fairy-tale-like personifications where the land "leans down" "to lift the sea from under." What size are these protagonists? In what world and time is that action occurring? These are the kinds of questions her poems invite us to feel. Her unique understanding of the symbiotic relationship between the shifting nature of duration—how long a thing lasts or takes to "take place"—and the reality-status of such a thing in the world, radically opens up different regions in what we conventionally feel to be the unbreakable realm called "reality." And yet she is so soft-spoken, one might, without closely enacted reading, never notice.

The Fish

I caught a tremendous fish
and held him beside the boat
half out of water, with my hook
fast in a corner of his mouth.
He didn't fight.
He hadn't fought at all.
He hung a grunting weight,
battered and venerable
and homely. Here and there
his brown skin hung in strips
like ancient wallpaper,
and its pattern of darker brown
was like wallpaper:
shapes like full-blown roses
stained and lost through age.
He was speckled with barnacles,
fine rosettes of lime,
and infested
with tiny white sea-lice,
and underneath two or three
rags of green weed hung down.
While his gills were breathing in
the terrible oxygen
—the frightening gills,
fresh and crisp with blood,
that can cut so badly—
I thought of the coarse white flesh
packed in like feathers,
the big bones and the little bones,
the dramatic reds and blacks
of his shiny entrails,
and the pink swim-bladder
like a big peony.
I looked into his eyes
which were far larger than mine
but shallower, and yellowed,
the irises backed and packed
with tarnished tinfoil
seen through the lenses
of old scratched isinglass.
They shifted a little, but not
to return my stare.
—It was more like the tipping
of an object toward the light.
I admired his sullen face,
the mechanism of his jaw,
and then I saw
that from his lower lip
—if you could call it a lip—
grim, wet, and weaponlike,
hung five old pieces of fish-line,
or four and a wire leader
with the swivel still attached,
with all their five big hooks
grown firmly in his mouth.
A green line, frayed at the end
where he broke it, two heavier lines,
and a fine black thread
still crimped from the strain and snap
when it broke and he got away.
Like medals with their ribbons
frayed and wavering,
a five-haired beard of wisdom
trailing from his aching jaw.
I stared and stared
and victory filled up
the little rented boat,
from the pool of bilge
where oil had spread a rainbow
around the rusted engine
to the bailer rusted orange,
the sun-cracked thwarts,
the oarlocks on their strings,
the gunnels—until everything
was rainbow, rainbow, rainbow!
And I let the fish go.

[1946]

The Map

Land lies in water; it is shadowed green.
Shadows, or are they shallows, at its edges
showing the line of long sea-weeded ledges
where weeds hang to the simple blue from green.
Or does the land lean down to lift the sea from under,
drawing it unperturbed around itself?
Along the fine tan sandy shelf
is the land tugging at the sea from under?

The shadow of Newfoundland lies flat and still.
Labrador's yellow, where the moony Eskimo
has oiled it. We can stroke these lovely bays,
under a glass as if they were expected to blossom,
or as if to provide a clean cage for invisible fish.
The names of seashore towns run out to sea,
the names of cities cross the neighboring mountains
—the printer here experiencing the same excitement
as when emotion too far exceeds its cause.
These peninsulas take the water between thumb and finger
like women feeling for the smoothness of yard-goods.

Mapped waters are more quiet than the land is,
lending the land their waves' own conformation:
and Norway's hare runs south in agitation,
profiles investigate the sea, where land is.
Are they assigned, or can the countries pick their colors?
—What suits the character or the native waters best.
Topography displays no favorites; North's as near as West.
More delicate than the historians' are the map-makers' colors.

[1946]

The Armadillo

For Robert Lowell

This is the time of year
when almost every night
the frail, illegal fire balloons appear.
Climbing the mountain height,

rising toward a saint
still honored in these parts,
the paper chambers flush and fill with light
that comes and goes, like hearts.

Once up against the sky it's hard
to tell them from the stars—
planets, that is—the tinted ones:
Venus going down, or Mars,

or the pale green one. With a wind,
they flare and falter, wobble and toss;
but if it's still they steer between
the kite sticks of the Southern Cross,

receding, dwindling, solemnly
and steadily forsaking us,
or, in the downdraft from a peak,
suddenly turning dangerous.

Last night another big one fell.
It splattered like an egg of fire
against the cliff behind the house.
The flame ran down. We saw the pair

of owls who nest there flying up
and up, their whirling black-and-white
stained bright pink underneath, until
they shrieked up out of sight.

The ancient owls' nest must have burned.
Hastily, all alone,
a glistening armadillo left the scene,
rose-flecked, head down, tail down,

and then a baby rabbit jumped out,
short-eared, to our surprise.
So soft!—a handful of intangible ash
with fixed, ignited eyes.

Too pretty, dreamlike mimicry!
O falling fire and piercing cry
and panic, and a weak mailed fist
clenched ignorant against the sky!

[1965]

Crusoe in England

A new volcano has erupted,
the papers say, and last week I was reading
where some ship saw an island being born:
at first a breath of steam, ten miles away;
and then a black fleck—basalt, probably—
rose in the mate's binoculars
and caught on the horizon like a fly.
They named it. But my poor old island's still
un-rediscovered, un-renamable.
None of the books has ever got it right.

Well, I had fifty-two
miserable, small volcanoes I could climb
with a few slithery strides—
volcanoes dead as ash heaps.
I used to sit on the edge of the highest one
and count the others standing up,
naked and leaden, with their heads blown off.
I'd think that if they were the size
I thought volcanoes should be, then I had
become a giant;
and if I had become a giant,
I couldn't bear to think what size
the goats and turtles were,
or the gulls, or the overlapping rollers
—a glittering hexagon of rollers
closing and closing in, but never quite,
glittering and glittering, though the sky
was mostly overcast.

My island seemed to be
a sort of cloud-dump. All the hemisphere's
left-over clouds arrived and hung
above the craters—their parched throats
were hot to touch.
Was that why it rained so much?
And why sometimes the whole place hissed?
The turtles lumbered by, high-domed,

hissing like teakettles.
(And I'd have given years, or taken a few,
for any sort of kettle, of course.)
The folds of lava, running out to sea,
would hiss. I'd turn. And then they'd prove
to be more turtles.
The beaches were all lava, variegated,
black, red, and white, and gray;
the marbled colors made a fine display.
And I had waterspouts. Oh,
half a dozen at a time, far out,
they'd come and go, advancing and retreating,
their heads in cloud, their feet in moving patches
of scuffed-up white.
Glass chimneys, flexible, attenuated,
sacerdotal beings of glass…I watched
the water spiral up in them like smoke.
Beautiful, yes, but not much company.

I often gave way to self-pity.
"Do I deserve this? I suppose I must.
I wouldn't be here otherwise. Was there
a moment when I actually chose this?
I don't remember, but there could have been."
What's wrong about self-pity, anyway?
With my legs dangling down familiarly
over a crater's edge, I told myself
"Pity should begin at home." So the more
pity I felt, the more I felt at home.

The sun set in the sea; the same odd sun
rose from the sea,
and there was one of it and one of me.
The island had one kind of everything:
one tree snail, a bright violet-blue
with a thin shell, crept over everything,
over the one variety of tree,
a sooty, scrub affair.
Snail shells lay under these in drifts
and, at a distance,
you'd swear that they were beds of irises.

There was one kind of berry, a dark red.
I tried it, one by one, and hours apart.
Sub-acid, and not bad, no ill effects;
and so I made home-brew. I'd drink
the awful, fizzy, stinging stuff
that went straight to my head
and play my home-made flute
(I think it had the weirdest scale on earth)
and, dizzy, whoop and dance among the goats.
Home-made, home-made! But aren't we all?
I felt a deep affection for
the smallest of my island industries.
No, not exactly, since the smallest was
a miserable philosophy.

Because I didn't know enough.
Why didn't I know enough of something?
Greek drama or astronomy? The books
I'd read were full of blanks;
the poems—well, I tried
reciting to my iris-beds,
"They flash upon that inward eye,
which is the bliss…" The bliss of what?
One of the first things that I did
when I got back was look it up.

The island smelled of goat and guano.
The goats were white, so were the gulls,
and both too tame, or else they thought
I was a goat, too, or a gull.
Baa, baa, baa and *shriek, shriek, shriek,*
*baa…shriek…baa…*I still can't shake
them from my ears; they're hurting now.
The questioning shrieks, the equivocal replies
over a ground of hissing rain
and hissing, ambulating turtles
got on my nerves.

When all the gulls flew up at once, they sounded
like a big tree in a strong wind, its leaves.
I'd shut my eyes and think about a tree,

an oak, say, with real shade, somewhere.
I'd heard of cattle getting island-sick.
I thought the goats were.
One billy-goat would stand on the volcano
I'd christened *Mont d'Espoir* or *Mount Despair*
(I'd time enough to play with names),
and bleat and bleat, and sniff the air.
I'd grab his beard and look at him.
His pupils, horizontal, narrowed up
and expressed nothing, or a little malice.
I got so tired of the very colors!
One day I dyed a baby goat bright red
with my red berries, just to see
something a little different.
And then his mother wouldn't recognize him.

Dreams were the worst. Of course I dreamed of food
and love, but they were pleasant rather
than otherwise. But then I'd dream of things
like slitting a baby's throat, mistaking it
for a baby goat. I'd have
nightmares of other islands
stretching away from mine, infinities
of islands, islands spawning islands,
like frogs' eggs turning into polliwogs
of islands, knowing that I had to live
on each and every one, eventually,
for ages, registering their flora,
their fauna, their geography.

Just when I thought I couldn't stand it
another minute longer, Friday came.
(Accounts of that have everything all wrong.)
Friday was nice.
Friday was nice, and we were friends.
If only he had been a woman!
I wanted to propagate my kind,
and so did he, I think, poor boy.
He'd pet the baby goats sometimes,
and race with them, or carry one around.
—Pretty to watch; he had a pretty body.

And then one day they came and took us off.

Now I live here, another island,
that doesn't seem like one, but who decides?
My blood was full of them; my brain
bred islands. But that archipelago
has petered out. I'm old.
I'm bored, too, drinking my real tea,
surrounded by uninteresting lumber.
The knife there on the shelf—
it reeked of meaning, like a crucifix.
It lived. How many years did I
beg it, implore it, not to break?
I knew each nick and scratch by heart,
the bluish blade, the broken tip,
the lines of wood-grain on the handle…
Now it won't look at me at all.
The living soul has dribbled away.
My eyes rest on it and pass on.

The local museum's asked me to
leave everything to them:
the flute, the knife, the shrivelled shoes,
my shedding goatskin trousers
(moths have got in the fur),
the parasol that took me such a time
remembering the way the ribs should go.
It still will work but, folded up,
looks like a plucked and skinny fowl.
How can anyone want such things?
—And Friday, my dear Friday, died of measles
seventeen years ago come March.

[1976]

One Art

The art of losing isn't hard to master;
so many things seem filled with the intent
to be lost that their loss is no disaster.

Lose something every day. Accept the fluster
of lost door keys, the hour badly spent.
The art of losing isn't hard to master.

Then practice losing farther, losing faster:
places, and names, and where it was you meant
to travel. None of these will bring disaster.

I lost my mother's watch. And look! my last, or
next-to-last, of three loved houses went.
The art of losing isn't hard to master.

I lost two cities, lovely ones. And, vaster,
some realms I owned, two rivers, a continent.
I miss them, but it wasn't a disaster.

—Even losing you (the joking voice, a gesture
I love) I shan't have lied. It's evident
the art of losing's not too hard to master
though it may look like (*Write* it!) like disaster.

[1976]

In the Waiting Room

In Worcester, Massachusetts,
I went with Aunt Consuelo
to keep her dentist's appointment
and sat and waited for her
in the dentist's waiting room.
It was winter. It got dark
early. The waiting room
was full of grown-up people,
arctics and overcoats,
lamps and magazines.
My aunt was inside
what seemed like a long time
and while I waited I read
the *National Geographic*
(I could read) and carefully
studied the photographs:
the inside of a volcano,
black, and full of ashes;
then it was spilling over
in rivulets of fire.
Osa and Martin Johnson
dressed in riding breeches,
laced boots, and pith helmets.
A dead man slung on a pole
—"Long Pig," the caption said.
Babies with pointed heads
wound round and round with string;
black, naked women with necks
wound round and round with wire
like the necks of light bulbs.
Their breasts were horrifying.
I read it right straight through.
I was too shy to stop.
And then I looked at the cover:
the yellow margins, the date.

Suddenly, from inside,
came an *oh!* of pain
—Aunt Consuelo's voice—
not very loud or long.
I wasn't at all surprised;
even then I knew she was
a foolish, timid woman.
I might have been embarrassed,
but wasn't. What took me
completely by surprise
was that it was *me*:
my voice, in my mouth.
Without thinking at all
I was my foolish aunt,
I—we—were falling, falling,
our eyes glued to the cover
of the *National Geographic*,
February, 1918.

I said to myself: three days
and you'll be seven years old.
I was saying it to stop
the sensation of falling off
the round, turning world
into cold, blue-black space.
But I felt: you are an *I*,
you are an *Elizabeth*,
you are one the *them*.
Why should you be one, too?
I scarcely dared to look
to see what it was I was.
I gave a sidelong glance
—I couldn't look any higher—
at shadowy gray knees,
trousers and skirts and boots
and different pairs of hands
lying under the lamps.
I knew that nothing stranger

had ever happened, that nothing
stranger could ever happen.
Why should I be my aunt,
or me, or anyone?
What similarities—
boots, hands, the family voice
I felt in my throat, or even
the *National Geographic*
and those awful hanging breasts—
held us all together
or made us all just one?
How—I didn't know any
word for it—how "unlikely"…
How had I come to be here,
like them, and overhear
a cry of pain that could have
got loud and worse but hadn't?

The waiting room was bright
and too hot. It was sliding
beneath a big black wave,
another, and another.

Then I was back in it.
The War was on. Outside,
in Worcester, Massachusetts,
were night and slush and cold,
and it was still the fifth
of February, 1918.

[1976]

May Swenson

(1913-1989) b. b. Logan, Utah, United States

Disc 2

Track 47–49

Anna Thilda May Swenson was born on May 28, 1913, the first of ten children, to an immigrant Swedish couple, Margaret and Dan Arthur Swenson, who settled there as Mormon converts. The family's first language, and hers, was Swedish. Swenson later put her bilingual skills to use as a translator of Swedish poetry, including *Windows and Stones: Selected Poems of Tomas Tranströmer* in 1972. Swenson's father was a professor of mechanical engineering at the State University at Logan, from which she received a bachelor's degree in English in 1939, after which she worked as a reporter for a Salt Lake City newspaper.

Swenson soon moved to New York City, which marked the beginning of her literary career. She worked as a stenographer but chiefly wrote "quite extraordinary poetry," according to Elizabeth Bishop, who met Swenson at Yaddo in 1950 (Bishop also considered her "awfully cute").They remained lifelong friends. By 1952 Swenson's work began appearing in *Poetry, The New Yorker*, and other magazines, and eventually in *Paris Review, The Atlantic Monthly*, and *The Hudson Review*. Her first collection, *Another Animal*, was published by Scribner's in 1954.

In 1959, after several teaching jobs, Swenson became an editor at New Directions, a position she held for seven years until she resigned to write full time. As book succeeded book—*A Cage of Spines* (1958), *To Mix with Time: New and Selected Poems* (1963), *Half Sun Half Sleep* (1967), *Iconographs* (1970), and *In Other Words* (1987) among them, so did her honors, most notably the Shelley Poetry Award, a Guggenheim fellowship, an Amy Lowell Traveling Scholarship, the Bollingen Prize for poetry, and in 1987 a John D. and Catherine T. MacArthur Fellowship. She was a Chancellor of the Academy of American Poets from 1980 until her death. Harold Bloom called her "one of the three best woman poets of the twentieth century" along with Marianne Moore and Elizabeth Bishop. Critics admired her "eye for detail" *(Time)*, her search for clarity, and her ability to use nature as an expression of sexuality. Poet Dennis Sampson described Swenson as "mischievous, inquisitive in the extreme, totally given over to the task of witnessing the physical world." Although she never concealed her sexual identity, she rejected offers to be represented in anthologies of lesbian writing.

Surprisingly, most anthologists during her lifetime failed to include her. Some may not have been able to take seriously her typographical experiments in poems where she was attempting to suggest her subjects graphically on the page. Or perhaps one should say "feel her subjects," because the typography in such poems is once again an attempt to enter them. Her volume *Iconographs* (1970) is composed entirely of such poems, most of which had been available earlier in journals. Her interest in science, especially space travel, is especially evident in *Iconographs* and in her collection *Half Sun Half Sleep*. In an essay first published in 1966 she defined the experience of poetry as "based in a craving to get through the curtains of things as they *appear,* to things as they *are,* and then into the larger, wilder space of things as they *are becoming.*" The definition was meant to apply to all poetry, but it applies more specifically to her typographical poems.

Swenson died in Oceanview, Delaware, on December 4, 1989 and is buried in her hometown of Logan. A collection of Swenson's prose pieces, *Made with Words*, appeared in 1990, the year after her death. It included short stories, a one-act play *(The Floor)* which had a New York production in 1966, interviews, and book reviews, as well as a selection of her letters to Elizabeth Bishop. Among her other legacies is an annual poetry contest in her name conducted by the University of Utah Press. The writer Rozanne Knudson, her literary executor, was her partner for twenty-three years.

Grace Schulman on May Swenson

> *Body my house*
> *my horse my hound*
> *what will I do*
> *when you are fallen*
> *Where will I sleep*
> *How will I ride*
> *What will I hunt . . .*

From the day I first read May Swenson's "Question" aloud, those lines have stalked me, and perhaps they always will. They are hypnotic, having the rhythmic pull of a chant, the tone of awe. They terrify with the shocking awareness that my body is not the real me. They follow with insistent questions—"what will I do," "How will I ride," "What will I hunt," "Where can I go"—all ironic because they cannot be answered.

Some years after I first read the poem, I saw an early version, scribbled and crossed out, line after discarded line, its wonder gone. "Body" was the name of Swenson's dog, her "good bright dog," as he is referred to, briefly, in the final draft. The original version dwelled on the poignant but more limited subject of its death.

That discovery, though daunting at first, did not trouble me for long. The poet was an endless reviser. Unexpectedly, in contrast to the mysterious aura of her poems, her composition was methodical. She kept a file filled with drafts, handwritten and typed, of nearly everything she wrote, sometimes as many as twenty sheets per poem. She placed them in folders, dated, the first being the draft she retyped and sent to an editor.

Swenson is a master at her craft. Whether her subjects are commonplace or unfamiliar, she presents them with an urgency that heightens their impact. Often her poems, like "Question," are pitched low, having the tone of chatty, intimate speech, and at the same time, the music of charms, spells, and ritual dances.

It's about the ball the bat & the mit
Ball hits bat or hits mit
Bat doesn't hit ball Bat meets it
Ball bounces off bat flies air or
thuds ground dud or it →
fits mit

Bat wants for ball to mate
Ball hates to take bat's bait
Bat flirts ball's late don't keep the date
goes home thwack to mit
goes out back to mit

mit fits ball but not all
the time Sometimes ball
quits mit falls in disgrace
That's about "the bases loaded"
about the ~~~~ "exploded"

It's about the ball the bat the mit
the base and the fan
It's done
on a diamond and for fun
It's about Home and it's about Run

5/25/69

May Swenson wrote this initial draft of her poem *Analysis of Baseball* in the car on the way home from a Yankees game.

May Swenson is a poet of endless curiosity. With nothing less than pure wonder, she considers the Statue of Liberty, Washington Square, the sight of land from a plane. In "A Watch," the poet recalls its repair in a shop where she "felt privileged but also pained to watch the operation." With gleaming word-play ("my ticker going lickety-split"), she regards the watch as it becomes, metaphorically, a patient undergoing surgery.

Her intellectual probing is accompanied by a passionate identification with her subjects. She is fascinated with technology, such as anti-matter, electronic sound, DNA, and the miraculous first photo of the entire planet Earth taken from above the moon, this last in a poem called "Orbiter 5 Shows How Earth Looks from the Moon." Cast in the shape of the earth photo, that poem is striking for language that fairly leaps out of its picture ("A woman in the earth. / A man in the moon."). Nature, especially, enchants this poet: the lion's yearning, autumn's "bruise-reds." In "The Woods at Night," she sees "The binocular owl, / fastened to a limb / like a lantern / all night long."

Swenson's love poems are vivid and moving. They are low-spoken, seductive, and sly, but with outcries such as: "Burn radiant sex born scorpion need." In them, she regards the human body in a way that enlarges the dread of its loss. The best of them are poems of intense love between women, composed at a time when that subject was rare in poetry. Sadly, they were written in the closet and published only after her death. Their lesbian imagery is subtle and brilliantly dramatized: "I open to your dew, / beginning in the spring again . . ." ("Annual"); "I exist in your verdant garden . . . I unfurled in your rich soil" ("You Are"). And this, from "Neither Wanting More":

To feel your breast
rise with a sigh
to hold you mirrored
in my eye
Neither wanting more
Neither asking why

Most remarkable, here and elsewhere, is Swenson's intimacy with the natural world. "At Truro" finds the poet so close to the sea as to read her own biography in the encroaching waves. She sees herself as a crab, a coral, a sea worm, until, caught like a fish to dry on land, she strikes a dark note: "In brightness I lost track / of my underworld / of ultraviolet wisdom." But the sea remains in her, as we learn at the poem's startling conclusion: "As if the sun were blind / again I feel the suck / of the sea's dark mind." Like other of her poems, this one compels, haunts, surprises, catches us unaware. Swenson is at once a magician, a shaman, a close friend, an intelligent companion. To read her is to be enthralled. I, for one, will never stop.

May Swenson in Cape Cod

Body my house
my horse my hound
what will I do
when you are fallen

Where will I sleep
How will I ride
What will I hunt

Where can I go
without my mount
all eager and quick
How will I know
in thicket ahead
is danger or treasure
when Body my good
bright dog is dead

How will it be
to lie in the sky
without roof or door
and wind for an eye

With cloud for shift
how will I hide?

[1954]

The Watch

CD 2 / TRACK 49

When I
took my
watch to the watchfixer I
felt privileged but also pained to watch the operation. He
had long fingernails and a voluntary squint. He
fixed a magnifying cup over his
squint eye. He
undressed my
watch. I
watched him
split her
in three layers and lay her
middle—a quivering viscera—in a circle on a little plinth. He
shoved shirtsleeves up and leaned like an ogre over my
naked watch. With critical pincers he
poked and stirred. He
lifted out little private things with a magnet too tiny for me
to watch almost. "Watch out!" I
almost said. His
eye watched, enlarged, the secrets of my
watch, and I
watched anxiously. Because what if he
touched her
ticker too rough, and she
gave up the ghost out of pure fright? Or put her
things back backwards so she'd
run backwards after this? Or he
might lose a minuscule part, connected to her

exquisite heart, and mix her
up, instead of fix her.
And all the time,
all the time-
pieces on the walls, on the shelves, told the time,
told the time
in swishes and ticks,
swishes and ticks
and seemed to be gloating, as they watched and told. I
felt faint, I
was about to lose my
breath—my
ticker going lickety-split—when watchfixer clipped her
three slices together with a gleam and two flicks of his
tools like chopsticks. He
spat out his
eye, lifted her
high, gave her
a twist, set her
hands right, and laid her
little face, quite as usual, in its place on my
wrist.

[1963]

At Truro

The sea is unfolding scrolls
and rolling them up again.
It is an ancient diary

the waves are murmuring.
The words are white curls,
great capitals are seen

on the wrinkled swells.
Repeated rhythmically
it seems to me I read

my own biography.
Once I was a sea bird
With beak a sharp pen,

I drew my signature on air.
There is a chapter when,
a crab, I slowly scratched

my name on a sandy page,
and once, a coral, wrote
a record of my age

on the wall of a water-grotto.
When I was a sea worm
I never saw the sun,

but flowed, a salty germ,
in the bloodstream of the sea.
There I left an alphabet

but it grew dim to me.
Something caught me in its net,
took me from the deep

book of the ocean, weaned me,
put fin and wing to sleep,
made me stand and made me

face the sun's dry eye.
On the shore of intellect
I forgot how to fly

above the wave, below it.
When I touched my foot
to land's thick back,

it stuck like stem or root.
In brightness I lost track
of my underworld

of ultraviolet wisdom.
My fiery head furled
up its cool kingdom

and put night away.
The sea is unfolding scrolls,
and rolling them up.

As if the sun were blind
again I feel the suck
of the sea's dark mind.

[1964]

Orbiter 5 Shows How Earth Looks From the Moon

ORBITER 5 SHOWS
HOW EARTH LOOKS FROM THE MOON

There's a woman in the earth, sitting on
her heels. You see her from the back, in three-
quarter profile. She has a flowing pigtail. She's
holding something in her right hand—some holy jug. Her left arm is thinner,
in a gesture like a dancer. She's the Indian Ocean. Asia is
light swirling up out of her vessel. Her pigtail points to Europe
and her dancer's arm is the Suez Canal. She is a woman
in a square kimono, bare feet tucked beneath the tip of Africa. Her tail of long hair is
the Arabian Peninsula.

A woman in the earth.

A man in the moon.

[1967]

July 4th

Gradual bud and bloom and seedfall speeded up
are these mute explosions in slow motion.

From vertical shoots above the sea, the fire
flowers open, shedding their petals.

Black waves, turned more than moonwhite, pink
ice, lightning blue, echo our gasps of admiration

as they crash and hush. Another bush ablaze
snicks straight up. A gap like heartstop between

the last vanished particle and the thuggish boom.
And the thuggish boom repeats in stutters

from sandhill hollows in the shore. We want
more. A twirling sun, or dismembered chrysanthemum

bulleted up, leisurely bursts, in an instant
timestreak is suckswooped back to its core.

And we want more: we want red giant, white dwarf,
black hole, extinct, orgasmic, all in one!

[1972]

The Woods at Night

The binocular owl,
fastened to a limb
like a lantern
all night long,

sees where all
the other birds sleep:
towhee under leaves,
titmouse deep

in a twighouse,
sapsucker gripped
to a knothole lip,
redwing in the reeds,

swallow in the willow,
flicker in the oak—
but cannot see poor
whippoorwill!

under the hill
in deadbrush nest,
who's awake, too—
with striken eye

flayed by the moon
her brindled breast
repeats, repeats, repeats its plea
for cruelty.

[1978]

Robert Hayden

(1913–1980) b. Detroit, Michigan, United States

Disc 2
Tracks 50–52

Robert Hayden was born Asa Bundy Sheffey on August 4, 1913. His parents, Asa and Ruth Sheffy, had separated before his birth. Unable to raise him, his mother gave him over to foster parents named William and Sue Ellen Hayden; because the Haydens lived next door, she was able to visit her son frequently throughout his childhood. Hayden would later remember these visits from his mother as the most edifying and enjoyable moments of his upbringing, for the relations with his adoptive family were quite strained. After completing high school, Hayden entered Detroit City College (now Wayne State University) on a scholarship allegedly obtained with the assistance of a woman who had seen him reading a book of Countee Cullen's poetry while standing in a welfare line. However, even with the scholarship, the costs of college proved too much for Hayden and he was forced to drop out in 1936, one credit short of graduation. Having already published a few poems in various literary magazines, Hayden was able to get a job with the Work Progress Administration researching black history and culture, especially the abolition movement and the Underground Railroad. Much of this research would inform his later poetry.

In June 1940, Hayden married Erma Inez Morris, a music teacher and concert pianist, and published his first volume of poems, *Heart-Shape in the Dust*. Published locally, it received only minimal attention from the literary community, and Hayden himself would later criticize the volume. Hayden enrolled in the University of Michigan at Ann Arbor to pursue graduate studies in 1942, the same year that poet W.H. Auden began teaching there. Auden would become an enormous influence on Hayden's poetry from that time on. After serving as a teaching assistant for two years, Hayden was able to obtain a professorship at Fisk University in 1946. Hayden continued to write poetry and publish volumes throughout the 1940s and '50s, but they were never very widely distributed and he continued to go largely unnoticed. It was not until the 1960s that his literary reputation began to take root, and in 1966, it blossomed: Hayden received the Grand Prix de la Poésie at the First World Festival of Negro Arts in Senegal for his volume *Ballad of Remembrance*. That same year, he was appointed Senegal's Poet Laureate. Now with an international audience, Hayden republished a selection of his best work from the last several decades. His *Selected Poems* (1966) brought him instant acclaim as a poet of rare artistry—and as one of the leading African-American poets of the day. The most trenchant criticism of his poetry, however, came from within the black literary community itself, as politically motivated poets condemned Hayden for not taking a more vociferous stance on racial issues in his work.

Despite this condemnation, Hayden's reputation reached new proportions in the 1970s. In 1975, he was elected to the Academy of American Poets and, in that same year, he was appointed Poetry Consultant to the Library of Congress (later renamed Poet Laureate), becoming the first African-American ever to hold that position. He continued to teach and to publish poems, many of them his best, until his death in Ann Arbor in 1980. Although he did live to receive the kind of respect as a poet that he sought throughout his career, he is only now beginning to receive widespread recognition as one of his generation's greatest practitioners of the art.

Marilyn Nelson on Robert Hayden

The father whose name Robert Hayden briefly bore left the family prior to his birth; his mother gave him away to neighbors who renamed and raised him. Hayden's foster father was a hardworking, sternly devout Baptist; his foster mother bitter and disappointed. Hayden was a bookish child, forced by extreme nearsightedness to wear bottle-bottom-thick glasses. He was one of few African-American students in his high school.

In 1942, with his wife Erma pregnant with their only child, Maia, Hayden entered graduate school in English at the University of Michigan, where he studied with W.H. Auden. Auden recognized him as a fellow poet on the first day of class, asking the young Hayden to come to the front of the lecture hall to read a poem aloud. Auden was Hayden's mentor for several years. In 1943, Hayden's first published poem appeared in *Poetry Magazine,* and Hayden became a Baha'i. He then took a position at Fisk University in Nashville, one of the most highly respected of the traditionally black institutions of higher education. He taught for twenty-three years on the Fisk faculty, gently guiding a generation of younger African-American writers. Visitors today may be shown his modest former home just off the Fisk campus, and his annotated private library is dispersed in the Fisk library stacks, just waiting to be mined for a dissertation. During the cataclysm of the '60s, Hayden's serenity became so unfashionable that he was dismissed as "a pathetic irrelevance" by a generation of obtuse young militant black writers. When, after twenty-three years, he was replaced as writer-in-residence at Fisk by a novelist (whose work has largely been forgotten), Hayden moved back to Michigan to join the faculty of the University of Michigan.

Despite his relative isolation from the power-brokers of the African-American arts world, Hayden enjoyed a growing international reputation. He was awarded the Grand Prix de la Poésie at the pan-Diaspora First World Festival of Negro Arts held in Dakar in 1969, and was named Poet Laureate of Senegal. One imagines there may be some Hayden poems in French that have not yet been discovered by the American audience. In the following years, two major collections of his poems were published in the United States, he was elected a Fellow of the Academy of American Poets, and he served two two-year terms as Consultant in Poetry to the Library of Congress, the position now called Poet Laureate of the United States. He was the first African-American to hold that honor. He was further honored during this period by President Jimmy Carter in a formal White House ceremony. On February 24, 1980, the Center for Afro-American and African Studies at the University of Michigan hosted a national conference called "A Tribute to Robert Hayden." Ill with cancer, Hayden was unable to attend this gala event, but he was told about it and spoke with some of the poets and scholars who had come to wintry Detroit to celebrate him. Knowing he was dying, the conferees prayed for his peace. He died the following day at the age of sixty-two. A *tzaddik's* death: at peace with the world and with his Creator. The Baha'i Faith, central to Hayden's life and work, was founded by Husayn-Ali, a Persian nobleman born in 1817, known today as Baha'u'llah ("The Glory of God"). The basic tenets of Baha'u'llah's teaching are that God is One, that we are all one race, and that all major religions are paths leading toward the one center. Baha'ullah's coming was prepared by another great holy man, the Ba'b, the founder of a religion called the Babi movement, which spread like brush-fire in Iran, and was persecuted by the Muslim power elite. Baha'u'llah received the first of his revelations while imprisoned as an advocate of the Ba'b in Teheran's notorious "Black Pit" prison. He was released into exile. He spent the rest of his life outside of his native land, moving from Baghdad to Constantinople, Greece, Smyrna, Alexandria, Jaffa, Haifa, and finally arriving at Acre, in what is now Israel. The map of his exile forms a spiral encompassing the Middle East. Baha'u'llah's vision of history resembles Yeats' gyres: he taught that our age, the Millennial Century, is approaching a pivot-point; that the wrenching changes the world is experiencing are the necessary processes by which the human race will finally come to the realization of its capacity for humanness. Baha'u'llah received many revelations, which were recorded and authenticated at the time they were revealed: either written in Baha'u'llah's own flowing script or recorded in shorthand Arabic by a scribe, then transcribed with Baha'u'llah's oversight and approval.

Hayden is best known for his widely anthologized earlier poems, such as the semi-confessional "The Whipping" and "Those Winter Sundays." They are translucent, layered poems which can be savored again and again. His history poems are also well known, most notably his masterpiece, "Middle Passage." Less easily accessible, and for that reason less familiar, are the poems in which Hayden offers some of Baha'u'llah's teachings. One of these is "El-Hajj Malik El-Shabazz," Hayden's tribute to the brother formerly known as Malcolm X.

Like all of Hayden's history poems, this one is steeped in accurate detail. Hayden's poems are often bearers of precise words and of information. Readers unfamiliar with Malcolm's history will learn it here. Readers who have read Alex

Haley's brilliant *Autobiography of Malcolm X* or seen Denzel Washington's passion-ate and poignant film portrayal will understand more deeply Hayden's presenting as the climax of Malcolm's life that moment in his pilgrimage to Mecca when he received the revelation that people of different races can treat each other as equal members of one family. This is the point at which Malcolm Little/Malcolm X chose his true name. (*El-Hajj*: one who has been to Mecca; *Malik*: king; *El-Shabazz*: the black tribe which peacefully populated the earth until the birth of Yacub, the trick-ster scientist who created the first white people, according to the Black Muslim cre-ation myth.) The poem thus describes the fulcrum moment of Malcolm's life. Hayden presents Malcolm's moment of revelation, when he cries out "Labbayk! Labbayk!"—the Arabic expression of joyful submission to the will of God—as he arrives at the realization that changed his life. To a Baha'i, the wisdom of Malcolm's last teachings is precisely that taught by Baha'u'llah: "Allah the raceless in whose blazing Oneness all / were one."

One of Hayden's great unread poems, "Baha'u'llah in the Garden of Ridwan," describes the night before the Exiled One revealed himself and his mission to his fol-lowers. A Christian reader might compare this with Jesus' night in Gesthemene. The disciples sleep, the called one prays all night, and the universe is changed: "Within the rock the undiscovered suns / release their light."

Hayden's formalist training under Auden is readily apparent, the *continuo* of his music almost as constant as that of Emily Dickinson or Paul Lawrence Dunbar. The framework of most of his poems is traditional: the quatrain, the ballad, the sonnet, the tetrameter or pentameter iambic line. But Hayden's improvisations dance around traditional form with loose arpeggios of rhythm, rhymes so slant as to disappear.

Like that of his near peer, Gwendolyn Brooks, another virtuoso of poetic tech-nique, Hayden's work has been too often relegated to the ghetto of racial literature, his poems often read primarily for the light they shed on sociological or historical issues. He is so much more than that.

Those Winter Sundays

DISC 2, TRACK 51

Sundays too my father got up early
and put his clothes on in the blueblack cold,
then with cracked hands that ached
from labor in the weekday weather made
banked fires blaze. No one ever thanked him.

I'd wake and hear the cold splintering, breaking.
When the rooms were warm, he'd call,
and slowly I would rise and dress,
fearing the chronic angers of that house,

Speaking indifferently to him,
who had driven out the cold
and polished my good shoes as well.
What did I know, what did I know
of love's austere and lonely offices?

[1962]

Frederick Douglass

When it is finally ours, this freedom, this liberty, this beautiful
and terrible thing, needful to man as air,
usable as earth; when it belongs at last to all,
when it is truly instinct, brain matter, diastole, systole,
reflex action; when it is finally won; when it is more
than the gaudy mumbo jumbo of politicians;
this man, this Douglass, this former slave, this Negro
beaten to his knees, exiled, visioning a world
where none is lonely, none hunted, alien,
this man, superb in love and logic, this man
shall be remembered. Oh, not with statues' rhetoric,
not with legends and poems and wreaths of bronze alone,
but with the lives grown out of his life, the lives
fleshing his dream of the beautiful, needful thing.

[1962]

Homage to the Empress of the Blues

Because there was a man somewhere in a candystripe silk shirt,
gracile and dangerous as a jaguar and because a woman moaned
for him in sixty-watt gloom and mourned him Faithless Love
Twotiming Love Oh Love Oh Careless Aggravating Love,

She came out on the stage in yards of pearls, emerging like
a favorite scenic view, flashed her golden smile and sang.

Because grey laths began somewhere to show from underneath
torn hurdygurdy lithographs of dollfaced heaven;
and because there were those who feared alarming fists of snow
on the door and those who feared the riot-squad of statistics,

She came out on the stage in ostrich feathers, beaded satin,
and shone that smile on us and sang.

[1966]

El-Hajj Malik El-Shabazz

(Malcolm X)

O masks and metamorphoses of Ahab, Native Son

DISC 2, TRACK 52

I

The icy evil that struck his father down
and ravished his mother into madness
trapped him in violence of a punished self
struggling to break free.

As Home Boy, as Dee-troit Red,
he fled his name, became the quarry of
his own obsessed pursuit.

He conked his hair and Lindy-hopped,
zoot-suited jiver, swinging those chicks
in the hot rose and reefer glow.

His injured childhood bullied him.
He skirmished in the Upas trees
and cannibal flowers of the American Dream—

but could not hurt the enemy
powered against him there.

II

Sometimes the dark that gave his life
its cold satanic sheen would shift
a little, and he saw himself
floodlit and eloquent;

yet how could he, "Satan" in The Hole,
guess what the waking dream foretold?

Then false dawn of vision came;
he fell upon his face before
a racist Allah pledged to wrest him from
the hellward-thrusting hand of Calvin's Christ—

to free him and his kind
from Yakub's white-faced treachery.
He rose redeemed from all but prideful anger,
though adulterate attars could not cleanse
him of the odors of the pit.

III

Asalam alaikum!

He X'd his name, became his people's anger,
exhorted them to vengeance for their past;
rebuked, admonished them,

their scouger who
would shame them, drive them from
the lush ice gardens of their servitude.

Asalam alaikum!

Rejecting Ahab, he was Ahab's tribe.
"Strike through the mask!"

IV

Time. "The martyr's time," he said.
Time and the karate killer,
knifer, gunman. Time that brought
ironic trophies as his faith

twined sparking round the bole,
the fruit of neo-Islam.
"The martyr's time."

But first, the ebb time pilgrimage
toward revelation, hejira to
his final metamorphosis;

Labbayk! Labbayk!

He fell upon his face before
Allah the raceless in whose blazing Oneness all
were one. He rose renewed renamed, became
much more than there was time for him to be.

[1970]

Words in the Mourning Time

I

For King, for Robert Kennedy,
destroyed by those they could not save,
for King for Kennedy I mourn.
And for America, self-destructive, self-betrayed.

I grieve. Yet know the vanity
of grief—through power of
The Blessed Exile's
transilluminating word

aware of how these deaths, how all
the agonies of our deathbed childbed age
are process, major means whereby,
oh dreadfully, our humanness must be achieved.

II

Killing people to save, to free them?
With napalm lighting routes to the future?

III

He comes to my table in his hungry wounds
and his hunger. The flamed-out eyes,
their sockets dripping. The nightmare mouth.

He snatches food from my plate, raw
fingers bleeding, seizes my glass
and drinks, leaving flesh-fragments on its rim.

IV

Vietnam bloodclotted name in my consciousness
recurring and recurring
like the obsessive thought many midnights
now of my own dying

Vietnam and I think of the villages
mistakenly burning the schoolrooms devouring
their children and I think of those who
were my students
                          brutalized killing
wasted by horror
in ultimate loneliness
dying
                    Vietnam Vietnam

V

Oh, what a world we make,
oppressor and oppressed.

Our world—
this violent ghetto, slum
of the spirit raging against itself.

We hate kill destroy
in the name of human good
our killing and our hate destroy.

VI
Lord Riot
        naked
                in flaming clothes
cannibal ruler
         of anger's
               carousals
    sing hey nonny no
terror
     his tribute
           shriek of bloody glass
his praise
    sing wrathful sing vengeful
       sing hey nonny no
gigantic
     and laughing
          sniper on tower
I hate
    I destroy
       I am   I am
     sing hey nonny no
     sing burn baby burn

VII
voice in the wilderness

Know that love has chosen you
to live his crucial purposes.
Know that love has chosen you.

And will not pamper you nor spare;
demands obedience to all
the rigorous laws of risk,
does not pamper, will not spare.

Oh, master now love's instruments—
complex and not for the fearful,
simple and not for the foolish.
Master now love's instruments.

I who love you tell you this,
even as the pitiful killer waits for me,
I who love you tell you this.

VIII
Light and the
          distortions
               of light as
the flame-night
         dawns
            Zenith-time and the anger
unto death and the
         fire-focused
             image
of a man
      invisible man
          and black boy and native
son and the
      man who
         lives underground whose
name nobody
      knows
       harrowing havocking
running through
      holocaust
        seeking the
soul-country of his
       meaning

IX

As the gook woman howls
for her boy in the smouldering,
as the expendable Clean-Cut Boys
From Decent American Homes
are slashing off enemy ears for keepsakes;

as the victories are tallied up
with flag-draped coffins, plastic bodybags,
what can I say
but this, this:

We must not be frightened nor cajoled
into accepting evil as deliverance from evil.
We must go on struggling to be human,
though monsters of abstraction
police and threaten us.

Reclaim now, now renew the vision of
a human world where godliness
is possible and man
is neither gook nigger honkey wop nor kike

but man

                    permitted to be man.

X

and all the atoms cry aloud

    I bear Him witness now
Who by the light of suns beyond the suns beyond
    the sun with shrill pen

    revealed renewal of
the covenant of timelessness with time, proclaimed
    advent of splendor joy

    alone can comprehend
and the imperious evils of an age could not
    withstand and stars

    and stones and seas
acclaimed—His life its crystal image and
    magnetic field.

    I bear Him witness now—
mystery Whose major clues are the heart of man,
    the mystery of God:

    Baha'u'llah:
Logos, poet, cosmic hero, surgeon, architect
    of our hope of peace,

    wronged, exiled One,
chosen to endure what agonies of knowledge, what
    auroral dark

    bestowals of truth
vision power anguish for our future's sake.
    "I was but a man

    "like others, asleep upon
My couch, when, lo, the breezes of the All-Glorious
    were wafted over Me...."

    Called, as in dead of night
a dreamer is roused to help the helpless flee
    a burning house.

    I bear Him witness now:
towards Him our history in its disastrous quest
    for meaning is impelled.

[1970]

Muriel Rukeyser

(1913–1980) b. New York, New York, United States

Disc 2
Tracks 53–56

Muriel Rukeyser was born into a wealthy New York City family on December 15, 1913. She was educated early in life at the Fieldston School, before moving on to Vassar College. Among her fellow students at Vassar was the future poet Elizabeth Bishop. Rukeyser left Vassar after two years and attended Columbia University from 1930 to 1932. After completing college, Rukeyser worked on the staff of the magazine *Student Review* while cultivating her widely varied interests, from physics to psychology to Greek hymns, all of which inform her poetry.

Having reported on several life-altering incidents in her young adulthood, including the second Scottsboro trial, the Gauley Bridge tragedy, and the Spanish Civil War, Rukeyser became a social activist. Her sense of social and political responsibility would forever motivate her writing. During this period, Rukeyser married and separated from her husband shortly thereafter. In 1935, her first volume of poetry, *Theory of Flight* (a title taken from her experiences as a novice pilot, another of her many hobbies), was chosen by Stephen Vincent Benét for the Yale Younger Poets Series and created a name for her in the poetic world. Influenced by such contemporary writers as W.H. Auden as well as by Walt Whitman, John Milton, and the Bible, *Theory of Flight* juxtaposes the plight of the "common man's" America with the intellectual language of Academia.

During the next several years, Rukeyser traveled frequently and used her experiences in foreign lands to help inspire further volumes of poetry, which she turned out in almost shocking abundance. *Mediterranean* appeared in 1938, as did *U.S. 1*, followed by *A Turning Wind* in 1939. These volumes largely maintained her poetic stance and style while never losing their political nerve. In addition to poetry, Rukeyser also wrote biographies and children's books and translated such collections as *Selected Poems of Octavio Paz* and Bertolt Brecht's *Uncle Eddie's Moustache*. In 1945, she began teaching poetry workshops at the California Labor School, and two years later gave birth to her only child, a son named Bill, whom she raised independently. Unlike the frequently despairing and at best ambivalent poems of childbirth and motherhood by such later figures as Sylvia Plath and Anne Sexton, Rukeyser's poems on these themes have a distinctly hopeful tone and are marked by images of nurturing and fulfillment. In 1949, she published her well-regarded prose work, *The Life of Poetry*, a characteristically passionate analysis of poetry's role in modern life.

In the 1970s, a looser, freer form of verse replaced Rukeyser's earlier, tightly constructed, classical approach that owed so much to Auden and his school. This stylistic liberty in combination with her increasing involvement in social issues drew the attention of a new generation of readers, as perhaps did her teaching position at Sarah Lawrence College from 1956 to 1967. As an activist, Rukeyser was jailed for protesting the Vietnam War; later, she flew to Hanoi to protest the imprisonment and death sentence of poet Kim Chi-Ha. Her poetry empowered such poets as Adrienne Rich and Anne Sexton, and she was an inspiration to the women's movement. The motto "No More Masks!" was taken from her poem "The Poem as Mask." Rukeyser continued to publish poetry until her death in New York City in 1980, with later volumes including *Breaking Open* in 1973 and *The Gates* in 1976. As one of the noted and most productive poet-activists of the twentieth century, she is perhaps remembered as much for her political views and actions as for her art.

Sharon Olds on Muriel Rukeyser

In 1968, when Muriel Rukeyser read her poems at a gathering of poets against the Vietnam War, I was amazed by their directness and power, and deeply moved by her voice. It had an unusually wide range of tones, and a slight vibrato. It had an amber quality, a dark gold note—it was deep, but with highlights in it when it sailed up almost girlishly, full of hope or promise. When she read, tears came out of me easily, as if automatically—as if this had been the voice I was imprinted with when still in the shell. Now, more than thirty years later, I hear in the recordings the shape of the lips and tongue and palate and vibrant throat of someone who loves to eat, and to laugh—not a woman with a small mouth, not a woman afraid to open it. She begins each line on a fairly high note, a casting up and out of the shining arc (with its tensile strength, and its hunting), which falls, gradually, in a serious, gravitational curve, to mezzo or alto (no lifting, no questioning, or permission-seeking, at the end). And her voice always sounds physical, homemade, and of its time and place.

In 1974, I had the good fortune to become a member of her Poetry Appreciation class at the 92nd Street Y. She loved to listen as we read to each other—she really liked poetry! She would lean into it and listen very bodily. Sometimes when a poem seemed especially to please her she would smack her lips after reading it to us, as if savoring a favorite food.

In December 1974, Muriel gave a reading from her new book, *The Gates*, at the Y. Her students were all lined up in a row before her when, toward the end of "The Poem as Mask," she stepped out from behind the podium and held her book up in her hand and cried out, *"No more masks! No more mythologies!"* She actually raised her voice and held the book up over her head and came out from behind her support: not interested in physical infirmity or in relying on the podium in any way.

By the time I last heard her read, in April 1979, the state of her health was parlous. Afterwards, she sat down to talk, having stood to read—she would not read sitting down, though standing was not easy—the black plastic boot from her foot operation sticking out, her face ravaged, smiling, full of light. We stood around her, feeling the tonic quality of her presence, her attention to detail, her seriousness about our beloved art, her fun. "Excuse this," she said, gesturing to her foot, "it's temporary." This became our joke while we took her home: any difficulty with the traffic, the world, life, was dismissed with the phrase, "It's temporary," and laughter. Such was the attractiveness of Muriel's spirit. Getting to know her meant falling in love with courage.

Around that time, I heard of the Christopher Smart reading when many poets took turns reading *Jubilate Agno*. Muriel was reading heartily, with power and verve, and then gradually people noticed that there was no longer any space between her head and the podium. She had sunk down to some degree, and yet there was no diminution in the gusto with which she was reading, so no one stepped up—everyone was kind of mesmerized. Eventually they realized she had sunk to the floor, and someone mentioned an ambulance. But Muriel, lying there, said, "No, I want to finish the passage, I'd like a chair." One was found, and they lifted her into it, and brought down the microphone, and, as if nothing had happened, she continued on with the section and finished it. The audience cheered her the way we cheer someone who has fallen in a race, and gotten up, and gone on to win.

I heard her game, matter-of-fact life-force again the last time I saw her. When I walked her back after lunch, she got a phone call from her Swedish translator. "Yes," she said, "I am well, but lame in one foot." "*Yes*." "Yes, this is new, an operation and a stroke." "*Yes*." I can hear her blunt delivery and her strong vibrant voice on the word *yes*—the affirmation in it, an intonation almost of joy. Muriel attacked the word *yes* like a singer, giving it an insistent beginning followed by a falling, lyric closing. It had a ringing sound, like praise—even when describing the most recent of her "smiters."

It was what had first struck me about Muriel, the physical sound of her voice, the way her spirit resonated in it with a pulse of determination, hope, sex, belief, and humor, never distorting the facts—verifiable and inverifiable—which she saw with a scientist's eye and a lover's heart, and which she sang forth for us and continues to sing forth.

A letter from Rukeyser to Ezra Pound, dated July 20, 1932

Roxbury
July 20
1 9 3 2

Dear Ezra Pound,

Selden Rodman said that, hoping hard, he thought you might say something to us - for us. I'd like that very much: but, magazine article or not, I'd rather know what you were thinking about our sort of thing than what almost anybody else thought. It's a place-magazine that speaks about New England, and sends form-letters telling how to focus "economic, social, cultural trends" - a prescribing magazine that covers up the clinical attitude. All college people are doing it. There are five of us at a Connecticut farm, putting little stamps on things, and writing four issues whose viewpoint is meant to veer to challenge from liberalism by the fourth issue.

Officially, I should be asking you what, from your point of vantage, you see happening to New England as the nucleus breaks. Writing for myself - I am wanting to write to you, or listen to you talk, after the refractions of books like Margaret Anderson's and Lincoln Steffen's - and your own.

Our attack is from the place-poem, place-magazine side, after the person-poem, person-novel - and that all facing the avenue of group-works of one or another sort. Of course the validity of that is questionable. I came into the magazine as somebody who's been for my eighteen years in New York and subject to that education, wanting to see any one place whole. I wish you would say something about that. And about not wanting to be a short-sighted, long-winded romantic, even about writing, even about places and people, even about inflated causes.

Words like that are falling leaves turning under-foot. - I would like it if you'd answer - that simply.

Muriel Rukeyser

Night Feeding

DISC 2, TRACK 54

Deeper than sleep but not so deep as death
I lay there sleeping and my magic head
remembered and forgot.   On first cry I
remembered and forgot and did believe.
I knew love and I knew evil:
woke to the burning song and the tree burning blind,
despair of our days and the calm milk-giver who
knows sleep, knows growth, the sex of fire and grass,
and the black snake with gold bones.

Black sleeps, gold burns;   on second cry I woke
fully and gave to feed and fed on feeding.
Gold seed, green pain, my wizards in the earth
walked through the house, black in the morning dark.
Shadows grew in my veins, my bright belief,
my head of dreams deeper than night and sleep.
Voices of all black animals crying to drink,
cries of all birth arise, simple as we,
found in the leaves, in clouds and dark, in dream,
deep as this hour, ready again to sleep.

[1935]

from Letter to the Front

VII
To be a Jew in the twentieth century
Is to be offered a gift.   If you refuse,
Wishing to be invisible, you choose
Death of the spirit, the stone insanity.
Accepting, take full life.   Full agonies:
Your evening deep in labyrinthine blood
Of those who resist, fail, and resist; and God
Reduced to a hostage among hostages.

The gift is torment.   Not alone the still
Torture, isolation; or torture of the flesh.
That may come also.   But the accepting wish,
The whole and fertile spirit as guarantee
For every human freedom, suffering to be free,
Daring to live for the impossible.

[1944]

The Poem as Mask

Orpheus

DISC 2, TRACK 55

When I wrote of the women in their dances and wildness, it was a mask,
on their mountain, god-hunting, singing, in orgy,
it was a mask; when I wrote of the god,
fragmented, exiled from himself, his life, the love gone down with song,
it was myself, split open, unable to speak, in exile from myself.

There is no mountain, there is no god, there is memory
of my torn life, myself split open in sleep, the rescued child
beside me among the doctors, and a word
of rescue from the great eyes.

No more masks! No more mythologies!

Now, for the first time, the god lifts his hand,
the fragments join in me with their own music.

[1968]

Waiting for Icarus

DISC 2, TRACK 56

He said he would be back and we'd drink wine together
He said that everything would be better than before
He said we were on the edge of a new relation
He said he would never again cringe before his father
He said that he was going to invent full-time
He said he loved me that going into me
He said was going into the world and the sky
He said all the buckles were very firm
He said the wax was the best wax
He said Wait for me here on the beach
He said Just don't cry

I remember the gulls and the waves
I remember the islands going dark on the sea
I remember the girls laughing
I remember they said he only wanted to get away from me
I remember mother saying : Inventors are like poets,
                                        a trashy lot
I remember she told me those who try out inventions are worse
I remember she added : Women who love such are the worst of all
I have been waiting all day, or perhaps longer.
I would have liked to try those wings myself.
It would have been better than this.

[1973]

Ballad of Orange and Grape

After you finish your work
after you do your day
after you've read your reading
after you've written your say   —
you go down the street to the hot dog stand,
one block down and across the way.
On a blistering afternoon in East Harlem in the twentieth century.

Most of the windows are boarded up,
the rats run out of a sack   —
sticking out of the crummy garage
one shiny long Cadillac;
at the glass door of the drug-addiction center,
a man who'd like to break your back.
But here's a brown woman with a little girl dressed in rose
    and pink, too.

Frankfurters frankfurters sizzle on the steel
where the hot-dog-man leans   —
nothing else on the counter
but the usual two machines,
the grape one, empty, and the orange one, empty,
I face him in between.
A black boy comes along, looks at the hot dogs, goes on
    walking.

I watch the man as he stands and pours
in the familiar shape
bright purple in the one marked ORANGE
orange in the one marked GRAPE,
the grape drink in the machine marked ORANGE
and orange drink in the GRAPE.
Just the one word large and clear, unmistakable, on each
    machine.

I ask him: How can we go on reading
and make sense out of what we read?   —
How can they write and believe what they're writing,
the young ones across the street,
while you go on pouring grape into ORANGE
and orange into the one marked GRAPE   —?
(How are we going to believe what we read and we write and
    we hear and we say and we do?)

He looks at the two machines and he smiles
and he shrugs and smiles and pours again.
It could be violence and nonviolence
it could be white and black   women and men
It could be war and peace or any
binary system, love and hate, enemy, friend.
Yes and no, be and not-be, what we do and what we don't do.

On a corner in East Harlem
garbage, reading, a deep smile, rape,
forgetfulness, a hot street of murder,
misery, withered hope,
a man keeps pouring grape into ORANGE
and orange into the one marked GRAPE,
pouring orange into GRAPE and grape into ORANGE forever.

[1973]

William Stafford

(1914–1993) b. Hutchinson, Kansas, United States

Disc 3
Tracks 1–3

William Stafford was born on January 17, 1914, in Hutchinson, Kansas. His family moved frequently throughout his childhood, as his father searched for work. He remembered the Depression well. Despite their hardships, Stafford's father encouraged all his children in reading, and Stafford remembered the family bringing armloads of books back from the library each week. While working as a paperboy or field hand, Stafford attended high school and, briefly, junior college. He was writing regularly even then. He enrolled in the University of Kansas, working at various jobs to pay his way. He took active part in the struggles that later became the Civil Rights movement.

World War II brought Stafford to a troubled period in his life. He registered as a conscientious objector in 1942, and ended up at a series of alternative service camps in Arkansas, California, and Illinois. During this time, Stafford established the discipline of writing every morning, and in those years wrote a great number of poems, many of which are now considered among his best. During his California service in 1944, he met Dorothy Hope Frantz, a schoolteacher who taught and lived nearby. That same year, Stafford and Frantz were married; in time, they would raise four children together. Stafford was discharged in 1946 after serving four years, and the couple returned to Kansas where Stafford completed his master's degree. They returned to California in 1948, and Stafford took teaching jobs at various colleges, finally settling into Lewis and Clark College in Portland, Oregon, in 1956.

During this time, Stafford was publishing his poetry in literary magazines, and although the poems received much notice, it wasn't until 1960 that his first volume, titled *West of Your City*, was published, which was received well. But two years later, when he published his second volume, *Traveling Through the Dark*, it was instantly heralded. It received the National Book Award that year and established Stafford as a poet of the highest order. He received a Guggenheim Fellowship in 1966.

Stafford wrote poems and essays steadily the rest of his life. While teaching at Lewis and Clark, he embarked on reading tours often, gave poetry workshops and attended literary conferences. In 1970, Stafford served as the Poetry Consultant to the Library of Congress (later renamed Poet Laureate). His later volumes of poetry, such as *Allegiances* (1970) and *Someday, Maybe* (1973), remained lively and brilliant. Though he favored simple, "spoken" diction and rhythms, his poetry always embodied the complicated relationships between nature and society, and between our obligations and our affections. He never descended into didacticism despite his continuing commitment to political activism. The poet and novelist James Dickey called Stafford America's most prolific poet, and suggested that the reason for that was that Stafford was a "born poet" and poetry was the easiest way for him to communicate. He retired from teaching in 1980, but continued to write, travel, and give poetry readings until his death in 1993.

Robert Bly on William Stafford

Many critics have written of Bill Stafford's restless love of ordinary things—straw, feathers, dust—his forgiveness of small towns, his fierce opposition to war, his intricate urging for rigor and honesty in his and our judgment of each other. Here I want to write about his genius in sound and his relation to reverie. Gaston Bachelard says,

> When a dreamer of reveries has swept aside all the "preoccupations" which were encumbering his everyday life, when he has detached himself from the worry which comes to him from the worry of others....Suddenly such a dreamer is a *world dreamer*. Time is engulfed in the double depths of the dreamer and the world. The world is so majestic that nothing any longer happens there; the world reposes in its tranquility....

We'll look at Stafford's poem called "St. Matthew and All":

> *Lorene—we thought she'd come home. But*
> *it got late, and then days. Now*
> *it has been years. Why shouldn't she,*
> *if she wanted? I would: something comes*
> *along, a sunny day, you start walking;*
> *you meet a person who says, "Follow me,"*
> *and things lead on.*

Let's mention first the delicious perfume of pitches, that we can smell, a perfume of pitches that American Midwestern speech often carried before TV flooded the language.

Lorene—we thought she'd come home.

As we say the word "Lorene," we hear our pitch sharpen on the second syllable and again in "home." Now we can notice similar sharpenings in "late," "days," and "years."

Lorene—we thought she'd come home. But
it got late, and then days. Now
it has been years.

Stafford is paying careful attention to the way a Kansas neighbor might have continued the story:

Why shouldn't she,
if she wanted? I would:

A sweet riff follows:

something comes
along, a sunny day, you start walking;
you meet a person who says, "Follow me,"
and things lead on.

The lines seem modest, but the sounds are complicated. We're given one melody of pitches, and a second tune involving all sorts of n sounds. Stafford removes any possibility of judgment by saying "Why shouldn't she, / if she wanted? I would." Both melodies are resolved with a little trumpet-call: "things lead on."

The musicianship helps us perceive the quality of writing Bachelard calls "reverie." We don't need judgment for reverie. A woman disappears from her little town. There's something distressing about her sudden absence. Disappearances of this sort have happened before, and maybe the neighbors are not even aware that she is gone.

something comes
along, a sunny day, you start walking;
you meet a person who says, "Follow me,"
and things lead on.

Any one of us could meet a person who could convincingly say, "Follow me." He uses the phrase "your car." "The neighbors notice your car is gone." The melody ends, as the previous one did, with a three-beat conclusion.

They forget.

Wallace Stevens writes from reverie too. Things happen as if they were inevitable:

> *Twenty men crossing a bridge,*
> *Into a village,*
> *Are twenty men crossing twenty bridges,*
> *Into twenty villages.*

Each of us could have been one of those twenty men. Details seem not only natural, but musical:

The mandolin is the instrument
Of a place.

Stafford carries on memory and reverie by remembering "doubting Thomas," as we call him, who, according to some scholars, followed his strange love of Eastern subtleties, and went, after Jesus died, to India.

> *In the Bible it happened—fishermen, Levites.*
> *They just went away and kept going. Thomas,*
> *away off in India, never came back.*

Using a grammatical fragment, "In the Bible it happened—fishermen, Levites"—seems careless, but it is, musically, very nourishing and cunning. High pitches appear with "Bible" and "Levites," and a certain exhilaration enters the poem. The musical pitch goes down in "away" and back up with "going," then hits a new peak with "Thomas." The repetition of "in" and "en" syllables continues, and the sequence sweetly concludes with "India."

> *In the Bible it happened—fishermen, Levites.*
> *They just went away and kept going. Thomas,*
> *away off in India, never came back.*

We recognize in "never came back" the three-beat phrase again, ending the stanza.

> *But Lorene—it was a stranger maybe, and he*
> *said, "Your life, I need it." And nobody else did.*

The whole poem concludes with another three-beat phrase: "nobody else did." Many poems we all love carry a bitter or sarcastic bite; and those poems are fine. But this is the music of yearning. Such a music does not try to push us away, but it works to draw us—are we missing?—back into the community.

In another essay about Stafford's work, I wrote:

> By following the tiny impulses through the meadow of language, the writer may find himself or herself closer to "the self most centrally yours." It would be too much to claim that art, the practice of it, will establish a good, a serene, a superior self. No. But art will, if pursued for itself, bring into realization the "self most centrally yours." Writing poetry, then, doesn't make a poet such as Stafford a better person, only a more genuine *William*.

This yearning, the absence of judgment, and the pulling of us back into the community, are three of the gifts of reverie. Often in our literary criticism, with its recent obsession with literal facts, confession, and wit, we forget the genius of reverie. Reverie is not day-dreaming; instead it helps the poet become a *world dreamer*.

Of all the American poets of the last thirty years, I think William Stafford broods most about community—the "mutual life" we share, as black people and white people, pacifists and militarists, city people and small-town people.

> *If you don't know the kind of person I am*
> *and I don't know the kind of person you are*
> *a pattern that others made may prevail in the world...*
>
> *For it is important that awake people be awake,*
> *or a breaking line may discourage them back to sleep;*
> *the signals we give—yes or no, or maybe—*
> *should be clear: the darkness around us is deep.*

The Star in the Hills

DISC 3, TRACK 2

A star hit in the hills behind our house
up where the grass turns brown touching the sky.

Meteors have hit the world before, but this was near,
and since TV; few saw, but many felt the shock.
The state of California owns that land
(and out from shore three miles), and any stars
that come will be roped off and viewed on week days 8 to 5.

A guard who took the oath of loyalty and denied
any police record told me this:
"If you don't have a police record yet
you could take the oath and get a job
if California should be hit by another star."

"I'd promise to be loyal to California
and to guard any stars that hit it," I said,
"or any place three miles out from shore,
unless the star was bigger than the state—
in which case I'd be loyal to *it*."

But he said no exceptions were allowed,
and he leaned against the state-owned meteor
so calm and puffed a cork-tip cigarette
that I looked down and traced with my foot in the dust
and thought again and said, "OK—any star."

[1962]

Traveling Through the Dark

DISC 3, TRACK 3

Traveling through the dark I found a deer
dead on the edge of the Wilson River road.
It is usually best to roll them into the canyon:
that road is narrow; to swerve might make more dead.

By glow of the tail-light I stumbled back of the car
and stood by the heap, a doe, a recent killing;
she had stiffened already, almost cold.
I dragged her off; she was large in the belly.

My fingers touching her side brought me the reason—
her side was warm; her fawn lay there waiting,
alive, still, never to be born.
Beside that mountain road I hesitated.

The car aimed ahead its lowered parking lights;
under the hood purred the steady engine.
I stood in the glare of the warm exhaust turning red;
around our group I could hear the wilderness listen.

I thought hard for us all—my only swerving—,
then pushed her over the edge into the river.

[1962]

Passing Remark

In scenery I like flat country.
In life I don't like much to happen.

In personalities I like mild colorless people.
And in colors I prefer gray and brown.

My wife, a vivid girl from the mountains,
says, "Then why did you choose me?"

Mildly I lower my brown eyes—
there are so many things admirable people
    do not understand.

[1966]

Saint Matthew and All

Lorene—we thought she'd come home. But
it got late, and then days. Now
it has been years. Why shouldn't she,
if she wanted? I would: something comes
along, a sunny day, you start walking;
you meet a person who says, "Follow me,"
and things lead on.

Usually, it wouldn't happen, but sometimes
the neighbors notice your car is gone, the
patch of oil in the driveway, and it fades.
They forget.

In the Bible it happened—fishermen, Levites.
They just went away and kept going. Thomas,
away off in India, never came back.

But Lorene—it was a stranger maybe, and he
said, "Your life, I need it." And nobody else did.

[1973]

Report to Crazy Horse

All the Sioux were defeated. Our clan
got poor, but a few got richer.
They fought two wars. I did not
take part. No one remembers your vision
or even your real name. Now
the children go to town and like
loud music. I married a Christian.

Crazy Horse, it is not fair
to hide a new vision from you.
In our schools we are learning
to take aim when we talk, and we have
found out our enemies. They shift when
words do; they even change and hide
in every person. A teacher here says
hurt or scorned people are places
where real enemies hide. He says
we should not hurt or scorn anyone,
but help them. And I will tell you
in a brave way, the way Crazy Horse
talked: that teacher is right.

I will tell you a strange thing:
at the rodeo, close to the grandstand,
I saw a farm lady scared by a blown
piece of paper; and at the place
horses and policemen were no longer
frightening, but suffering faces were,
and the hunched-over backs of the old.

Crazy Horse, tell me if I am right:
these are the things we thought we were
doing something about.

In your life you saw many strange things,
and I will tell you another: now I salute
the white man's flag. But when I salute
I hold my hand alertly on the heartbeat
and remember all of us and how we depend
on a steady pulse together. There are those
who salute because they fear other flags
or mean to use ours to chase them:
I must not allow my part of saluting
to mean this. All of our promises,
our generous saying to each other, our
honorable intentions—those I affirm
when I salute. At these times it is like
shutting my eyes and joining a religious
colony at prayer in the gray dawn
in the deep aisle of a church.

Now I have told you about new times.
Yes, I know others will report
different things. They have been caught
by weak ways. I tell you straight
the way it is now, and it is our way,
the way we were trying to find.

The chokecherries along our valley
still bear a bright fruit. There is good
pottery clay north of here. I remember
our old places. When I pass the Musselshell
I run my hand along those old grooves in the rock.

[1973]

Randall Jarrell

(1914–1965) b. Nashville, Tennessee, United States

Disc 3
Tracks 4–6

Randall Jarrell was born in Nashville on May 6, 1914. Shortly after his birth, his parents moved to Los Angeles. Financial difficulties strained his parents' relationship and eventually they divorced; when his mother returned to Nashville, she brought Jarrell and his younger brother with her. From 1927 to 1931, Jarrell attended Hume-Fogg High School, where he excelled academically, became a skilled tennis player, and was active in both drama and journalism. A small National Youth Administration allowance enabled him to enroll at Vanderbilt University as a day student; while there, he edited the university's humor magazine, was captain of the tennis team, and was inducted into the Phi Beta Kappa Society. He studied under Robert Penn Warren and John Crowe Ransom, both respected poets associated with The Fugitive movement, and, although Jarrell never fully adopted their poetic agenda, their influence played a marked role in the development of his own aesthetic. In 1934, he published his first poem in *The American Review*.

After finishing his undergraduate degree, Jarrell remained at Vanderbilt as a graduate and accepted an assistant teaching position under Ransom at Kenyon College, Ohio. Here Jarrell met the fiction writer Peter Taylor and the poet Robert Lowell who were to become his closest friends and allies for the remainder of his life. He received his master's degree in 1938, and in the following year, he left Kenyon for a teaching position at the University of Texas. It was here that he met Mackie Langham, a colleague to whom he was married in 1940, and two years later his first book of poems was published, *Blood for a Stranger*.

During the war years, Jarrell enrolled in the Army Air Corps, but failed to qualify as a pilot. Instead, he instructed celestial navigation in Tucson, Arizona. His wartime experiences provided him with much inspiration for his next book of poetry, *Little Friend, Little Friend*, published in 1945. This book established Jarrell's reputation as a poet, and following his discharge, he spent a year working as the literary editor of *The Nation*. During this year, he also taught writing at Sarah Lawrence College, which became the model for the fictional Benton College, the setting for his single novel, 1954's satirical *Pictures from an Institution*. When his year at *The Nation* ended, Jarrell took a teaching position at the University of North Carolina-Greensboro. Although he remained there for the rest of his life, he took several leaves of absence, including a year teaching at Princeton and a two-year appointment as Poetry Consultant to the Library of Congress, (later renamed Poet Laureate).

Jarrell continued to publish poetry as well as essays and incisive, sometimes fiercely critical poetry reviews. His most famous book of poems, *The Woman at the Washington Zoo*, appeared in 1960 and won the National Book Award. He also translated Part I of Goethe's *Faust*, the Chekhov play *The Three Sisters*, and wrote several notable children's stories. In 1965, he suffered a severe depression, and after a suicide attempt, he entered Chapel Hill hospital for therapy. After his release, on October 14, 1965, Jarrell was out walking at dusk when he was struck by an automobile and killed instantly. The coroner declared the death accidental, but the full circumstances are not entirely clear. Today Jarrell is remembered most for his skillful, compassionate lyric poetry and his brilliant criticism, which have forever fixed him as a defining presence in postwar American poetry.

Peter Sacks on Randall Jarrell

Before listening to recordings of Randall Jarrell's voice, I'd already imagined the reed-like timbre emerging from his edgily oneiric poems, and from the wiry brilliance of his critical prose. A fairly high pitch in either case: in the poems, plangent with yearning or with an actual complaint whose potentially narcissistic frequencies hover within the trebles of a nostalgically recreated childhood ("The Lost World," "A Sick Child," etc.), or of the eerily radio-like remoteness of dead or alive wartime fliers (poems in *Little Friend, Little Friend*), or of the barely ventriloquized soprano arias of such monologues as "Seele im Raum," "The Woman at the Washington Zoo," or "Next Day"; while in the essays the wavelength is sharpened either by opinionated critique or by the thrill of espousal. I wasn't, however, prepared for the lambent flicker playing across the ghostly drawl, nor for the tentative short-breathed delicacy with which the clarinet-like lofting and crooning of the phrases is punctuated, nor for the quavery fraying when Jarrell's chronic sentiment of displacement cracks against the very limits (of recollection, fantasy, disenchantment, or self-transformation) which it both seeks and fears. Nor, finally, had I realized just how consistently this slender voice found its own tensile blends of litheness and frailty, of languid nervousness, of tenderness and near-frigidity, of faux-naif or wise-child pointedness capable of piercing the several veils between self-protection and sudden exposure, between reverie and terrified wakefulness.

"90 North" (1941) indicates the longitude on which many of Jarrell's rather entrapped, psychologically channeled poems would journey. (Soon the literal ruptures of war, and the invasive yet drifting asphyxias that marked America's postwar sense of freedom veined with urban and suburban paranoia, guilty power, commercially pumped and estranged desires, velocity, and blockage—these would bring to Jarrell's work the historical alertness James Dickey among others praised: "His poems give you the feel of a time, our time, as no other poetry of our century does, or could, even.") In "90 North," the sled-track of the psyche travels between polar opposites of "there" and "here," of wish-fulfillment and despair, of recollected childhood fantasy and terminal adult wretchedness. The North Pole of projected boyish dominion, in which the explorer attains what Yeats would have called the "heroic consummation

From my mother's sleep I
fell into the State
And hunched in its belly
Till my wet fur froze.
Six miles from earth, loosed
from its dream of life,
I woke to black flak and the
nightmare fighters.
When I died they washed me
out of the turret with a hose

To Mary — her very own poem — Randall

"The Death of the Ball Turret Gunner" handwritten by Jarrell and inscribed to his second wife, Mary

that he dreamed"—all death-wish and frozen fur—yields upon waking and aging to the yet more chilling "actual pole of my existence, / Where all that I have done is meaningless, / Where I die or live by accident alone / Where, living or dying, I am still alone." For a moment the vertigo is stunning, literal: "Turn as I please, my step is to the south. / The world—my world spins on this final point / Of cold and wretchedness." But unlike Elizabeth Bishop's partially cheerful concession to the vital, contingent world that awaits whoever chooses to leave the imaginary iceberg ("Good-bye, we say, good-bye") for a region "where waves give in to one another's waves," Jarrell's speaker commits himself to a desolation whose uncompromising extremity matches the polar absoluteness of dream: "I see at last that all the knowledge / I wrung from the darkness—that the darkness flung me— / Is worthless as ignorance: nothing comes from nothing, / The darkness from the darkness. Pain comes from the darkness / And we call it wisdom. It is pain."

For all the reiterative eloquence of these closing lines, with their hypnotic near-chiasmus, their echo of Lear, and their seemingly mature refusal of trope (Pain=Pain), the ending declines into exaggerated generalization. It is a young man's attempt to close the case with a dark, compensatory authority that has only marginally more empirical or general truth than the bright dream of ice. With regard to this issue of generalization, it is worth remembering how many of Jarrell's post-Freudian generation suffered from what they took to be the orphaning demise of High Modernism. If one comes to distrust the fictive, the visionary, and the metaphysical, and turns instead to the intractable data of autobiography and psychology, how then can a poet mediate between sheer contingency (Jarrell's "accident alone") on the one hand and a persuasive sense of the general on the other? Jarrell's master's thesis was titled "Implicit Generalization in Housman," and much of his own poetry searches desperately for some egress from the prison of exclusively personal experience and identity—via the use of personae, fairy tales, Chekhovian significant detail, translation, or by way of crying out for the kind of violent but passive metamorphosis ("change me, change me!") that does not require a greater strength or effort of will. At its worst, the result can be regressive and overwrought; but at best, Jarrell's intuitive sympathies and his sad, almost fixated love for the fugitive sweetness of life and for the marred innocence of dream, yield poems of stubborn fidelity to imaginary or lost worlds evoked with a crystalline grace.

Perhaps Child Randall's vicarious yet intimate participation (as instructor and tower-operator) in the fate of young airmen during the Second World War crossed with his ever-deepening devotion not just to the practice and criticism of poetry but also to the teaching of it (William Pritchard cites the poet's claim that he would pay to teach; and he was by all accounts a memorable and beloved teacher)—perhaps these leavened the otherwise flat and incipiently deep-frozen kind of revocation found in "90 North." If that poem reached a virtual pole defined by its withdrawn equidistance from the warmth of the tropics and from the zenith of idealization, a later poem like "Seele im Raum" (1950) provides a more flexible portrayal of the misalignment between an "actual" or "livable" life and an individual soul's dream or desire. The overt persona gives Jarrell greater control and modulation, as well as a more oxygenated mouthpiece through which to explore and partly release while also fortifying an anarchic, cracked, self-isolating part of the psyche.

"Seele im Raum" is the title of a poem by one of Jarrell's masters, Rainer Maria Rilke. It is not one of Rilke's better known poems, and Jarrell's decision not to translate the title (Soul in Space) preserves a degree of obscurity or recessiveness that emphasize the speaker's foreignness from her family and from her own nationality. She harbors an otherness that will not be translated away. Yes, she is a wife and mother, but she lives also with a hallucinated African antelope, the eland (idiosyncratically associated with the German word *elend*, meaning *wretched*), a private symbol of her own inarticulable being. This phantasmagoric companion is not the vocal "self" in its "skin of being—of what owns, is owned / In honor or dishonor," but rather "that raw thing, the being inside it / That has neither a wife, a husband, nor a child / But goes at last as naked from this world / As it was born into it." Not surprisingly, this psychotic menage is impossible to sustain. The eland is taken away, interred. But the speaker is defiantly haunted:

> *Shall I make sense or shall I tell the truth?*
> *Choose either—I cannot do both.*
> *…*
> *To be at all is to be wrong.*
> *Being is being old*
> *And saying, almost comfortably, across a table*
> *From—*
> *from what I don't know—*
> *in a voice*
> *Rich with a kind of longing satisfaction:*
> *"To own an eland! That's what I call life!"*

It's a far cry from the posthumous utterance of the soul in Rilke's poem. And yet Jarrell's forlorn psychologizing of what had been metaphysical in Rilke, does rise with near brio to its own candid salience. There's a vitality, however fractured, that shines from this personal calvary. It is a bright, solitary eminence, not easily separable from the one evoked in cheerier terms at the end of Elizabeth Bishop's memorial tribute to her dead friend: "I like to think of him as I saw him once after we had gone swimming together on Cape Cod; wearing only bathing trunks and a very queer straw cap with a big visor, seated on the crest of a high sand dune, writing in a notebook. It was a bright and dazzling day. Randall looked small and rather delicate, but bright and dazzling too. I felt quite sure that whatever he was writing would be bound to share the characteristics of the day and of the small man writing away so busily in the middle of it all."

90 North

At home, in my flannel gown, like a bear to its floe,
I clambered to bed; up the globe's impossible sides
I sailed all night—till at last, with my black beard,
My furs and my dogs, I stood at the northern pole.

There in the childish night my companions lay frozen,
The stiff furs knocked at my starveling throat,
And I gave my great sigh: the flakes came huddling,
Were they really my end? In the darkness I turned to my rest.

—Here, the flag snaps in the glare and silence
Of the unbroken ice. I stand here,
The dogs bark, my beard is black, and I stare
At the North Pole…
                         And now what? Why, go back.

Turn as I please, my step is to the south.
The world—my world spins on this final point
Of cold and wretchedness: all lines, all winds
End in this whirlpool I at last discover.

And it is meaningless. In the child's bed
After the night's voyage, in that warm world
Where people work and suffer for the end
That crowns the pain—in that Cloud-Cuckoo-Land

I reached my North and it had meaning.
Here at the actual pole of my existence,
Where all that I have done is meaningless,
Where I die or live by accident alone—

Where, living or dying, I am still alone;
Here where North, the night, the berg of death
Crowd me out of the ignorant darkness,
I see at last that all the knowledge

I wrung from the darkness—that the darkness flung me—
Is worthless as ignorance: nothing comes from nothing,
The darkness from the darkness. Pain comes from the darkness
And we call it wisdom. It is pain.

[1942]

The Death of the Ball Turret Gunner

DISC 3, TRACK 5

From my mother's sleep I fell into the State,
And I hunched in its belly till my wet fur froze.
Six miles from earth, loosed from its dream of life,
I woke to black flak and the nightmare fighters.
When I died they washed me out of the turret with a hose.

[1945]

Seele im Raum

It sat between my husband and my children.
A place was set for it—a plate of greens.
It had been there: I had seen it
But not somehow—but this was like a dream—
Not seen it so that I knew I saw it.
It was as if I could not know I saw it
Because I had never once in all my life
Not seen it. It was an eland.
An eland! *That* is why the children
Would ask my husband, for a joke, at Christmas:
"Father, is it Donner?" He would say, "No, Blitzen."
It had been there always. Now we put silver
At its place at meals, fed it the same food
We ourselves ate, and said nothing. Many times
When it breathed heavily (when it had tried
A long useless time to speak) and reached to me
So that I touched it—of a different size
And order of being, like the live hard side
Of a horse's neck when you pat the horse—
And looked with its great melting tearless eyes
Fringed with a few coarse wire-like lashes
Into my eyes, and whispered to me
So that my eyes turned backward in their sockets
And they said nothing—
                    many times
I have known, when they said nothing,
That it did not exist. If they had heard
They *could* not have been silent. And yet they heard;
Heard many times what I have spoken
When it could no longer speak, but only breathe—
When I could no longer speak, but only breathe.

And, after some years, the others came
And took it from me—it was ill, they told me—
And cured it, they wrote me: my whole city
Sent me cards like lilac-branches, mourning
As I had mourned—
                    and I was standing

By a grave in flowers, by dyed rolls of turf,
And a canvas marquee the last brown of earth.

It is over.
It is over so long that I begin to think
That it did not exist, that I have never—
And my son says, one morning, from the paper:
"An eland. Look, an eland!"
                    —It was so.

Today, in a German dictionary, I saw *elend*
And the heart in my breast turned over, it was—

It was a word one translates *wretched*.

It is as if someone remembered saying:
"This is an antimacassar that I grew from seed,"
And this were true.
                    And, truly,
One could not wish for anything more strange—
For anything more. And yet it wasn't *interesting*...
—It was worse than impossible, it was a joke.

And yet when it was, I *was*—
Even to think that I once thought
That I could see it is to feel the sweat
Like needles at my hair-roots, I am blind

—It was not even a joke, not even a joke.
Yet how can I believe it? Or believe that I
Owned it, a husband, children? Is my voice the voice
Of that skin of being—of what owns, is owned
In honor or dishonor, that is borne and bears—
Or of that raw thing, the being inside it
That has neither a wife, a husband, nor a child
But goes at last as naked from this world
As it was born into it—

And the eland comes and grazes on its grave.

                              This is senseless?
Shall I make sense or shall I tell the truth?
Choose either—I cannot do both.

I tell myself that. And yet it is not so,
And what I say afterwards will not be so:
To be at all is to be wrong.
                              Being is being old
And saying, almost comfortably, across a table
From—
          from what I don't know—
                              in a voice
Rich with a kind of longing satisfaction:
"To own an eland! That's what I call life!"

                                        [1950]

Next Day

Moving from Cheer to Joy, from Joy to All,
I take a box
And add it to my wild rice, my Cornish game hens.
The slacked or shorted, basketed, identical
Food-gathering flocks
Are selves I overlook. Wisdom, said William James,

Is learning what to overlook. And I am wise
If that is wisdom.
Yet somehow, as I buy All from these shelves
And the boy takes it to my station wagon,
What I've become
Troubles me even if I shut my eyes.

When I was young and miserable and pretty
And poor, I'd wish
What all girls wish: to have a husband,
A house and children. Now that I'm old, my wish
Is womanish:
That the boy putting groceries in my car

See me. It bewilders me he doesn't see me.
For so many years
I was good enough to eat: the world looked at me
And its mouth watered. How often they have undressed me,
The eyes of strangers!
And, holding their flesh within my flesh, their vile

Imaginings within my imagining,
I too have taken
The chance of life. Now the boy pats my dog
And we start home. Now I am good.
The last mistaken,
Ecstatic, accidental bliss, the blind

Happiness that, bursting, leaves upon the palm
Some soap and water—
It was so long ago, back in some Gay
Twenties, Nineties, I don't know…Today I miss
My lovely daughter
Away at school, my sons away at school,

My husband away at work—I wish for them.
The dog, the maid,
And I go through the sure unvarying days
At home in them. As I look at my life,
I am afraid
Only that it will change, as I am changing:

I am afraid, this morning, of my face.
It looks at me
From the rear-view mirror, with the eyes I hate,
The smile I hate. Its plain, lined look
Of gray discovery
Repeats to me: "You're old." That's all, I'm old.

And yet I'm afraid, as I was at the funeral
I went to yesterday.
My friend's cold made-up face, granite among its flowers,
Her undressed, operated-on, dressed body
Were my face and body.
As I think of her I hear her telling me

How young I seem; I *am* exceptional;
I think of all I have.
But really no one is exceptional,
No one has anything, I'm anybody,
I stand beside my grave
Confused with my life, that is commonplace and solitary.

[1965]

John Berryman

(1914–1972) b. McAlester, Oklahoma, United States

Disc 3
Tracks 7–10

John Berryman was born John Allyn Smith Jr. on October 25, 1914, in the rural town of McAlester, Oklahoma. He spent his first ten years there before moving to Florida, where his father hoped to take advantage of that state's economic boom. His expectations were not borne out, however, and the family suffered economically. This economic failure and a turbulent marriage brought Berryman's father to commit suicide by shooting himself outside his son's window on June 26, 1926. The trauma of that event would haunt Berryman for the rest of his life. Shortly thereafter, Berryman's mother married John Angus McAlpin Berryman, from whom the poet took his surname. Berryman, an excellent student, attended Columbia College, where he continued to excel and received a scholarship to study at Cambridge from 1936 to 1938. There he befriended W.H. Auden and Dylan Thomas, both of whom he admired greatly, and he even had the chance to meet his idol, W.B. Yeats.

Berryman returned to the U.S. and took a teaching position at Wayne State University. In 1940, his first published poems appeared in a small volume titled *Five Young American Poets*, a collection that also included work by Randall Jarrell. That same year, he began teaching at Harvard University. In 1942, he married Eileen Patricia Mulligan, and the next year he published his first collection, titled simply *Poems*, to mixed reviews. While teaching at Princeton University, a position he would hold for a decade, Berryman published his second volume of poetry, *The Dispossessed* (1948). The book introduced many of the themes and tensions that have become associated with Berryman's work, but it, too, received both praise and criticism.

Berryman's alcoholism gave rise to troubles in his marriage, and in 1946, he began the first of many extramarital affairs. His *Sonnets to Chris*, inspired by one of these relationships, was written in 1947 and published twenty years later. Also in the late 1940s and '50s, Berryman began writing critical prose as well as the long poem, *Homage to Mistress Bradstreet*. The poem appeared in the *Partisan Review* in 1953 and in book form three years later. *Homage* was an unqualified success. It earned Berryman a Guggenheim fellowship and led to a steady teaching position at the University of Minnesota. Although he took many extended leaves of absence, he remained there until his death. In 1954, Berryman fell in love with Elizabeth Ann Levine, a graduate student, and they married when Berryman and Mulligan divorced after a long separation. Berryman and Levine had a son before divorcing in 1959. Shortly thereafter, he married his third wife, Kathleen Donahue, a twenty-two-year-old introduced to him by another student with whom he had become romantically involved, and together they had two daughters.

During one of his leaves of absence, Berryman finished a volume of poetry in Dublin that was published in 1964 with the title *77 Dream Songs*. The book's groundbreaking, near-psychotic themes and stylistics catapulted Berryman to new levels of fame, winning him the Pulitzer Prize. He continued to add to the volume until it comprised over three hundred compressed, tragicomic, and dazzling lyrics finally republished in 1969 under the title *The Dream Songs*. The psychological deterioration depicted in *The Dream Songs* was not merely an artistic invention; it was, unfortunately, drawn from Berryman's life. Despite repeated efforts at rehabilitation, after a life of alcohol abuse and mental illness, Berryman committed suicide by throwing himself off a bridge in Minneapolis on January 7, 1972. Two years earlier, he had published his final volume of poetry, *Love and Fame*.

Elizabeth Spires on John Berryman

"I am interested only in people in crisis," John Berryman once said. "When I finish one I enter on another." And crisis is continually reflected in his poems, not only in their subjects and attitudes, but in the nervous energy of his oftentimes broken, disrupted syntax.

Without wanting to be reductive about the complex forces driving Berryman's art and psyche, undoubtedly his father's suicide when the poet was eleven years old shadowed him his entire life. It was a major factor, along with the poet's lifelong struggle with alcoholism, in Berryman's decision to take his own life when he was fifty-seven. (He once said that all the *Dream Songs* were about the death of his father.) It became the impossibly heavy burden, the "thing on Henry's heart / so heavy, if he had a hundred years / & more, & weeping, sleepless, in all them time / Henry could not make good."

But, in fact, in his art he *did* make good, writing wild, impassioned poems in which personal, intimate detail, sometimes masked, is set against a wider cultural, historical panorama. In his use of a distinctive American idiom, and in his informed interest in American history and politics, Berryman is, in a sense, the most American of poets. Named after his father John Allyn Smith, he subsequently took the last name of his stepfather, John Angus McAlpin Berryman, in the wake of his father's suicide. Thereafter, he became the American Everyman *in extremis*, struggling to come to terms, as the distressed boy in "The Ball Poem" must, with "The epistemology of loss, how to stand up / Knowing what every man must one day know / And most know many days, how to stand up…"

Berryman's best poems, of course, transcend the historical era in which he found himself, just as they transcend the painful, personal details of his autobiography. "Poetry is a terminal activity," he wrote, "taking place out near the end of things, where the poet's soul addresses one other soul only, never mind when. And it aims— never mind *either* communication or expression—at the reformation of the poet, as prayer does. In the grand cases—as in our century, Yeats and Eliot—it enables the poet gradually, again and again, to become almost another man…"

Certainly, in his poems, we can observe his soul's address to itself, to his alter ego "Henry" in *The Dream Songs*, to those closest to him, friends, wives, and lovers, and, finally, to God. The poems' continual sense of crisis and transformation bring to mind the existential, spiritual predicament of John Donne's *Holy Sonnets* and Gerard Manley Hopkins's *Dark Sonnets*: an isolated human being stranded on the edge of abyss, hoping through the grace of divine providence to weather the soul's dark night. Nervous, edgy, despairing, Berryman's poems can, nevertheless, move into regions of calm contemplation, as in his sequence "Eleven Addresses to the Lord," included in *Love and Fame*, a book published two years before his death.

Admittedly, Berryman is not the easiest of poets. How then to read his poems? If one listens to recordings of Berryman, the answer becomes obvious. *Read him out loud, slowly*, and with successive rereadings his poems will begin to take on an unexpected clarity and immediacy. Why is this? Because Berryman wrote as much for the ear as for the page, successfully melding the distinctive idioms of contemporary American speech with a more elevated, literary diction. In their dramatic conjoining of an upper and lower register, the poems owe a substantial debt to Shakespeare, of whom Berryman was a serious scholar. As Berryman evolved, he created a highly wrenched and wrought language that wanted, first and foremost, to *dramatically create the poem on an auditory level*. Of all those in his generation, it is perhaps Berryman who does this best.

Filling her compact & delicious body

with chicken páprika, she glanced at me

twice.

Fainting with interest, I hungered back

and only the fact of her husband & four other people

kept me from springing on her

or falling at her little feet and crying

'You are the hottest one for years of night

Henry's dazed eyes

have enjoyed, Brilliance.' I advanced upon

(despairing) my spumoni. —Sir Bones: is stuffed,

de world, wif feeding girls.

—Black hair, complexion Latin, jewelled eyes

downcast...The slob beside her feasts...What wonders is

she sitting on, over there?

The restaurant buzzes. She might as well be on Mars.

Where did it all go wrong? There ought to be a law against

                                    Henry.

—Mr. Bones: there is.

Corrected typescript of "4" from *The Dream Songs* by Berryman

The Ball Poem

DISC 3, TRACK 8

What is the boy now, who has lost his ball,
What, what is he to do? I saw it go
Merrily bouncing, down the street, and then
Merrily over—there it is in the water!
No use to say "O there are other balls":
An ultimate shaking grief fixes the boy
As he stands rigid, trembling, staring down
All his young days into the harbour where
His ball went. I would not intrude on him,
A dime, another ball, is worthless. Now
He senses first responsibility
In a world of possessions. People will take balls,
Balls will be lost always, little boy,
And no one buys a ball back. Money is external.
He is learning, well behind his desperate eyes,
The epistemology of loss, how to stand up.
Knowing what every man must one day know
And most know many days, how to stand up
And gradually light returns to the street,
A whistle blows, the ball is out of sight,
Soon part of me will explore the deep and dark
Floor of the harbour…I am everywhere,
I suffer and move, my mind and my heart move
With all that move me, under the water
Or whistling, I am not a little boy.

[1948]

4

from The Dream Songs

DISC 3, TRACK 9

Filling her compact & delicious body
with chicken páprika, she glanced at me
twice.
Fainting with interest, I hungered back
and only the fact of her husband & four other people
kept me from springing on her

or falling at her little feet and crying
"You are the hottest one for years of night
Henry's dazed eyes
have enjoyed, Brilliance." I advanced upon
(despairing) my spumoni.—Sir Bones: is stuffed,
de world, wif feeding girls.

—Black hair, complexion Latin, jewelled eyes
downcast…The slob beside her feasts…What wonders is
she sitting on, over there?
The restaurant buzzes. She might as well be on Mars.
Where did it all go wrong? There ought to be a law against
   Henry.
—Mr. Bones: there is.

[1964]

14

from The Dream Songs

Life, friends, is boring. We must not say so.
After all, the sky flashes, the great sea yearns,
we ourselves flash and yearn,
and moreover my mother told me as a boy
(repeatingly) "Ever to confess you're bored
means you have no

Inner Resources." I conclude now I have no
inner resources, because I am heavy bored.
Peoples bore me,
literature bores me, especially great literature,
Henry bores me, with his plights & gripes
as bad as achilles,

who loves people and valiant art, which bores me.
And the tranquil hills, & gin, look like a drag
and somehow a dog
has taken itself & its tail considerably away
into mountains or sea or sky, leaving
behind: me, wag.

[1964]

22

from The Dream Songs

Of 1826
I am the little man who smokes & smokes.
I am the girl who does know better but.
I am the king of the pool.
I am so wise I had my mouth sewn shut.
I am a government official & a goddamned fool.
I am a lady who takes jokes.

I am the enemy of the mind.
I am the auto salesman and lóve you.
I am a teenage cancer, with a plan.
I am the blackt-out man.
I am the woman powerful as a zoo.
I am two eyes screwed to my set, whose blind—

It is the Fourth of July.
Collect: while the dying man,
forgone by you creator, who forgives,
is gasping "Thomas Jefferson still lives"
in vain, in vain, in vain.
I am Henry Pussy-cat! My whiskers fly.

[1964]

"Sole Watchman"

from Eleven Addresses to the Lord

Sole watchman of the flying stars, guard me
against my flicker of impulse lust: teach me
to see them as sisters & daughters. Sustain
my grand endeavours: husbandship & crafting.

Forsake me not when my wild hours come;
grant me sleep nightly, grace soften my dreams;
achieve in me patience till the thing be done,
a careful view of my achievement come.

Make me from time to time the gift of the shoulder.
When all hurt nerves whine shut away the whiskey.
Empty my heart toward Thee.
Let me pace without fear the common path of death.

Cross am I sometimes with my little daughter:
fill her eyes with tears. Forgive me, Lord.
Unite my various soul,
sole watchman of the wide & single stars.

[1970]

Dylan Thomas

(1914–1953) b. Swansea, Wales

Disc 3

Tracks 11–13

Dylan Thomas, possibly the most renowned Welsh poet of all time, was born on October 27, 1914, in the Welsh seaport town of Swansea. A sickly child, Thomas received nearly all of his formal education at Swansea Grammar School, where his father was the senior English master. While Thomas performed poorly in other subjects, he excelled at English. He edited the school magazine, passionately studied D.H. Lawrence's poems, and appears to have begun composing his own poetry at an early age. While he never learned to read Welsh, his parents' native tongue, the rhythms and textures of that language exerted a marked influence on Thomas's writing. Dropping out of school at age sixteen, he worked briefly as a newspaper reporter with the *South Wales Daily Post*. In 1933, he published his first poem in a major literary magazine and decided to pursue a literary career. He moved to London in 1934; later that year, at the age of twenty, Thomas published his first collection of poems. Comprising a handful of tempestuous, sensuous, and mystical lyrics, *Eighteen Poems* received wide acclaim and announced the young Thomas as a poet of much promise.

In early 1936, Thomas met Caitlin MacNamara, a writer and acclaimed free-style dancer, whom he married a year later. Later in 1936, he published his second collection, *Twenty-Five Poems*, and the book established his reputation as one of the premier poets of the day. Thomas and his wife briefly moved to Laugharne, Wales, which would eventually become a permanent home for them after a period of rambling. Despite Thomas's many publications and growing popularity throughout the '30s—bolstered by his radio broadcasts beginning in 1937—his earnings were never steady. Financial troubles and alcohol abuse affected his marriage, which was always turbulent, as well as his personal relationships. His writing, however, continued to flourish. During this period, Thomas published such works as *Portrait of the Artist as a Young Dog* (1940), a collection of autobiographical short stories; *Deaths and Entrances* (1946), a volume of poems containing many of his best-remembered, including "Fern Hill" and *The Map of Love* (1939).

In 1947, Thomas suffered a nervous breakdown and moved with Caitlin to Oxford. After recuperating, he returned to Wales in 1949, and in the following year he began the first of his famous American tours. Thomas's reputation had been established early in America, and his readings on and off college campuses were extremely popular. He followed the 1950 tour with additional tours in 1952 and 1953. On his last visit to America, Thomas composed what is perhaps his most celebrated single work, the radio drama titled *Under Milk Wood*. He read this "play for voices" publicly with five other readers in Cambridge, Massachusetts, on May 14, 1953, and by chance, an audience member recorded the reading. *Under Milk Wood* would not appear in book form until after Thomas's death.

On November 9, 1953, Thomas died in New York City. A lifelong heavy drinker, his death was brought on by a case of acute alcohol poisoning in combination with an excessive dose of morphine sulphate administered by a doctor. Many of his works were published posthumously, including *A Child's Christmas in Wales* (1955) and *Notebooks* (1968). In light of its tremendous and enduring artistic achievements, it is impossible to categorize Thomas's life as either triumphant or tragic. It was, like his poetry, both.

Glyn Maxwell on Dylan Thomas

Dylan Thomas is among those poets—along with the likes of Lord Byron, Edgar Allan Poe, and Sylvia Plath—who is as often remembered for the manner of his life and death as for the splendor of his verse. These are the poets whose lives adhere most closely to the culture's prejudices about the calling: the devil-may-cares who drink life to the dregs, the tortured obsessives who self-destruct, those whom the gods destroy. They become iconic figures, even caricatures, which always has the effect of obscuring their true worth.

In the case of Dylan Thomas, the legend makes him seem like a figure on the edge of society, a misfit, a divine drunk, whereas in fact he lived his life very much at the public heart of things. Welsh culture treats the Poet not as a lonely spirit in the hills—as did, say, the English Romantic movement—but as an oracle for the nation, a voice deep in the language, while by temperament Thomas was exceedingly social and gregarious. The London pubs he frequented were generally to be found in the vicinity of the BBC, for which he was a brilliant and popular broadcaster. He was a memorable reader of his poetry. In addition, he worked extensively in film and left behind, in the dreamlike *Under Milk Wood*, one of the best plays written by a poet in the twentieth century.

All true poems have a pitch, a level at which they communicate with the reader. Some chatty and intimate, some like sermons or harangues, others as natural as conversation. Nearly all of Thomas's verse is pitched high. If Robert Frost's verse can be imagined as a man speaking trenchantly outdoors, or Philip Larkin's as a world-weary chap in reflective mood on a bar-stool, Thomas's seems to sweep down from the pulpit or the organ-loft. His lines are musical and muscular. They are often strange, they are on occasion opaque. It is a verse that sings, that seems to trust the deepest cadences of language to carry the pulse of meaning. This can make it difficult, but even when difficult, it is usually rewarding, and on occasions sublime.

Like the Ancient Mariner's hand on the arm of the Wedding-Guest, all Thomas's poems start by seizing one's attention. This can be done through the sheer individual oddity of the line ("The seed-at-zero shall not storm…") or by sudden exclamation or command ("Foster the light…" "Friend by enemy I call you out…" "Hold

The boathouse in Laugharne, Wales, where Thomas lived

Thomas's writing desk in the boathouse

hard, these ancient minutes…") or by high, almost scriptural, pronouncement ("This bread I break was once the oat…" "And death shall have no dominion…") It is a formal poetry, usually stanzaic, but it draws as much on the older alliterative traditions of English verse as it does on later resources such as rhyme and pentameter. Indeed Thomas's love of sound-patterns—"And green and golden as I was huntsman and herdsman"—derives from a more ancient source than most canonical English poetry: the highly complex repeating forms of old Welsh verse. In the century before Thomas, only Gerard Manley Hopkins displays a similar ancestry, so strong a faith and so deep a delight in the fiber of language itself.

Given such a pitch of intensity, it is not surprising that Thomas's themes are elemental: birth, loss, death. If anything is common to every poem, it is a burning sense of mortality, an amazement at the vigour of life or a heightened dismay at its brevity. It is a corporeal poetry, never far from an awareness of blood and bones and nakedness. Its fury for life produced the best villanelle in the language, which pleads over and over: "Do not go gentle into that good night…" Christ's Passion haunts the work, spreads out its scope, sharpens the mortal sense. That feeling of all life as a painful flash of beauty reaches its height at the close of "Fern Hill":

Oh as I was young and easy in the mercy of his means,
Time held me green and dying
Though I sang in my chains like the sea.

The too-brief story of Dylan Thomas may lend these lines some poignancy, but they would lose none of their magnificence had an old man written them.

And Death Shall Have No Dominion

And death shall have no dominion.
Dead men naked they shall be one
With the man in the wind and the west moon;
When their bones are picked clean and the clean bones gone,
They shall have stars at elbow and foot;
Though they go mad they shall be sane,
Though they sink through the sea they shall rise again;
Though lovers be lost love shall not;
And death shall have no dominion.

And death shall have no dominion.
Under the windings of the sea
They lying long shall not die windily;
Twisting on racks when sinews give way,
Strapped to a wheel, yet they shall not break;
Faith in their hands shall snap in two,
And the unicorn evils run them through;
Split all end up they shan't crack;
And death shall have no dominion.

And death shall have no dominion.
No more may gulls cry at their ears
Or waves break loud on the seashores;
Where blew a flower may a flower no more
Lift its head to the blows of the rain;
Though they be mad and dead as nails,
Heads of the characters hammer through daisies;
Break in the sun till the sun breaks down,
And death shall have no dominion.

[1936]

Fern Hill

Now as I was young and easy under the apple boughs
About the lilting house and happy as the grass was green,
     The night above the dingle starry,
       Time let me hail and climb
     Golden in the heydays of his eyes,
And honoured among wagons I was prince of the apple towns
And once below a time I lordly had the trees and leaves
       Trail with daisies and barley
     Down the rivers of the windfall light.

And as I was green and carefree, famous among the barns
About the happy yard and singing as the farm was home,
     In the sun that is young once only,
       Time let me play and be
     Golden in the mercy of his means,
And green and golden I was huntsman and herdsman, the calves
Sang to my horn, the foxes on the hills barked clear and cold,
       And the sabbath rang slowly
     In the pebbles of the holy streams.

All the sun long it was running, it was lovely, the hay
Fields high as the house, the tunes from the chimneys, it was air
     And playing, lovely and watery
       And fire green as grass.
     And nightly under the simple stars
As I rode to sleep the owls were bearing the farm away,
All the moon long I heard, blessed among stables, the night-jars
     Flying with the ricks, and the horses
       Flashing into the dark.

And then to awake, and the farm, like a wanderer white
With the dew, come back, the cock on his shoulder: it was all
     Shining, it was Adam and maiden,
       The sky gathered again
     And the sun grew round that very day.
So it must have been after the birth of the simple light

In the first, spinning place, the spellbound horses walking warm
    Out of the whinnying green stable
      On to the fields of praise.

And honoured among foxes and pheasants by the gay house
Under the new made clouds and happy as the heart was long,
    In the sun born over and over,
      I ran my heedless ways,
    My wishes raced through the house high hay
And nothing I cared, at my sky blue trades, that time allows
In all his tuneful turning so few and such morning songs
    Before the children green and golden
      Follow him out of grace,

Nothing I cared, in the lamb white days, that time would take me
Up to the swallow thronged loft by the shadow of my hand,
    In the moon that is always rising,
      Nor that riding to sleep
    I should hear him fly with the high fields
And wake to the farm forever fled from the childless land.
Oh as I was young and easy in the mercy of his means,
    Time held me green and dying
    Though I sang in my chains like the sea.

[1946]

Among Those Killed in the Dawn Raid Was a Man Aged a Hundred

DISC 3, TRACK 13

When the morning was waking over the war
He put on his clothes and stepped out and he died,
The locks yawned loose and a blast blew them wide,
He dropped where he loved on the burst pavement stone
And the funeral grains of the slaughtered floor.
Tell his street on its back he stopped a sun
And the craters of his eyes grew springshoots and fire
When all the keys shot from the locks, and rang.
Dig no more for the chains of his grey-haired heart.
The heavenly ambulance drawn by a wound
Assembling waits for the spade's ring on the cage.
O keep his bones away from that common cart,
The morning is flying on the wings of his age
And a hundred storks perch on the sun's right hand.

[1946]

In My Craft or Sullen Art

In my craft or sullen art
Exercised in the still night
When only the moon rages
And the lovers lie abed
With all their griefs in their arms,
I labour by singing light
Not for ambition or bread
Or the strut and trade of charms
On the ivory stages
But for the common wages
Of their most secret heart.

Not for the proud man apart
From the raging moon I write
On these spindrift pages
Nor for the towering dead
With their nightingales and psalms
But for the lovers, their arms
Round the griefs of the ages,
Who pay no praise or wages
Nor heed my craft or art.

[1946]

Do Not Go Gentle into That Good Night

Do not go gentle into that good night,
Old age should burn and rave at close of day;
Rage, rage against the dying of the light.

Though wise men at their end know dark is right,
Because their words had forked no lighting they
Do not go gentle into that good night.

Good men, the last wave by, crying how bright
Their frail deeds might have danced in a green bay,
Rage, rage against the dying of the light.

Wild men who caught and sang the sun in flight,
And learn, too late, they grieved it on its way,
Do not go gentle into that good night.

Grave men, near death, who see with blinding sight
Blind eyes could blaze like meteors and be gay,
Rage, rage against the dying of the light.

And you, my father, there on the sad height,
Curse, bless, me now with your fierce tears, I pray.
Do not go gentle into that good night.
Rage, rage against the dying of the light.

[1952]

Robert Lowell

(1917–1977) b. Boston, Massachusetts, United States

Disc 3
Tracks 14–16

Robert Lowell was born into a prominent Boston family on March 1, 1917. Graced with many famous family members—including poets James Russell and Amy Lowell—the Lowells boasted an illustrious history stretching back for generations. Lowell attended Boston private schools, St. Mark's Preparatory School, and then enrolled in Harvard University. Harvard was his family's traditional alma mater, but Lowell remained there for only two years. After meeting Allen Tate, a respected poet of the Fugitive movement, in 1937, Lowell decided to transfer to Kenyon College in order to study under John Crowe Ransom, another member of the movement. He graduated Kenyon in 1940, but not before befriending Randall Jarrell and Peter Taylor, both of whom went on to successful and influential writing careers of their own. Nineteen forty was a turning point in other ways for Lowell as well. That year, he married the novelist and short-story writer Jean Stafford. Breaking another of his family's longstanding traditions, Lowell converted from Protestantism to Roman Catholicism, an event that had a definite and marked influence on his life and his poetry.

Lowell and Stafford ventured together to Louisiana, where Lowell studied with Cleanth Brooks and Robert Penn Warren at Louisiana State University. Shortly thereafter, they moved to Monteagle, Tennessee, where they shared a house with Allen Tate and his wife. The outbreak of World War II prompted Lowell to volunteer for military service in 1941, but he was rejected at that time due to his poor eyesight. Nonetheless, a conscription notice came for him in 1943. By that time, Lowell had undergone another ideological conversion and declared himself a conscientious objector. This protest marked the beginning of Lowell's career in political activism. He went to prison as a result of his refusal to serve, and during this time he finished his first volume of poetry, *Land of Unlikeness*, which was published in 1944. The publication of his second book, *Lord Weary's Castle* (1946), led to his recognition as one of the top poets of his day and earned him a Pulitzer Prize in 1947.

Lowell was divorced from Stafford in 1948, but remarried a year later to Elizabeth Hardwick, a novelist from Kentucky. His next book of poetry, *The Mills of the Kavanaughs*, appeared in 1951 to mostly unfavorable reviews. Lowell and Hardwick moved to Europe, but Lowell began suffering from mental breakdowns and depression. He was ultimately hospitalized in 1954, shortly after his mother's death. He returned to America that year and began lecturing at various universities. His fourth collection, *Life Studies*, widely considered his highest accomplishment, restored his reputation when it appeared in 1959. A landmark work in many ways, the unabashedly autobiographical and incalculably influential *Life Studies* gave rise to the poetic trend now known as "confessionalism." With this success to bolster him, Lowell embarked on a series of projects, including translations, stage adaptations, and many antiwar demonstrations. Lowell even declined an invitation to the White House as a way to protest the Vietnam War.

Lowell continued to write poetry until his death, and his later collections include some of his finest work. *The Dolphin*, for which he won a second Pulitzer Prize, *History*, and *For Lizzie and Harriet* all appeared in 1973. He spent most of his remaining years in England with his third wife, Caroline Blackwood, an English writer and aristocrat. He was on his way to visit Elizabeth Hardwick in New York when he died of heart failure on September 12, 1977.

Frank Bidart on Robert Lowell

Because Robert Lowell is widely, perhaps indelibly associated with the term "confessional," it seems appropriate and even necessary to discuss how "confessional" poetry is not confession. How Lowell's candor is an illusion created by art. He always insisted that his so-called confessional poems were in significant ways invented. The power aimed at in *Life Studies* is the result not of accuracy but the illusion of accuracy, the result of arrangement and invention.

Lowell in his *Paris Review* interview with Frederick Seidel says that the illusion of "reality" in a "confessional" poem *is an aesthetic effect*. Seidel: "These poems, I gather from what you said earlier, did take as much working over as the earlier ones." Lowell's response:

They were just as hard to write. They're not always factually true. There's a good deal of tinkering with fact. You leave out a lot, and emphasize this and not that. Your actual experience is a complete flux. I've invented facts and changed things, and the whole balance of the poem was something invented. So there's a lot of artistry, I hope, in the poems. Yet there's this thing: if a poem is autobiographical—and this is true of any kind of autobiographical writing and of historical writing—you want the reader to say, this is true. In something like Macaulay's *History of England*, you think you're really getting William III. That's as good as a good plot in a novel. And so there was always that standard of truth which you wouldn't ordinarily have in poetry—the reader was to believe he was getting the *real* Robert Lowell.

What fascinates in these sentences is the forthrightness with which Lowell treats the sensation that the autobiographical or historical writer aims at, *This is true*, as an aesthetic effect—as possessing power *because* the writing gives the reader the illusion that it is true. *Life Studies* aims at this effect. The illusion that the poem is not art but a report on life, that the reader is getting "the *real* Robert Lowell," is not a central concern in all of Lowell's books (not central, for example, to *Near the Ocean* or *Lord Weary's Castle*), but lies at the heart of the power of autobiography and history. Art that constantly reminds one that it is art, that it is constructed and could have been constructed in another way, forgoes this power (ideally, for power of another kind).

The "realist" author serves an accuracy that is not the accuracy of fact: Lowell says in the final paragraph of the same interview, "Almost the whole problem of writing poetry is to get it back to what you feel." That takes, he says, "maneuvering." Here is an example of maneuvering, from "To Speak of Woe That Is in Marriage":

> *It's the injustice...he is so unjust—*
> *whiskey-blind, swaggering home at five.*
> *My only thought is how to keep alive.*
> *What makes him tick? Each night now I tie*
> *ten dollars and his car key to my thigh...*

I've taught this poem many times in class, and I always ask the class—why does she tie ten dollars and his car key to her thigh? (I teach at Wellesley College, so this is asked of a group of women.) The answers usually are about evenly divided between the idea that she does this to protect her escape if he again becomes violent, and the idea that she thereby requires sexual intimacy from him before he can escape and (in the words of the poem) "free-lanc[e] out along the razor's edge." Each motive is possible (she fears him; she is fascinated by him), and they are opposites. I don't think that, from the poem, one can know which is true. Does *she* know? Are both true?

I once brought this passage up with Lowell. He smiled rather sheepishly and said that his wife had never done that, that it was told him by the wife of Delmore Schwartz.

Crucial to the texture of a Lowell poem, throughout his career, are these images or actions or *things* that resist a single meaning, that haunt because, dense with meaning, they also elude meaning. Autobiography promises that the walls of a house will dissolve, the veil that separates us from what is real will be at last lifted. In a Lowell poem, what the reader is offered—with at times startling candor—is an invented world dense with the luminous opacity of life.

Typescript of "Home After Three Months Away" with Lowell's revisions

Skunk Hour

DISC 3, TRACK 15

[For Elizabeth Bishop]

Nautilus Island's hermit
heiress still lives through winter in her Spartan cottage;
her sheep still graze above the sea.
Her son's a bishop. Her farmer
is first selectman in our village;
she's in her dotage.

Thirsting for
the hierarchic privacy
of Queen Victoria's century,
she buys up all
the eyesores facing her shore,
and lets them fall.

The season's ill—
we've lost our summer millionaire,
who seemed to leap from an L.L. Bean
catalogue. His nine-knot yawl
was auctioned off to lobstermen.
A red fox stain covers Blue Hill.

And now our fairy
decorator brightens his shop for fall;
his fishnet's filled with orange cork,
orange, his cobbler's bench and awl;
there is no money in his work,
he'd rather marry.

One dark night,
my Tudor Ford climbed the hill's skull;
I watched for love-cars. Lights turned down,
they lay together, hull to hull,
where the graveyard shelves on the town....
My mind's not right.

A car radio bleats,
"Love, O careless Love...." I hear
my ill-spirit sob in each blood cell,
as if my hand were at its throat....
I myself am hell;
nobody's here—

only skunks, that search
in the moonlight for a bite to eat.
They march on their soles up Main Street:
white stripes, moonstruck eyes' red fire
under the chalk-dry and spar spire
of the Trinitarian Church.

I stand on top
of our back steps and breathe the rich air—
a mother skunk with her column of kittens swills the
                                        garbage pail.
She jabs her wedge-head in a cup
of sour cream, drops her ostrich tail,
and will not scare.

[1958]

Home After Three Months Away

Gone now the baby's nurse,
a lioness who ruled the roost
and made the Mother cry.
She used to tie
gobbets of porkrind in bowknots of gauze—
three months they hung like soggy toast
on our eight foot magnolia tree,
and helped the English sparrows
weather a Boston winter.

Three months, three months!
Is Richard now himself again?
Dimpled with exaltation,
my daughter holds her levee in the tub.
Our noses rub,
each of us pats a stringy lock of hair—
they tell me nothing's gone.
Though I am forty-one,
not forty now, the time I put away
was child's-play. After thirteen weeks
my child still dabs her cheeks
to start me shaving. When
we dress her in her sky-blue corduroy,
she changes to a boy,
and floats my shaving brush
and washcloth in the flush....
Dearest, I cannot loiter here
in lather like a polar bear.

Recuperating, I neither spin nor toil.
Three stories down below,
a choreman tends our coffin's length of soil,
and seven horizontal tulips blow.
Just twelve months ago,
these flowers were pedigreed
imported Dutchmen; now no one need
distinguish them from weed.
Bushed by the late spring snow,
they cannot meet
another year's snowballing enervation.

I keep no rank nor station.
Cured, I am frizzled, stale and small.

[1959]

"To Speak of Woe That Is in Marriage"

"It is the future generation that presses into being by means of these exuberant feelings and supersensible soap bubbles of ours."

Schopenhauer

"The hot night makes us keep our bedroom windows
    open.
Our magnolia blossoms. Life begins to happen.
My hopped up husband drops his home disputes,
and hits the streets to cruise for prostitutes,
free-lancing out along the razor's edge.
This screwball might kill his wife, then take the
    pledge.
Oh the monotonous meanness of his lust....
It's the injustice...he is so unjust—
whiskey-blind, swaggering home at five.
My only thought is how to keep alive.
What makes him tick? Each night now I tie
ten dollars and his car key to my thigh....
Gored by the climacteric of his want,
he stalls above me like an elephant."

[1959]

For the Union Dead
"Relinquunt Omnia Servare Rem Publicam."

The old South Boston Aquarium stands
in a Sahara of snow now. Its broken windows are boarded.
The bronze weathervane cod has lost half its scales.
The airy tanks are dry.

Once my nose crawled like a snail on the glass;
my hand tingled
to burst the bubbles
drifting from the noses of the cowed, compliant fish.

My hand draws back. I often sigh still
for the dark downward and vegetating kingdom
of the fish and reptile. One morning last March,
I pressed against the new barbed and galvanized

fence on the Boston Common. Behind their cage,
yellow dinosaur steamshovels were grunting
as they cropped up tons of mush and grass
to gouge their underworld garage.

Parking spaces luxuriate like civic
sandpiles in the heart of Boston.
A girdle of orange, Puritan-pumpkin colored girders
braces the tingling Statehouse,

shaking over the excavations, as it faces Colonel Shaw
and his bell-cheeked Negro infantry
on St. Gaudens' shaking Civil War relief,
propped by a plank splint against the garage's earthquake.

Two months after marching through Boston,
half the regiment was dead;
at the dedication,
William James could almost hear the bronze Negroes breathe.

Their monument sticks like a fishbone
in the city's throat.
Its Colonel is as lean
as a compass-needle.

He has an angry wrenlike vigilance,
a greyhound's gentle tautness;
he seems to wince at pleasure,
and suffocate for privacy.

He is out of bounds now. He rejoices in man's lovely,
peculiar power to choose life and die—
when he leads his black soldiers to death,
he cannot bend his back.

On a thousand small town New England greens,
the old white churches hold their air
of sparse, sincere rebellion; frayed flags
quilt the graveyards of the Grand Army of the Republic.

The stone statues of the abstract Union Soldier
grow slimmer and younger each year—
wasp-wasted, they doze over muskets
and muse through their sideburns…

Shaw's father wanted no monument
except the ditch,
where his son's body was thrown
and lost with his "niggers."

The ditch is nearer.
There are no statues for the last war here;
on Boylston Street, a commercial photograph
shows Hiroshima boiling

over a Mosler Safe, the "Rock of Ages"
that survived the blast. Space is nearer.
When I crouch to my television set,
the drained faces of Negro school-children rise like balloons.

Colonel Shaw
is riding on his bubble,
he waits
for the blesséd break.

The Aquarium is gone. Everywhere,
giant finned cars nose forward like fish;
a savage servility
slides by on grease.

[1960]

Epilogue

Those blessèd structures, plot and rhyme—
why are they no help to me now
I want to make
something imagined, not recalled?
I hear the noise of my own voice:
The painter's vision is not a lens,
it trembles to caress the light.
But sometimes everything I write
with the threadbare art of my eye
seems a snapshot,
lurid, rapid, garish, grouped,
heightened from life,
yet paralyzed by fact.
All's misalliance.
Yet why not say what happened?
Pray for the grace of accuracy
Vermeer gave to the sun's illumination
stealing like the tide across a map
to his girl solid with yearning.
We are poor passing facts,
warned by that to give
each figure in the photograph
his living name.

[1977]

Gwendolyn Brooks

(1917–2000) b. Topeka, Kansas, United States

Disc 3
Tracks 17-20

Gwendolyn Brooks was born in Topeka, Kansas, on June 7, 1917. Her father, David Anderson Brooks, was the son of a runaway slave. Her mother, Keziah Corinne Brooks, had traveled to her own mother's home in Topeka shortly before giving birth. One month later, Brooks was brought home to Chicago, where she would live throughout her life. Brooks attended one of Chicago's leading white high schools, Hyde Park High School, but later transferred to the all-black Wendell Phillips High School, and then to the integrated Englewood High School. After receiving her diploma, she attended Wilson Junior College, graduating in 1936.

Brooks's love of poetry made itself known at an early age, as did her talent. In 1930, at the age of thirteen, she published her first poem, "Eventide," in *American Childhood*. While still in high school, Brooks met the poets James Weldon Johnson and Langston Hughes, who both encouraged her literary ambitions. Johnson urged Brooks to familiarize herself with the work of such Modernists as T.S. Eliot, Ezra Pound, and E.E. Cummings, and Hughes went on to mention her several times in the column he wrote for the black newspaper, the *Chicago Defender*. In 1934, Brooks became an adjunct staff member of the newspaper and wrote a regular poetry column. In 1939, she married Henry Blakely, a writer who would later publish his own volume of poetry, and one year later gave birth to Henry, the first of the couple's two children. (Their daughter, Nora, was born in 1951.) Brooks's formally adept poetry portraying the everyday lives of black Chicagoans began receiving wide recognition in the early 1940s. In 1945, her first book of poems, *A Street in Bronzeville*, brought her instant critical and popular success.

Brooks became the first black poet to receive the Pulitzer Prize when her second collection, *Annie Allen*, was awarded the Prize in 1950. In 1953, Brooks published *Maud Martha*, an under-appreciated, lyrical novel comprising a series of precise, poignant vignettes. In 1960, Brooks published *The Bean Eaters*, another book of well-crafted lyrics, some of which address racial issues explicitly. The fact of her blackness began occupying an increasingly significant place in Brooks's work, especially following her participation in the Second Black Writers' Conference at Fisk University in 1967. This development is reflected in her next collection, *In the Mecca*, which appeared in 1968. That same year, following the death of Carl Sandburg, Brooks was named Poet Laureate of Illinois, a post that she held until her death. Brooks chose not to publish her next book, *Rio*, with her mainstream publisher, Harper & Row, but with Broadside Press, a small, black-owned press. She continued to publish with small presses throughout the 1970s and '80s, including the autobiographical prose collection *Report from Part One* (1972), a collection of reminiscences, interviews, and short, powerful political pieces, and *Blacks* (1987), a collection of her work from over three decades.

From 1985 to 1986, before the publication of *Blacks*, Brooks served as Poetry Consultant to the Library of Congress (later renamed Poet Laureate). She received numerous other honors throughout her career, including an American Academy of Arts and Letters Award, The Frost Medal, and fellowships from the National Endowment for the Arts, the Academy of American Poets, and the Guggenheim Foundation. In 1994 and 1995, she received her highest honor when she was chosen as the Jefferson Lecturer by the National Endowment for the Humanities and received the National Medal of Arts. After a lifetime of writing unforgettable poetry and decades dedicated to raising political consciousness, Brooks died of cancer on December 3, 2000.

Sonia Sanchez on Gwendolyn Brooks

For a long time I've pondered this thing that we do called writing. I've looked at my words sometimes as if they belonged to a stranger. The truth is as you grow older, as time passes, you stare at some of your words as if you have only a passing acquaintance with them. But each time I read Miss Brooks, each time I revisit her poems, they climb up on my knees and sit in tight contentment. They speak to me of form and color, patterns and dawns. They talk of myths; they tell me where the flesh lives; where a troop of young heroes and sheroes "lean back in chairs, beautiful. Impudent. Ready for life." Where the young "Live not for battles won. / live not for the-end-of-the-song. / Live in the along."

I never have to ask where are the flowers? Sun? Where are the mothers? Fathers? Where are the old marrieds? Where are the children "adjudged the leastwise of the land"? Where are the riots? The Sermon on the Warpland? Where are the prophets? Where is Pepita? Where are they who "flail in the hot time"? Where is the sound "that we are each other's harvest"?

I see them in her poems that breathe women in a blaze of upsweeps and backyards and ballads, in her children dancing between urine and violets, in her singing to us between the sleeping and the waking.

I have gotten lost sometimes in this journey called life, in which nothing moved, when I gathered up our daytime hysteria, when I looked at the country's delirium, when I tried to disagree with my blood, and I heard her poems turning away from funerals, feasting on rain and laughter, walking toward life with serious hands, heard her footsteps gathering around us, and she came tongued by fire and water and bone, and she came from where the drum sings, and she came reclaiming our most sacred ashes, and her love carved the journey of this woman-sail.

And as she entered into our twenty-first century bloodstream, paddling a river of risks, she became the color of bells, set sail on the wind and sailed home. Said hello to our own good-byes.

A Song in the Front Yard

DISC 3, TRACK 18

I've stayed in the front yard all my life.
I want a peek at the back
Where it's rough and untended and hungry weed grows.
A girl gets sick of a rose.

I want to go in the back yard now
And maybe down the alley,
To where the charity children play.
I want a good time today.

They do some wonderful things.
They have some wonderful fun.
My mother sneers, but I say it's fine
How they don't have to go in at quarter to nine.
My mother, she tells me that Johnnie Mae
Will grow up to be a bad woman.
That George'll be taken to Jail soon or late
(On account of last winter he sold our back gate).

But I say it's fine. Honest, I do.
And I'd like to be a bad woman, too,
And wear the brave stockings of night-black lace
And strut down the streets with paint on my face.

[1945]

kitchenette building

DISC 3, TRACK 19

We are things of dry hours and the involuntary plan,
Grayed in, and gray. "Dream" makes a giddy sound, not strong
Like "rent," "feeding a wife," "satisfying a man."

But could a dream send up through onion fumes
Its white and violet, fight with fried potatoes
And yesterday's garbage ripening in the hall,
Flutter, or sing an aria down these rooms

Even if we were willing to let it in,
Had time to warm it, keep it very clean,
Anticipate a message, let it begin?

We wonder. But not well! not for a minute!
Since Number Five is out of the bathroom now,
We think of lukewarm water, hope to get in it.

[1945]

We Real Cool

**The Pool Players.
Seven at the Golden Shovel.**

DISC 3, TRACK 20

We real cool. We
Left school. We

Lurk late. We
Strike straight. We

Sing sin. We
Thin gin. We

Jazz June. We
Die soon.

[1960]

The Boy Died in My Alley

The Boy died in my alley
Without my Having Known.
Policeman said, next morning,
"Apparently died Alone"

"You heard a shot?" Policeman said.
Shots I hear and Shots I hear.
I never see the Dead.

The Shot that killed him yes I heard
as I heard the Thousand shots before;
careening tinnily down the nights
across my years and arteries.

Policeman pounded on my door.
"Who is it?" "POLICE!" Policeman yelled.
"A Boy was dying in your alley.
A Boy is dead, and in your alley.
And have you known this Boy before?"

I have known this Boy before.
I have known this Boy before, who
ornaments my alley.
I never saw his face at all.
I never saw his futurefall.
But I have known this Boy.

I have always heard him deal with death.
I have always heard the shout, the volley.
I have closed my heart-ears late and early.
And I have killed him ever.

I joined the Wild and killed him
with knowledgeable unknowing.
I saw where he was going.
I saw him Crossed. And seeing,
I did not take him down.

He cried not only "Father!"
but "Mother!
Sister!
Brother."
The cry climbed up the alley.
It went up to the wind.
It hung upon the heaven
for a long
stretch-strain of Moment.

The red floor of my alley
is a special speech to me.

[1981]

Speech to the Young
Speech to the Progress-Toward
(Among Them Nora and Henry III)

Say to them,
say to the down-keepers,
the sun-slappers,
the self-soilers,
the harmony-hushers,
"Even if you are not ready for day
it cannot always be night."
You will be right.
For that is the hard home-run.
Live not for battles won.
Live not for the-end-of-the-song.
Live in the along.

[1991]

Robert Duncan

(1919–1988) b. Oakland, California, United States

Disc 3
Tracks 21–23

Robert Duncan was born Edward Howard Duncan on January 7, 1919, in Oakland, California. Duncan's mother died in childbirth, and when his father found it impossible to care for his son while working as a day laborer, he put Duncan up for adoption. Edwin Joseph Symmes and Minnehaha Harris, the couple who raised Duncan, practiced Theosophy and even consulted astrological charts before adopting him. Their devoutly held mystical and philosophical views would forever influence Duncan's poetry. Duncan began writing at an early age, and with the encouragement of a high-school teacher, decided upon a career in poetry during his teens. Beginning in 1938, he attended the University of California, Berkeley on a scholarship. He left after two years to attend North Carolina's Black Mountain College, but quickly abandoned those plans. Instead, he moved to Philadelphia to live with his male lover, a former instructor at Berkeley, but soon relocated to Woodstock, New York, to a commune. He was drafted in 1941, but was discharged while still in training camp because of his sexual orientation.

Although Duncan had female as well as male lovers and was even married briefly, he identified himself as homosexual. In 1944, he published an article titled "The Homosexual in Society" in the journal *Politics*. Calling for social unity based on love and acceptance, Duncan compared the homosexual's struggle for acceptance with that of African-Americans and Jews. A theosophical belief in the "essential oneness" of creation informed much of Duncan's poetry as well as his politics; among other major influences on his development as a poet, Duncan included the work of Jack Spicer, Denise Levertov, H.D., Edith Sitwell, and Robert Creeley. In 1946, Duncan left New York and returned to study medieval and Renaissance literature at Berkeley. The San Francisco Renaissance (a movement related to the Beat movement) was in its early stages at this time, and the work of Robin Blaser and Kenneth Rexroth held particular importance for Duncan. In 1947, he published his first collection of poems, *Heavenly City, Earthly City* to mediocre reviews. That same year, Duncan met poet-scholar Charles Olson. The two formed a close friendship, and Duncan adopted much of the aesthetic ideals touched on in Olson's famous essay, "Projective Verse." Duncan continued to publish books of poems and was invited to teach at Black Mountain College in 1955. While there, Duncan wrote most of what would become his first widely heralded collection, 1960's *The Opening of the Field*. The book synthesized the spiritualism Duncan had inherited from his adoptive parents, the elements of a recovered and reconfigured romanticism, and the Black Mountain aesthetic into a singular, rhetorically elevated style.

Duncan's poetry continued to receive high praise from critics. His next volume, *Roots and Branches*, was equally well crafted but used more elegant language; in 1968, his *Bending the Bow* addressed political and social concerns and, though well thought of, was criticized by some for its bald-faced denunciation of warmongering. As a result, Duncan vowed not to publish another volume for fifteen years. He wrote *Ground Work: Before the War* during that time. Published in 1984, the volume showed Duncan at the height of his powers and won the first-ever National Poetry Award. The follow-up volume, 1987's *Ground Work II: In the Dark*, focused on the interplay of life and death and seemed to presage Duncan's succumbing to kidney disease in 1988. Duncan is remembered as a member of many different schools of poetry who managed to avoid conforming to any single one of them, producing a personal, maverick style that resists replication.

Michael Palmer
Robert Duncan

Michael Palmer on Robert Duncan

Robert Duncan was born in Oakland, California, in 1919. His mother died at his birth, and he was adopted into a spiritualist family steeped in the lore of Theosophy. While not a practicing spiritualist himself, Duncan was forever impressed by the sense of a mythic continuum. His own mature poetics would manifest both a belief in the visionary possibilities of the poetic imagination and a vast, syncretic, personal scholarship.

Duncan himself identified with what has come to be called the exploratory counter-tradition in American poetry and letters, which he interpreted as a subset of an eternal, bardic *Traditio* encompassing the work of such poets as Blake and Shelley, Nerval, Rimbaud and Mallarmé, Dante and the Troubadours, Rumi, Pindar, and many more. It is an ancient tradition of the endlessly new, of the always and the never before, one of songs circulating in nonlinear time, in a kind of enduring, resistant, Orphic conversation. His poetics were largely articulated through two different, yet equally crucial, poetic movements. Initially, in Berkeley, he became associated with the poets of the Berkeley Renaissance, such as Jack Spicer, Robin Blaser, Madeleine Gleason, and others. In their company, he would further develop his store of sometimes hermetic imagery and his taste for a heightened poetic rhetoric, romantic in its origins, yet crossed with a Modernist, experimental sensibility. His work would be forever marked by this paradox. In fact, it might be seen as the characteristic signature of both his poetry and his extensive writings in poetics, and it is much in evidence in "Often I Am Permitted to Return to a Meadow" and "The Sentinels." His second, seminal association was with the "Black Mountain Poets," principally Denise Levertov, Charles Olson, and Robert Creeley. Through his correspondence and conversations with them, he refined his personal sense of a projective, open-field verse, with its dynamic relationship between the oral and the textual, the body and the page, their natures enfolded by the breath's (or the "spirit's") own measure. The result would be a poetry of folds, intersections, and errancy, rather than one of a linear, narrative line. It would be a poetry faithful in all respects to his master Dante's idea of "polysemy," of multiple valences and currents, of figures beneath figures, and of an indeterminate journey, "where the straight way was lost."

Yet, as in Dante, it would also be a journey toward a source of light, an origin, or "place of first permission." The poem then becomes a site not so much for personal reflection or confession, or a naturalistic representation of the world, as for a search for poetry's "truths in their wild state," as the philosopher Gilles Deleuze phrases it.

"Often I Am Permitted to Return to a Meadow" occupies a very particular place within Duncan's body of work. It is the *opening* poem in Duncan's first collection from a time of full poetic maturity, *The Opening of the Field* (1960). It is usually read, correctly I think, as both an enactment of, and a multidimensional statement on, his poetics, and it introduces the thematic images of the book: dream and dance, the play of shadow and light, the field and its folds, the romantic quest for a primal source of the poetic imagination and poetic thought. Through the turnings and folds of its syntax, it attempts to create its own "poetic logic," a logic not of deduction and formal argument, but of multiple associations amid the play of harmonies and disharmonies within the poem's highly charged, open-ended field of signification. The image of the field, Duncan tells us in an unpublished preface to the volume, issues from his recurring childhood "Atlantis dream," a dream of the lost city and the lost mother, and of deluge. It is a dream of darkness and light intermingled, catastrophe and hope conjoined. In the field or meadow itself, that place of "first permission," children dance in a circle. Yet as Duncan well knew from his research in folklore, the ditty they recite resonates with conflicting historical meanings. What we now register as a song of innocence, "Ring Around the Rosy," derives from an era of pestilence, that of one of the bubonic plague epidemics in England. It speaks or sings of infection and death ("All fall down"). So the place of permission and initiation into language, the site of song unconstrained, is also one of terror and foreboding and a reminder of mortality.

"The Sentinels" (from Duncan's final collection, *Ground Work II*) is still another dream song in which disparate forces irresolubly contend. The poem represents a descent into a crepuscular, wordless, nearly indiscernible world over which earth owls preside, as sentinels. It is a world of "after-light," a zone where waking and dream, conscious and unconscious uneasily meet, mingle, and intertwine; a world of mute memory ("silent as a family photograph"), ghosts and traces, through which the poet, himself wraith-like, passes, interrupting the silence with the scratching of his pen. The owl (should we think of Minerva's owl?) is always the "bird of poetry" in Duncan's work, yet here, in this sequence of fragments or dream recollections, we have owls "clumpt" "in ancient burrows" in the earth, "so near to death," as if buried but not quite. Infernal beings, they preside over an Orphic world the poet must enter to find the "secrets of the earth," that "owl-thought…hidden in all things." It is a placeless place, prior to language, from which the measures of the poem arise. From there the poet returns to the upper, waking world, harboring the figures and forms he has been given.

"If Love Broke," handwritten manuscript by Duncan

Poetry, A Natural Thing

    Neither our vices nor our virtues
further the poem. "They came up
    and died
just like they do every year
    on the rocks."

    The poem
feeds upon thought, feeling, impulse,
    to breed   itself,
a spiritual urgency at the dark ladders leaping.

This beauty is an inner persistence
    toward the source
striving against (within) down-rushet of the river,
    a call we heard and answer
in the lateness of the world
    primordial bellowings
from which the youngest world might spring,

salmon not in the well where the
    hazelnut falls
but at the falls battling, inarticulate,
    blindly making it.

This is one picture apt for the mind.

A second: a moose painted by Stubbs,
where last year's extravagant antlers
    lie on the ground.
The forlorn moosey-faced poem wears
    new antler-buds,
    the same,

"a little heavy, a little contrived",

his only beauty to be
    all moose.

[1960]

The Structure of Rime I

I ask the unyielding Sentence that shows Itself forth in the language
as I make it,

>   Speak! For I name myself your master, who come to serve.
>   Writing is first a search in obedience.

There is a woman who resembles the sentence. She has a place in
memory that moves language. Her voice comes across the waters from a shore
I don't know to a shore I know, and is translated into words belonging to
the poem:

>   *Have heart,* the text reads,
>   *you that were heartless.*
>   *Suffering joy or despair*
>   *you will suffer the sentence*
>   *a law of words moving*
>   *seeking their right period.*

I saw a snake-like beauty in the living changes of syntax.

>   *Wake up,* she cried.
>   *Jacob wrestled with Sleep—you who fall into Nothingness*
>   *and dread sleep.*
>   *He wrestled with Sleep like a man reading a strong*
>   *sentence.*

I will not take the actual world for granted, I said.

>   *Why not?* she replied.
>   *Do I not withhold the song of birds from you?*
>   *Do I not withhold the penetrations of red from you?*
>   *Do I not withhold the weight of mountains from you?*
>   *Do I not withhold the hearts of men from you?*
>
>   *I alone long for your demand.*
>   *I alone measure your desire.*

O Lasting Sentence,
sentence after sentence I make in your image. In the feet that measure
the dance of my pages I hear cosmic intoxications of the man I will be.

Cheat at this game? she cries.
The world is what you are.
    Stand then
so I can see you, a fierce destroyer of images.

Will you drive me to madness
    only there to know me?
vomiting images into the place of the Law!

[1960]

DISC 3, TRACK 23

Often I Am Permitted to Return to a Meadow

as if it were a scene made-up by the mind,
that is not mine, but is a made place,

that is mine, it is so near to the heart,
an eternal pasture folded in all thought
so that there is a hall therein

that is a made place, created by light
wherefrom the shadows that are forms fall.

Wherefrom fall all architectures I am
I say are likenesses of the First Beloved
whose flowers are flames lit to the Lady.

She it is Queen Under The Hill
whose hosts are a disturbance of words within words
that is a field folded.

It is only a dream of the grass blowing
east against the source of the sun
in an hour before the sun's going down

whose secret we see in a children's game
of ring a round of roses told.

Often I am permitted to return to a meadow
as if it were a given property of the mind
that certain bounds hold against chaos,

that is a place of first permission,
everlasting omen of what is.

[1960]

The Sentinels

Earth owls in ancient burrow clumpt
the dream presents.   I could return to look.
No other fragment remains.   I wanted owls
and brought them back.   The grey-brown earth-
haunted grass and bush and bushy birds
so near to death, silent as a family photograph,
still as if the sound of a rattle were missing,
the owls shifting into the stillness, thicket and hole
alive, impassive witnesses thrive there
as ever—I've but to close my eyes and go.
The rest of that field and the company
I was among in that place are lost—ghost folk,
passing among whom I was a wraith,
awake, studious, writing, the blur
marrd and almost erased,   unmarkt events.
It was night and cold and the light there
was an after-light.   I wrapt my naked body
in my comforter against that wind.   I
do not—I can not—I will not, trying,
recite the rest.   It was grey day in an absence of the sun.
It was a place without a rattling sound,
a deaf waiting room this place is close upon.
The scratching of my pen and my bending thought
move from this margin and return.   Morning shrinks.
The owls shiver down into the secrets of an earth
I began to see when I lookt into the hole I feard
and then saw others in the clump of grass.
I was dreaming and where I dreamt a light had gone out
and in that light they blind their sight and sit
sentinel upon the brooding of owl-thought, counselings
I remember ever mute and alive, hidden in all things.

[1987]

Jack Kerouac

(1922–1969) b. Lowell, Massachusetts, United States

Disc 3
Track 24–26

Following the publication in 1957 of *On the Road*, Jack Kerouac became the hip ideal of an entire generation of young people. He was born Jean-Louis Lebris de Kerouac on March 12, 1922, in the declining mill town of Lowell, Massachusetts. His French-Canadian parents spoke Québécois French, and Jack, as he came to be called, did not learn English until the age of six. The death of his nine-year-old elder brother from rheumatic fever was a traumatic shock from which Kerouac never fully recovered. A Columbia University athlete, he later joined the Navy but was unable to find his niche. In New York he hung out with Allen Ginsberg, William Burroughs, and other figures of what would become known as the Beat Generation, including Edie Parker, to whom he was briefly married. Most important, he met his friend and sometime lover Neal Cassady, the model for Dean Moriarty, the protagonist of *On the Road*.

In San Francisco he befriended Gary Snyder, the poet and Zen Buddhist who inspired Kerouac to strive toward enlightenment. He married again, this time to Joan Haverty, a union that lasted eight months and ended acrimoniously. It was while he was married that his travels with Cassady resulted in *On the Road*, the first draft of which he completed at breakneck speed, in only three weeks. But his way of life exacted a toll: he began to suffer bouts of depression and became addicted to alcohol and drugs. Even so, his output was prodigious and included the poems of *Mexico City Blues*. A final marriage, to Stella Sampas in 1966, lasted for the short time until his death. His attachment to his mother had always been strong; after leaving California he moved into her house in Northport, Long Island, and never again left her. But it had no effect on reducing the consumption of whiskey and cheap wine which contributed to his death. He died at her home, which was then in St. Petersburg, Florida, on October 21, 1969.

Still, the seeming randomness, even zaniness, of Kerouac's work should be understood in the context of his early life, which included writing comic strips and little novels from the age of eight, and reading Jack London, Ernest Hemingway, William Saroyan, and Thomas Wolfe in his teens. "Then I read Joyce and wrote a whole juvenile novel like *Ulysses*..." That was all well before "reading the marvelous free narrative letters of Neal Cassady...." Unconventional as this "training" was, this early experience with language informed the later work which has come to define him.

Like Ginsberg's "Howl" (1956), *On the Road* not only created a sensation: it came as a shock to readers whose sense of literature had been conditioned by the attendant formalities of most British and American verse in mid-century. And it paved the way for the reception of Kerouac's own poetry. Kerouac's poems, as in the choruses of *Mexico City Blues*, tended to be short and frequently haiku-like. His San Francisco readings prompted midwest poet Michael McClure to proclaim: "I think of Jack as having written the greatest religious poem in the 20th century, which is *Mexico City Blues*."

Jason Shinder on Jack Kerouac

Much of Kerouac's poetry sounds to me like a horn player trying the scale while tuning up. As a "jazz poet," he aims for free association of the mind into a limitless "blow-on subject sea of thought" where "words sing/what mind/brings."

Pestiferating at moon squid
  Salt flat tip fly toe
    tat   sand traps
With cigar smoking interesteds
     puffing at the
       stroll

Written as a fast-paced series of recollections, one bit of memory and sensation piling up on another, "MacDougal Street Blues" and many of his other poems remind me that poetry (and life) is not always a problem to be solved, but a reality to be experienced.

As an alternative to the traditional principles of "good poetry" (where every word and punctuation bears a burden of meaning and purpose), Kerouac sacrificed order and form for what he thought would yield a greater truth about life, especially the unresolvable tangle of modern society. This undoing of order in art was also a necessary source of creativity; reminding us that the basis of free expression is often the unleashing of feelings and thoughts without regard for approval from any individual and/or organized collective or government.

Above all, Kerouac's "order-less" poems aim to offer us the intensity of the moment:

> *Brang!—blong!—trucks*
> *Break glass i the dog barking*
> *Street—dwang, wur,*
> *Ta ta ta*
>   *ta ta*

In his rush to capture the intensity and immediacy of everything he encountered with accessible "everyday" language, Kerouac sometimes gave all experience the same significance, leaving little room for a definitive analysis. Yet I'm always greatly inspired by his courage and candor in putting down the unaccustomed, imperfect rhythm and details of his life exactly the way he immediately saw it and lived it.

The idea of letting thoughts and feelings come forth unimpeded is, of course, an age-old Romantic belief. William Blake claimed he wrote *Milton* without effort, listening to a voice within him. W.B. Yeats based "A Vision" on automatic writing. André Breton and the Surrealists sought to tap into the unconscious through automatic writing and free association. Kerouac's effort to write freely was, however, inspired to a great degree by a letter he received in 1951 from his friend Neal Cassady. Written while Cassady was high on Benzedrine, the letter was a forty-page single-spaced missive about a love affair. Its rushing images and thoughts without chronology or overall coherence captivated Kerouac.

In his essay *The Essentials of Spontaneous Prose* (1953), Kerouac shares his passion for this method. He tells the would-be writer not to worry about using exact words. "Write excitedly...in accordance...with laws of orgasm...write outwards swimming in a sea of language...to release and exhaustion," he instructs. The more effortless the writing, the more true it would be, he claimed.

> *Alone – Nobody's alone*
> *For more than a minute.*
>   *Growl, low, tenorman*
>   *Work out your tune till the day*
>   *Is break, smooth out the rough night,*
> *Wail, ...*

Much of the poetry of the Beat Generation (the generation of disaffected young people who had come to majority during and shortly after World War II) was inspired by Kerouac's "wail," as in these excerpts from *Mexico City Blues*. While the young "beatniks" were making the middle class uneasy with their drug use, sexual promis-

In 1988 the city of San Francisco renamed the alley behind City Lights Bookstore "Jack Kerouac Street."

cuity, and scornful attitude toward "regular" employment, Kerouac was leading a group of poets, including Gregory Corso, John Clellon Holmes, Diane DiPrima, Michael McClure, Edie Parker, Lawrence Ferlinghetti, and Allen Ginsberg to transcribe the scene with "free deviation (association) of mind."

"My own poetry," Allen Ginsberg wrote in his introduction to Kerouac's book, *Poems of All Sizes*, "is modeled on Kerouac's practice of tracing his mind's thoughts and sounds directly on the page." Ginsberg's seminal poem "Howl," named as such by Kerouac, about the desperate quest for meaning and vision in a seemingly mad universe, was created, in good part, with Kerouac's hands-on support as detailed in their correspondence at the time.

Like Ginsberg and his other "beat" contemporaries, Kerouac favored us with subjects that were not readily recognized in the poetry of his time, including drugs, race, hallucinations, money, poverty, crime, and sexuality, as well as driving fast cars, movie-going, blues, rock and roll, friends, and just hanging out. Yet all of the subjects of his verse were connected by something else—the Buddhist-friendly idea that life was an illusion and therefore not worth fretting about. Many of his poems became philosophical statements (sacrificing inspired spontaneity) about life being out of one's control.

– And you seek to achieve
Greater satisfaction
Which is already impossible

It was often all or nothing, and at the end of the Buddhist road all and nothing were the same thing.

How do I know that I'm dead.
*   Because I'm alive*
*   and I got work to do*

I often find the essence of Kerouac's poetic inclinations in his haiku. Working within the limits of a short form, he could be spontaneous, surprising, ironic, humorous, experience-based, and philosophical, with the added focus, discrimination, and power of compression and a relatively unified image.

Kerouac proposed the idea of a "western haiku" that would be "very simple and free of all poetic trickery and make a little picture."

Nightfall—too dark
*   to read the page,*
Too cold

Following each other,
*   my cats stop*
When it thunders

Spring evening—
*   the two*
Eighteen year old sisters

His attempt to transform the traditional Japanese haiku (three lines: five, seven and five syllables respectively) to one that transcended its conditions of conformity was part of his lifelong pursuit to imagine "a new style for American culture." It is a vision that still has an inescapable hold on the imagination and curiosity of our society, especially the young, as evidenced perhaps most strikingly by the establishment of the successful graduate writing school, The Jack Kerouac School of Disembodied Poetics, co-founded by poet/writer Ann Waldman and Allen Ginsberg.

Although best known for his novels, including the celebrated *On The Road*, the heart of this "new style for American culture" included his life-long pursuit of poetry with the publication of more than eight collections in his lifetime and posthumously, including *Mexico City Blues* (a poem in 242 choruses), *Heaven and Other Poems,* and *Poems of All Sizes*. And at the heart of his poetry was a call "to blow as deep as you want…. for the true blue song of man." As for me, such singing is a kind of unthinking, a tune that gets me back to the basic, feeling self.

MacDougal Street Blues

Canto Uno

The goofy foolish
        human parade
Passing on Sunday
        art streets
Of Greenwich Village

Pitiful drawings of
        images on an
        iron fence
        ranged there
        by selfbelieving
        artists
        with no hair
        and black berets
        showing green seas
        eating at rock
        and Pleiades
        of Time

Pestiferating at moon squid
    Salt flat tip fly toe
            tat   sand traps
        With cigar smoking interesteds
                puffing at the
                    stroll
I mean sincerely
    naive sailors buying prints
Women with red banjos
    On their handbags
    And arts handicrafty
    Slow shuffling
    art-ers of Washington Sq
        Passing in what they think
    Is a happy June afternoon
Good God the Sorrow
    They dont even listen to me when
    I try to tell them they will die

They say "Of course I know
I'll die, why should you mention
It now—Why should I worry
About it—it'll happen
    It'll happen—Now
    I want a good time—
    Excuse me—
    It's a beautiful happy June
    Afternoon I want to walk in—

Why are you so tragic & gloomy?"
And on the corner at the
            Pony Stables
Of Sixth Ave & 4th
Sits Bodhisattva Meditating
In Hobo Rags
    Praying at Joe Gould's chair
For the Emancipation

Of the shufflers passing by,
Immovable in Meditation
He offers his hand & feet
    To the passers by
And nobody believes
That there's nothing to believe in.
Listen to Me.
There is no sidewalk artshow
    No strollers are there

No poem here, no June
    afternoon of Oh
But only   Imagelessness
Unrepresented on the iron fence
Of bald artists
    With black berets
    Passing by

One moment less than this
Is future Nothingness Already

The Chess men are silent, assembling
Ready for funny war—
Voices of Washington Sq Blues
    Rise to my Bodhisattva Poem
        Window
    I will describe them:
    E y t k e y   ee
        S a la   o s o
            F r   up   t u r t

Etc.
No need, no words to
        describe
The sound of Ignorance—
They are strolling to
        their death
Watching the Pictures of Hell
Eating Ice Cream
        of Ignorance
On wood sticks
That were once sincere
        in trees—
But I cant write, poetry,
    just prose

I mean
 This is prose
    Not poetry
        But I want
            To be sincere

[1955]

7th Chorus from
Orizaba 210 Blues

Brang!—blong!—trucks
Break glass i the dog barking
Street—dwang, wur,
Ta ta ta
  ta ta
Me that was weaned in the
    heaven's machine
Me that was wailed
  in the wild bar
called fence
Me that repeated & petered
The meter & lost 2 cents
Me that was fined
To be hined
And refined
    Ay
        Me that was
        Whoo ee
        The owl
        On the fence

[1956]

from *Book of Haikus*

CD 3 / TRACK 26

Snap yr finger,
   stop the world!
— Rain falls harder

Nightfall—too dark
   to read the page,
Too cold

In my medicine cabinet
   the winter fly
Has died of old age

Following each other,
   my cats stop
When it thunders

Spring evening—
   the two
Eighteen year old sisters

The postman is late
   —The toilet window
Is shining

Wash hung out
   by moonlight
  —Friday night

Empty baseball field
   —A robin,
Hops along the bench

Black bird – no!
   bluebird – pear
Branch still jumping

My rumpled couch
   —The lady's voice
Next door

The bottoms of my shoes
   are clean
From walking in the rain

Bee, why are you
   staring at me?
I'm not a flower!

The barn, swimming
   in a sea
Of windblown leaves

Glow worm sleeping
   on this flower,
Your light's on!

Spring night—
   a leaf falling
From my chimney

[1956-1959]

from [Biographical Résumé, Fall 1957]

When I was 4 my brother Gerard was 9, at his deathbed several nuns took down his last words about Heaven and went away with the notes, which I've never seen. They said he was a little saint. My father was a printer, in his plant I often made little one page newspapers, typesetting them and printing them on a hand press (Racetrack News).

I wrote my first novel at age 11, in a 5¢ notebook, about an orphan boy running away, floating down a river in a boat... I went to parochial school in little black stockings and pants (St Louis de France & St Joseph in Lowell Mass). In high school, football, which led me (via scouts) to Columbia varsity but I quit football to write (because one afternoon, before scrimmage, I heard Beethoven fifth symphony and it had begun to snow and I knew I wanted to be a Beethoven instead of an athlete)... First serious writing at 18, influenced by Hemingway and Saroyan and Whitman... Spent 3 years on first full novel (1100-page Town and City) which was cut to 400 pages by Harcourt-Brace and thereby reduced from a mighty (over-long, windy, but sincere) black book of sorrows into a "saleable" ordinary novel...(Never again editorship for me.) My father died in my arms in 1946, alone in house with me, told me to take care of my mother, which I do. After Town and City, I wrote On the Road but it was rejected (1951) so spent 6 years on the road writing whatever came into my head, hopping freights, hitchhiking, working as railroad brakeman, deck hand and scullion on merchant ships, hundreds of assorted jobs, government fire lookout. Slept in mountains and desert in my sleepingbag. My chief activity (seriously) is praying that all living things and all things may go to Heaven. It is said in ancient sutras, that if this prayer and wish is sincere, the deed is already accomplished. I'll buy that.

In a recent reading appearance at Village Vanguard I was universally attacked, but all I did was stand there and read my heart out, not caring how I looked or what anybody thought, and I am satisfied because the dishwasher (an old Negro named Elton Stratton) said: "All I wanta do is get 2 quarts of whiskey and lie down in bed and listen to you read to me." Also, the musicians (Lee Konitz, Billy Bauer, Wilbur Little) said I was "singing" when I read and said they heard the music, and since I consider myself a jazz poet, I am satisfied with that. What intelligentsia says makes little difference, as I've always spent my time in skid row or in jazz joints or with personal poet madmen and never cared what "intelligentsia" thinks. My love of poetry is love of joy.

[1957]

99th Chorus from
Mexico City Blues

My father, Leo Alcide Kérouac
Comes in the door of the porch
On the way out to downtown red,
 (where Neons Redly-Brownly Flash
An aura over the city center
As seen from the river where we lived)
— "Prap – prohock!" he's coughing,
    Busy, "Am," bursting to part
    the seams of his trousers with power
    of assembled intentions.
                "B-rrack – Brap?"
(as years later GJ would imitate him,
"your father, Zagg, he goes along,
  Bre-hack! Brop?" Raising
      his leg, bursting his face
          to rouge outpop huge mad eyes
          of "big burper balloons
          of the huge world")
To see if there's any mail in the box
My father shoots 2 quick glances
Into all hearts of the box,
No mail, you see the flash of his anxious
Head looking in the void for nothing.

[1959]

114th Chorus from
Mexico City Blues

Everything is perfect, dear friend.
When you wrote the letter
I was writing you one,
I checked on the dates,
Just about right, and One.

You dont have to worry
      about colics & fits
From me any more
      or evermore either

You dont have to worry bout death.
Everything you do, is like your hero
The Sweetest angelic tenor of man
Wailing sweet bop
On a front afternoon
When not leading the band
And every note plaintive,
Every note Call for Loss
        of out Love and Mastery –
        just so, eternalized –

You are a great man
I've gone inside myself
And there to find you
        And little ants too

[1959]

Rimbaud

Arthur!
On t'appela pas Jean!
Born in 1854 cursing Charle-
ville thus paving the way for
the abominable murderousnesses
of Ardennes –
No wonder your father left!
So you entered school at 8
—Proficient little Latinist you!
In October of 1869
Rimbaud is writing poetry
in Greek French –
Takes a runaway train

to Paris without a ticket,
the miraculous Mexican Brakeman
throws him off the fast
train, to Heaven, which
he no longer travels because
Heaven is everywhere –
Nevertheless the old fags
intervene –
Rimbaud nonplussed Rimbaud
trains in the green National
Guard, proud, marching
in the dust with his heroes –
hoping to be buggered,
dreaming of the ultimate Girl.
— Cities are bombarded as
he stares & stares & chews
his degenerate lip & stares
with gray eyes at
Walled France –

André Gill was forerunner
to André Gide –
Long walks reading poems
in the Genet Haystacks –
The Voyant is born,
the deranged seer makes his
first Manifesto,
gives vowels colors
& consonants carking care,
comes under the influence
of old French Fairies
who accuse him of constipation
of the brain & diarrhea
of the mouth –
Verlaine summons him to Paris
with less aplomb than he
did banish girls to
Abyssinia –
"Merde!" screams Rimbaud
at Verlaine salons –
Gossip in Paris – Verlaine Wife
is jealous of a boy
with no seats to his trousers
— Love sends money from Brussels
— Mother Rimbaud hates
the importunity of Madame
Verlaine – Degenerate Arthur
is suspected of being a poet
by now –
Screaming in the barn
Rimbaud writes Season in Hell,
his mother trembles –
Verlaine sends money & bullets
into Rimbaud –
Rimbaud goes to the police
& presents his innocence
like the pale innocence
of his divine, feminine Jesus
— Poor Verlaine, 2 years
in the can, but could have
got a knife in the heart

— Illuminations! Stuttgart!
Study of Languages!
On foot Rimbaud walks
& looks thru the Alpine
passes into Italy, looking
        for clover bells, rabbits,
        Genie Kingdoms & ahead
        of him nothing but the old
            Canaletto death of sun
            on old Venetian buildings
— Rimbaud studies language
— hears of the Alleghanies,
of Brooklyn, of last
        American Plages –
His angel sister dies –
        Vienne! He looks at pastries
        & pets old dogs! I hope!
This mad cat joins
            the Dutch Army
            & sails for Java
commanding the fleet
        at midnight
        on the bow, alone,
        no one hears his Command
but every fish shining
        in the sea – August is no
time to stay in Java –
        Aiming at Egypt, he's again
hungup in Italy so he goes
back home to deep armchair
but immediately he goes
again, to Cyprus, to
        run a gang of quarry

workers, — what did he
        look like now, this Later
        Rimbaud? – Rock dust
& black backs & hacks
        of coughers, the dream rises
in the Frenchman's Africa
mind, — Invalids from
    the tropics are always
        loved – The Red Sea
        in June, the coast clanks
        of Arabia – Havar,
        Havar, the magic trading
        post – Aden, Aden,
            South of Bedouin –
            Ogaden, Ogaden, never
            known – (Meanwhile
            Verlaine sits in Paris
    over cognacs wondering
what Arthur looks like
    now, & how bleak their
eyebrows because they believed
in earlier eyebrow beauty –
Who cares? What kinda
Frenchmen are these?
Rimbaud, hit me over the
head with that rock!

Serious Rimbaud composes
elegant & learned articles
for National Geographic
Societies, & after wars
commands Harari Girl

(Ha Ha !) back
to Abbyssinia, & she
was young, had black
    eyes, thick lips, hair
    curled, & breasts like
    polished brown with
    copper teats & ringlets
    on her arms & joined
     her hands upon her
     central loin & had
     shoulders as broad as
     Arthur's & little ears
— A girl of some
    caste, in Bronzeville –

Rimbaud also knew
thinbonehipped Polynesians
with long tumbling hair
  & tiny tits & big feet

    Finally he starts
trading illegal guns
    in Tajoura
    riding in caravans, mad,
with a belt of gold
    around his waist –
Screwed by King Menelek!
The Shah of Shoa!
    The noises of these names
     in that noisy French
     mind!

    Cairo for the summer,
bitter lemon wind
& kisses in the dusty park
   where girls sit folded
    at dusk thinking
    nothing –

    Havar! Havar!
    By litter to Zeyla
    he's carried moaning his
    birthday – the boat
    returns to chalk castle
    Marseilles sadder than
    time, than dream,
    sadder than water
— Carcinoma, Rimbaud
   is eaten by the disease
of overlife – They cut
off his beautiful leg –

He dies in the arms
  of Ste. Isabelle
   his sister
& before rising to Heaven
sends his francs
  to Djami, Djami
  the Havari boy
    his body servant
    8 years in the African
    Frenchman's Hell,
    & it all adds up
     to nothing, like

    Dostoevsky, Beethoven
     or Da Vinci –
So, poets, rest awhile
  & shut up:
Nothing ever came
  of nothing.

[1960]

Philip Larkin

(1922–1985) b. Coventry, England

Disc 3
Tracks 27–29

Philip Larkin was born in Coventry, England, on August 9, 1922, the son of Eva and Sydney Larkin, who served as Coventry's City Treasurer. Larkin attended the King Henry VIII School in Coventry from 1930 to 1940 and then enrolled in St. John's College, Oxford. By the time he arrived at Oxford, Larkin had already begun realizing his literary talents and inclinations, having been a regular contributor to and coeditor of his school's magazine in Coventry. Strongly influenced by W. H. Auden and W. B. Yeats, Larkin continued to write while at college, publishing his first poem in a national magazine, *The Listener*, in November of his first year there. Larkin excelled in English and graduated in 1943, having been prevented from serving in the military service after failing an eyesight test. That same year, three of his poems appeared in the anthology *Oxford Poetry 1942–43*. After graduating, Larkin wrote prose as well as poetry while working as a librarian in Shropshire. In 1945, he published his first book of poems, *The North Ship*, but it failed to generate much attention. While it has never been considered a particularly strong volume, *The North Ship* nonetheless hints at the stylistic approaches and thematic concerns of Larkin's later poetry.

Larkin followed his poetic debut with two novels: *Jill* in 1946 and *A Girl in Winter* in 1947. Neither novel met with any success. Throughout the late '40s, Larkin held positions at various university libraries while completing courses that would qualify him as a professional librarian, and in 1950, he accepted a position at Queen's University in Belfast. He attempted to publish another volume of poetry in 1948, but had been unable to find a publisher; as a result, he privately printed poems from 1951 to 1954 and sent them to critics, hoping to build a reputation for himself, but they went unnoticed and unremarked-upon. However, this streak of bad luck would soon come to an end. In one of the more remarkable turnarounds in literary history, Larkin's 1955 volume, *The Less Deceived*, instantly established him as the leading poet of a new generation of voices, a group that would come to be known as "The Movement." This group of poets championed the technique of building strong, unique poems out of the everyday details of life, and Larkin, largely influenced by the poetry of Thomas Hardy, proved himself a master of this style. In addition to Larkin, figures associated with The Movement include Kingsley Amis, Donald Davie, and Thom Gunn.

Also in 1955, Larkin was appointed Librarian to the University of Hull, a position he would hold for almost three decades. While leading what some might consider an unexciting life as a librarian, Larkin turned out more collections of poems that proved the reputation that *The Less Deceived* earned him was well deserved. In 1964, he published *The Whitsun Weddings*, which was awarded the Queen's Gold Medal for Poetry and *High Windows* in 1974. A longtime aficionado of American jazz, Larkin also published many reviews for *The Daily Telegraph*. In time, these reviews were collected in the book *All What Jazz: A Record Diary*, published in 1970. Although Larkin wrote very little during the '70s and '80s (*High Windows* was his last full volume), it is a sign of the high quality of his work that he continued to receive numerous honors throughout those years. These include many honorary doctorates, most notably one from Oxford in 1984, and a nomination for Poet Laureate, a position he declined to hold because of the daunting amount of publicity associated with it. He remained in Hull until his death from cancer on December 2, 1985.

Mary Jo Salter

Philip Larkin

Mary Jo Salter on Philip Larkin

One may as well begin at the end, as Larkin did. (Perhaps no poet of the twentieth century was more fixated on old age, death, the looming end of us in every blooming day.) In "The Old Fools," a helplessly funny/sad poem from his last and best book, *High Windows*, he confronts mind-crippling senescence in a tone that fairly snarls:

> *What do they think has happened, the old fools,*
> *To make them like this? Do they somehow suppose*
> *It's more grown-up when your mouth hangs open and drools,*
> *And you keep on pissing yourself, and can't remember*
> *Who called this morning?*

The curt tag to that first stanza ("Why aren't they screaming?") crystallizes its series of miserable questions so beautifully that, shocking ourselves, we laugh.

If we had begun at the beginning, we would already have noted that he was born on August 9, 1922, to parents with just enough poetry in them to name their only son after Philip Sidney, and was baptized in Coventry Cathedral, a national treasure destroyed by German bombs while he was a student at Oxford. (That event may account partly for the resigned spiritual longings and patriotism of his most famous poem, "Church-Going.") The bickering union of a depressive mother chained to domesticity and a dour, Nazi-sympathizing father turned him forever against marriage; a fiercely lonely childhood turned him, less explicably, against children. Though he could be as amusing as his most important model, W.H. Auden, Larkin seems never to have been truly young or heedlessly happy.

Dying at sixty-three, not long after a diagnosis of cancer, he never reached the dotage he dreaded—although at fifty-one, the age at which he composed "The Old Fools," he seemed "somehow old as the hills" to a poet five years his senior, Robert Lowell. If he seems always old to us, that's due not only to his bald, wobbly-chinned, stooped homeliness, or to his duty-bound, if admirable, long career as librarian at the University of Hull. His poems themselves precociously, and ever after, confronted the bodily decrepitude that W.B. Yeats, another of Larkin's first models, had reminded us is wisdom. "On Being Twenty-Six," a poem Larkin never collected, confided with unintentional humor that he "feared these present years, / The middle twenties / When deftness disappears…"

In an adulthood of reading and rereading Larkin, I've had some dozen favorites in addition to "The Old Fools," but I always cling to memorized bits of this one (like "the million-petalled flower / Of being here") with a wondering shake of the head. How does its lyricism survive its snarl? I return to the poem, too, for its nearly complete inventory of Larkin's figurative universe: the flower, the dance, the wedding, "toad" hands (recalling "the toad *work*" which he railed against, and yet preferred to idleness, in two poems), sun, rain, the book, the armchair, the "blown bush at the window" (calling up the wind in "High Windows" and "Mr. Bleaney" and "Talking in Bed" and "Sad Steps"). The only recurrent Larkin image which "The Old Fools" lacks is that lonely moon that shows up in poems like "Dockery and Son" and again in "Sad Steps" ("Groping back to bed after a piss / I part thick curtains, and am startled by / The rapid clouds, the moon's cleanliness").

I like something *un*characteristic too about "The Old Fools." In contrast to most of Larkin's poems, which exact an iambic, graceful obedience to the poet's will, this one gallops. Or it seems to try to, stumbling along on its cane. Making his way with unpredictable anapests ("Start speeding away from each other for ever") and feminine rhyme ("they're for it" / "ignore it"), Larkin bumps with the surest craftsmanship into levity and out of it, making his subject bearable and unbearable.

The poem's success hinges on all of these devices, but you could argue that the most important trick it plays is with a pronoun. Throughout, we're asked to imagine what "they" must be thinking (in much the manner that Larkin looks at the unemployed in "Toads Revisited" and exclaims, "Think of being them!"). At the last moment, in a poem that has provided us with various syntactic and formal parallelisms, almost all of them contained in long sentences, the tables turn abruptly:

> *…Can they never tell*
> *What is dragging them back, and how it will end?*
> *Not at night?*
> *Not when the strangers come? Never, throughout*
> *The whole hideous inverted childhood? Well,*
> *We shall find out.*

"They" have become "we," and we must read the whole poem again to face what we knew. Larkin's conversational, seemingly offhand "Well" deceives, of course: it's a set-up rhyme for what we didn't want, ourselves, ever to be able to "tell."

Perhaps I'm striving to find sentiment or human feeling in a poet who offers so little of it. Most of the people Larkin likes wholeheartedly are figures of nostalgia, as in "MCMXIV" or "Dublinesque." And yet the prophet of solitude and even of selfishness, the reluctant invitee of "Vers de Société" who wants to shrug off all social life as "filled / with forks and faces" does end up going to dinner. He may view himself as cowardly, in poem after poem, for accepting the terms (the job, the dance, the dinner party) on which we join with others; and yet alone in his room he wrote outward, thinking not only "they" but "we."

Places, Loved Ones

No, I have never found
The place where I could say
This is my proper ground,
Here I shall stay;
Nor met that special one
Who has an instant claim
On everything I own
Down to my name;

To find such seems to prove
You want no choice in where
To build, or whom to love;
You ask them to bear
You off irrevocably,
So that it's not your fault
Should the town turn dreary,
The girl a dolt.

Yet, having missed them, you're
Bound, none the less, to act
As if what you settled for
Mashed you, in fact;
And wiser to keep away
From thinking you still might trace
Uncalled-for to this day
Your person, your place.

[1954]

The Whitsun Weddings

That Whitsun, I was late getting away:
    Not till about
One-twenty on the sunlit Saturday
Did my three-quarters-empty train pull out,
All windows down, all cushions hot, all sense
Of being in a hurry gone. We ran
Behind the backs of houses, crossed a street
Of blinding windscreens, smelt the fish-dock; thence
The river's level drifting breadth began,
Where sky and Lincolnshire and water meet.

All afternoon, through the tall heat that slept
    For miles inland,
A slow and stopping curve southwards we kept.
Wide farms went by, short-shadowed cattle, and
Canals with floatings of industrial froth;
A hothouse flashed uniquely: hedges dipped
And rose: and now and then a smell of grass
Displaced the reek of buttoned carriage-cloth
Until the next town, new and nondescript,
Approached with acres of dismantled cars.

At first, I didn't notice what a noise
    The weddings made
Each station that we stopped at: sun destroys
The interest of what's happening in the shade,
And down the long cool platforms whoops and skirls
I took for porters larking with the mails,
And went on reading. Once we started, though,
We passed them, grinning and pomaded, girls
In parodies of fashion, heels and veils,
All posed irresolutely, watching us go,

As if out on the end of an event
    Waving goodbye
To something that survived it. Struck, I leant
More promptly out next time, more curiously,
And saw it all again in different terms:
The fathers with broad belts under their suits
And seamy foreheads; mothers loud and fat;

An uncle shouting smut; and then the perms,
The nylon gloves and jewellery-substitutes,
The lemons, mauves, and olive-ochres that

Marked off the girls unreally from the rest.
    Yes, from cafés
And banquet-halls up yards, and bunting-dressed
Coach-party annexes, the wedding-days
Were coming to an end. All down the line
Fresh couples climbed aboard: the rest stood round;
The last confetti and advice were thrown,
And, as we moved, each face seemed to define
Just what it saw departing: children frowned
At something dull; fathers had never known

Success so huge and wholly farcical;
    The women shared
The secret like a happy funeral;
While girls, gripping their handbags tighter, stared
At a religious wounding. Free at last,
And loaded with the sum of all they saw,
We hurried towards London, shuffling gouts of steam.
Now fields were building-plots, and poplars cast
Long shadows over major roads, and for
Some fifty minutes, that in time would seem

Just long enough to settle hats and say
    I nearly died,
A dozen marriages got under way.
They watched the landscape, sitting side by side
—An Odeon went past, a cooling tower,
And someone running up to bowl—and none
Thought of the others they would never meet
Or how their lives would all contain this hour.
I thought of London spread out in the sun,
Its postal districts packed like squares of wheat:

There we were aimed. And as we raced across
    Bright knots of rail
Past standing Pullmans, walls of blackened moss
Came close, and it was nearly done, this frail
Travelling coincidence; and what it held
Stood ready to be loosed with all the power
That being changed can give. We slowed again,
And as the tightened brakes took hold, there swelled
A sense of falling, like an arrow-shower
Sent out of sight, somewhere becoming rain.

[1958]

Wild Oats

About twenty years ago
Two girls came in where I worked—
A bosomy English rose
And her friend in specs I could talk to.
Faces in those days sparked
The whole shooting-match off, and I doubt
If ever one had like hers:
But it was the friend I took out,

And in seven years after that
Wrote over four hundred letters,
Gave a ten-guinea ring
I got back in the end, and met
At numerous cathedral cities
Unknown to the clergy. I believe
I met beautiful twice. She was trying
Both times (so I thought) not to laugh.

Parting, after about five
Rehearsals, was an agreement
That I was too selfish, withdrawn,
And easily bored to love.
Well, useful to get that learnt.
In my wallet are still two snaps
Of bosomy rose with fur gloves on.
Unlucky charms, perhaps.

[1962]

This Be the Verse

They fuck you up, your mum and dad.
    They may not mean to, but they do.
They fill you with the faults they had
    And add some extra, just for you.

But they were fucked up in their turn
    By fools in old-style hats and coats,
Who half the time were soppy-stern
    And half at one another's throats.

Man hands on misery to man.
    It deepens like a coastal shelf.
Get out as early as you can,
    And don't have any kids yourself.

[1971]

The Old Fools

What do they think has happened, the old fools,
To make them like this? Do they somehow suppose
It's more grown-up when your mouth hangs open and drools,
And you keep on pissing yourself, and can't remember
Who called this morning? Or that, if they only chose,
They could alter things back to when they danced all night,
Or went to their wedding, or sloped arms some September?
Or do they fancy there's really been no change,
And they've always behaved as if they were crippled or tight,
Or sat through days of thin continuous dreaming
Watching light move? If they don't (and they can't), it's strange:
          Why aren't they screaming?

At death, you break up: the bits that were you
Start speeding away from each other for ever
With no one to see. It's only oblivion, true:
We had it before, but then it was going to end,
And was all the time merging with a unique endeavour
To bring to bloom the million-petalled flower
Of being here. Next time you can't pretend
There'll be anything else. And these are the first signs:
Not knowing how, not hearing who, the power
Of choosing gone. Their looks show that they're for it:
Ash hair, toad hands, prune face dried into lines—
          How can they ignore it?

Perhaps being old is having lighted rooms
Inside your head, and people in them, acting.
People you know, yet can't quite name; each looms
Like a deep loss restored, from known doors turning,
Setting down a lamp, smiling from a stair, extracting
A known book from the shelves; or sometimes only
The rooms themselves, chairs and a fire burning,
The blown bush at the window, or the sun's
Faint friendliness on the wall some lonely
Rain-ceased midsummer evening. That is where they live:
Not here and now, but where all happened once.
          This is why they give

An air of baffled absence, trying to be there
Yet being here. For the rooms grow farther, leaving
Incompetent cold, the constant wear and tear
Of taken breath, and them crouching below
Extinction's alp, the old fools, never perceiving
How near it is. This must be what keeps them quiet:
The peak that stays in view wherever we go
For them is rising ground. Can they never tell
What is dragging them back, and how it will end? Not at night?
Not when the strangers come? Never, throughout
The whole hideous inverted childhood? Well,
          We shall find out.

[1973]

Denise Levertov

(1923–1997) b. Ilford, England

Disc 3

Tracks 30–32

Denise Levertov was born on October 24, 1923, in the town of Ilford in Essex, England. Her Welsh mother descended from a line of mystics, and her Russian father was raised as a Hasidic Jew but later converted to Christianity and became an Anglican priest. Levertov grew up in a book-loving, book-filled household. Her mother read Tolstoy and Dickens aloud to the family, and Levertov received all of her instruction at home, except for classes in classical ballet. Undoubtedly this lively, spiritual, literary atmosphere encouraged Levertov's writing, which began when she was five. Entranced by the poetry of T.S. Eliot, she sent him some of her own work at age twelve, and Eliot returned it to her with his advice and encouragement. Five years later, her first published poem appeared in *Poetry Quarterly*. During World War II, Levertov cared for injured veterans returning from the front, and in 1946, she published her first full volume of poetry, *The Double Image*, comprising poems written between the ages of seventeen and twenty-one. Though it brought her to the attention of readers and critics, it did not bring her the fame or renown that her later work would.

Nineteen forty-eight marked a major turning point in Levertov's life, both personally and poetically. Married to the American writer Mitchell Goodman, she left her native England and moved to America, settling in New York City. Here, largely influenced by the poetry of William Carlos Williams, she began work on new poems that captured a more "American" sensibility. The traditional English forms of *The Double Image* were dropped in favor of open, experimental forms and a riskier, more expressive range of diction. Within a year, Levertov gave birth to her first son, and by 1956 she became a naturalized U.S. citizen. America proved tremendously stimulating to Levertov. She tapped into the Transcendentalist ideals of Thoreau and Emerson; found inspiration in the poetry of Ezra Pound, Robert Creeley, and Wallace Stevens; and like so many others, learned from Charles Olson's seminal essay, "Projective Verse." The first of her American books, *Here and Now* and *Overland to the Islands*, appeared in 1956 and 1958, respectively. In 1959, poet and publisher James Laughlin accepted her next book, *With Eyes at the Back of Our Heads*, for publication with New Directions Press, and she continued to publish with them for the remainder of her life. In 1960, her work was included in Donald Allen's inestimably important anthology, *The New American Poetry: 1945–1960*.

Throughout the course of the 1960s, Levertov produced five more volumes of poetry and became a political activist. Although she apparently perceived the Beats as sexist, she absorbed the spirit of the Beat movement; her poetry grew increasingly socially aware and prone to passages of sweeping sorrow and rage. In 1965, *Poetry* magazine ran her highly influential essay, "Some Notes on Organic Form." In the essay she drew a distinction between free verse, whose primary formal concern was to maintain freedom from all constriction, and "organic" verse, whose primary formal concern was to remain faithful to the nature of perception and experience. Her own "organic" verse continued to evolve politically through the 1970s and '80s. Beginning in 1982, she was a professor at Stanford University, a position she held for a decade; upon retiring, she relocated to Seattle, Washington, and remained a vital, productive poet until her death from lymphoma on December 20, 1997. Her last volumes include *Breathing the Water* (1987), *A Door in the Hive* (1989), *Evening Train* (1992), *The Sands of the Well* (1996), and the posthumously published *This Great Unknowing: Last Poems* (1999).

Nancy Willard

Denise Levertov

Nancy Willard on Denise Levertov

When people ask me, "How do you teach poetry?" I say, "Start by giving your students a poem that speaks to them in so clear and astonishing a voice they might carry it with them for the rest of their lives." This makes me feel like a doctor dispensing prescriptions for an underfed imagination. Take two poems by Denise Levertov, to be read at bedtime. No limit on refills.

The poem I share most frequently is "Come Into Animal Presence." Of course the title calls us to enter the poem itself. But more important, the first line (which is also the title) calls on us to celebrate the non-human world in all its mystery ("sacred" is the word she uses), a world not captive to human purposes and desires, much as Blake does when he considers the tiger and asks, "What immortal hand or eye / dare frame thy fearful symmetry?" The last four lines of Levertov's poem remind us that such joy is ours for the seeing:

> *holiness does not dissolve, it is a presence*
> *of bronze, only the sight that saw it*
> *faltered and turned from it.*
> *An old joy returns in holy presence.*

Many years ago, when my husband and I visited Denise Levertov in Temple, Maine, we were both struck by the indivisible connection between her life and her work. The weathered wooden table where she often wrote stood in the yard, and it was while she sat at this table, she told us, that a deer stepped out of the woods, walked toward her, and stood still. She felt he had honored her with a visit. She knew the woods well, both the earth and the air of it. During our walk there, as she picked wild mushrooms for our supper, her seeing went beyond the recognition of the edible kinds to a keen pleasure in seeing and touching them. To this day, when I read "O Taste and See," I remember that walk in the woods. I remember the sneakers she told us carried the oil of poison ivy on them for a year. I remember the cold stream across the road where we washed up for supper.

Handwritten manuscript of "Come Into Animal Presence" illustrated by Levertov and inscribed to William Carlos Williams

Denise Levertov is the poet laureate of rabbits and serpents, llamas and armadillos, cats and dragonflies, pigs, clouds, willows, and wells. She has seen these things and a thousand others, and in her poems she urges us to bear witness to the earth itself. Her voice invites us into her poems the way a good storyteller at a party widens the conversation to include strangers. A poem that touches one wave in the great sea of readers sends out rings from the center that carry a single line far out of the poet's sight. In "The Secret," Levertov shows the marvelous journey a poem makes. She opens with the promise of a story.

Two girls discover
the secret of life
in a sudden line of
poetry.

But when the poet says, "I who don't know the / secret wrote / the line," we understand that in poetry, it's more important to share a secret than to tell it and more important to reveal a mystery than to solve it. If she loves her readers for finding the secret she can't find, she also loves them for forgetting it so that

a thousand times, till death
finds them, they may
discover it again, in other
lines…

So many of her poems seem to stop on a journey. If the journey is joyful, it's because of what the traveler has made from sorrow. Not long after I read the announcement of Denise Levertov's death in 1997, I came across a poem of hers that my memory had misplaced. Same poem, but telling now a different story, as I read of the girl who

stepped out of her youth's brocade slippers
and set out barefoot, strong from her years of
pleasure,
to wander the roads of the second half of her life.
—*"An Embroidery, (II)"*
(from Andrew Lang and H.J. Ford)

Come Into Animal Presence

Come into animal presence.
No man is so guileless as
the serpent. The lonely white
rabbit on the roof is a star
twitching its ears at the rain.
The llama intricately
folding its hind legs to be seated
not disdains but mildly
disregards human approval.
What joy when the insouciant
armadillo glances at us and doesn't
quicken his trotting
across the track into the palm brush.

What is this joy? That no animal
falters, but knows what it must do?
That the snake has no blemish,
that the rabbit inspects his strange surroundings
in white star-silence? The llama
rests in dignity, the armadillo
has some intention to pursue in the palm-forest.
Those who were sacred have remained so,
holiness does not dissolve, it is a presence
of bronze, only the sight that saw it
faltered and turned from it.
An old joy returns in holy presence.

[1961]

The Secret

Two girls discover
the secret of life
in a sudden line of
poetry.

I who don't know the
secret wrote
the line. They
told me

(through a third person)
they had found it
but not what it was
not even

what line it was. No doubt
by now, more than a week
later, they have forgotten
the secret,

the line, the name of
the poem. I love them
for finding what
I can't find,

and for loving me
for the line I wrote,
and for forgetting it
so that

a thousand times, till death
finds them, they may
discover it again, in other
lines

in other
happenings. And for
wanting to know it,
for

assuming there is
such a secret, yes,
for that
most of all.

[1964]

Talking to Grief

Ah, grief, I should not treat you
like a homeless dog
who comes to the back door
for a crust, for a meatless bone.
I should trust you.

I should coax you
into the house and give you
your own corner,
a worn mat to lie on,
your own water dish.

You think I don't know you've been living
under my porch.
You long for your real place to be readied
before winter comes. You need
your name,
your collar and tag. You need
the right to warn off intruders,
to consider
my house your own
and me your person
and yourself
my own dog.

[1978]

A Woman Alone

When she cannot be sure
which of two lovers it was with whom she felt
this or that moment of pleasure, of something fiery
streaking from head to heels, the way the white
flame of a cascade streaks a mountainside
seen from a car across a valley, the car
changing gear, skirting a precipice,
climbing...
When she can sit or walk for hours after a movie
talking earnestly and with bursts of laughter
with friends, without worrying
that it's late, dinner at midnight, her time
spent without counting the change...
When half her bed is covered with books
and no one is kept awake by the reading light
and she disconnects the phone, to sleep till noon...
Then
selfpity dries up, a joy
untainted by guilt lifts her.
She has fears, but not about loneliness;
fears about how to deal with the aging
of her body—how to deal
with photographs and the mirror. She feels
so much younger and more beautiful
than she looks. At her happiest
—or even in the midst of
some less than joyful hour, sweating
patiently through a heatwave in the city
or hearing the sparrows at daybreak, dully gray,
toneless, the sound of fatigue—

a kind of sober euphoria makes her believe
in her future as an old woman, a wanderer,
seamed and brown,
little luxuries of the middle of life all gone,
watching cities and rivers, people and mountains,
without being watched; not grim nor sad,
an old winedrinking woman, who knows
the old roads, grass-grown, and laughs to herself...
She knows it can't be:
that's Mrs. Doasyouwouldbedoneby from
                              The Water-Babies,
no one can walk the world any more,
a world of fumes and decibels.
But she thinks maybe
she could get to be tough and wise, some way,
anyway. Now at least
she is past the time of mourning,
now she can say without shame or deceit,
O blessed Solitude.

[1978]

Her Sadness

When days are short,
mountains already
white-headed, the west
red in its branchy
leafless nest, I know

more than a simple
sow should know.

I know
the days of a pig—

and the days of dogbrothers, catpigs,
cud-chewing cowfriends—
are numbered,

even the days of
Sylvia the Pet,

even the days
of humans are numbered.
Already

laps are denied me,
I cannot be cuddled,
they scratch my ears
as if I were anypig, fattening for bacon.

I shall grow heavier still,
even though I walk
for miles with my Humans,
through field and forest.

Mortality
weighs on my shoulders,
I know
too much about Time for a pig.

[1981]

Allen Ginsberg
(1926–1997) b. Newark, New Jersey, United States

Disc 3

Tracks 33–35

Allen Ginsberg was born on June 3, 1926, in Newark, New Jersey. His father, Louis Ginsberg, taught high school, wrote poetry, and was fairly widely published, and appears to have been a moderate socialist. His mother, Naomi, was a radical communist, a nudist, and mentally unstable. Fascinated by poems since his childhood, especially those of Walt Whitman, Ginsberg chose what seems, in retrospect, a surprising course of study at Columbia University: labor law. Ginsberg attended Columbia in the early 1940s and, while there, forged crucial friendships with writers William S. Burroughs, Neal Cassady, and Jack Kerouac, all major figures in the Beat movement to come. Ginsberg began exploring the wilder possibilities that college life in New York City had to offer; he cruised gay bars, experimented with drugs, and associated with Times Square's subculture. Having dropped legal studies, Ginsberg again embraced his truest passion, poetry, and with Kerouac he believed that their exuberant behavior would open up for them another, poetic way of seeing, or "New Vision," as they called it. Ginsberg received his B.A. from Columbia in 1948 and remained in New York until 1953, when he moved to San Francisco with a letter of introduction from William Carlos Williams, fellow New Jersey native, in hand.

In San Francisco, Ginsberg joined poet and translator Kenneth Rexroth's circle of emerging literary talent. The turning point in Ginsberg's literary career came in 1955. In October of that year, Ginsberg read in the Six Gallery reading series, and his powerful, heart-stopping delivery of the landmark poem "Howl" brought him instant popularity. A passionately rhythmic, breath-taking diatribe against materialism, hypocrisy, spiritual bankruptcy, and other symptoms of society's malaise, "Howl" spoke on behalf of an entire generation in much the same way that T.S. Eliot's *The Waste Land* did in the early 1920s. The poem was destined to become one of the most widely read poems of the twentieth century. After a series of highly publicized obscenity trials, Lawrence Ferlinghetti's City Lights Books finally published *Howl and Other Poems* in October 1956.

Ginsberg's poetic reputation soared, and he became the leading voice of the new Beat movement. A loosely organized group of artists mostly living in San Francisco, the Beats rose to prominence in the 1950s, and their young-spirited, rebellious, and vaguely mystical work proved widely influential throughout the '60s. *Time* and *Life* magazines ran articles on the Beats, adding to the attention brought to the movement by the "Howl" lawsuit. Many books followed Ginsberg's debut, including 1961's *Kaddish and Other Poems*, whose title poem mourns the poet's mother's death, and 1963's *Reality Sandwiches*. Also during this period, Ginsberg began a love affair with poet Peter Orlovsky that would endure, on and off, for decades. Throughout the '60s and '70s, Ginsberg studied Zen Buddhism and traveled internationally as an antiwar demonstrator and unofficial ambassador for the youthful Beat movement. Always outspoken, he rarely failed to provoke controversy. In the '70s, Ginsberg cofounded the Jack Kerouac School of Disembodied Poetics at the Naropa Institute with poet Anne Waldman, and later taught at Brooklyn College as a Distinguished Professor. His later collections include *Planet News, 1961–1967* (1968), the National Book Award–winning *The Fall of America* (1973), *Plutonian Ode* (1982), and *Collected Poems, 1947–1980* (1984).

Ginsberg lived according to his own ideals and kept writing incomparable poetry until his death in New York City on April 5, 1997.

C. K. Williams on Allen Ginsberg

It's difficult to realize now just how controversial Allen Ginsberg's great poem "Howl" was when it was first published: it was actually brought to trial on a charge of obscenity. In truth, it was much more the poem's aggravating and mostly accurate challenge to the moral conformism of the post–World War II epoch that so fractured American sensibilities; Ginsberg himself described "the…screams of disgruntled mediocrity, screams which lasted three years before subsiding into a raped moan."

Ginsberg's genius had much to do with his vision of himself as both poet and prophet, as he conceived his principal poetic models, Blake and Whitman, to have been. And prophet he surely was. His call for personal and aesthetic openness, for "the true gaiety & excess of Freedom," as he put it, became a well-publicized element of the cultural revolutions of the 1960s, revolutions which enacted many of the shifts of perception which Ginsberg was certainly among the first to promulgate: a more open sexuality, both hetero- and homosexual; a more tolerant notion of personal identity in everything from dress to drugs; a legitimization of popular culture as an expression of spiritual aspiration, particularly music, at first jazz, then rock and roll; a nonviolence grounded in Ginsberg's serious commitment to Buddhism; and finally a withering contempt for capitalist mores, what he called the "Nightmare of Moloch!" The first line of "Howl," "I saw the best minds of my generation destroyed by madness, starving hysterical naked…" became an anthem for that era, and Ginsberg came to represent opposition to any oppressive mode of thought and behavior, at first in the United States and then through much of the world. When he visited what was then Czechoslovakia during the Cold War, he was hailed by large crowds as a hero—a public figure who incarnated the political freedoms forbidden to the peoples of the Soviet bloc.

It's also sometimes hard, given all his notoriety, to appreciate just how fine a poet Ginsberg really was. But it is as a poet that he defined himself, and surely it is as a poet that he takes his place in literature and history. His ambitious poetic conceptions, and the devices he developed for his work—long lines, open stanzas, propulsive Whitmanesque cadences, and a nearly Dionysian drive toward an unrestrained, ecstatic rhetoric—produced in his major poems a unique fusion of the political and the poetic, the intimate and public, the meditative and ecstatic. There is really nothing like either "Howl" or "Kaddish" in poetry. "Howl" is indeed just that; a cry of rage and frustration, but at the same time an expression of enormous sympathy and compassion. Conceived as an address to his friend, Carl Solomon, who was in a mental hospital, Ginsberg reenacts Whitman's call for a true democratic inclusiveness, one that will account for as many representative lives as possible, from every segment of society. It has qualities of both the epic in its scope, and the lyric in its sheer musical force.

In "Kaddish," using as a model the structure and incantatory rhythms of the Jewish prayer for the dead, Ginsberg recounts, in what seems at first a disjointed, chaotic manner, the tragic story of his mother's ever worsening mental illness, which finally destroyed her, and nearly him. Ginsberg was strongly influenced by the artists of the irrational; Arthur Rimbaud, the French prodigy, who promulgated a "derangement of the senses," and Antonin Artaud, the wild dramaturge, in particular offered him examples of non-rational expressions of experience, and "Kaddish" puts their methods to good use. The apparently arbitrary bits of detail and narrative accumulate to form a dense dramatic mass, which, along with the poem's intensity of language and its nearly frightening commitment to truth, create a luminous enactment not only of Ginsberg's family's trials, but of the entire social cultural moment of his childhood and youth.

The adjunct to the poem, "Hymmnn," is a panegyric to a God who is certainly not the God of whom any established religion has ever conceived: "Blessed be He in homosexuality!" it chants, "Blessed be He in Paranoia!" "Hymmnn" ends with this brilliantly idiosyncratic God fused with the crows at the cemetery where Ginsberg's mother is buried: "Lord Lord Lord caw caw caw Lord Lord Lord caw caw caw Lord," Ginsberg chants to his divinity of tolerance and redemption, in a unique and thrilling affirmation of poetic inspiration.

Howl album cover from 1969

Howl

For Carl Solomon

I

I saw the best minds of my generation destroyed by
    madness, starving hysterical naked,
dragging themselves through the negro streets at
    dawn looking for an angry fix,
angelheaded hipsters burning for the ancient
    heavenly connection to the starry dynamo in the
    machinery of night,
who poverty and tatters and hollow-eyed and high sat
    up smoking in the supernatural darkness of
    cold-water flats floating across the tops of cities
    contemplating jazz,
who bared their brains to Heaven under the El and
    saw Mohammedan angels staggering on tenement
    roofs illuminated,
who passed through universities with radiant cool
    eyes hallucinating Arkansas and Blake-light
    tragedy among the scholars of war,
who were expelled from the academies for crazy &
    publishing obscene odes on the windows of the
    skull,
who cowered in unshaven rooms in underwear,
    burning their money in wastebaskets and listening
    to the Terror through the wall,
who got busted in their pubic beards returning
    through Laredo with a belt of marijuana for
    New York,
who ate fire in paint hotels or drank turpentine in
    Paradise Alley, death, or purgatoried their torsos
    night after night
with dreams, with drugs, with waking nightmares,
    alcohol and cock and endless balls,
incomparable blind streets of shuddering cloud and
    lightning in the mind leaping toward poles of
    Canada & Paterson, illuminating all the
    motionless world of Time between,

Peyote solidities of halls, backyard green tree
    cemetery dawns, wine drunkenness over the
    rooftops, storefront boroughs of teahead
    joyride neon blinking traffic light, sun and
    moon and tree vibrations in the roaring
    winter dusks of Brooklyn, ashcan rantings
    and kind king light of mind,
who chained themselves to subways for the endless
    ride from Battery to holy Bronx on benzedrine
    until the noise of wheels and children
    brought them down shuddering mouth-
    wracked and battered bleak of brain all
    drained of brilliance in the drear light of Zoo,
who sank all night in submarine light of Bickford's
    floated out and sat through the stale beer
    afternoon in desolate Fugazzi's, listening to
    the crack of doom on the hydrogen jukebox,
who talked continuously seventy hours from park to
    pad to bar to Bellevue to museum to the
    Brooklyn Bridge,
a lost battalion of platonic conversationalists
    jumping down the stoops off fire escapes off
    windowsills off Empire State out of the moon,
yacketayakking screaming vomiting whispering facts
    and memories and anecdotes and eyeball
    kicks and shocks of hospitals and jails and wars,
whole intellects disgorged in total recall for seven
    days and nights with brilliant eyes, meat for
    the Synagogue cast on the pavement,
who vanished into nowhere Zen New Jersey leaving a
    trail of ambiguous picture postcards of
    Atlantic City Hall,
suffering Eastern sweats and Tangerian bone-grindings
    and migraines of China under junk-withdrawal in
    Newark's bleak furnished room,
who wandered around and around at midnight in the
    railroad yard wondering where to go, and went,
    leaving no broken hearts,

who lit cigarettes in boxcars boxcars boxcars
racketing through snow toward lonesome farms in
grandfather night,

who studied Plotinus Poe St. John of the Cross
telepathy and bop kabbalah because the cosmos
instinctively vibrated at their feet in Kansas,

who loned it through the streets of Idaho seeking
visionary indian angels who were visionary
indian angels,

who thought they were only mad when Baltimore
gleamed in supernatural ecstasy,

who jumped in limousines with the Chinaman of
Oklahoma on the impulse of winter midnight
streetlight smalltown rain,

who lounged hungry and lonesome through Houston
seeking jazz or sex or soup, and followed the
brilliant Spaniard to converse about America
and Eternity, a hopeless task, and so took ship
to Africa,

who disappeared into the volcanoes of Mexico leaving
behind nothing but the shadow of dungarees
and the lava and ash of poetry scattered in
fireplace Chicago,

who reappeared on the West Coast investigating
the FBI in beards and shorts with big pacifist eyes
sexy in their dark skin passing out
incomprehensible leaflets,

who burned cigarette holes in their arms protesting
the narcotic tobacco haze of Capitalism,

who distributed Supercommunist pamphlets in
Union Square weeping and undressing while the
sirens of Los Alamos wailed them down, and
wailed down Wall, and the Staten Island ferry
also wailed,

who broke down crying in white gymnasiums naked
and trembling before the machinery of other
skeletons,

who bit detectives in the neck and shrieked with
delight in policecars for committing no crime
but their own wild cooking pederasty and
intoxication,

who howled on their knees in the subway and
were dragged off the roof waving genitals and
manuscripts,

who let themselves be fucked in the ass by saintly
motorcyclists, and screamed with joy,

who blew and were blown by those human
seraphim, the sailors, caresses of Atlantic and
Caribbean love,

who balled in the morning in the evenings in
rosegardens and the grass of public parks and
cemeteries scattering their semen freely to
whomever come who may,

who hiccuped endlessly trying to giggle but wound
up with a sob behind a partition in a Turkish
Bath when the blond & naked angel came to
pierce them with a sword,

who lost their loveboys to the three old shrews of
fate the one eyed shrew of the heterosexual
dollar the one eyed shrew that winks out of
the womb and the one eyed shrew that does
nothing but sit on her ass and snip the intellectual
golden threads of the craftsman's loom,

who copulated ecstatic and insatiate with a bottle of
beer a sweetheart a package of cigarettes a
candle and fell off the bed, and continued
along the floor and down the hall and ended
fainting on the wall with a vision of ultimate
cunt and come eluding the last gyzym of
consciousness,

who sweetened the snatches of a million girls
trembling in the sunset, and were red eyed in the
morning but prepared to sweeten the snatch
of the sunrise, flashing buttocks under barns
and naked in the lake,

who went out whoring through Colorado in myriad
 stolen night-cars, N.C., secret hero of these
 poems, cocksman and Adonis of Denver—joy
 to the memory of his innumerable lays of girls
 in empty lots & diner backyards, moviehouses'
 rickety rows, on mountaintops in caves or with
 gaunt waitresses in familiar roadside lonely
 petticoat upliftings & especially secret gas-station
 solipsisms of johns, & hometown alleys too,

who faded out in vast sordid movies, were shifted in
 dreams, woke on a sudden Manhattan, and
 picked themselves up out of basements hung-
 over with heartless Tokay and horrors of Third
 Avenue iron dreams & stumbled to unemployment
 offices,

who walked all night with their shoes full of blood on
 the snowbank docks waiting for a door in the
 East River to open to a room full of steam-heat
 and opium,

who created great suicidal dramas on the apartment
 cliff-banks of the Hudson under the wartime
 blue floodlight of the moon & their heads shall
 be crowned with laurel in oblivion,

who ate the lamb stew of the imagination or digested
 the crab at the muddy bottom of the rivers of
 Bowery,

who wept at the romance of the streets with their
 pushcarts full of onions and bad music,

who sat in boxes breathing in the darkness under the
 bridge, and rose up to build harpsichords in
 their lofts,

who coughed on the sixth floor of Harlem crowned
 with flame under the tubercular sky surrounded
 by orange crates of theology,

who scribbled all night rocking and rolling over lofty
 incantations which in the yellow morning were
 stanzas of gibberish,

who cooked rotten animals lung heart feet tail borsht
 & tortillas dreaming of the pure vegetable
 kingdom,

who plunged themselves under meat trucks looking
 for an egg,

who threw their watches off the roof to cast their ballot
 for Eternity outside of Time, & alarm clocks fell
 on their heads every day for the next decade,

who cut their wrists three times successively
 unsuccessfully, gave up and were forced to open
 antique stores where they thought they were
 growing old and cried,

who were burned alive in their innocent flannel suits
 on Madison Avenue amid blasts of leaden
 verse & the tanked-up clatter of the iron
 regiments of fashion & the nitroglycerine shrieks
 of the fairies of advertising & the mustard gas
 of sinister intelligent editors, or were run
 down by the drunken taxicabs of Absolute
 Reality,

who jumped off the Brooklyn Bridge this actually
 happened and walked away unknown and
 forgotten into the ghostly daze of Chinatown
 soup alleyways & firetrucks, not even one
 free beer,

who sang out of their windows in despair, fell out of
 the subway window, jumped in the filthy
 Passaic, leaped on negroes, cried all over the
 street, danced on broken wineglasses barefoot
 smashed phonograph records of nostalgic
 European 1930s German jazz finished the
 whiskey and threw up groaning into the
 bloody toilet, moans in their ears and the
 blast of colossal steamwhistles,

who barreled down the highways of the past journeying
 to each other's hotrod-Golgotha jail-solitude watch
 or Birmingham jazz incarnation,

who drove crosscountry seventytwo hours to find out
 if I had a vision or you had a vision or he had
 a vision to find out Eternity,

who journeyed to Denver, who died in Denver, who
    came back to Denver & waited in vain, who
    watched over Denver & brooded & loned in
    Denver and finally went away to find out the
    Time, & now Denver is lonesome for her heroes,
who fell on their knees in hopeless cathedrals praying
    for each other's salvation and light and breasts,
    until the soul illuminated its hair for a second,
who crashed through their minds in jail waiting for
    impossible criminals with golden heads and
    the charm of reality in their hearts who
    sang sweet blues to Alcatraz,
who retired to Mexico to cultivate a habit, or Rocky
    Mount to tender Buddha or Tangiers to boys
    or Southern Pacific to the black locomotive
    or Harvard to Narcissus to Woodlawn to the
    daisychain or grave,
who demanded sanity trials accusing the radio of
    hypnotism & were left with their insanity &
    their hands & a hung jury,
who threw potato salad at CCNY lecturers on
    Dadaism and subsequently presented themselves
    on the granite steps of the madhouse with shaven
    heads and harlequin speech of suicide,
    demanding instantaneous lobotomy,
and who were given instead the concrete void of
    insulin Metrazol electricity hydrotherapy
    psychotherapy occupational therapy pingpong &
    amnesia,
who in humorless protest overturned only one symbolic
    pingpong table, resting briefly in catatonia,
returning years later truly bald except for a wig of
    blood, and tears and fingers, to the visible
    madman doom of the wards of the madtowns
    of the East,
Pilgrim State's Rockland's and Greystone's foetid halls,
    bickering with the echoes of the soul, rocking
    and rolling in the midnight solitude-bench
    dolmen-realms of love, dream of life a nightmare,
    bodies turned to stone as heavy as the moon,

with mother finally ******, and the last fantastic
    book flung out of the tenement window, and the
    last door closed at 4 A.M. and the last
    telephone slammed at the wall in reply and the
    last furnished room emptied down to the last
    piece of mental furniture, a yellow paper rose
    twisted on a wire hanger in the closet, and
    even that imaginary, nothing but a hopeful
    little bit of hallucination—
ah, Carl, while you are not safe I am not safe, and now
    you're really in the total animal soup of time—
and who therefore ran through the icy streets
    obsessed with a sudden flash of the alchemy of
    the use of the ellipsis catalogue a variable meas-
    ure and the vibrating plane,
who dreamt and made incarnate gaps in Time &
    Space through images juxtaposed, and trapped the
    archangel of the soul between 2 visual images
    and joined the elemental verbs and set the
    noun and dash of consciousness together
    jumping with sensation of Pater Omnipotens
    Aeterna Deus
to recreate the syntax and measure of poor human
    prose and stand before you speechless and
    intelligent and shaking with shame, rejected yet
    confessing out the soul to conform to the rhythm of
    thought in his naked and endless head,
the madman bum and angel beat in Time, unknown,
    yet putting down here what might be left to say
    in time come after death,
and rose reincarnate in the ghostly clothes of jazz in
    the goldhorn shadow of the band and blew
    the suffering of America's naked mind for
    love into an eli eli lamma lamma sabacthani
    saxophone cry that shivered the cities down
    to the last radio
with the absolute heart of the poem of life butchered
    out of their own bodies good to eat a thousand years.

II

What sphinx of cement and aluminum bashed open
    their skulls and ate up their brains and imagination?
Moloch! Solitude! Filth! Ugliness! Ashcans and
    unobtainable dollars! Children screaming under
    the stairways! Boys sobbing in armies! Old men
    weeping in the parks!
Moloch! Moloch! Nightmare of Moloch! Moloch the
    loveless! Mental Moloch! Moloch the heavy
    judger of men!
Moloch the incomprehensible prison! Moloch the
    crossbone soulless jailhouse and Congress of
    sorrows! Moloch whose buildings are judgment!
    Moloch the vast stone of war! Moloch the
    stunned governments!
Moloch whose mind is pure machinery! Moloch
    whose blood is running money! Moloch whose
    fingers are ten armies! Moloch whose breast is
    a cannibal dynamo! Moloch whose ear is a
    smoking tomb!
Moloch whose eyes are a thousand blind windows!
    Moloch whose skyscrapers stand in the long
    streets like endless Jehovahs! Moloch whose
    factories dream and croak in the fog! Moloch
    whose smokestacks and antennae crown the cities!
Moloch whose love is endless oil and stone! Moloch
    whose soul is electricity and banks! Moloch
    whose poverty is the specter of genius! Moloch
    whose fate is a cloud of sexless hydrogen! Moloch
    whose name is the Mind!
Moloch in whom I sit lonely! Moloch in whom I dream
    Angels! Crazy in Moloch! Cocksucker in
    Moloch! Lacklove and manless in Moloch!
Moloch who entered my soul early! Moloch in whom I
    am a consciousness without a body! Moloch
    who frightened me out of my natural ecstasy!
    Moloch whom I abandon! Wake up in Moloch!
    Light streaming out of the sky!

Moloch! Moloch! Robot apartments! invisible
    suburbs! skeleton treasuries! blind capitals!
    demonic industries! spectral nations! invincible
    madhouses! granite cocks! monstrous bombs!
They broke their backs lifting Moloch to Heaven!
    Pavements, trees, radios, tons! lifting the city
    to Heaven which exists and is everywhere
    about us!
Visions! omens! hallucinations! miracles! ecstasies!
    gone down the American river!
Dreams! adorations! illuminations! religions! the
    whole boatload of sensitive bullshit!
Breakthroughs! over the river! flips and crucifixions!
    gone down the flood! Highs! Epiphanies!
    Despairs! Ten years' animal screams and suicides!
    Minds! New loves! Mad generation! down on the
    rocks of Time!
Real holy laughter in the river! They saw it all! the
    wild eyes! the holy yells! They bade farewell! They
    jumped off the roof! to solitude! waving!
    carrying flowers! Down to the river! into the
    street!

III

Carl Solomon! I'm with you in Rockland
    where you're madder than I am
I'm with you in Rockland
    where you must feel very strange
I'm with you in Rockland
    where you imitate the shade of my mother
I'm with you in Rockland
    where you've murdered your twelve secretaries
I'm with you in Rockland
    where you laugh at this invisible humor
I'm with you in Rockland
    where we are great writers on the same
    dreadful typewriter
I'm with you in Rockland
    where your condition has become serious
    and is reported on the radio

I'm with you in Rockland
    where the faculties of the skull no longer
    admit the worms of the senses
I'm with you in Rockland
    where you drink the tea of the breasts of the
    spinsters of Utica
I'm with you in Rockland
    where you pun on the bodies of your nurses
    the harpies of the Bronx
I'm with you in Rockland
    where you scream in a straightjacket that
    you're losing the game of the actual pingpong of the
    abyss
I'm with you in Rockland
    where you bang on the catatonic piano the
    soul is innocent and immortal it should
    never die ungodly in an armed madhouse
I'm with you in Rockland
    where fifty more shocks will never return
    your soul to its body again from its pilgrimage
    to a cross in the void
I'm with you in Rockland
    where you accuse your doctors of insanity
    and plot the Hebrew socialist revolution
    against the fascist national Golgotha
I'm with you in Rockland
    where you will split the heavens of Long Island
    and resurrect your living human Jesus from
    the superhuman tomb
I'm with you in Rockland
    where there are twentyfive thousand mad
    comrades all together singing the final stanzas
    of the Internationale
I'm with you in Rockland
    where we hug and kiss the United States
    under our bedsheets the United States that
    coughs all night and won't let us sleep

I'm with you in Rockland
    where we wake up electrified out of the coma
    by our own souls' airplanes roaring over the
    roof they've come to drop angelic bombs the
    hospital illuminates itself   imaginary walls
    collapse   O skinny legions run outside   O starry-
    spangled shock of mercy the eternal war is here
    O victory forget your underwear we're free
I'm with you in Rockland
    in my dreams you walk dripping from the sea-
    journey on the highway across America in tears
    to the door of my cottage in the Western night

[1956]

A Supermarket in California

What thoughts I have of you tonight, Walt Whitman, for I walked down the sidestreets under the trees with a headache self-conscious looking at the full moon.

In my hungry fatigue, and shopping for images, I went into the neon fruit supermarket, dreaming of your enumerations!

What peaches and what penumbras! Whole families shopping at night! Aisles full of husbands! Wives in the avocados, babies in the tomatoes!—and you, García Lorca, what were you doing down by the watermelons?

I saw you, Walt Whitman, childless, lonely old grubber, poking among the meats in the refrigerator and eyeing the grocery boys.

I heard you asking questions of each: Who killed the pork chops? What price bananas? Are you my Angel?

I wandered in and out of the brilliant stacks of cans following you, and followed in my imagination by the store detective.

We strode down the open corridors together in our solitary fancy tasting artichokes, possessing every frozen delicacy, and never passing the cashier.

Where are we going, Walt Whitman? The doors close in an hour. Which way does you beard point tonight?

(I touch your book and dream of our odyssey in the supermarket and feel absurd.)

Will we walk all night through solitary streets? The trees add shade to shade, lights out in the houses, we'll both be lonely.

Will we stroll dreaming of the lost America of love past blue automobiles in driveways, home to our silent cottage?

Ah, dear father, graybeard, lonely old courage-teacher, what America did you have when Charon quit poling his ferry and you got out on a smoking bank and stood watching the boat disappear on the black waters of Lethe?

[1956]

America

America I've given you all and now I'm nothing.
America two dollars and twentyseven cents January
    17, 1956.
I can't stand my own mind.
America when will we end the human war?
Go fuck yourself with your atom bomb.
I don't feel good don't bother me.
I won't write my poem till I'm in my right mind.
America when will you be angelic?
When will you take off your clothes?
When will you look at yourself through the grave?
When will you be worthy of your million
    Trotskyites?
America why are your libraries full of tears?
America when will you send your eggs to India?
I'm sick of your insane demands.
When can I go into the supermarket and buy what
    I need with my good looks?
America after all it is you and I who are perfect not
    the next world.
Your machinery is too much for me.
You made me want to be a saint.
There must be some other way to settle this
    argument.
Burroughs is in Tangiers I don't think he'll come
    back it's sinister.
Are you being sinister or is this some form of
    practical joke?
I'm trying to come to the point.
I refuse to give up my obsession.
America stop pushing I know what I'm doing.
America the plum blossoms are falling.
I haven't read the newspapers for months, everyday
    somebody goes on trial for murder.
America I feel sentimental about the Wobblies.
America I used to be a communist when I was a
    kid I'm not sorry.
I smoke marijuana every chance I get.

I sit in my house for days on end and stare at the roses
    in the closet.
When I go to Chinatown I get drunk and never get laid.
My mind is made up there's going to be trouble.
You should have seen me reading Marx.
My psychoanalyst thinks I'm perfectly right.
I won't say the Lord's Prayer.
I have mystical visions and cosmic vibrations.
America I still haven't told you what you did to Uncle
    Max after he came over from Russia.
I'm addressing you.
Are you going to let your emotional life be run by Time
    Magazine?
I'm obsessed by Time Magazine.
I read it every week.
Its cover stares at me every time I slink past the corner
    candystore.
I read it in the basement of the Berkeley Public Library.
It's always telling me about responsibility. Businessmen
    are serious. Movie producers are serious. Everybody's
    serious but me.
It occurs to me that I am America.
I am talking to myself again.

Asia is rising against me.
I haven't got a chinaman's chance.
I'd better consider my national resources.
My national resources consist of two joints of marijuana
    millions of genitals an unpublishable private
    literature that jetplanes 1400 miles an hour and
    twentyfive-thousand mental institutions.
I say nothing about my prisons nor the millions of
    underprivileged who live in my flowerpots under the
    light of five hundred suns.
I have abolished the whorehouses of France, Tangiers is
    the next to go.
My ambition is to be President despite the fact that I'm
    a Catholic.

America how can I write a holy litany in your silly mood?
I will continue like Henry Ford my strophes are as
    individual as his automobiles more so they're all
    different sexes.
America I will sell you strophes $2500 apiece $500 down
    on your old strophe

America free Tom Mooney
America save the Spanish Loyalists
America Sacco & Vanzetti must not die
America I am the Scottsboro boys.
America when I was seven momma took me to
    Communist Cell meetings they sold us garbanzos
    a handful per ticket a ticket costs a nickel and
    the speeches were free everybody was angelic
    and sentimental about the workers it was all so
    sincere you have no idea what a good thing the
    party was in 1835 Scott Nearing was a grand old
    man a real mensch Mother Bloor the Silk-
    strikers' Ewig Weibliche made me cry I once saw
    the Yiddish orator Israel Amter plain. Everybody
    must have been a spy.
America you don't really want to go to war.
America it's them bad Russians.
Them Russians them Russians and them Chinamen.
    And them Russians.
The Russia want to eat us alive. The Russia's power
    mad. She wants to take our cars from out our
    garages.
Her wants to grab Chicago. Her needs a Red
    Reader's Digest. Her want our auto plants in
    Siberia. Him big bureaucracy running our
    fillingstations.
That no good. Ugh. Him make Indians learn read.
    Him need big black niggers. Hah. Her make us
    all work sixteen hours a day. Help.
America this is quite serious.
America this is the impression I get from looking in
    the television set.
America is this correct?
I'd better get right down to the job.
It's true I don't want to join the Army or turn lathes
    in precision parts factories, I'm nearsighted and
    psychopathic anyway.
America I'm putting my queer shoulder to the
    wheel.

[1956]

Frank O'Hara

(1926–1966) b. Baltimore, Maryland, United States

Disc 3
Tracks 36–38

Frank O'Hara was born in Baltimore on March 27, 1926. His parents, Katherine Broderick and Russell Joseph O'Hara, had married in Grafton, Massachusetts, in 1925 and moved to Baltimore shortly thereafter, perhaps to conceal a prenuptial pregnancy from their morally strict Irish-Catholic families. (O'Hara always believed that he had been born in July, three months after his official date of birth.) Eighteen months later, Katherine and Russell O'Hara returned to Grafton with their son, and O'Hara spent most of his early years there. Musically gifted, he studied piano at the renowned New England Conservatory from 1941 to 1944. After serving in the Navy from 1944 to 1946, he attended Harvard University on the GI Bill and continued his musical studies. While O'Hara began writing poetry at Harvard, music composition and art appear to have been his original loves. Before graduating in 1950, however, O'Hara changed his major to English. O'Hara went on to graduate school at the University of Michigan, Ann Arbor, and received his master's in comparative literature in 1951. He then moved to New York City.

O'Hara soon found employment at New York's Museum of Modern Art, where he was to work for the remainder of his life. At this time, he published his first volume, *A City in Winter and Other Poems*, appearing in 1952. The book received a favorable response from both critics and the public. He also began publishing critical essays on art, primarily on abstract expressionists, in the magazine *Art News*. He built a reputation as an enthusiastic and insightful art critic, and his growing literary reputation drew him into the center of the emerging "New York School." A loosely defined group influenced by Abstract Expressionist art, the American and Russian Modernist movements, and French poetry from Baudelaire to the Surrealists, the New York School included the poets John Ashbery, Kenneth Koch, and James Schuyler. By turns urbane, philosophical, and colloquial, The New York School poets corresponded to a group of similarly avant-garde painters, comprising such well-known artists as Jackson Pollock, Franz Kline, and Willem de Kooning. O'Hara formed friendships with many of these painters and drew inspiration from all of them. Recognized largely as a spontaneous poet whose poems convey an instant of time or feeling, he also became known for his collaborations with painter friends such as Larry Rivers, Joe Brainard, and Al Leslie.

Five more books of poetry followed his debut volume, including the spirited and utterly original *Meditations in an Emergency*, published in 1957. Critical responses to *Meditations* were largely unfavorable, but the book—with such poems as "Chez Jane" and "For James Dean"—would become O'Hara's signature accomplishment during his lifetime. Two more collections, *Seventh Avenue* and *Odes*, appeared in 1960, and also in that year, O'Hara's work was included in Donald Allen's now-legendary anthology, *The New American Poetry: 1945–1960*. Only Allen Ginsberg received more pages in this anthology, an indication of its importance in establishing his reputation. O'Hara would publish two more collections before his death, *Lunch Poems* in 1964 and *Love Poems (Tentative Title)* in 1965. The poems in these last volumes, like all O'Hara's poetry, embrace popular culture and embody an attractive in-the-moment jubilance and freedom of expression previously unknown in American poetry. His huge influence can be detected in much contemporary poetry. He died on the morning of July 24, 1966, due to injuries suffered after being hit by a dune buggy while vacationing on Fire Island, New York.

David Lehman on Frank O'Hara

"You just go on your nerve," Frank O'Hara wrote in "Personism," a poetic manifesto that parodies the whole genre of poetic manifestos and manages nevertheless to state the poet's credo. "If someone's chasing you down the street with a knife you just run, you don't turn around and shout, 'Give it up! I was a track star for Mineola Prep.'" This is vintage O'Hara: defiantly witty, funny, and strategically self-deprecating in a way that woos the reader. He has style, he has nerve. Not only can he make you laugh, he can also make you realize that laughter is a serious part of the business of being a poet.

O'Hara rejects the prevailing notion of what constitutes poetic excellence. Not for him the poetry of intricate stanzas and world-weary resignation. He writes in the free-wheeling American vernacular, often with exclamatory wonder. His poems sound like a man talking and are fairly bursting with the details of his daily life. They make it seem the height of glamour to be a poet in New York City in the 1950s and early '60s.

O'Hara championed the great avant-garde art of his time. He stood in relation to the New York Schools of painting and poetry in the 1950s and early '60s as the poet Guillaume Apollinaire stood in relation to Cubism in the Paris of the teens. O'Hara could provoke paintings—and participate in them as model, collaborator, or kibbitzer—with the same seeming ease with which he dashed off what he disarmingly dubbed his "I do this I do that" poems. What made him so singular a presence among painters was his native generosity of spirit, which transcended the usual factions. When everyone else was either for Pollock or de Kooning, as if it were a choose-up stickball game between the two titans of Abstract Expressionism, O'Hara refused to take sides. At the Museum of Modern Art, where he worked his way up from postcard clerk to curator, he was planning major retrospectives on both painters when he died, a casualty of a freak dune buggy accident on a Fire Island beach, in July 1966. At his funeral, the painter Larry Rivers estimated that some sixty New Yorkers, himself included, considered the poet to be their best friend.

O'Hara and his pals who made up the New York School of Poets (a name none of them liked) prove that poetry can derive its inspiration from the example of the visual arts rather than from mainstream literary influences. He is himself the

O'Hara (second from left) admires a lamp sculpture by Larry Rivers with (left to right) John Ashbery, Patsy Southgate, Bill Berkson, and Kenneth Koch.

nearest thing in poetry to an Action Painter. Feeling that poems could be as immediate and spontaneous as phone calls, O'Hara developed an improvisatory style capable of recording a "meditation in an emergency" or a reverie triggered by the headline of an afternoon paper. His poems chronicle his impressions and experiences, but more immediately they chronicle their own coming into existence. Cosmopolitan, witty, and open to life, they establish the distinctive O'Hara tone: two-fifths melancholy, three-fifths joy. He found a way to write about himself and his trials that make his wounded narcissism—"the catastrophe of my personality," as he put it in a poem titled "Mayakovsky"—seem "beautiful" and "interesting" and "modern."

My favorite photograph of O'Hara shows him emerging from the swivel door of the Museum of Modern Art. This is the O'Hara of the daily poems, on a hot date with the muse of 53rd Street, looking lucky, tie blowing out behind him in the wind: "and the light seems to be eternal / and joy seems to be inexorable / I am foolish enough always to find it in wind."

Reading his poems can fill an otherwise sane citizen with the sudden overwhelming urge to be a poet.

Why I Am Not a Painter

I am not a painter, I am a poet.
Why? I think I would rather be
a painter, but I am not. Well,

for instance, Mike Goldberg
is starting a painting. I drop in.
"Sit down and have a drink" he
says. I drink; we drink. I look
up. "You have SARDINES in it."
"Yes, it needed something there."
"Oh." I go and the days go by
and I drop in again. The painting
is going on, and I go, and the days
go by. I drop in. The painting is
finished. "Where's SARDINES?"
All that's left is just
letters, "It was too much." Mike says.

But me? One day I am thinking of
a color: orange. I write a line
about orange. Pretty soon it is a
whole page of words, not lines.
Then another page. There should be
so much more, not of orange, of
words, of how terrible orange is
and life. Days go by. It is even in
prose, I am a real poet. My poem
is finished and I haven't mentioned
orange yet. It's twelve poems, I call
it ORANGES. And one day in a gallery
I see Mike's painting, called SARDINES.

[1956]

Poem
(Hate Is Only One of Many Responses)

Hate is only one of many responses
true, hurt and hate go hand in hand
but why be afraid of hate, it is only there
think of filth, is it really awesome
neither is hate
don't be shy of unkindness, either
it's cleansing and allows you to be direct
like an arrow that feels something

out and out meanness, too, lets love breathe
you don't have to fight off getting in too deep
you can always get out if you're not too scared

an ounce of prevention's
enough to poison the heart
don't think of others
until you have thought of yourself, are true

all of these things, if you feel them
will be graced by a certain reluctance
and turn into gold

if felt be me, will be smilingly deflected
by your mysterious concern

[1959]

The Day Lady Died

It is 12:20 in New York a Friday
three days after Bastille day, yes
it is 1959 and I go get a shoeshine
because I will get off the 4:19 in Easthampton
at 7:15 and then go straight to dinner
and I don't know the people who will feed me

I walk up the muggy street beginning to sun
and have a hamburger and a malted and buy
an ugly NEW WORLD WRITING to see what the poets
in Ghana are doing these days
                              I go on to the bank
and Miss Stillwagon (first name Linda I once heard)
doesn't even look up my balance for once in her life
and in the GOLDEN GRIFFIN I get a little Verlaine
for Patsy with drawings by Bonnard although I do
think of Hesiod, trans. Richmond Lattimore or
Brendan Behan's new play or *Le Balcon* or *Les Nègres*
of Genet, but I don't, I stick with Verlaine
after practically going to sleep with quandariness

and for Mike I just stroll into the PARK LANE
Liquor Store and ask for a bottle of Strega and
then I go back where I came from to 6th Avenue
and the tobacconist in the Ziegfeld Theatre and
casually ask for a carton of Gauloises and a carton
of Picayunes, a NEW YORK POST with her face on it

and I am sweating a lot by now and thinking of
leaning on the john door in the 5 SPOT
while she whispered a song along the keyboard
to Mal Waldron and everyone and I stopped breathing

[1959]

Ave Maria

Mothers of America
          let your kids go to the movies!
get them out of the house so they won't know what you're up to
it's true that fresh air is good for the body
                but what about the soul
that grows in darkness, embossed by silvery images
and when you grow old as grow old you must
             they won't hate you
they won't criticize you they won't know
           they'll be in some glamorous country
they first saw on a Saturday afternoon or playing hookey

they may even be grateful to you
          for their first sexual experience
which only cost you a quarter
         and didn't upset the peaceful home
they will know where candy bars come from
           and gratuitous bags of popcorn
as gratuitous as leaving the movie before it's over
with a pleasant stranger whose apartment is in the Heaven on Earth Bldg
near the Williamsburg Bridge
         oh mothers you will have made the little tykes
so happy because if nobody does pick them up in the movies
they won't know the difference
        and if somebody does it'll be sheer gravy
and they'll have been truly entertained either way
instead of hanging around the yard
        or up in their room
           hating you
prematurely since you won't have done anything horribly mean yet
except keeping them from the darker joys
        it's unforgivable the latter
so don't blame me if you won't take this advice
        and the family breaks up
and your children grow old and blind in front of a TV set
         seeing
movies you wouldn't let them see when they were young

        [1960]

Poem
(Lana Turner Has Collapsed!)

DISC 3, TRACK 38

Lana Turner has collapsed!
I was trotting along and suddenly
it started raining and snowing
and you said it was hailing
but hailing hits you on the head
hard so it was really snowing and
raining and I was in such a hurry
to meet you but the traffic
was acting exactly like the sky
and suddenly I see a headline
LANA TURNER HAS COLLAPSED!
there is no snow in Hollywood
there is no rain in California
I have been to lots of parties
and acted perfectly disgraceful
but I never actually collapsed
oh Lana Turner we love you get up

[1962]

Anne Sexton

(1928–1974) b. Newton, Massachusetts, United States

Disc 3
Tracks 39–41

Anne Sexton was born Anne Gray Harvey on November 9, 1928, in Newton, Massachusetts. She attended Rogers Hall Preparatory School in Lowell followed by one year at a Boston finishing school called The Garland School. In 1948, at age nineteen, she eloped with Alfred Muller Sexton, son of a prominent Chestnut Hill family and student at Colgate University, and the couple relocated from Boston to Baltimore, from Baltimore to San Francisco, and then finally back to Massachusetts. Sexton worked briefly as a fashion model for the Boston-based Hart Agency, and in 1953, she gave birth to the first of her two daughters, Linda Gray Sexton. In the following year, she was diagnosed with severe depression and was hospitalized at the Westwood Lodge after suffering an intense mental breakdown. Released from the hospital, Sexton eventually gave birth to her second daughter, Joyce Ladd Sexton, in 1955. Another mental breakdown followed. Sexton was rehospitalized and, later that year, she attempted suicide.

While recovering from this second breakdown, Sexton's therapist, Dr. Martin Orne, recommended that she compose poetry as a form of therapy. She enrolled in several workshops, attended the Antioch Writers' Conference in Ohio where she worked with W.D. Snodgrass in 1958, and eventually was accepted into the graduate writing program at Boston University. There, Sexton studied under Robert Lowell and befriended fellow students Sylvia Plath, George Starbuck, and Maxine Kumin. Gaining a reputation as a poet, she was invited to deliver a lecture at Harvard University in 1959. Her first book of poems, *To Bedlam and Part Way Back*, appeared in 1960; sexy, wry, moving, at times audacious, and always formally adept, the book introduced Sexton's signature style and was nominated for a National Book Award. From 1961 to 1962, Sexton taught at the Radcliffe Institute for Independent Study, and shortly thereafter published her second book, *All My Pretty Ones*, which was also nominated for a National Book Award. With her reputation secured, Sexton began to receive several awards for her poetry, including a Pulitzer Prize for what many consider her finest single book, the 1967 volume *Live or Die*. Tragically, Sexton's psychological problems never fully vanished, and she attempted suicide several times throughout her life, even in the midst of all her success. Her always controversial work grew even more so as she began publishing such poems as "In Celebration of My Uterus" and "The Ballad of the Lonely Masturbator." In 1971, she published *Transformations*, a wildly popular book of hip, slangy poems based on the fairy tales of Andersen and Grimm.

Sexton received numerous honorary degrees and held many teaching positions throughout her career. She finally attained a full professorship—Colgate University's Crashaw Chair in Literature—in 1972. In the following year, she divorced her husband, suffered yet another mental breakdown, and was again hospitalized. On October 4, 1974, released from the hospital, and writing and publishing new poetry, Anne Sexton committed suicide by asphyxiation in the garage of her house. While her legacy may be somewhat overshadowed by that of her friend and fellow "confessional" poet Sylvia Plath, Sexton's enormous poetic accomplishments cannot be underestimated. Her unmistakable, decidedly feminine voice and frank, authoritative treatment of such subject matter as menstruation and abortion have secured for Sexton a permanent place in the annals of American poetry.

Kay Ryan on Anne Sexton

Anne Sexton is the author of ravishing poetry supercharged with primitive power, poetry that bangs big pots and pans, that is incautious, that runs headlong, and will stumble.

Anne Sexton makes me think hard about this business of stumbling, or *unevenness*, because she is sublimely uneven. There is an immense distance between hitting and missing in her work; it can happen in a *line*. In Sexton's hands, unevenness becomes a surprising source of power. Think about it; unevenness has a terrific *alerting* capacity. Careening along Sexton's narrative line at breakneck speed, the reader never knows when she will drop into a pothole. The work is bumpy and immediate. Add to this, Sexton is always holding this special black ace: she's been certified crazy and can crack up again right in front of you. Her power is *part threat,* which may be cheating, but cheating is fair in poetry.

Sexton cannot *not* be bold. There is something *cartoonlike* in her poems—simple line drawings with a ton of *ZAP!*s and *POW!*s. She inclines to drumming accents and simple, vivid words. She is grand by refusing to be conventionally serious. She is grandstanding, diva tragic, and outrageous—which of course means she has left the place for real grandeur wide open in you, an empty hole, undefended. So she can come along and roll a cannonball into it.

I'm glad to be thinking about Anne Sexton long past the fuss over her subject matter—madness, suicide, abortion, divorce, uteruses, and whatnot. Now it is possible to sort among the zillions of poems born of Sexton's example and identify those who wrote lasting poems that incidentally had exploding-woman subjects. Sexton did. Read Sexton's "The Operation" and you will weep for the pale imitations done in this vein after her. The technique is spare and forceful with short, hard words, tight management of rhyme and a terrific sense of order. The story is incontestably Sexton's, but the feelings are everyone's. In some way that makes a deep difference, Sexton is more *visceral* than *emotional*.

Poetry has got to be supersaturated. All poetry deemed "lasting" during its moment has this quality. But it takes a while to know what it was overfull of: the temporal or the eternal? What is it that "dates" a poem? Interestingly, it may not be the

ANNE SEXTON
14 BLACK OAK ROAD
WESTON, MASSACHUSETTS 02193

14, June 1965

Dear William Cookson,

I am pleased to be included in your
issue of American poetry. I cannot give you anything new
as so much of my new work has appeared in England that
the others came out in the U.S. But, of course, I would
be pleased if you could find your way to print some of
the enclosed. They are actually quite new anyhow. As you
will see from publication dates. There is the matter
of copyrite. You must, I fear, write to both these
magazines and ask for the copyrite assignment. Then,
later, I would like you reasign it to me. I know that
it is actually in the U.S. always listed as copyrite,
Hudson Review, 1965 and in the case of Harper's it says,
Harper's Magazine, 1965. What that all means I don't
know. My publishers always take care of it. You might,
if you don't know all about it either, consult Jon
Stallworthy at The Oxford University Press.

All this copyrite business is to
much for me...but I do know that I stand some sort of
chance of losing the poems, AND getting into trouble with
Houghton Mifflin Co. and or Oxford Press(if they intend
to continue publishing my work) if I don'r get the matter
legal and straight.

Aside from that. I do hope you will
like some of the enclosed. Please send me a copy of the
issue... even a couple if you can afford them.

I am enjoying Agenda and reading
with great interest.

Sincerely yours,

Anne Sexton

Letter from Sexton to William
Cookson, founder of the British
poetry magazine, *Agenda*, dated
June 14, 1965

little pull-date stickers of old technology (Sexton's "wind up the clock" sounds antique already) or even a time's hot topics (her firecrackers lit in the mouths of the frogs of propriety are taken for granted now). Rather, datedness may lie in a particular moment's concept of the timeless. By that I mean, what may give away the striving heart of the poet may be the *conventional* way she tries to survive her time. That's where Anne Sexton sails: she can barely survive the day; the hell with her time. And rewarded by the gods of irony, she does survive her time.

At her best, Anne Sexton commands with an irresistible ease. An odd thing to say, you might think, since she is so nervy and subject to collapse. But when she gets it going right, I feel the weightlessness that means poetry to me. Suffering and torment are neither canceled nor exploited; they are—strangely—elements, along with language and design, of a new configuration that we forever know as the beautiful.

The Truth the Dead Know

For my mother, born March 1902, died March 1959
and my father, born February 1900, died June 1959

Gone, I say and walk from church,
refusing the stiff procession to the grave,
letting the dead ride alone in the hearse.
It is June. I am tired of being brave.

We drive to the Cape. I cultivate
myself where the sun gutters from the sky,
where the sea swings in like an iron gate
and we touch. In another country people die.

My darling, the wind falls in like stones
from the whitehearted water and when we touch
we enter touch entirely. No one's alone.
Men kill for this, or for as much.

And what of the dead? They lie without shoes
in their stone boats. They are more like stone
than the sea would be if it stopped. They refuse
to be blessed, throat, eye and knucklebone.

[1959]

Her Kind

I have gone out, a possessed witch,
haunting the black air, braver at night;
dreaming evil, I have done my hitch
over the plain houses, light by light:
lonely thing, twelve-fingered, out of mind.
A woman like that is not a woman, quite.
I have been her kind.

I have found the warm caves in the woods,
filled them with skillets, carvings, shelves,
closets, silks, innumerable goods;
fixed the suppers for the worms and the elves:
whining, rearranging the disaligned.
A woman like that is misunderstood.
I have been her kind.

I have ridden in your cart, driver,
waved my nude arms at villages going by,
learning the last bright routes, survivor
where your flames still bite my thigh
and my ribs crack where your wheels wind.
A woman like that is not ashamed to die.
I have been her kind.

[1960]

The Operation

1

After the sweet promise,
the summer's mild retreat
from mother's cancer, the winter months of her death,
I come to this white office, its sterile sheet,
its hard tablet, its stirrups, to hold my breath
while I, who must, allow the glove its oily rape,
to hear the almost mighty doctor over me equate
my ills with hers
and decide to operate.

It grew in her
as simply as a child would grow,
as simply as she housed me once, fat and female.
Always my most gentle house before that embryo
of evil spread in her shelter and she grew frail.
Frail, we say, remembering fear, that face we wear
in the room of the special smells of dying, fear
where the snoring mouth gapes
and is not dear.

There was snow everywhere.
Each day I grueled through
its sloppy peak, its blue-struck days, my boots
slapping into the hospital halls, past the retinue
of nurses at the desk, to murmur in cahoots
with hers outside her door, to enter with the outside
air stuck on my skin, to enter smelling her pride,
her upkeep, and to lie
as all who love have lied.

No reason to be afraid,
my almost mighty doctor reasons.
I nod, thinking that woman's dying
must come in seasons,
thinking that living is worth buying.
I walk out, scuffing a raw leaf,
kicking the clumps of dead straw
that were this summer's lawn.
Automatically I get in my car,
knowing the historic thief
is loose in my house
and must be set upon.

2

Clean of the body's hair,
I lie smooth from breast to leg.
All that was special, all that was rare
is common here. Fact: death too is in the egg.
Fact: the body is dumb, the body is meat.
And tomorrow the O.R. Only the summer was sweet.

The rooms down the hall are calling
all night long, while the night outside
sucks at the trees. I hear limbs falling
and see yellow eyes flick in the rain. Wide eyed
and still whole I turn in my bin like a shorn lamb.
A nurse's flashlight blinds me to see who I am.

The walls color in a wash
of daylight until the room takes its objects
into itself again. I smoke furtively and squash
the butt and hide it with my watch and other effects.
The halls bustle with legs. I smile at the nurse
who smiles for the morning shift. Day is worse.

Scheduled late, I cannot drink
or eat, except for yellow pills
and a jigger of water. I wait and think
until she brings two mysterious needles: the skills
she knows she knows, promising, soon you'll be out.
But nothing is sure. No one. I wait in doubt.

I wait like a kennel of dogs
jumping against their fence. At ten
she returns, laughs and catalogues
my resistance to drugs. On the stretcher, citizen
and boss of my own body still, I glide down the halls
and rise in the iron cage toward science and pitfalls.

The great green people stand
over me; I roll on the table
under a terrible sun, following their command
to curl, head touching knee if I am able.
Next, I am hung up like a saddle and they begin.
Pale as an angel I float out over my own skin.

I soar in hostile air
over the pure women in labor,
over the crowning heads of babies being born.
I plunge down the backstair
calling *mother* at the dying door,
to rush back to my own skin, tied where it was torn.
Its nerves pull like wires
snapping from the leg to the rib.
Strangers, their faces rolling like hoops, require
my arm. I am lifted into my aluminum crib.

3
Skull flat, here in my harness,
thick with shock, I call mother
to help myself, call toe of frog,
that woolly bat, that tongue of dog;
call God help and all the rest.
The soul that swam the furious water
sinks now in flies and the brain
flops like a docked fish and the eyes
are flat boat decks riding out the pain.

My nurses, those starchy ghosts,
hover over me for my lame hours
and my lame days. The mechanics
of the body pump for their tricks.
I rest on their needles, am dosed

and snoring amid the orange flowers
and the eyes of visitors. I wear,
like some senile woman, a scarlet
candy package ribbon in my hair.

Four days from home I lurk on my
mechanical parapet with two pillows
at my elbows, as soft as praying cushions.
My knees work with the bed that runs
on power. I grumble to forget the lie
I ought to hear, but don't. God knows
I thought I'd die—but here I am,
recalling mother, the sound of her
good morning, the odor of orange and jam.

All's well, they say. They say I'm better.
I lounge in frills or, picturesque,
I wear bunny pink slippers in the hall.
I read a new book and shuffle past the desk
to mail the author my first fan letter.
Time now to pack this humpty-dumpty
back the frightened way she came
and run along, Anne, and run along now,
my stomach laced up like a football
for the game.

[1962]

For My Lover, Returning to His Wife

She is all there.
She was melted carefully down for you
and cast up from your childhood,
cast up from your one hundred favorite aggies.

She has always been there, my darling.
She is, in fact, exquisite.
Fireworks in the dull middle of February
and as real as a cast-iron pot.

Let's face it, I have been momentary.
A luxury. A bright red sloop in the harbor.
My hair rising like smoke from the car window.
Littleneck clams out of season.

She is more than that. She is your have to have,
has grown you your practical your tropical growth.
This is not an experiment. She is all harmony.
She sees to oars and oarlocks for the dinghy,

has placed wild flowers at the window at breakfast,
sat by the potter's wheel at midday,
set forth three children under the moon,
three cherubs drawn by Michelangelo,

done this with her legs spread out
in the terrible months in the chapel.
If you glance up, the children are there
like delicate balloons resting on the ceiling.

She has also carried each one down the hall
after supper, their heads privately bent,
two legs protesting, person to person,
her face flushed with a song and their little sleep.

I give you back your heart.
I give you permission—

for the fuse inside her, throbbing
angrily in the dirt, for the bitch in her
and the burying of her wound—
for the burying of her small red wound alive—

for the pale flickering flare under her ribs,
for the drunken sailor who waits in her left pulse,
for the mother's knee, for the stockings,
for the garter belt, for the call—

the curious call
when you will burrow in arms and breasts
and tug at the orange ribbon in her hair
and answer the call, the curious call.

She is so naked and singular.
She is the sum of yourself and your dream.
Climb her like a monument, step after step.
She is solid.

As for me, I am a watercolor.
I wash off.

[1969]

Rumpelstiltskin

Inside many of us
is a small old man
who wants to get out.
No bigger than a two-year-old
whom you'd call lamb chop
yet this one is old and malformed.
His head is okay
but the rest of him wasn't Sanforized.
He is a monster of despair.
He is all decay.
He speaks up as tiny as an earphone
with Truman's asexual voice:
I am your dwarf.
I am the enemy within.
I am the boss of your dreams.
No. I am not the law in your mind,
the grandfather of watchfulness.
I am the law of your members,
the kindred of blackness and impulse.
See. Your hand shakes.
It is not palsy or booze.
It is your Doppelgänger
trying to get out.
Beware…Beware…

There once was a miller
with a daughter as lovely as a grape.
He told the king that she could
spin gold out of common straw.
The king summoned the girl
and locked her in a room full of straw
and told her to spin it into gold
or she would die like a criminal.
Poor grape with no one to pick.
Luscious and round and sleek.
Poor thing.
To die and never see Brooklyn.

She wept,
of course, huge aquamarine tears.
The door opened and in popped a dwarf.
He was ugly as a wart.
Little thing, what are you? she cried.
With his tiny no-sex voice he replied:
I am a dwarf.
I have been exhibited on Bond Street
and no child will ever call me Papa.
I have no private life.
If I'm in my cups
the whole town knows by breakfast
and no child will ever call me Papa.
I am eighteen inches high.
I am no bigger than a partridge.
I am your evil eye
and no child will ever call me Papa.
Stop this Papa foolishness,
she cried. Can you perhaps
spin straw into gold?
Yes indeed, he said,
that I can do.
He spun the straw into gold
and she gave him her necklace
as a small reward.
When the king saw what she had done
he put her in a bigger room of straw
and threatened death once more.
Again she cried.
Again the dwarf came.
Again he spun the straw into gold.
She gave him her ring
as a small reward.
The king put her in an even bigger room
but this time he promised
to marry her if she succeeded.
Again she cried.

Again the dwarf came.
But she had nothing to give him.
Without a reward the dwarf would not spin.
He was on the scent of something bigger.
He was a regular bird dog.
Give me your first-born
and I will spin.
She thought: Piffle!
He is a silly little man.
And so she agreed.
So he did the trick.
Gold as good as Fort Knox.

The king married her
and within a year
a son was born.
He was like most new babies,
as ugly as an artichoke
but the queen thought him a pearl.
She gave him her dumb lactation,
delicate, trembling, hidden,
warm, etc.
And then the dwarf appeared
to claim his prize.
Indeed! I have become a papa!
cried the little man.
She offered him all the kingdom
but he wanted only this—
a living thing
to call his own.
And being mortal
who can blame him?

The queen cried two pails of sea water.
She was as persistent
as a Jehovah's Witness.
And the dwarf took pity.
He said: I will give you
three days to guess my name
and if you cannot do it
I will collect your child.
The queen sent messengers

throughout the land to find names
of the most unusual sort.
When he appeared the next day
she asked: Melchior?
Balthazar?
But each time the dwarf replied:
No! No! That's not my name.
The next day she asked:
Spindleshanks? Spiderlegs?
But it was still no-no.
On the third day the messenger
came back with a strange story.
He told her:
As I came around the corner of the wood
where the fox says good night to the hare
I saw a little house with a fire
burning in front of it.
Around that fire a ridiculous little man
was leaping on one leg and singing:
Today I bake.
Tomorrow I brew my beer.
The next day the queen's only child will be mine.
Not even the census taker knows
that Rumpelstiltskin is my name...
The queen was delighted.
She had the name!
Her breath blew bubbles.

When the dwarf returned
she called out:
Is your name by any chance Rumpelstiltskin?
He cried: The devil told you that!
He stamped his right foot into the ground
and sank in up to his waist.
Then he tore himself in two.
Somewhat like a split broiler.
He laid his two sides down on the floor,
one part soft as a woman,
one part a barbed hook,
one part papa,
one part Doppelgänger.

[1971]

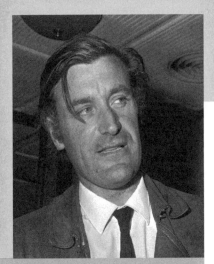

Ted Hughes
(1930–1998) b. Mytholmroyd, Yorkshire, England

Disc 3

Track 42–44

Edward James Hughes was born on August 17, 1930. His father was a carpenter, and his sister Olwyn would later become important as his agent. But during his childhood it was his brother Gerald, eight years older, who taught him hunting, fishing, camping, an appreciation of wildlife and exploring the outdoors, all of which would later inform Ted's poetry. When the family moved to the village of Mexborough, the landscape of moors also entered his poems.

After two years in the Royal Air Force, he entered Pembroke College, Cambridge, graduating in 1954. He moved to London, but returned most weekends to visit friends in Cambridge. He considered teaching English in Australia, in part because his brother Gerald had settled there, but kept postponing the move. He did commit, along with some friends in Cambridge, to launching a magazine, *St. Botolph's Review.*

The launching date was February 26, 1956. It was a long, drunken party, during which Hughes and an American Fulbright scholar named Sylvia Plath met and were immediately attracted to each other. He kissed her, ripped off her hairband and earrings, kissed her again on the neck, and then, as his biographer Elaine Feinstein tells it, "Plath bit him so long and hard on his cheek that blood was running down his face . . ." Thus began the most celebrated, productive, controversial relationship in contemporary literary history. They married the following June.

Over the next several months both Hughes and Plath had poems published in many of the same acclaimed journals and magazines, and Hughes made recordings for the BBC. In June 1957 they went to the United States, where Plath taught at Smith College, and Hughes taught at the University of Massachusetts in Amherst. They spent an impoverished year in Boston before returning to England in December of 1959. Their first child, Frieda, was born in April. That summer they sublet their London flat to Canadian poet David Wevill and his wife Assia, and moved to Court Green, a thatched cottage in North Tawton, Devon. A second child, Nicholas, was born in January, 1962.

Hughes began an affair with Assia Weevil, and Plath asked him to leave in August of 1962. Plath moved to a flat in London during the coldest winter in memory and on February 11, 1963, gassed herself in the kitchen oven. In the preceding few months she feverishly wrote the poems that comprised the collection *Ariel.* Following Plath's suicide, Hughes was blamed by many for his wife's death and vilified for editing Plath's poems in ways that appeared to protect his own reputation. Hughes's life with Assia Wevill was also difficult. At first they continued living in the same flat where the suicide had occurred, then began a series of moves back and forth between London and Court Green, sometimes separated, sometimes together. In 1965, Assia gave birth to Alexandra Tatiana Eloise Wevill, known as Shura. In London, in 1969, she gassed herself and Shura. In 1970 Hughes married Carol Orchard; they continued living at Court Green. Throughout his life he had been reticent about his relationship with Plath, but in 1998, he published *Birthday Letters,* a final book of poems that tells the story of their courtship and life in an unflinching way. His death on October 28 of that year came as a shock: He had kept private his struggle with cancer for eighteen months.

The large body of work Hughes left established him early on as an important poet of his generation. His first, prize-winning collection, *The Hawk in the Rain* (1957) was prominently reviewed in America by Galway Kinnell, W.S. Merwin, and Philip Booth, among others. By the time of *Crow* (1970), it was clear that he had few rivals on either side of the Atlantic. In 1984 Hughes became Poet Laureate. Twelve days before he died, he received the Order of Merit from Queen Elizabeth.

Christopher Reid on Ted Hughes

"The Thought-Fox" is one of those poems that, while it stands somewhat apart from an author's main work—perhaps because it stands apart—it seems to allow unusually intimate access to his or her creative resources. "The Thought-Fox," indeed, is about creation: the act of coaxing a living creature out of its natural habitat and onto the page. In *Poetry in the Making*, the book about writing that began as a series of radio talks for schools, Ted Hughes likened the composition of a poem to the capture of a wild animal. It was not an idle analogy. In his early childhood, Hughes had learned about animals from his brother Gerald, who was his elder by ten years and who had taken him on explorations of the West Yorkshire countryside, teaching him to track its wildlife. The "sudden sharp hot stink of fox" that "enters the dark hole of the head" at the climax of this poetic effort would have been a familiar sensation to Hughes, the by-now seasoned layer of animal traps. The unmistakable bestial reek certified artistic success.

For all its vividness, however, the Thought-Fox remains a figment, a creature of allegory. The stillborn lamb in "February 17th" is quite different. By the time he wrote this poem, Hughes had become a farmer. He places the date of its composition, "17 February 1974," at its foot, suggesting that he wrote it, exactly in the manner of a verse diary-entry, immediately after the event it describes. It is almost shocking in its fascinated attention to the separate stages of the thwarted struggle. In contrast to the successful conjuring performed in "The Thought-Fox," it presents a failure to achieve life; and yet, from the first glimpse of its head as the "blackish lump" that "bobs" at its mother's "rear-end" to its final "hacked-off" state, the lamb could hardly be more vitally present. In effect, the poem reverses the paradoxical proposition of "The Thought-Fox," that an imagined creature can have the force of a truly living one, by celebrating the will and energy expressed in even the most defeated attempt to assist at a birth.

Crow, from which "Crow's First Lesson" is taken, shows yet another aspect of Hughes's bestiary. The book contains the poems that he was able to salvage from an incomplete epic about the Crow, written during the unhappiest period of his life, after the suicide of his first wife, Sylvia Plath, and during the collapse of his relationship with Assia Wevill, who had supplanted Plath and who would in turn kill herself. Anti-hero Crow is as much a human being as he is a bird, and behind the violent and scurrilous knockabout of his adventures, which are recounted in a language of deliberate baseness, lies a complete mythology derived from the folktales of Celtic Britain and Ireland. Hughes, the close, occasionally empathetic observer of animal life, is replaced here by the witness of far more appalling happenings. Yet, in a poem like "Crow's First Lesson," isn't there enacted something like the same attempt at understanding? Isn't God's failure to cajole the word "Love" out of Crow's mouth a little like the farmer's inability to help the lamb "get born"?

Creation, birth, first lessons in love: these are topics that Hughes was able to address through the description of animal behavior, whether realistic or anthropomorphically stylized. "The Howling of Wolves," which he once told an inquirer was connected in his mind with the music of J.S. Bach, occupies intermediate territory and, like "The Thought-Fox," seems to equate creativity with creaturely essence. "A Pink Wool Knitted Dress," however, is exclusively and wholly human in its concerns. Recollecting, years later, the events of his and Sylvia Plath's wedding day, it describes another kind of beginning: a rite of initiation at which the bride was "transfigured" and claimed to have seen "the heavens open / And show riches, ready to drop on us." Hughes's genius in this poem is to question this benediction at the very moment his own eyes looked into those of his new wife and saw their pupils as "great cut jewels / Jostling their tear-flames, truly like big jewels / Shaken in a dice-cup and held up to me." There is hardly a poem of Hughes's that does not either mention eyes or describe their constant negotiation with the world, and both of the two that he reads here are eloquent examples.

The Thought-Fox

I imagine this midnight moment's forest:
Something else is alive
Beside the clock's loneliness
And this blank page where my fingers move.

Through the window I see no star:
Something more near
Though deeper within darkness
Is entering the loneliness:

Cold, delicately as the dark snow,
A fox's nose touches twig, leaf;
Two eyes serve a movement, that now
And again now, and now, and now

Sets neat prints into the snow
Between trees, and warily a lame
Shadow lags by stump and in hollow
Of a body that is bold to come

Across clearings, an eye,
A widening deepening greenness,
Brilliantly, concentratedly,
Coming about its own business

Till, with a sudden sharp hot stink of fox
It enters the dark hold of the head.
The window is starless still; the clock ticks,
The page is printed.

[1957]

The Howling of Wolves

Is without world.

What are they dragging up and out on their long leashes of sound
That dissolve in the mid-air silence?

Then crying of a baby, in this forest of starving silences,
Brings the wolves running.
Tuning of a viola, in this forest delicate as an owl's ear,
Brings the wolves running – brings the steel traps clashing and slavering,
The steel furred to keep it from cracking in the cold,
The eyes that never learn how it has come about
That they must live like this,

That they must live

Innocence crept into minerals.

The wind sweeps through and the hunched wolf shivers.
It howls you cannot say whether out of agony or joy.

The earth is under its tongue,
And dead weight of darkness, trying to see through its eyes.
The wolf is living for the earth.
But the wolf is small, it comprehends little.

It goes to and fro, trailing its haunches and whimpering horribly.

It must feed its fur.

The night snows stars and the earth creaks.

[1967]

Crow's First Lesson

God tried to teach Crow how to talk.
"Love," said God. "Say, Love."
Crow gaped, and the white shark crashed into the sea
And went rolling downwards, discovering its own depth.

"No, no," said God. "Say Love. Now try it. LOVE."
Crow gaped, and a bluefly, a tsetse, a mosquito
Zoomed out and down
To their sundry flesh-pots.

"A final try," said God. "Now, LOVE."
Crow convulsed, gaped, retched and
Man's bodiless prodigious head
Bulbed out onto the earth, with swivelling eyes,
Jabbering protest –

And Crow retched again, before God could stop him.
And woman's vulva dropped over man's neck and tightened.
The two struggled together on the grass.
God struggled to part them, cursed, wept –

Crow flew guiltily off.

[1970]

February 17

CD 3 / TRACK 44

A lamb could not get born. Ice wind
Out of a downpour dishclout sunrise. The mother
Lay on the mudded slope. Harried, she got up
And the blackish lump bobbed at her back-end
Under her tail. After some hard galloping,
Some manoeuvring, much flapping of the backward
Lump head of the lamb looking out,
I caught her with a rope. Laid her, head uphill
And examined the lamb. A blood-ball swollen
Tight in its black felt, its mouth gap
Squashed crooked, tongue stuck out, black-purple,
Strangled by its mother. I felt inside,
Past the noose of mother-flesh, into the slippery
Muscled tunnel, fingering for a hoof,
Right back to the port-hole of the pelvis.
But there was no hoof. He had stuck his head out too early
And his feet could not follow. He should have
Felt his way, tip-toe, his toes
Tucked up under his nose
For a safe landing. So I kneeled wrestling
With her groans. No hand could squeeze past
The lamb's neck into her interior
To hook a knee. I roped that baby head
And hauled till she cried out and tried
To get up and I saw it was useless. I went
Two miles for the injection and a razor.
Sliced the lamb's throat-strings, levered with a knife
Between the vertebrae and brought the head off
To stare at its mother, its pipes sitting in the mud
With all earth for a body. Then pushed
The neck-stump right back in, and as I pushed
She pushed. She pushed crying and I pushed gasping.

And the strength
Of the birth push and the push of my thumb
Against that wobbly vertebra were deadlock,
A to-fro futility. Till I forced
A hand past and got a knee. Then like
Pulling myself to the ceiling with one finger
Hooked in a loop, timing my effort
To her birth push groans, I pulled against
The corpse that would not come. Till it came.
And after it the long, sudden, yolk-yellow
Parcel of life
In a smoking slither of oils and soups and syrups –
And the body lay born, beside the hacked-off head.

                                   17th February 1974

                                              [1974]

A Pink Wool Knitted Dress

In your pink wool knitted dress
Before anything had smudged anything
You stood at the altar. Bloomsday.

Rain – so that a just-bought umbrella
Was the only furnishing about me
Newer than three years inured.
My tie – sole, drab, veteran R.A.F. black –
Was the used-up symbol of a tie.
My cord jacket – thrice-dyed black, exhausted,
Just hanging on to itself.

I was a post-war, utility son-in-law!
Not quite the Frog-Prince. Maybe the Swineherd
Stealing this daughter's pedigree dreams
From under her watchtowered searchlit future.

No ceremony could conscript me
Out of my uniform. I wore my whole wardrobe –
Except for the odd, spare, identical item.
My wedding, like Nature, wanted to hide.
However – if we were going to be married
It had better be Westminster Abbey. Why not?
The Dean told us why not. That is how
I learned that I had a Parish Church.
St George of the Chimney Sweeps.
So we squeezed into marriage finally.
You mother, brave even in this
U.S. Foreign Affairs gamble,
Acted all bridesmaids and all guests,
Even – magnanimity – represented

My family
Who had heard nothing about it.
I had invited only their ancestors.
I had not even confided my theft of you
To a closest friend. For Best Man – my squire
To hold the meanwhile rings –
We requisitioned the sexton. Twist of the outrage:
He was packing children into a bus,
Taking them to the Zoo – in that downpour!
All the prison animals had to be patient
While we married.

You were transfigured.
So slender and new and naked,
A nodding spray of wet lilac.
You shook, you sobbed with joy, you were ocean depth
Brimming with God.
You said you saw the heavens open
And show riches, ready to drop upon us.
Levitated beside you, I stood subjected
To a strange tense: the spellbound future.

In that echo-gaunt, weekday chancel
I see you
Wrestling to contain your flames
In your pink wool knitted dress
And in your eye-pupils – great cut jewels
Jostling their tear-flames, truly like big jewels
Shaken in a dice-cup and held up to me.

[1998]

Etheridge Knight

(1931–1991) b. Corinth, Mississippi, United States

Disc 3
Tracks 45–47

Etheridge Knight was born on April 19, 1931, in Corinth, Mississippi, and was raised with his five brothers and sisters in Paducah, Kentucky. Though he dropped out of school in the eighth grade, Knight was self-educated and took an almost scholarly interest in the language and customs of pool halls, poker games, juke joints, and other local hangouts and gatherings. In environments such as these, Knight came to master the art of "playing the dozens," or "toast," a traditional African-American form of long, improvised, and frequently ribald poetry rooted in storytelling. The reciter needed strong rhyming skills (most toasts were in rhyming couplets) as well as a lightning-quick imagination: competitive audience members would frequently interject new material that the reciter had to weave into his narrative. Knight enlisted in the Army in 1947 and served as a medical technician. On active duty during the Korean War, Knight suffered a shrapnel wound that resurrected an earlier addiction to drugs and alcohol. After his discharge from the Army in 1951, Knight turned to crime to support his habits.

In 1960, Knight was convicted of robbery and began serving an eight-year sentence in the Indiana State Prison. While confined there, Knight read *The Autobiography of Malcolm X* and the poetry of Langston Hughes. Already accomplished at playing the dozens, Knight began investing his narratives with a more sophisticated, nuanced understanding of character, subject, and language. Telling these narratives proved therapeutic for Knight. Determined to perfect his craft, he sought out and won help and admiration from Gwendolyn Brooks, who visited him in prison, as well as from poets Sonia Sanchez and Dudley Randall, whose Broadside Press published Knight's first book, *Poems from Prison*, in 1968. A passionately felt tribute to freedom and redemption, the book includes such unforgettable emotional and introspective pieces as "The Idea of Ancestry." *Poems from Prison* was a major success, and is considered by some his highest achievement.

Also in 1968, Knight was released from prison and married Sanchez. Together with such writers as Randall, Amiri Baraka, and Haki Madhubuti, Knight and Sanchez embraced the community-based ideals of the Black Arts Movement. Knight's popularity began to rise; he performed numerous readings and gave Free People's Poetry Workshops that were open for everyone. From 1969 to 1972, he was a writer-in-residence at the University of Pittsburgh, University of Hartford, and Lincoln University. In 1970, Knight edited the anthology *Black Voices from Prison*, and in 1972 he was awarded a National Endowment for the Arts grant. Before the publication of his second collection, *Belly Songs and Other Poems*, Knight and Sanchez divorced.

Although he was not a prolific writer, Knight continued throughout the 1970s to write poems that balanced traditional metrical devices with the rhythms of black street talk and blues. He remarried twice, once to Mary Ann McNally, with whom he had two children, and once to Charlene Blackburn, with whom he had one child. Knight's personal difficulties persisted, however, including his trouble with drugs and drinking. In 1980, he published *Born of a Woman: New and Selected Poems*, and settled in Memphis. In 1987, *The Essential Etheridge Knight* received the American Book Award, and in 1990, he received a B.A. in American Poetry and Criminal Justice from Martin Center University in Indianapolis. By the time of his death on March 10, 1991, Knight was recognized as a major African-American poet who created a living connection between his powerful, purposeful poems and his audience.

Elizabeth Alexander on Etheridge Knight

The poet and critic Edward Hirsch describes the impact of the long line in English poetry with eloquent precision:

> Blank verse offers the normative line in English poetry, the line closer to actual speech (as both Wordsworth and Frost perceived), and so one tends to feel that lines extending well beyond five beats and ten syllables are also going beyond the parameters of oral utterance, or over them, beyond speech itself. The long lines widen the space for reverie, they have a dreamlike associativeness, as in the early poems of W.B. Yeats. Or else they radiate an oracular feeling of prophetic utterance.

This "feeling of prophetic utterance" is in full flower in Etheridge Knight's great poem, "The Idea of Ancestry." His long lines race forward with river force and speed: "Taped to the wall of my cell are 47 pictures," he begins, and moves from there through a catalogue of family members such as an uncle who shares Knight's name and

> *...disappeared when he was 15, just took*
> *off and caught a freight (they say). He's discussed each year*
> *when the family has a reunion, he causes uneasiness in*
> *the clan, he is an empty space...*

Knight uses commas where grammatical logic calls for periods, again animating the swift movement from "the brown / hills and red gullies of mississippi," back to "grandmother's backyard," to Memphis, and then to a bunk in a cell in an Indiana prison where the speaker meditates on his place and legacy. That long line in American poetry is obviously the bequest of Walt Whitman, and it also illustrates something about American space and spaciousness, of its huge geographical divides and spans of the Great Migration, reaching across great distance and marking "the space between" where the emotional life of families takes place. The long line is also a spoken line, an orated line, a church line, and it rolls and unfolds in the manner of the black preachers whose grandiloquent speaking style has left such a strong imprint on the culture.

Etheridge Knight was born in Mississippi in 1931 and, like so many other African-Americans of his generation, his family made the migration from South to North, away from chronic racial violence and towards, it was hoped, greater promise in the North. He entered the Army and served in Korea, where he received a serious shrapnel wound and became addicted to pain-deadening narcotics. He was unable to shake his addiction, turned to crime, and subsequently was sent to prison. In jail, he began writing poetry, which caught the eye of Gwendolyn Brooks, among others. His first book, *Poems from Prison*, was published by the late Dudley Randall's legendary Broadside Press, based in Detroit. The author's photograph on that book shows a bespectacled Knight sitting straight on a single bed with his legs crossed in an Indiana State Prison cell, with the quote, "I died in Korea from a shrapnel wound and narcotics resurrected me. I died in 1960 from a prison sentence and poetry brought me back to life." He made a life in poetry, publishing several books of his own poems as well as an edited collection of other prison poems, and received praise and renown in the form of NEA and Guggenheim fellowships and poet-in-residencies.

Knight is known in part as a "prison poet," and his lean prison haikus are a radical reimagining of what the form can be. His characters are truly unforgettable, like the mythopoetic Hard Rock who was "known not to take no shit / From nobody." Other poems are peopled with the likes of Flukum, Freckle-faced Gerald, and the Reverend Gatemouth Moore. These characters process life's pains in different ways. Take, for example, "A Poem for Black Relocation Centers":

Handwritten poem on a paper plate by Knight

> Flukum couldn't stand the strain. Flukum
> wanted inner and outer order, so
> he joined the army where U.S. Manuals made
> everything plain—even how to button his shirt,
> and how to kill the yellow men...

And then, of course, is "Shine, King of the Cats." At the time of his death, Knight was working on a collection of black toasts; his ear was well-tuned to the wicked pleasures of the boasts and toasts of folk heroes such as Shine, who jumped off the sinking *Titanic* and saved himself while all the white folks went down. In "Dark Prophecy: I Sing of Shine," Knight writes of

> *...how the millionaire banker stood on the deck*
> *and pulled from his pockets a million dollar check*
> *saying Shine Shine save poor me*
> *and I'll give you all the money a black boy needs—*
> *how Shine looked at the money and then at the sea*
> *and said jump in mothafucka and swim like me—*
> *And Shine swam on—Shine swam on...*

His poems are often profane, but he speaks a lingua franca that is absolutely true to his characters and that seizes the vernacular spirit to great effect. The blues of "Feeling Fucked Up" are so low-down and blue ("Lord she's gone done left me done packed / up and split") that when he read it to a group of incarcerated women in a prison outside Philadelphia, they made him read it over and over and over again because it spoke to them so deeply and directly.

Knight in blue mode wonders what art can possibly make happen in a world full of pain. In "The Violent Space (or when your sister sleeps around for money)," the poet-figure says to his beloved, drug-using prostitute sister,

> *...here we are:*
> *You and I and this poem.*
> *And what should I do? Should I squat*
> *In the dust and make strange markings on the ground?*
> *Shall I chant a spell to drive the demon away?*
> *...*
> *And what do I do. I boil my tears in a twisted spoon*
> *And dance like an angel on the point of a needle.*
> *I sit counting syllables like Midas gold.*
> *I am not bold. I cannot yet take hold of the demon*
> *and lift his weight from you black belly,*
> *So I grab the air and sing my song.*
> *(But the air cannot stand my singing long.)*

The use of parentheses marks an ongoing, wryly pragmatic conversation with the self and an often unjust God. The poet's open-mouthed "song" is neither salvation nor salve, though the poet wishes it could accomplish more.

What does it mean to be part of a family? That is the enormous question Knight asks, in the end. "I know / their dark eyes, they know mine. I know their style, / they know mine. I am all of them, they are all of me; / they are farmers, I am a thief, I am me, they are thee," he writes, in "The Idea of Ancestry." The jazzy back and forth captures how a person navigates the waters of genealogy, how one is and is not of the tribe, the community, singularly oneself while simultaneously part of the larger whole. That rhetorical pattern is repeated at the end of the poem to great effect: "I pace my cell or flop on my bunk / and stare at the 47 black faces across the space. I am all of them, / they are all of me, I am me, and they are thee, and I have no children / to float in the space between." Knight marks an existential inner space in this poem that helps us think about "the space between": the space between bars from which a prisoner speaks as well as the spaces in African-American historical and family memory that have been erased in the Middle Passage, so starkly a "space between." The space between one station of life and another, soldier and civilian, overseas and then back home, with no place to belong. In and out of prison. Between South and North, country and industry, "ancestry a process, not mere inheritance." Here is his poetic dedication to the collection "Born of a Woman": ─────

This book is dedicated to my Father,
Etheridge "BuShie" Knight, whose name
Nobody really / knew, not even my mother.
She said his name was one / thing, his
Social security card said an / other. And,
Dead at 45—he ain't saying nothing.

This is "the space between" that Knight makes audible, too often "whereabouts unknown."

Drink, drugs, and smoke took their toll on Knight. He died before he should have, and left his admiring readers wishing for so much more of that true-blue, close-to-the-bone voice which speaks as directly as the morning sunlight blazing through a small chink in a prison wall somewhere. The space between here and there, drug jags and sobriety, haze and clarity, self and other—the space between.

The Idea of Ancestry

1

Taped to the wall of my cell are 47 pictures: 47 black
faces: my father, mother, grandmothers (1 dead), grand-
fathers (both dead), brothers, sisters, uncles, aunts,
cousins (1st & 2nd), nieces, and nephews. They stare
across the space at me sprawling on my bunk. I know
their dark eyes, they know mine. I know their style,
they know mine. I am all of them, they are all of me;
they are farmers, I am a thief, I am me, they are thee.

I have at one time or another been in love with my mother,
1 grandmother, 2 sisters, 2 aunts (1 went to the asylum),
and 5 cousins. I am now in love with a 7-yr-old niece
(she send me letters in large block print, and
her picture is the only one that smiles at me).

I have the same name as 1 grandfather, 3 cousins, 3 nephews,
and 1 uncle. The uncle disappeared when he was 15, just took
off and caught a freight (they say). He's discussed each year
when the family has a reunion, he causes uneasiness in
the clan, he is an empty space. My father's mother, who is 93
and who keeps the Family Bible with everybody's birth dates
(and death dates) in it, always mentions him. There is no
place in her Bible for "whereabouts unknown."

2

Each fall the graves of my grandfathers call me, the brown
hills and red gullies of mississippi send out their electric
messages, galvanizing my genes. Last yr / like a salmon quitting
the cold ocean-leaping and bucking up his birth stream / I
hitchhiked my way from LA with 16 caps in my pocket and a
monkey on my back. And I almost kicked it with the kinfolks.
I walked barefooted in my grandmother's backyard / I smelled the old
land and the woods / I sipped cornwhiskey from the fruit jars with the men /
I flirted with the women / I had a ball till the caps ran out
and my habit came down. That night I looked at my grandmother
and split / my guts were screaming for junk / but I was almost
contented / I had almost caught up with me.
(The next day in Memphis I cracked a croaker's crib for a fix.)

This yr there is a gray stone wall damming my stream, and when
the falling leaves stir my genes, I pace my cell or flop on my bunk
and stare at 47 black faces across the space. I am all of them,
they are all of me, I am me, they are thee, and I have no children
to float in the space between.

[1968]

Hard Rock Returns to Prison from the Hospital for the Criminal Insane

Hard Rock / was / "known not to take no shit
From nobody," and he had the scars to prove it:
Split purple lips, lumbed ears, welts above
His yellow eyes, and one long scar that cut
Across his temple and plowed through a thick
Canopy of kinky hair.

The WORD / was / that Hard Rock wasn't a mean nigger
Anymore, that the doctors had bored a hole in his head,
Cut out part of his brain, and shot electricity
Through the rest. When they brought Hard Rock back,
Handcuffed and chained, he was turned loose,
Like a freshly gelded stallion, to try his new status.
And we all waited and watched, like a herd of sheep,
To see if the WORD was true.

As we waited we wrapped ourselves in the cloak
Of his exploits: "Man, the last time, it took eight
Screws to put him in the Hole." "Yeah, remember when he
Smacked the captain with his dinner tray?" "He set
The record for time in the Hole—67 straight days!"
"Ol Hard Rock! man, that's one crazy nigger."
And then the jewel of a myth that Hard Rock had once bit
A screw on the thumb and poisoned him with syphilitic spit.

The testing came, to see if Hard Rock was really tame.
A hillbilly called him a black son of a bitch
And didn't lose his teeth, a screw who knew Hard Rock
From before shook him down and barked in his face.
And Hard Rock did *nothing*. Just grinned and looked silly,
His eyes empty like knot holes in a fence.

And even after we discovered that it took Hard Rock
Exactly 3 minutes to tell you his first name,
We told ourselves that he had just wised up,
Was being cool; but we could not fool ourselves for long,
And we turned away, our eyes on the ground. Crushed.
He had been our Destroyer, the doer of things
We dreamed of doing but could not bring ourselves to do,
The fears of years, like a biting whip,
Had cut deep bloody grooves
Across our backs.

[1968]

Belly Song

—for the Daytop Family

DISC 3, TRACK 47

"You have made something
Out of the sea that blew
And rolled you on its salt bitter lips.
It nearly swallowed you.
But I hear
You are tough and harder to swallow than most..."

—S. Mansfield

1

And I   and I / must admit
that the sea in you
    has sung / to the sea / in me
and I   and I / must admit
that the sea in me
    has fallen / in love
    with the sea in you
because you have made something
out of the sea
    that nearly swallowed you

And this poem
This poem
This poem / I give / to you.
This poem is a song / I sing / I sing / to you
from the bottom
    of the sea
      in my belly

This poem / is a song / about FEELINGS
about the Bone of feeling
about the Stone of feeling
    And the Feather of feeling

2

This poem
This poem
This poem / is /
a death / chant
and a grave / stone
and a prayer for the dead:
    for young Jackie Robinson.
a moving Blk / warrior who walked
among us
    with a wide / stride—and heavy heels
moving   moving   moving
thru the blood and mud and shit of Vietnam
moving   moving   moving
thru the blood and mud and dope of America
    for Jackie / who was /

a song
and a stone
and a Feather of feeling
    now dead
and / gone / in this month of love

This poem
This poem / is / a silver feather
and the sun-gold / glinting / green hills breathing
river flowing...

3
This poem
This poem
This poem / is / for ME—for me
and the days / that lay / in the back / of my mind
when the sea / rose up /
    to swallow me
and the streets I walked
    were lonely streets
    were stone / cold streets

This poem
This poem / is /
for me / and the nights
    when I
wrapped my feelings
    in a sheet of ice
and stared
        at the stars
            thru iron bars
                and cried
in the middle of my eyes…

This poem
This poem
This poem / is / for me
    and my woman
    and the yesterdays
when she opened
        to me like a flower
        But I fell on her
        like a stone
I fell on her like a stone…

4
And now—in my 40th year
    I have come here
to this House of Feelings
to this Singing Sea
and I   and I / must admit
that the sea in me
    has fallen / in love
with the sea in you
because the sea
that now sings / in you
    is the same sea
that nearly swallowed you—
    and me too.

Dark Prophecy: I Sing of Shine

And, yeah, brothers
while white / america sings about the unsink-
able molly brown
(who was hustling the titanic
when it went down)
I sing to thee of Shine
the stoker who was hip enough to flee the fucking ship
and let the white folks drown
with screams on their lips
(jumped his black ass into the dark sea, Shine did,
broke free from the straining steel).
Yeah, I sing to thee of Shine
and how the millionaire banker stood on the deck
and pulled from his pockets a million dollar check
saying Shine Shine save poor me
and I'll give you all the money a black boy needs—
how Shine looked at the money and then at the sea
and said jump in mothafucka and swim like me—
And Shine swam on—Shine swam on—
and how the banker's daughter ran naked on the deck
with her pink tits trembling and her pants roun her neck
screaming Shine Shine save poor me
and I'll give you all the pussy a black boy needs—
how Shine said now pussy is good and that's no jive
but you got to swim not fuck to stay alive—
And Shine swam on Shine Swam on—

How Shine swam past a preacher afloating on a board
crying save *me* nigger Shine in the name of the Lord—
and how the preacher grabbed Shine's arm and broke his stroke—
how Shine pulled his shank and cut the preacher's throat—
And Shine swam on—Shine swam on—
And when the news hit shore that the titanic had sunk
Shine was up in Harlem damn near drunk

[1973]

The Violent Space
(or when your sister sleeps around for money)

Exchange in greed the ungraceful signs. Thrust
The thick notes between green apple breasts.
Then the shadow of the devil descends,
The violent space cries and angel eyes,
Large and dark, retreat in innocence and in ice.
(Run sister run—the Bugga man comes!)

The violent space cries silently,
Like you cried wide years ago
In another space, speckled by the sun
And the leaves of a green plum tree,
And you were stung
By a red wasp and we flew home.
(Run sister run—the Bugga man comes!)

Well, hell, lil sis, wasps still sting.
You are all of seventeen and as alone now
In your pain as you were with the sting
On your brow.
Well, shit, lil sis, here we are:
You and I and this poem.
And what should I do? should I squat
In the dust and make strange markings on the ground?
Shall I chant a spell to drive the demon away?
(Run sister run—the Bugga man comes!)

In the beginning you were the Virgin Mary,
And you are the Virgin Mary now.
But somewhere between Nazareth and Bethlehem
You lost your name in the nameless void.
"O Mary don't you weep don't you moan"
O Mary shake your butt to the violent juke,
Absorb the demon puke and watch the white eyes pop,
(Run sister run—the Bugga man comes!)

And what do I do. I boil my tears in a twisted spoon
And dance like an angel on the point of a needle.
I sit counting syllables like Midas gold.
I am not bold. I cannot yet take hold of the demon
And lift his weight from you black belly,
So I grab the air and sing my song.
(But the air cannot stand my singing long.)

[1973]

Sylvia Plath

(1932–1963) b. Jamaica Plain, Massachusetts, United States

Disc 3
Tracks 48–50

Sylvia Plath was born in Jamaica Plain, Massachusetts, on October 27, 1932. Her German-born father, Otto, held a professorship at Boston University and her mother, Aurelia, taught high school. In 1940, her father died of complications brought on by diabetes, and subsequently the family moved to Wellesley. Having published her first poem at age eight and another poem in *Seventeen* while still in high school, Plath continued to write poems and short stories at Smith College, which she began attending on scholarships in 1951. While at Smith, Plath wrote more than four hundred poems, and in 1952, she co-won a celebrated short-story contest sponsored by *Mademoiselle* magazine. The next year, *Mademoiselle* offered her a summer internship at their offices in New York City. She accepted, but the intense atmosphere of magazine publishing magnified the already pronounced depressive tendencies that many maintain she had inherited from her father. In August 1953, after a grueling series of electroshock treatments, Plath attempted suicide. She was placed in an institution for rehabilitation. Her experiences that summer would serve as the basis of her largely autobiographical novel, *The Bell Jar*.

Six months later, apparently recovered, Plath returned to Smith College and graduated summa cum laude in 1955. The next year, she left America for England, having won a Fulbright Scholarship to study for two years at Cambridge. In Cambridge, Plath met the English poet Ted Hughes, whom she married in June 1956. Though the marriage eventually disintegrated, at its outset the two poets profoundly influenced and enriched each other's writing. After taking a degree at Cambridge, Plath returned to the States and a job as Instructor in English at Smith College; Hughes found work teaching at the University of Massachusetts. Both found academic life incompatible with writing, and they moved to Boston the next year. Plath enrolled in Robert Lowell's writing workshop at Boston University where she met Anne Sexton, whose work, with its subjective intensity, later affected her own. Meanwhile, Hughes's first collection, *The Hawk in the Rain*, had not only won him acclaim in England and America but also brought in enough prize money to enable the poets to travel widely in America before they returned to London. Here, in the spring of 1960, Plath gave birth to a daughter, and in the same year, Knopf published her first collection, *The Colossus and Other Poems*. For a first book of poems it was received with moderate praise; a few critics commented on the achieved formality of the poems, others found the subject matter depressing. Only in retrospect was it perceived that the seven-part "Poem for a Birthday" prefigured many of the hauntingly dark and violent themes later to be developed in *Ariel*.

In the fall of 1961, the Hugheses moved to a thatched manor house in rural Devon where, in February 1962, Plath gave birth to a son. Childbirth was a spur to her work, and for a while she and her husband divided daily child-minding and writing duties. The marriage, however, was strained to its breaking point, and when Hughes began an affair with a friend in London, Plath insisted that he move out. It was in the wake of his departure from Devon that Plath began to produce the excruciatingly powerful, almost hallucinatory yet often wryly comical poems that stunned the literary world when *Ariel* was published in 1965.

In December 1962, attempting to begin a new life with her children, Plath moved to a flat near London's Primrose Hill. Tragically, she succumbed to suicidal depression only two months later. She died on the morning of February 11, 1963. Considered by many as a feminist heroine and martyr, she was undoubtedly one of the most original and influential poets of the twentieth century.

Anne Stevenson on Sylvia Plath

It is surely one of literary history's kinder ironies that Sylvia Plath, who slipped out of the world at thirty, will be remembered for as long as poetry itself is remembered. No poet of modern times, or probably of any time, has made a more spectacular impression on her readers. She has attained a sort of superstar status even among people who care little for poetry, but are familiar all the same with the story of Plath's breakdown and suicide attempt as a student at Smith College, and her marriage, with its tragic denouement, to the English poet and former laureate, Ted Hughes. To a certain extent, Plath's huge reputation makes it difficult not to read her poetry in the light of the psychological autobiography she confided so vividly to her journals— all of which, with the exception of two lost ones, have been published. Yet the poetry she drew from her personal history breathes out an unquenchable life of its own. Serious student of T.S. Eliot that she was, she conscientiously studied the work of older poets she admired—among them, W.B. Yeats, W.H. Auden, and Dylan Thomas—and passed on this "modernist" tradition, though utterly transformed, to the present.

Plath is remarkable among women poets, then, not because she created a desperate mythology of death that she hoped would enable her to live, and not because the fury that radiates from some of her poems prefigures the violent feminism that took hold in America and Britain after her suicide, but because the flow, grit, and beauty of her lines, together with the surreal dreamlike quality of her images, are simply unforgettable. Famous poems such as "Daddy," written to exorcise crushing resentments against father and husband, and "Lady Lazarus" with its aggressive assertion of regeneration, rejoice in so much verbal energy that the justice or injustice of the poet's accusations cease to matter. What lasts is a voice that defies human defeat on a universal scale.

Approaching genius in Sylvia Plath's poetry is the painterly and auditory skill with which she constructed the birth-after-death imagery that began to dominate her writing after electric shock treatment had jarred her back to the world in 1953, "patched for the road" but not "cured" after her first suicide attempt. Slow-moving adagio lines—"This is the light of the mind, cold and planetary...The grasses unload

Sick room tulips   Sylvia Plath ①

These tulips are too excitable, it is winter here
Look how white everything is, the walls, my bed
tight white, the sheets & light blankets fit me like an eyelid
And my head is (a pupil between the pillow & sheet-cuff.
    opens like
Stupidly as a pupil, it has to take everything in.

These tulips are too excitable, it is winter here:
Look how white everything is, how quiet, how snowed-in
I am learning peacefulness, just lying quietly by myself
As the light lies on these white walls, this bed, these hands
I am nobody; I have nothing to do with explosions
I have given my name & my day-clothes up to the nurses
I have given my history to the anaesthetist, my body to surgeons

They have propped my head between the pillow & sheet-cuff
like an ... eye, between two white lids that will not shut:
Stupid pupil, it has to take everything in: the tulips
The nurses pass & pass, they are no trouble
They pass the way gulls ... in their white caps
Doing things with their hands, one just the same as another
So it is impossible to tell how many there are.
My body is a pebble to them, they tend it as water
tends to the pebbles it must run over, smoothing them gently
They bring me numbness in their bright needles, they bring me sleep.
Now I have lost myself I am sick of baggage
my overnight bag like a black patent-leather pill box
my husband & child smiling out of the family photo,
their smiles catch onto my skin, little smiling hooks
I have let things slip, I ... a thirtyyear-old cargo boat ...
hanging onto my name & address stubbornly as ...
Scared & bare on the green plastic-pillowed trolley
I watched ... : they tied up my hair
... bandage they taped
my wedding ring to my finger with white adhesive
I watched my teasets, my bureaus of linen, my books
sink & the water went over my head
out of sight
They swabbed me clear of my cosy associations
I am a nun now, I have never been so pure.

Handwritten manuscript of "Tulips"
with revisions by Plath

their griefs on my feet as if I were God" ("The Moon and the Yew Tree")—contrast like slow movements in Beethoven with the clipped staccato of lines like: "By the roots of my hair some god got hold of me. / I sizzled in his blue volts like a desert prophet" ("Hanging Man"). Even poems about the births of her children abound with images and sounds that are more surreal—or echoingly distant—than personal. Who else would have likened a newborn baby to a "New statue / in a drafty museum" ("Morning Song"), or depicted the world into which she has brought an infant son as a mine full of "waxy stalactites" in which "raggy shawls, cold homicides…weld to me like plums" ("Nick and the Candle Stick")? Plath's is almost a fifteenth-century vision of the world as hell, though, unlike Hieronymous Bosch, she expressed love and grief as memorably as horror in her poems as in "Candles":

How shall I tell anything at all
To this infant still in a birth-drowse?

and "Nick and the Candlestick":

Love, love,
I have hung our cave with roses.
With soft rugs

The last of Victoriana…
You are the one
Solid the spaces lean on, envious.
You are the baby in the barn.

Sylvia Plath's poetry is all of a piece. Its moments of tenderness work upon the heart as surely as its moments of terror and harsh resentment. And despite her exaggerated tone and the extreme violence of some of her imagery, Plath did, courageously, open a door to reality. What other poet of the twentieth century has presented us with more disturbing insights, not only into the unspeakable dealings of its Hitlers, Stalins, and Milosevics, but into a dangerously dehumanized "virtual" world that our televisions and computers could so easily persuade us was worth cultivating at the cost of our flawed, human dependence upon love?

Tulips

The tulips are too excitable, it is winter here.
Look how white everything is, how quiet, how snowed-in.
I am learning peacefulness, lying by myself quietly
As the light lies on these white walls, this bed, these hands.
I am nobody; I have nothing to do with explosions.
I have given my name and my day-clothes up to the nurses
And my history to the anesthetist and my body to surgeons.

They have propped my head between the pillow and the sheet-cuff
Like an eye between two white lids that will not shut.
Stupid pupil, it has to take everything in.
The nurses pass and pass, they are no trouble,
They pass the way gulls pass inland in their white caps,
Doing things with their hands, one just the same as another,
So it is impossible to tell how many there are.

My body is a pebble to them, they tend it as water
Tends to the pebbles it must run over, smoothing them gently.
They bring me numbness in their bright needles, they bring me sleep.
Now I have lost myself I am sick of baggage——
My patent leather overnight case like a black pillbox,
My husband and child smiling out of the family photo;
Their smiles catch onto my skin, little smiling hooks.

I have let things slip, a thirty-year-old cargo boat
Stubbornly hanging on to my name and address.
They have swabbed me clear of my loving associations.
Scared and bare on the green plastic-pillowed trolley
I watched my teaset, my bureaus of linen, my books
Sink out of sight, and the water went over my head.
I am a nun now, I have never been so pure.

I didn't want any flowers, I only wanted
To lie with my hands turned up and be utterly empty.
How free it is, you have no idea how free——
The peacefulness is so big it dazes you,
And it asks nothing, a name tag, a few trinkets.
It is what the dead close on, finally; I imagine them
Shutting their mouths on it, like a Communion tablet.

The tulips are too red in the first place, they hurt me.
Even through the gift paper I could hear them breathe
Lightly, through their white swaddlings, like an awful baby.
Their redness talks to my wound, it corresponds.
They are subtle: they seem to float, though they weigh me down,
Upsetting me with their sudden tongues and their color,
A dozen red lead sinkers round my neck.

Nobody watched me before, now I am watched.
The tulips turn to me, and the window behind me
Where once a day the light slowly widens and slowly thins,
And I see myself, flat, ridiculous, a cut-paper shadow
Between the eye of the sun and the eyes of the tulips,
And I have no face, I have wanted to efface myself.
The vivid tulips eat my oxygen.

Before they came the air was calm enough,
Coming and going, breath by breath, without any fuss.
Then the tulips filled it up like a loud noise.
Now the air snags and eddies round them the way a river
Snags and eddies round a sunken rust-red engine.
They concentrate my attention, that was happy
Playing and resting without committing itself.

The walls, also, seem to be warming themselves.
The tulips should be behind bars like dangerous animals;
They are opening like the mouth of some great African cat,
And I am aware of my heart: it opens and closes
Its bowl of red blooms out of sheer love of me.
The water I taste is warm and salt, like the sea,
And comes from a country far away as health.

[1961]

Morning Song

Love set you going like a fat gold watch.
The midwife slapped your footsoles, and your bald cry
Took its place among the elements.

Our voices echo, magnifying your arrival. New statue.
In a drafty museum, your nakedness
Shadows our safety. We stand round blankly as walls.

I'm no more your mother
Than the cloud that distills a mirror to reflect its own slow
Effacement at the wind's hand.

All night your moth-breath
Flickers among the flat pink roses. I wake to listen:
A far sea moves in my ear.

One cry, and I stumble from bed, cow-heavy and floral
In my Victorian nightgown.
Your mouth opens clean as a cat's. The window square

Whitens and swallows its dull stars. And now you try
Your handful of notes;
The clear vowels rise like balloons.

[1961]

I Am Vertical

But I would rather be horizontal.
I am not a tree with my root in the soil
Sucking up minerals and motherly love
So that each March I may gleam into leaf,
Nor am I the beauty of a garden bed
Attracting my share of Ahs and spectacularly painted,
Unknowing I must soon unpetal.
Compared with me, a tree is immortal
And a flower-head not tall, but more startling,
And I want the one's longevity and the other's daring.

Tonight, in the infinitesimal light of the stars,
The trees and flowers have been strewing their cool odors.
I walk among them, but none of them are noticing.
Sometimes I think that when I am sleeping
I must most perfectly resemble them—
Thoughts gone dim.
It is more natural to me, lying down.
Then the sky and I are in open conversation,
And I shall be useful when I lie down finally:
Then the trees may touch me for once, and the
    flowers have time for me.

[1961]

Daddy

DISC 3, TRACK 49

You do not do, you do not do
Any more, black shoe
In which I have lived like a foot
For thirty years, poor and white,
Barely daring to breathe or Achoo.

Daddy, I have had to kill you.
You died before I had time——
Marble-heavy, a bag full of God,
Ghastly statue with one gray toe
Big as a Frisco seal

And a head in the freakish Atlantic
Where it pours bean green over blue
In the waters off beautiful Nauset.
I used to pray to recover you.
Ach, du.

In the German tongue, in the Polish town
Scraped flat by the roller
Of wars, wars, wars.
But the name of the town is common.
My Polack friend

Says there are a dozen or two.
So I never could tell where you
Put your foot, your root,
I never could talk to you.
The tongue stuck in my jaw.

It stuck in a barb wire snare.
Ich, ich, ich, ich,
I could hardly speak.
I thought every German was you.
And the language obscene

An engine, an engine
Chuffing me off like a Jew.
A Jew to Dachau, Auschwitz, Belsen.
I began to talk like a Jew.
I think I may well be a Jew.

The snows of the Tyrol, the clear beer of Vienna
Are not very pure or true.
With my gipsy ancestress and my weird luck
And my Taroc pack and my Taroc pack
I may be a bit of a Jew.

I have always been scared of *you*,
With your Luftwaffe, your gobbledygoo.
And your neat mustache
And your Aryan eye, bright blue.
Panzer-man, panzer-man, O You——

Not God but a swastika
So black no sky could squeak through.
Every woman adores a Fascist,
The boot in the face, the brute
Brute heart of a brute like you.

You stand at the blackboard, daddy,
In the picture I have of you,
A cleft in your chin instead of your foot
But no less a devil for that, no not
Any less the black man who

Bit my pretty red heart in two.
I was ten when they buried you.
At twenty I tried to die
And get back, back, back to you.
I thought even the bones would do.

But they pulled me out of the sack,
And they stuck me together with glue.
And then I knew what to do.
I made a model of you,
A man in black with a Meinkampf look

And a love of the rack and the screw.
And I said I do, I do.
So daddy, I'm finally through.
The black telephone's off at the root,
The voices just can't worm through.

If I've killed one man, I've killed two——
The vampire who said he was you
And drank my blood for a year,
Seven years, if you want to know.
Daddy, you can lie back now.

There's a stake in your fat black heart
And the villagers never liked you.
They are dancing and stamping on you.
They always *knew* it was you.
Daddy, daddy, you bastard, I'm through.

[1962]

Lady Lazarus

I have done it again.
One year in every ten
I manage it—

A sort of walking miracle, my skin
Bright as a Nazi lampshade,
My right foot

A paperweight,
My face a featureless, fine
Jew linen.

Peel off the napkin
O my enemy.
Do I terrify?—

The nose, the eye pits, the full set of teeth?
The sour breath
Will vanish in a day.

Soon, soon the flesh
The grave cave ate will be
At home on me

And I a smiling woman.
I am only thirty.
And like the cat I have nine times to die.

This is Number Three.
What a trash
To annihilate each decade.

What a million filaments.
The peanut-crunching crowd
Shoves in to see

Them unwrap me hand and foot—
The big strip tease.
Gentlemen, ladies

These are my hands
My knees.
I may be skin and bone,

Nevertheless, I am the same, identical woman.
The first time it happened I was ten.
It was an accident.

The second time I meant
To last it out and not come back at all.
I rocked shut

As a seashell.
They had to call and call
And pick the worms off me like sticky pearls.

Dying
Is an art, like everything else.
I do it exceptionally well.

I do it so it feels like hell.
I do it so it feels real.
I guess you could say I've a call.

It's easy enough to do it in a cell.
It's easy enough to do it and stay put.
It's the theatrical

Comeback in broad day
To the same place, the same face, the same brute
Amused shout:

"A miracle!"
That knocks me out.
There is a charge

For the eyeing of my scars, there is a charge
For the hearing of my heart—
It really goes.

And there is a charge, a very large charge
For a word or a touch
Or a bit of blood

Or a piece of my hair or my clothes.
So, so, Herr Doktor.
So, Herr Enemy.

I am your opus,
I am your valuable,
The pure gold baby

That melts to a shriek.
I turn and burn.
Do not think I underestimate your great concern.

Ash, ash—
You poke and stir.
Flesh, bone, there is nothing there—

A cake of soap,
A wedding ring,
A gold filling.

Herr God, Herr Lucifer
Beware
Beware.

Out of the ash
I rise with my red hair
And I eat men like air.

[1962]

Index

About the Contributors

Editors

Elise Paschen

Elise Paschen is the author of *Houses: Coasts* and *Infidelities*, winner of the Nicholas Roerich Poetry Prize, and her poems have appeared in numerous magazines and anthologies. A graduate of Harvard University, she holds M.Phil. and D.Phil. degrees in twentieth century literature from Oxford University. Former Executive Director of the Poetry Society of America, she is the co-founder of *Poetry in Motion*, a nationwide program that places poetry in subways and buses, and the co-editor of *Poetry In Motion*, and *Poetry in Motion from Coast to Coast*. She is also editor of The New York Times best-selling *Poetry Speaks to Children*. Dr. Paschen teaches in the Writing Program at The School of the Art Institute of Chicago.

Rebekah Presson Mosby

Rebekah Presson Mosby produced and hosted *New Letters on the Air* for 13 years on National Public Radio, interviewing writers and artists. She was nominated for a Grammy Award for her work as producer / editor of the 4CD box set, *Poetry on Record: 98 Poets Read Their Work (1888-2006)*, and edited the poetry box sets, *In Their Own Voices: A Century of Recorded Poetry* and *Our Souls Have Grown Deep Like the Rivers: Black Poets Read Their Work*. Mosby has also produced a Living History for Colgate University and selected work for the poetry room at the National Museum of Women in the Arts in Dallas. At present, Mosby is teaching a course in Radio Writing at Colgate University in Hamilton, New York.

Series Editor

Dominique Raccah

Dominique Raccah is founder, president, and publisher of Sourcebooks, a leading independent publisher outside of Chicago. Today Sourcebooks is the world's leading publisher of poetry in book-and-audio form, and also publishes nonfiction and fiction. Raccah first envisioned *Poetry Speaks* in 1997 as an interactive, engaging way to experience spoken and written poetry. In 2005 she brought poetry to younger readers with the NY Times bestseller *Poetry Speaks to Children*.

Narrator

Charles Osgood

Charles Osgood, often referred to as CBS News' poet-in-residence, has been anchor of *CBS News Sunday Morning* since 1994. He also anchors and writes *The Osgood File*, his daily news commentary broadcast on the CBS Radio Network. He was inducted into the *Broadcasting and Cable* Hall of Fame in 2000, and the National Association of Broadcasters Hall of Fame in 1999. Osgood has received numerous awards including the 2005 Paul White Award for lifetime contribution to electronic journalism, three Peabody Awards, three Emmys, and a Marconi Radio Award. He is the author of six books including *Defending Baltimore Against Enemy Attack* and *The Osgood Files*, and recently edited *Funny Letters from Famous People* and *Kilroy Was Here*.

Advisory Editors

Rita Dove

Rita Dove is the author of seven books of poetry, a volume of short stories, a novel, essays (*The Poet's World*, 1995), and the play *The Darker Face of the Earth*. She served as United States Poet Laureate from 1993 to 1995 and has received numerous literary and academic honors, including the 1987 Pulitzer Prize in Poetry, the NAACP Great American Artist Award, the Heinz Award, and the National Humanities Medal. She is currently Commonwealth Professor of English at the University of Virginia in Charlottesville.

Dana Gioia

Dana Gioia, Chairman of the National Endowment for the Arts, received his B.A. and M.B.A. from Stanford University. He also completed an M.A. at Harvard where he studied with poets Robert Fitzgerald and Elizabeth Bishop. Gioia is the author of *Can Poetry Matter? Essays on Poetry and American Culture* as well as two previous collections of poetry, *The Gods of Winter* and *Daily Horoscope*, and *Nosferatu*, a libretto. His third book, *Interrogations at Noon*, won the 2002 American Book Award. He lives in Santa Rosa, California.

Robert Pinsky

Robert Pinsky served as United States Poet Laureate from 1997–2000, the first to serve three consecutive terms. His *The Sounds of Poetry* (1998) was nominated for a National Book Award in Criticism. Creator and director of the Favorite Poem Project and poetry editor at *SLATE*, he also teaches in the graduate writing program at Boston University. His most recent collection of poems is *Jersey Rain* (2000).

Essayists

Elizabeth Alexander

Elizabeth Alexander is the author of three poetry collections, *The Venus Hottentot, Body of Life*, and *Antebellum Dream Book*. Her awards include a National Endowment for the Arts Fellowship, a Pushcart Prize, the Quantrell Award for Excellence in Undergraduate Teaching at the University of Chicago, and the George Kent Award, given by Gwendolyn Brooks. She teaches at Yale University.

Agha Shahid Ali

Agha Shahid Ali is on the poetry faculty of the M.F.A./Ph.D. creative writing program at the University of Utah, and is the author of several volumes of poetry. His most recent credits are *Ravishing DisUnities: Real Ghazals in English* and *Rooms Are Never Finished*.

Charles Bernstein

Charles Bernstein is the author of more than twenty collections of poetry and essays. His most recent books include *Republics of Reality: 1975–1995*, and *My Way: Speeches and Poems*, and, as editor, *Close Listening: Poetry and the Performed Word*. Bernstein is David Gray Professor of Poetry and Letters at SUNY-Buffalo, where he is director of the Poetics Program.

Frank Bidart

Frank Bidart's books are collected in *In the Western Night: Collected Poems 1965–1990*. Among other honors, he has received the Lila Acheson Wallace/Reader's Digest Fund Writer's Award, the Morton Dauwen Zabel Award given by the American Academy of Arts and Letters, the Shelley Award, the Lannan Literary Award, and the Wallace Stevens Award. He teaches at Wellesley College. Bidart is the editor (with David Gewanter) of Robert Lowell's collected poems.

Robert Bly

As a poet, editor, and translator, Robert Bly has had a profound impact on the shape of American poetry. He is the author of more than thirty books of poetry, including *The Night Abraham Called to the Stars* (2001). He has also edited a selection of William Stafford's poems, *The Darkness Around Us Is Deep*. Bly's honors include Guggenheim, Rockefeller, and National Endowment for the Arts fellowships.

Rosellen Brown

The most recent of Rosellen Brown's five novels are *Half a Heart* and *Before and After*. She has published three books of poetry, *Some Deaths in the Delta, Cora Fry*, and *Cora Fry's Pillow Book*. She lives in Chicago.

Rafael Campo

Rafael Campo teaches and practices internal medicine at Beth Israel Deaconess Medical Center and Harvard Medical School in Boston. His most recent book, *DIVA* (1999), written with the support of a Guggenheim fellowship, was a finalist for both the National Book Critics Circle Award and the Paterson Poetry Prize.

Billy Collins

Billy Collins is the 2001–2002 United States Poet Laureate. He is the author of seven books of poetry. His latest book is *Sailing Alone Around the Room*, a collection of new and selected poems published by Random House. He teaches at Lehman College (CUNY) and is a visiting writer at Sarah Lawrence College.

Forrest Gander

Forrest Gander's most recent books of poems are *Science & Steepleflower* and *Torn Awake* from New Directions. Among his translations are the two collections, *Immanent Visitor: The Selected Poems of Jaime Saenz* (with Kent Johnson) and *No Shelter: Selected Poems of Pura López Colomé*. Gander is professor of English Literature and director of the Graduate Program in Creative Writing at Brown University.

Jorie Graham

Jorie Graham has received numerous awards for her work, including the 1996 Pulitzer Prize for poetry for *The Dream of the Unified Field: Selected Poems 1974–1994*. She was recently appointed Boylston Professor at Harvard University and currently divides her time between Iowa and Massachusetts.

Susan Hahn

Susan Hahn is the author of five books of poetry and two plays. She is the editor of *TriQuarterly* magazine.

Joy Harjo

Joy Harjo is a poet, musician, writer, and performer. She has published several books including her recently released *A Map to the Next World: Poems and Tales*. She has also coedited an anthology of Native American women's writing, *Reinventing the Enemy's Language: Native Women's Writing of North America*. She is a saxophone player and performs solo and with her band Joy Harjo and Poetic Justice. She currently teaches at UCLA and lives in Honolulu.

Robert Hass

Robert Hass's books of poetry include *Sun Under Wood: New Poems* (1996), *Human Wishes* (1989), *Praise* (1979), and *Field Guide* (1973). He has also co-translated several volumes of poetry with Czeslaw Milosz, most recently *Facing the River* (1995), and is author or editor of several other collections of essays and translation, including *The Essential Haiku: Versions of Basho, Buson, and Issa* (1994) and *Twentieth Century Pleasures: Prose on Poetry* (1984). He is a former United States Poet Laureate.

Seamus Heaney

Seamus Heaney received the Nobel Prize in Literature in 1995. A resident of Dublin since 1976, he teaches regularly at Harvard University. His recent publications include *Electric Light* (2001), *Beowulf* (2000), *Diary of One Who Vanished* (2000), and *Opened Ground* (1998).

Anthony Hecht

Anthony Hecht recently published two new volumes of poems, *Flight Among the Tombs* (1996), and *The Darkness and the Light* (2001). He was awarded the Pulitzer Prize, the Eugenio Montale Award, and the Robert Frost Medal by the Poetry Society of America. A collection of essays, *Melodies Unheard*, is forthcoming.

Edward Hirsch

Edward Hirsch's seven books include *On Love: Poems* (1998) and *How to Read a Poem and Fall in Love with Poetry* (1999). He is a 1998 MacArthur Fellow and teaches in the Creative Writing Program at the University of Houston.

John Hollander

John Hollander, Sterling Professor of English, Yale University, is the author of eighteen books of poetry, including, most recently, *Figurehead, Tesserae, Selected Poetry,* and a new edition of his earlier *Reflections on Espionage*. He has also published nine volumes of criticism, the most recent being *The Work of Poetry* and *The Poetry of Everyday Life*. He has edited or coedited twenty-one books, including *American Poetry: The Nineteenth Century* and *The Oxford Anthology of English Literature*.

Richard Howard

Richard Howard is the author of numerous collections of poetry and translation including, most recently *Trappings*. He has received a MacArthur Fellowship, the Pulitzer Prize, and the Academy of Arts and Letters Literary Award, among other prizes. He is poetry editor of *The Paris Review* and *Western Humanities Review* and Professor of Practice in the School of the Arts (Writing Division) of Columbia University.

Galway Kinnell

Galway Kinnell is a former MacArthur fellow and has been state poet of Vermont. In 1982, his *Selected Poems* won the Pulitzer Prize and the National Book Award. He is the translator, with Hannah Liebmann, of *The Essential Rilke*. Kinnell teaches at New York University, where he is the Erich Maria Remarque Professor of Creative Writing. His most recent book is *A New Selected Poems* (2000).

David Lehman

David Lehman is the author most recently of *The Daily Mirror* (2000), a book of poems, and *The Last Avant-Garde: The Making of the New York School of Poets* (1999). He is the series editor of *The Best American Poetry*, which he initiated in 1988. He teaches on the core faculty of the graduate writing programs at the New School in New York City and at Bennington College in Vermont.

Brad Leithauser

Brad Leithauser is the author of five novels, most recently *A Few Corrections* (2001) and four books of poems, including *The Odd Last Thing She Did* (1998). He shares the Emily Dickinson Chair in the Humanities at Mount Holyoke College with his wife, Mary Jo Salter.

Glyn Maxwell

Glyn Maxwell was born in 1962 in Hertfordshire, England. He studied English at Oxford and poetry at Boston University. Among the honors he has received are the Somerset Maugham Prize and the E.M. Forster Prize, which he was awarded in 1997 by the American Academy of Arts and Letters. Maxwell now lives with his wife and their daughter in the United States, where he teaches at Amherst College.

Peter McDonald

Peter McDonald is a poet and critic, born in Belfast in 1962. He has taught for many years in British universities, and is currently Christopher Tower Tutor in English Poetry at Christ Church, Oxford. He is the author of three volumes of poetry, and has written critical books on Louis MacNeice and on modern Irish poetry.

W. S. Merwin

W. S. Merwin's new and selected poems, *Migration*, won the 2005 National Book Award for Poetry. His most recent book of translations is Jean Follain's *Transparence of the World* (2003). Both are from Copper Canyon Press. Copper Canyon will publish "The Book of Fables"—short, pure fictions—in 2007.

Paul Muldoon

Paul Muldoon was born in 1951 in County Armagh, Northern Ireland, and educated in Armagh and at the Queen's University of Belfast. From 1973 to 1986 he worked in Belfast as a radio and television producer for the British Broadcasting Corporation. Since 1987 he has lived in the United States, where he is now Howard G.B. Clark '21 Professor at Princeton University and Chair of the Lewis Center for the Creative and Performing Arts. Between 1999 and 2004 he was Professor of Poetry at the University of Oxford. Paul Muldoon's main collections of poetry are *New Weather* (1973), *Mules* (1977), *Why Brownlee Left* (1980), *Quoof* (1983), *Meeting The British* (1987), *Madoc: A Mystery* (1990), *The Annals of Chile* (1994), *Hay* (1998), *Poems 1968-1998* (2001), *Moy Sand and Gravel* (2002), and *Horse Latitudes* (2006).

Marilyn Nelson

Marilyn Nelson's third book, *The Homeplace*, was a finalist for the 1991 National Book Award and won the 1992 Annisfield-Wolf Award. Her fifth book, *The Fields of Praise: New and Selected Poems*, was a finalist for the 1997 National Book Award and won the 1998 Poets' Prize. Her newest book, *Carver*, was published in 2001. She is professor of English at the University of Connecticut, Storrs.

Sharon Olds

Sharon Olds teaches at New York University and is, with Jane Cooper and Audre Lorde, a New York State Poet Laureate Emerita. Her most recent poetry collection is *Blood, Tin, Straw* (1999). Her numerous honors include a National Endowment for the Arts grant; a Guggenheim Foundation Fellowship; the San Francisco Poetry Center Award; and the National Book Critics Circle Award.

Michael Palmer

Michael Palmer was born in New York City. He is the recipient of two grants from the Literature Program of the National Endowment for the Arts, and was a Guggenheim Fellow 1989–90. He has published eight books of poetry. His most recent book of poetry is *The Promises of Glass* (2000). A prose work, *The Danish Notebook*, appeared in the fall of 1999. He lives in San Francisco.

Molly Peacock

Molly Peacock, one of the originators of "Poetry in Motion" on the nation's subways and buses, is the author of four books of poems, including *Raw Heaven*, *Take Heart*, and *Original Love*, as well as a memoir, *Paradise Piece by Piece*. Her most recent book is *How to Read a Poem & Start a Poetry Circle*. She currently serves as poet-in-residence at the Cathedral of St. John the Divine.

Christopher Reid

Christopher Reid is the author of a number of books of poems, from *Arcadia* (1979) to *Mr Mouth* (2006). His edition of the *Letters of Ted Hughes* appeared in 2007. From 1991 to 1999, he was Poetry Editor at Faber and Faber, in London, and he is now Professor in Creative Writing at the University of Hull.

Kay Ryan

Kay Ryan is the author of five books of poetry, most recently *Say Uncle* (2000). Her work has been published in *The New Yorker*, *The Atlantic*, *The Paris Review*, *The New Republic*, and *The Best of the Best of American Poetry*, among other places. Kay Ryan lives in the San Francisco Bay area and is the reviewer and advisory editor for *Ruminator Review*. She teaches at the College of Marin.

Peter Sacks

Peter Sacks is the author of four collections of poems, most recently *Natal Command* (1997) and *O Wheel* (2000), as well as of *The English Elegy: Studies in the Genre from Spenser to Yeats*, and of several essays on poetry, and on painting. He is a professor in the Department of English and American Literature and Language at Harvard University.

Mary Jo Salter

Mary Jo Salter is the author of four books of poems, including *A Kiss in Space* (1999). She is also a coeditor of *The Norton Anthology of Poetry, Fourth Edition* (1996). She shares the Emily Dickinson Chair in the Humanities at Mount Holyoke College with her husband, Brad Leithauser.

Sonia Sanchez

Sonia Sanchez is a poet, mother, activist, and a national and international lecturer on black culture and literature, women's liberation, peace, and racial justice. She is the author of more than sixteen books, including *Homecoming, We a BaddDDD People, Homegirls and Handgrenades, Does Your House Have Lions?*, and, most recently, *Shake Loose My Skin*. She was the first presidential fellow at Temple University and she held the Laura Carnell Chair in English at Temple University.

Grace Schulman

Grace Schulman's newest poetry collection is *The Broken String* (from Houghton Mifflin, 2007). Her latest books of poems are *Days of Wonder: New and Collected Poems* (2002 and *The Paintings of Our Lives* (2001). She is editor of The Poems of Marianne Moore (Viking, 2003), and Distinguished Professor of English, Baruch College, C. U. N. Y. Honors for her poetry include a Guggenheim Fellowship, the Aiken Taylor Award, and the Delmore Schwartz Award.

Jason Shinder

Jason Shinder's books include *The Poem That Changed America: "Howl" Fifty Years Later, Lights, Camera, Poetry!* and *Best American Movie Writing*, of which he is the Series Editor. His poetry includes *Every Room We Ever Slept In* (a 1985 NY Public Library Noted Book) and, most recently, *Among Women* (short-listed for the 2001 National Book Award for Poetry). He is also the director of The Writing Program at Sundance Institute.

Elizabeth Spires

Elizabeth Spires is the author of four collections of poetry, including *Worldling* (1995). The recipient of a Guggenheim Foundation Fellowship and a Whiting Award, she holds the chair for distinguished achievement at Goucher College in Baltimore.

Anne Stevenson

Anne Stevenson, author of *Bitter Flame: A Life of Sylvia Plath*, was born in England of American parents and educated at the University of Michigan. After bringing out two volumes of poetry in the United States, she settled in Britain where she published *Travelling Behind Glass*. Her *Collected Poems* was published in 1996. Her most recent book of poems is *Granny Scarecrow* (2000).

Mark Strand

Mark Strand lives in Chicago and teaches in the Committee on Social Thought at the University of Chicago. He is the author of ten books of poems, the most recent of which is *Blizzard of One* (1998), as well as books of translation, fiction, and criticism. Mark Strand is a former United States Poet Laureate.

Richard Wilbur

Richard Wilbur's latest book of poems, *Mayflies*, came out in 2000. In September of that year, his most recent translation from Molière—*The Bungler*—had its world premiere at the Long Wharf Theatre in New Haven. He won the Pulitzer Prize in 1989 for his *New and Collected Poems*. Richard Wilbur is a former United States Poet Laureate.

Nancy Willard

Nancy Willard is the author of eleven books of poetry, two novels, and two collections of essays. Among her recent titles are *Swimming Lessons* and *The Tale I Told Sasha*. She teaches at Vassar College.

C. K. Williams

C. K. Williams has written eight collections of poetry, the most recent of which, *Repair*, was awarded the Pulitzer Prize. Among his many awards and honors are an American Academy of Arts and Letters Award, a Guggenheim Fellowship, the Lila Wallace-Reader's Digest Award, the PEN/Voelcker Award for Poetry, and a Pushcart Prize. He teaches in the Writing Program at Princeton University.

C. D. Wright

C. D. Wright's most recent collection is *Deepstep Come Shining* (1998). She is currently in collaboration with photographer Deborah Luster on a book titled *One Big Self: Prisoners of Louisiana*. Wright's awards include the Poetry Center Book Award, the Witter Bynner Prize from the American Academy and Institute of Arts and Letters, a General Electric Award for the literary essay, a Whiting, and a Guggenheim Award. She lives in Rhode Island.

Al Young

San Francisco Bay Area–based poet-novelist-essayist Al Young was named Poet Laureate of California in 2005, and is the author of more than twenty books. Among his honors: Guggenheim, Fulbright, NEA Fellowships, The Joseph Henry Jackson Award, and Stanford's Wallace Stegner Writing Fellowship. Young's titles include *Heaven: Collected Poems 1956–1990, The Sound of Dreams Remembered: Poems 1990–2000, Conjugal Visits, Mingus Mingus: Two Memoirs* (with Janet Coleman), *African American Literature: A Brief Introduction and Anthology*, the novels *Who Is Angelina?, Seduction By Light*, and *Sitting Pretty*. His newest book is *Something About the Blues*.

Acknowledgments

The publisher and editors wish to give heartfelt thanks to the advisory editors on *Poetry Speaks Expanded*, Rita Dove, Dana Gioia, and Robert Pinsky, whose brilliance and keen judgment were irreplaceable during the process of assembling this book and audio collection.

We were fortunate to have a group of poets of the highest caliber who contributed such marvelous essays and who lent their insight on the forty-seven poets featured in these pages. We would be remiss if we did not thank all of them for their unique contributions. Their efforts on behalf of *Poetry Speaks Expanded* cannot be underestimated. Each gave us invaluable help in thinking through the project in important and better ways. Also, due to difficulties in obtaining rights to the audio recordings, we were unable to include an essay on Marianne Moore written by Gloria Vando. We owe her our thanks as well.

Many thanks are also due to our narrator, Charles Osgood, who lent his incomparable voice to take us on an audio journey from Tennyson to Plath, and to his marvelous assistant, Karen Beckers.

We wouldn't have been able to conceive of this book had it not been for the extensive audio archives of the Library of Congress, Harvard University, and Yale University. In particular, we would like to thank Bryan Cornell, Brad McCoy, and Sam Brylawski at the Library of Congress; Don Share and Larissa Glasser at Harvard University; and Richard Warren at Yale University. Special thanks also to Richard Carrington and his staff at The Poetry Archive in the United Kingdom, for their assistance in obtaining one of the recordings of Ted Hughes.

For the handwritten manuscripts and letters of the poets, we must thank Thomas Ford and Leslie Morris at the Houghton Library at Harvard University; Rozanne Knudson, literary executor of the estate of May Swenson; Jennifer Lawyer at the Beinecke Library at Yale University; and Isaac Gewirtz, Diana Burnham, and Stephen Crook at the Berg Collection at the New York Public Library.

We also want to extend our thanks to Judy Noyes at the Case Library at Colgate University; Toby Oakes at the British Library of Congress; Michael Coyle at Colgate University; Chuck Haddix at the Marr Sound Archive at the University of Missouri–Kansas City; James McKinley and Robert Stewart of *New Letters on the Air*; Stephen Dunning; and Joe Berk at Pathways of Sound.

National Video's Sharon J. DiTullio and engineers Brian Beatrice and Chris Fina, as well as the staff of Dubway Studios and engineer Chris Abell, provided outstanding service in the recording of Charles Osgood's narration.

We owe a large debt of gratitude to Timothy Donnelly, who contributed the excellent biographies of the poets in the original edition, and Bruce Berlind who wrote several additional biographies for this update. We also wish to thank Aaron Fagan, Daniel Hall, Ellen Rachlin, and Bill Berkson for their help in putting together the various pieces of this project. Our personal thanks for their help and support go to Stuart Brainerd, Dewey F. Mosby, and Ray Bennett.

Finally, thanks to everyone at Sourcebooks who contributed their talents in making *Poetry Speaks Expanded* the wonderful book that it is—in particular, editors Todd Green, Todd Stocke, John Cominos, Alex Lubertozzi, Jennifer Fusco, and Jon Malysiak; graphic designers Megan Dempster and Tressa Minervini; print coordinator Dawn Weinfurtner; assistant to the publisher Vanessa Domoleczny; and editorial interns Theresa Kurzeja, Elizabeth Lhost, Lyron Bennett, Jay Diehl, Laura Kuhn, Andrew Logemann, and Tara Thompson.

Permissions

Audio Credits

W.H. Auden: "If I Could Tell You," licensed from Arthur Luce Klein & Associates Inc. "In Memory of W.B. Yeats" is from the Brander Matthews Collection, Rare Book and Manuscript Library, Columbia University. "Musée des Beaux Arts," licensed from the Estate of W.H. Auden. Used by permission of the Estate of W.H. Auden.

John Berryman: "The Ball Poem" from *Short Poems* by John Berryman. Copyright ©1967 by John Berryman. Dream Songs #4 and #22 from 77 *Dream Songs* by John Berryman. Copyright © 1964 by John Berryman. Copyright renewed 1992 by Kate Berryman. Reprinted by permission of Farrar, Straus and Giroux, LLC.

Elizabeth Bishop: "Crusoe in England" and "The Fish" from *The Complete Poems 1927–1979* by Elizabeth Bishop. Copyright © 1979, 1983 by Alice Helen Methfessel. Reprinted by permission of Farrar, Straus and Giroux, LLC.

Louise Bogan: "The Dream" and "Song for the Last Act" from *The Blue Estuaries* by Louise Bogan. Copyright © 1968 by Louise Bogan. Copyright renewed 1996 by Ruth Limmer. Reprinted by permission of Farrar, Straus and Giroux, LLC.

Gwendolyn Brooks: "We Real Cool," "Song in the Front Yard," "kitchenette building" "Speech to the Young" by Gwendolyn Brooks. Used by permission of Brooks Permissions.

Robert Browning: "How They Brought the Good News From Ghent to Aix." Courtesy of the Library of Congress.

E.E. Cummings: "anyone lived in a pretty how town" and "as freedom is a breakfastfood." Copyright © 1940, 1968, 1991 by the Trustees for the E.E Cummings Trust, from *Complete Poems: 1904–1962* by E.E. Cummings, edited by George J. Firmage. Used by permission of Liveright Publishing Corporation.

H.D. (Hilda Doolittle): Excerpt of "Helen In Egypt" by H.D., from *Helen In Egypt*, copyright © 1961 by Norman Holmes Pierson. Used by permission of New Directions Publishing Corporaton. Licensed from Arthur Luce Klein & Associates Inc.

Robert Duncan: "Often I Am Permitted to Return to a Meadow" and "Poetry, A Natural Thing" by Robert Duncan © 2007 by the Estate of Robert Duncan, reproduced with permission.

T.S. Eliot: "The Love Song of J. Alfred Prufrock" and "La Figlia Che Piange." Used by permission of Faber and Faber Ltd, London.

Robert Frost: "The Oven Bird," "The Silken Tent," "The Road Not Taken," "Nothing Gold Can Stay," "Stopping by Woods on a Snowy Evening." Used by permission of the Estate of Robert Lee Frost.

Allen Ginsberg: "Howl" and "A Supermarket in California" copyright © 1955 by Allen Ginsberg. Included with the permission of The Wylie Agency, Inc.

Robert Graves: "To Juan at the Winter Solstice," "The Blue-Fly," "The Castle" courtesy of AP Watt Ltd., on behalf of the Robert Graves Copyright Trust. Courtesy of the Academy of American Poets.

Robert Hayden: "Those Winter Sundays" and "El Hajj Malik El-Shabazz." Excerpted from *Collected Poems* by Robert Hayden. Copyright © 1985 by Robert Hayden. With permission of Liveright Publishing Corporation.

Langston Hughes: "The Negro Speaks of Rivers," "The Weary Blues," "Mother to Son," "Harlem [2]" by Langston Hughes. Used by permission of Harold Ober Associates Incorporated.

Ted Hughes: "The Thought-Fox" and "February 17" from *Collected Poems* by Ted Hughes. Copyright © 2003 by The Estate of Ted Hughes. Reprinted by permission of Farrar, Straus & Giroux, LLC. "February 17" courtesy of BBC Worldwide Americas Inc.

Laura (Riding) Jackson: "Death As Death" and "Nothing So Far" from *The Poems of Laura Riding* by Laura (Riding) Jackson. Copyright © 1938, 1980. Used by permission of the Laura (Riding) Jackson Board of Literary Management and the Woodberry Poetry Room, Harvard University.

Randall Jarrell: "The Death of the Ball Turret Gunner" and "Seele im Raum" from *The Complete Poems* by Randall Jarrell. Copyright © 1969, renewed 1997 by Mary von S. Jarrell. Reprinted by permission of Farrar, Straus and Giroux, LLC.

Robinson Jeffers: "The Day Is a Poem" and "Oh, Lovely Rock" by Robinson Jeffers. Used by permission of Jeffers Literary Properties.

James Joyce: "Anna Livia Plurabelle." Writings of James Joyce are reproduced with the permission of the Estate; © copyright the Estate of James Joyce.

Jack Kerouac: "MacDougal Street Blues" and "American Haikus" reprinted by permission of Sll/sterling Lord Literistic, Inc. Copyright by Jack Kerouac. Courtesy of Rhino Entertainment Company.

Etheridge Knight: "The Idea of Ancestry" and "Belly Song" from *The Essential Etheridge Knight* by Etheridge Knight. Copyright © 1986. Used by permission of the University of Pittsburgh Press. Taken from the album *So My Soul Can Sing* (Watershed Tapes WTC-212, 1986). Used by permission of The Watershed Foundation.

Philip Larkin: "The Old Fools." Used by permission of Faber and Faber Ltd, London and the Yale Collection of Historical Sound Recordings, Yale University Music Library. "Places, Loved Ones" from *The Less Deceived* by Philip Larkin. Recorded by permission of The Marvell Press, England and Australia.

Denise Levertov: "The Secret" by Denise Levertov, from *Poems 1960–1967*, copyright © 1966 by Denise Levertov. "Her Sadness" by Denise Levertov, from *Candles in Babylon*, copyright © 1982 by Denise Levertov. Used by permission of New Directions Publishing Corporation and the Woodberry Poetry Room, Harvard University.

Robert Lowell: "Home After Three Months Away" and "Skunk Hour" from *Colected Poems* by Robert Lowell. Copyright © 2003 by Harriet Lowell and Sheridan Lowell. Reprinted by permission of Farrar, Straus and Giroux, LLC and reproduced with the permission of the Department of English of Yale University, from a copy in the Yale Collection of Historical Sound Recordings, Yale University Music Library.

Louis MacNeice: "Conversation" and "Meeting Point" from *The Collected Poems of Louis MacNeice* by Louis MacNeice, edited by E.R. Dodds. Copyright © 1979 The Estate of Louis MacNeice. Used by permission of David Higham Associates Limited and reproduced with the permission of the Department of English of Yale University, from a copy in the Yale Collection of Historical Sound Recordings, Yale University Music Library.

Edna St. Vincent Millay: "Recuerdo," "I Shall Forget You Presently My Dear," and "Childhood Is the Kingdom Where Nobody Dies" from *The*

Collected Poems of Edna St. Vincent Millay, HarperCollins Publishers. Copyright © 1922, 1931, 1942, 1950, 1958 by Edna St. Vincent Millay and Norma Millay Ellis. All rights reserved. Used by permission of Elizabeth Barnett, literary executor. The recordings of Edna St. Vincent Millay reading her poetry are used by permission of the Edna St. Vincent Millay Society.

Ogden Nash: "I Do, I Will, I Have" and "I Must Tell You About My Novel." Used by permission of Curtis Brown Ltd. Copyright © 1948 by Ogden Nash, Renewed All rights reserved.

Frank O'Hara: "Ave Maria" and "Poem (Lana Turner Has Collapsed!)." Used by permission of Maureen Granville-Smith, Administratrix of the Estate of Frank O'Hara and the Poetry/Rare Books Collection, SUNY Buffalo.

Dorothy Parker: "One Perfect Rose," "Résumé," and "Afternoon." Used by permission of The National Association for the Advancement of Colored People (NAACP). Licensed from Arthur Luce Klein & Associates, Inc.

Sylvia Plath: "Daddy" and "Lady Lazarus" by Sylvia Plath. (p) 1975 Credo Records, under license from Pathways of Sound.

Ezra Pound: "Hugh Selwyn Mauberly" and "Cantico Del Sole" by Ezra Pound, from *Personae*, copyright © 1926 by Ezra Pound. "XLV" by Ezra Pound, from *The Cantos of Ezra Pound*, copyright © 1934, 1938 by Ezra Pound. Used by permission of New Directions Publishing Corporation and the Woodberry Poetry Room, Harvard University.

John Crowe Ransom: "Captain Carpenter" and "Bells for John Whiteside's Daughter" from *Selected Poems, Third Edition, Revised and Enlarged* by John Crowe Ransom, copyright 1924, 1927 by Alfred A. Knopf Inc. and renewed 1952, 1955 by John Crowe Ransom. Used by permission of Alfred A. Knopf, a division of Random House Inc.

Theodore Roethke: "The Waking," "My Papa's Waltz," "I Knew a Woman" by Theodore Roethke from the recording entitled *Words for the World: Poems of Theodore Roethke*, Folkways 09736, provided courtesy of Smithsonian Folkways Recordings. Copyright © 1962. Used by Permission.

Muriel Rukeyser: "The Poem as Mask," "Waiting for Icarus," "Night Feeding," from the *Collected Poems* by Muriel Rukeyser. Copyright © 1978 Muriel Rukeyser. Used by permission of International Creative Management Inc.

Carl Sandburg: "Grass" and "Cool Tombs" from *Cornhuskers* by Carl Sandburg, copyright 1918 by Holt, Rinehart and Winston and renewed 1946 by Carl Sandburg. "107" from *The People, Yes* by Carl Sandburg, copyright 1936 by Harcourt Inc. and renewed 1964 by Carl Sandburg. Recorded by permission of Harcourt Inc.

Anne Sexton: "The Operation" and "The Truth the Dead Know" from *All My Pretty Ones* by Anne Sexton. Copyright © 1962 by Anne Sexton, renewed 1990 by Linda G. Sexton. Recorded by permission of Sll/Sterling Lord Literistic Inc.

William Stafford: "Traveling Through the Dark" and "The Star in the Hills." Used by permission of the Estate of William Stafford.

Gertrude Stein: "She Bowed to Her Brother" and "Christian Berard" from *Portraits And Prayers* by Gertrude Stein. Copyright by the Estate of Gertrude Stein. Used by permission of Levin & Gann. Licensed from Arthur Luce Klein & Associates Inc.

Wallace Stevens: "Fabliau of Florida," "Not Ideas About the Thing, But the Thing Itself," "Bantams in Pine-Woods." Used by permission of the Estate of Wallace Stevens and the Woodberry Poetry Room, Harvard University. Licensed from Arthur Luce Klein & Associates Inc. This acknowledgment is to the sensible joy of experiencing imaginative work. For *one* human race, art in every form bridges gaps of human perception about our place in the larger world.

May Swenson: "Question" and "The Watch" used with the permission of The Literary Estate of May Swenson. Courtesy of the Academy of American Poets.

Alfred, Lord Tennyson: "The Charge of the Light Brigade" and "'The Bugle Song." Used by permission of the Yale Collection of Historical Sound Recordings, Yale University Music Library.

Dylan Thomas: "Fern Hill" and "Among Those Killed in The Dawn Raid Was a Man Aged a Hundred" from *The Poems of Dylan Thomas* by Dylan Thomas, copyright © 1943 by New Directions Publishing Corporation. Used by permission of New Directions Publishing Corporation and Harold Ober Associates Incorporated.

Melvin B. Tolson: "An Ex-Judge at the Bar" and "Dark Symphony" from *Rendezvous With America* by Melvin B. Tolson. Copyright © 1944 Melvin B. Tolson. Used by permission of Melvin B. Tolson Jr.

Walt Whitman: "America." Courtesy of the Walt Whitman Quarterly Review, University of Iowa.

William Carlos Williams: "The Red Wheelbarrow," "Queen-Anne's-Lace," "To Elsie" from *Collected Poems 1939–1962, Volume II* by William Carlos Williams, copyright © 1944 by William Carlos Williams. Used by permission of New Directions Publishing Corporation.

William Butler Yeats: "Coole Park and Ballylee, 1931," and "The Lake Isle of Innisfree." Used by permission of A P Watt Ltd. on behalf of Michael B. Yeats. "Coole Park and Ballylee, 1931," "The Lake Isle of Innisfree used by permission of A P Watt Ltd on behalf of Gráinne Yeats, Executrix of the Estate of Michael Butler Yeats.

The Library of Congress provided audio segments for the following poets:
W.H. Auden ("Musée des Beaux Arts")
John Berryman
Elizabeth Bishop
Louise Bogan
Gwendolyn Brooks
Robert Browning
E.E. Cummings
T.S. Eliot
Robert Frost
Allen Ginsberg ("A Supermarket in California")
Robert Graves ("The Castle")
Robert Hayden
Langston Hughes
Randall Jarrell
Robinson Jeffers
Ogden Nash
John Crowe Ransom
Muriel Rukeyser
Anne Sexton
William Stafford ("The Star in the Hills")
Wallace Stevens ("So-And-So Reclining on Her Couch")
May Swenson
Dylan Thomas
Melvin B. Tolson
William Carlos Williams

Audio Engineering
Audio produced at Earmark Inc. Remastering and production engineer: Len Perskie.
Charles Osgood narration produced at National Video Center and Dubway Studios. Production engineers: Brian Beatrice and Chris Fina, and Chris Abell.

Photo Credits

All credits listed by page number, in the order indicated on pages.

Every effort has been made to correctly attribute all the materials reproduced in this book. If any errors have been made, we will be happy to correct them in future editions.

Alfred, Lord Tennyson 1 Rischgitz/Archive Photos; 4 bMS Eng 952.1 (217) by permission of the Houghton Library, Harvard University **Robert Browning** 9 Bettmann/Corbis; 11 Archive Photos; The Henry W. and Albert A. Berg Collection of English and American Literature, The Research Libraries of The New York Public Library, Astor, Lenox and Tilden Foundations **Walt Whitman** 16 Corbis; 19 by permission of the Houghton Library, Harvard University **William Butler Yeats** 30 Bettmann/Corbis; 32 bMS Eng 338.12 (13) by permission of the Houghton Library, Harvard University **Gertrude Stein** 38 American Stock/Archive Photos; 40 TimePix **Robert Frost** 46 E.O. Hoppé/Corbis; 48 Dmitri Kessel/TimePix **Carl Sandburg** 53 George Tames/New York Times Co/Archive Photos; 55 Bernard Hoffman/TimePix; Carl Sandburg State Historic Site **Wallace Stevens** 60 Bettmann/Corbis; 62 fMS Am 1333 by permission of the Houghton Library, Harvard University; Beinecke Rare Book and Manuscript Library, Yale University **James Joyce** 67, 69 © Bettmann/CORBIS **William Carlos Williams** 75 Archive Photos; 77 Beinecke Rare Book and Manuscript Library, Yale University **Ezra Pound** 81 Bettmann/Corbis; 84 Beinecke Rare Book and Manuscript Library, Yale University **Hilda Doolittle** 89 Bettmann/Corbis; 91 Beinecke Rare Book and Manuscript Library, Yale University **Robinson Jeffers** 95 Bettmann/Corbis; 97 The Henry W. and Albert A. Berg Collection of English and American Literature, The Research Libraries of The New York Public Library, Astor, Lenox and Tilden Foundations; 98 TimePix **John Crowe Ransom** 104 Bettmann/Corbis **T.S. Eliot** 112 Express Newspapers/B090/Archive Photos; 114 Archive Photos **Edna St. Vincent Millay** 122 Archive Photos **Dorothy Parker** 128 Bettmann/Corbis **E.E. Cummings** 134 Archive Photos; 136 bMS Am 1823.7 (5) by permission of the Houghton Library, Harvard University **Robert Graves** 141 © Bettmann/CORBIS **Louise Bogan** 149 Bettmann/Corbis **Melvin B. Tolson** 154 Courtesy of Melvin B. Tolson Jr. **Laura (Riding) Jackson** 161 Courtesy of the Laura (Riding) Jackson Board of Literary Management and Cornell University **Langston Hughes** 166 Corbis; 168 Beinecke Rare Book and Manuscript Library, Yale University **Ogden Nash** 173 Bettmann/Corbis; 176 Archive Photos **W.H. Auden** 181 Jerry Cooke/Corbis; 183 The Henry W. and Albert A.

Berg Collection of English and American Literature, The Research Libraries of The New York Public Library, Astor, Lenox and Tilden Foundations **Louis MacNeice** 188 The National Portrait Gallery, London **Theodore Roethke** 195 Bettmann/Corbis **Elizabeth Bishop** 201 Bettmann/Corbis; 203 bMS Am 1905 (2863) by permission of the Houghton Library, Harvard University; Copyright © 1979, 1983 by Alice Helen Methfessel. Reprinted by permission of Farrar, Straus and Giroux, LLC. **May Swenson** 212, 214, 215 Courtesy of the Estate of May Swenson **Robert Hayden** 222 Pach/Corbis **Muriel Rukeyser** 206 Oscar White/Corbis; 234 Beinecke Rare Book and Manuscript Library, Yale University **William Stafford** 239 Courtesy of the Estate of William Stafford **Randall Jarrell** 247 Archive Photos; 249 The Henry W. and Albert A. Berg Collection of English and American Literature, The Research Libraries of The New York Public Library, Astor, Lenox and Tilden Foundations; Copyright © 1969, renewed 1997 by Mary von S. Jarrell. Reprinted by permission of Farrar, Straus and Giroux, LLC. **John Berryman** 255 Bettmann/Corbis; 257 The Henry W. and Albert A. Berg Collection of English and American Literature, The Research Libraries of The New York Public Library, Astor, Lenox and Tilden Foundations; Copyright © 1964 by John Berryman. Copyright renewed © 1992 by Kate Berryman. Reprinted by permission of Farrar, Straus and Giroux, LLC. **Dylan Thomas** 261 Picture Post/Archive Photos; 263 The Observer/Archive Photos; Express/Archive Photos **Robert Lowell** 268 Bettmann/Corbis; 270 bMS Am 1905 (2202) by permission of the Houghton Library, Harvard University; Copyright © 2003 by Harriet Lowell and Sheridan Lowell. Reprinted by permission of Farrar, Straus and Giroux, LLC. **Gwendolyn Brooks** 276 Bettmann/Corbis **Robert Duncan** 281 Chris Felver/Archive Photos; 283 The Henry W. and Albert A. Berg Collection of English and American Literature, The Research Libraries of The New York Public Library, Astor, Lenox and Tilden Foundations **Jack Kerouac** 288, 291 © Bettmann/CORBIS **Philip Larkin** 302 The Observer/Archive Photos **Denise Levertov** 309 Chris Felver/Archive Photos; 311 Beinecke Rare Book and Manuscript Library, Yale University **Allen Ginsberg** 315 Frank Capri/Saga/Archive Photos; 317 courtesy of Fantasy Records **Frank O'Hara** 327 Kenward Elmslie; 329 Mario Schifano **Anne Sexton** 334 Bettmann/Corbis; 336 Beinecke Rare Book and Manuscript Library, Yale University **Ted Hughes** 343 Associated Press **Etheridge Knight** 351 Courtesy of the University of Pittsburgh Press; 353 MSS-016 Ward M. Canaday Center, University of Toledo **Sylvia Plath** 361 Bettmann/Corbis; 363 MS Am 1780 (1) permission of the Houghton Library, Harvard University